THE KINGDOM
OF THE TWO SICILIES
1734-1861

Also by Louis Mendola

The Peoples of Sicily
A Multicultural Legacy

Sicilian Genealogy and Heraldry

Sicilian Studies
A Guide and Syllabus for Educators

Sicily's Rebellion against King Charles
The Story of the Sicilian Vespers
(Sicilian Medieval Studies)

Frederick, Conrad and Manfred of Hohenstaufen, Kings of Sicily
The Chronicle of Nicholas of Jamsilla
(Sicilian Medieval Studies)

The Kingdom of Sicily 1130-1860

Sicilian Court Culture 1061-1266
(Time Traveler's Guides)

Norman-Arab-Byzantine
Palermo, Monreale and Cefalù
(Time Traveler's Guides)

Sicily
The Time Traveler's Guide
(Time Traveler's Guides)

The Kingdom of the Two Sicilies 1734-1861

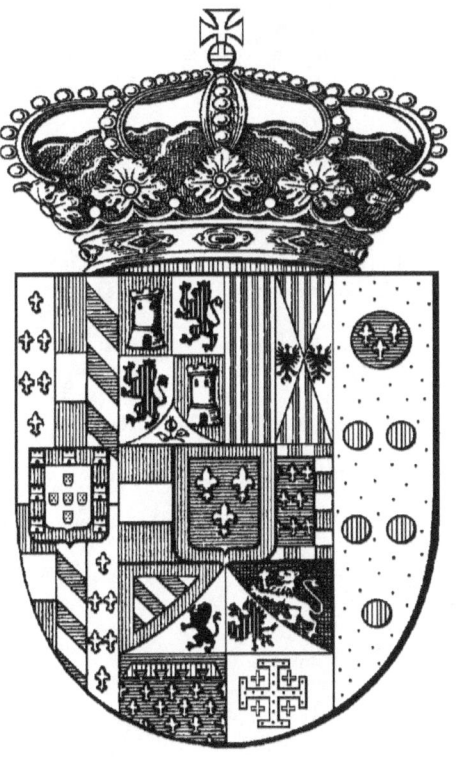

Louis Mendola

Copyright © 2020 Louis A. M. Mendola. All rights reserved.

Published by Trinacria Editions, New York.

This book may not be reproduced by any means whatsoever, either traditionally or electronically (digitally), in whole or in part, including illustrations, photographs and maps, in any form beyond the fair-use copying permitted by the United States Copyright Law and except by reviewers for the public press (magazines, newspapers and their websites), without written permission from the copyright holder.

The right of Louis Mendola to be identified as the author of this work has been asserted by him in accordance with the Copyright, Design and Patents Act, 1988 (UK).

Some material contained herein, authored by Louis A. M. Mendola, was previously published in *The Kingdom of Sicily 1130-1860* © 2015 Louis A. M. Mendola and is used by permission.

Legal Deposit: Library of Congress, British Library (and Bodleian Libraries, Cambridge University Library, Trinity College Library, National Libraries of Scotland and Wales), Italian National Libraries (Rome, Florence).

This book was assigned a Library of Congress Control Number (USA) on 10 June 2020. It was registered with Bibliographic Data Services (UK) on 12 June 2020.

Translations, maps, coats of arms, genealogical tables and cover design by the author. The text of this monograph was peer reviewed.

ORCID identifier Louis A. Mendola: 0000-0002-1965-6072.

Printed in the United States of America on acid-free paper.

10 9 8 7 6 5 4 3

ISBN 9781943639342 (print)
ISBN 9781943639359 (ebook)

Library of Congress Control Number 2020940311

A CIP catalogue record for this book is available from the British Library.

PROLOGUE

Born in Sicily in 1901, the author's grandmother, Maria, was conversant with its history and made occasional reference to such details as the fact that her island was conquered by many peoples during its three millennia of written memory. Maria was fluent in Italian, English and French, and proficient in Sicilian and Neapolitan. A competent Latinist, she was quite knowledgeable of ecclesiastical history. Very little in her formal education was left to chance.

When I was fourteen, I happened to mention something to her that I had read about the unification of Italy and Giuseppe Garibaldi, only to be taken aback by her reaction. Scrutinizing me through her steely blue eyes as she bristled at my ignorance, she uttered words I have never forgotten: "Don't believe everything you read, dear boy. History is written by the victors."

More than a simple rebuttal, her response was a fusillade of facts refuting most of what I thought I knew, casting my misplaced certitude into a sea of doubt. Her remarks transcended mere iconoclasm. What followed was nothing less than an object lesson in the value of epistemology, eyewitness accounts and corrective revisionism in the writing of history.

One detail she told me about had come down to her from her father, Niccolò, whom I had met shortly before his death at ninety-seven but only vaguely remember because I was so young at the time.

Niccolò's father, Vincenzo, was a royal messenger of the Kingdom of the Two Sicilies, beginning his career during the reign of King Ferdinand II. The riders in this military "pony express" were army officers armed with revolvers and ready to defend themselves against bandits and other potential adversaries. Vincenzo's travels took him around Sicily and sometimes into Calabria.

He was in Sicily when it was invaded in 1860, but the more interesting part of the story is what happened after the island was formally annexed, when his son, Niccolò, whom I was destined to meet in another place and time, attended a Dominican school. This was about twenty years following the invasion.

Niccolò was educated by teachers who presented *two* versions of unification history. In those days, the "official" history in the texts approved by the incipient state was studied only perfunctorily. More time was dedicated to the *actual* history, the verbal account drawn from recent memory of events. The typical Dominican friar teaching the course would close his history book at a certain point and say to his students something like, "Now, boys, I'm going to tell you what *really* happened in 1860."

This seems to have been a fairly widespread practice in Sicily's Catholic schools for some years, certainly outside the major cities, beyond the censorship of the civil authorities. Granted that its presentation may have reflected the clergy's natural antipathy toward the anticlerical government that confiscated ecclesiastical property, it nevertheless dealt with factual events. In Niccolò's case, it was bolstered by his father, Vincenzo.

PROLOGUE

That the "Black Friars" were teaching corrective history as recently as 1880 is nearly as significant as what they were teaching. Clearly, they didn't accept the official accounts of events unequivocally, in a state of unbridled awe, for they knew better. That was natural. Indeed, their religious order, present in Sicily since the thirteenth century, had seen plenty of dynasties come and go. The same was true of my forebears.

Maria's forceful remarks were the impetus for my study of the Kingdom of the Two Sicilies, encouraging me to question convenient clichés while recognizing that no written record can ever tell the whole story.

I only regret that a book like this one had not yet been written when that conversation took place so many years ago.

— Louis Mendola

Montefranco, Sicily
May 2020

Courtesy Metropolitan Museum of Art

REGINE MARGARETE SICVLORVM

This pendant (described on page 65) was worn by Queen Margaret, who received it in 1177. Crafted in Canterbury, it is conserved in New York. This is the oldest surviving royal jewelry from the kingdom founded by Roger of Hauteville in 1130.

PREFACE

To many, the Kingdom of the Two Sicilies is an undiscovered country.

Even the reader well-acquainted with European history might be forgiven for not immediately recognizing the ironic phrase "Two Sicilies," for the maps indicate only one island called *Sicily*. There are even occasional references to "the Sicilies," without the number specified, as if there were three or four Sicilies.

The kingdom — but not its people — vanished with the unification of Italy a decade before the unification of Germany during the second half of the nineteenth century.

The realm eventually known as the *Two Sicilies* traces its origin to a kingdom founded by Roger II, scion of the Hauteville dynasty of Normandy, in 1130. Ten years later, he instituted a legal code, the Assizes of Ariano, to delineate royal authority and bring cohesion to the laws of the polyglot realm. Coterminous to the ancient *Magna Graecia*, the Kingdom of Sicily encompassed the island of Sicily and most of the Apennine Peninsula south of Rome. Its capital was multicultural Palermo, a prosperous city of Muslim Arabs, Byzantine

Greeks and feudal Normans. In an earlier time, Longobard rulers came to be called kings of *Italy*, but during the Norman era there was no polity identified by that name. Instead, the peninsula's central regions dwelled under papal authority while those farther north answered to the Holy Roman Emperor.

This gave rise to political complexities that popes found threatening during the first half of the thirteenth century when the emperor, Roger's grandson Frederick II, was also the King of Sicily. In 1282, the War of the Vespers left the Kingdom of Sicily divided, with two kings — one in Naples and the other in Palermo — claiming the entire kingdom, hence the *Two Sicilies* and two kings of "Sicily."

Despite marital alliances between the Angevins of the peninsula and the Aragonese of the island, reunification proved difficult, eventually leaving the peninsular kingdom to be identified with the name of its growing capital, Naples. In that context, the term *Neapolitan* sometimes referred to the entire Kingdom of Naples.

By the end of the thirteenth century, the gradual but real amalgamation of the Arabs, Byzantines, Normans and Lombards of southern Italy had begun to coalesce into cohesive cultures vaguely identifiable as Neapolitan and Sicilian, each with its own distinctive Romance language. Decades before the birth of Dante Alighieri and his Tuscan tongue, the Sicilian School of poetry gave us the first literary vernacular of Italy. Southern Italy also boasted other languages, such as Calabrian.

Into the fifteenth century, despite the literary influences of the Renaissance, some of what was written in the twin kingdoms of Naples and Sicily was recorded in these languages rather than formal Latin or stylish Tuscan. Though their use was officially discouraged from the time Italy was unified in 1860 until the fall of the Italian monarchy following the Second World War, Neapolitan and Sicilian are still spoken by millions of Italians. Neapolitan was the mother tongue of the four

Bourbon monarchs who reigned during the nineteenth century.

Before embarking upon our discovery of the Kingdom of the Two Sicilies, we shall cast an eye over the history that came before it, but thereafter our emphasis will be the period beginning around 1700. There were several significant benchmarks. In 1735, Charles III was crowned in Palermo, reuniting the twin kingdoms of Naples and Sicily in a "personal union." In 1759, when this singular sovereign left to assume the Spanish crown inherited from an elder half-brother, he ceded these realms to his son, Ferdinand I. Interestingly, his pragmatic sanction confirming this transfer of power refers to the Two Sicilies by name, yet it was Ferdinand who formally, legally unified the two kingdoms in 1816 following the Congress of Vienna, which largely re-drew the map of Europe. This is the nation state that survived until 1860.

For a few years, Charles continued to advise his young son from Madrid, sending missives to the boy's counsellors and even using his not-so-invisible hand to influence the appointment of ministers. This was not unnatural. Nevertheless, the ideologies and policies of father and son eventually diverged. Where Charles was an early proponent of the United States of America, corresponding with George Washington and sponsoring the construction of a church in New York, Ferdinand came to support Great Britain. Ferdinand was never a great ideologue, nor were his descendants.

Charles, on the other hand, was clearly the most competent monarch that any of the Italian states, from Piedmont to Sicily, saw after 1700, and certainly the most inspired. Metternich famously referred to Italy as "a geographical expression." He never could have used the same terms to describe the Kingdom of the Two Sicilies.

"See Naples and die," went a familiar saying about the third-largest metropolis in Europe. When it was annexed to the nascent Kingdom of Italy, the Kingdom of the Two Sicilies, the largest and most populous of the pre-unitary Italian states, boasted more gold in its treasury than all the other monarchies combined. It had Italy's largest royal palace, at Caserta outside Naples, and could claim greater industrialization than the other Italian nations. It had the first public pension plan in Italy, the first welfare payment system for the poor and unemployed, and the first glass recycling program. These things would not be introduced in the neoteric Kingdom of Italy for decades, and the very fact of their existence in the erstwhile Kingdom of the Two Sicilies was ignored or even hidden.

Although those other monarchies, and the unitary state established in 1861, shall be mentioned in these pages from time to time for the sake of comparison, neither the Two Sicilies or its culture can be defined "dialectically" by the other pre-unitary states of Italy, as if there were a thesis, antithesis, or anything like a unifying synthesis.

Globalization has left us a world full of localized identities subsumed by a few larger ones. Much like the Romans of old, the citizens of the world are embraced by a communal culture which, in the end, sometimes proves as divisive as it is unifying. Just enough of the individual still exists for uniqueness to occasionally emerge from hidden niches. In this milieu, little Italy's role is not political, economic or technological but cultural, her pretensions to power long extinguished. The Italian language is spoken by no more than one half of one percent of the world's population.

Outside Italy, general Italian history is only rarely studied formally as a subject unto itself, usually in introductory courses at universities. More often, it is considered in the context of the Roman Empire, the Roman Catholic Church, the Renaissance or the Mafia.

Yet a large number of nonfiction books are published about Italy, ranging from history and art to tourism and cuisine. Several of the author's books have been used as texts in specialized courses and one work, *Sicilian Studies,* a guide for instructors seeking to formulate syllabi, recommends a number of books by competent historians.

Discovering the Kingdom of the Two Sicilies and its Siculo-Neapolitan culture is a rare opportunity awaiting a few curious *cognoscenti* among the greater number of Italophiles.

To those of us having roots there, the kingdom reflects something far greater than itself because its cultural, social and historic origins are older, being linked to an ethnic identity formed in the Middle Ages, if not earlier. The Introduction considers this based on the anthropological concept of an *ethnie* while concisely outlining perceptions of the Two Sicilies in the context of Italian unification and incisive, if ambivalent, attitudes about that nineteenth-century movement. Chapter 1 casts a cursory glance over the long history that formed the identity of a people, with a special emphasis on the medieval kingdom that shaped the customs and culture of the modern monarchy.

Several ideas related to identity permeate this field, and two of these occur fairly frequently in academic literature. *Sicilianità* is a general sense of Sicilian culture rooted in the Middle Ages. *Nazione Napoletana* is a post-medieval phrase that identifies the city of Naples as the social, economic, political and cultural focal point of the entire Kingdom of Naples. Neither term need encumber our study but it is noteworthy that each reflects attitudes seen to emerge following the separation of the two kingdoms after 1282, a reminder that there could be said to exist two sub-groups, Neapolitan and Sicilian, within the larger Siculo-Neapolitan ethnie. This, of course, coincides with the two major languages that originated in southern Italy.

This work does not presume the reader's prior knowledge of southern Italy. It is a survey but also a ready reference to a subject that was generally ignored by encyclopedias, and by Italians themselves, until the advent of the internet.

Some readers will see the political submersion of the Two Sicilies as a metaphor for many other lands and peoples, not only in Europe and the Mediterranean but around the world, that now appertain to larger nations. Bitterness, wars and insurrections are the fruits of those unwilling unions. That eminently significant conversation shall be left to others.

A territory identified with a certain culture or ethnie can be conquered. Cultures can be suppressed or, at the other extreme, popularized and "appropriated." Important works of art defining a culture can be removed from their place in one country and taken to another. The population associated with a certain culture can be displaced or even exterminated. The Siculo-Neapolitan culture of the Two Sicilies survives in its place of birth; much of it has even been propagated outside Italy. This is true even if it is viewed as *two* ethnic cultures: Neapolitan and Sicilian.

The story told in these pages ends in early 1861. What survives, and what is most pertinent today, is the cultural spirit that flourished in the Kingdom of the Two Sicilies, ranging from its literature and languages to its faith traditions and cuisine. This reflects the ethnicity of southern Italy. The House of Bourbon of the Two Sicilies, like all of our dynasties, beginning with the Hautevilles who founded the kingdom, is part of an indelible social identity, but so are the ordinary folk that lived in the kingdom.

It could — and shall — be argued that certain monarchs, like the Bourbons, who actually resided in the kingdom are more integral to that identity than those who ruled from afar.

It is easy enough to point to the obvious aspects of social culture identified with a certain place and its people, even if one may well enjoy spaghetti and pizza without knowing exactly where these foods originated. Yet the Kingdom of the Two Sicilies bequeaths us some unique, if less tangible, legacies. As we shall see, there are phrases like "on this side of the lighthouse" and references to "the thousand cities." There is currency based on the ducat established by King Roger II in 1140, a unit of measurement used in coinage until 1861.

When your author's first article about this subject was written back in 1986, shortly following the return, in death, of the last king and queen to Naples, there was, as yet, very little published about the kingdom in English or even Italian. That has changed.

Some of what appears in these pages was drawn from the author's original research in Italy. For example, in connection with genealogical research, the consultation of vital statistics registers and other documents recorded in the years immediately before and after the unification indicate an essentially uniform level of literacy throughout Italy at something between twenty and thirty percent; this is explained in a lengthy endnote. However, much that is reported here results from the efforts of other diligent historians; the endnotes and bibliography are full of references to such work.

The years since around 2000 have seen a tsunami of monographs and papers published on such topics as Sicily's Norman era and Italy's *Risorgimento,* including many in English. It so happens that these areas of study act as "bookends" by defining the parameters of seven centuries of monarchical history, the topic of an earlier work, *The Kingdom of Sicily 1130-1860.*

What might be considered the first "history" of the Kingdom of Sicily, from its Norman origins into the reign of Frederick II, is the *Ferraris Chronicle* completed at a monastery near Naples in 1228. The detail and scope of that medieval narrative, finally published in English in 2017, make it somewhat broader than the typical annal or chronicle.

It is appropriate to inform the reader of what is relevant, or not, to the subject of this work, the first volume written in English, in the original, on the history of the Kingdom of the Two Sicilies.

This history is both social and political in orientation. Although, for convenience, most chapters are linked to specific reigns, this work is not biographical; for dynastic history, Sir Harold Acton's two books about the Neapolitan Bourbons have generally withstood the test of time quite well and are highly recommended. While many topics are, of necessity, mentioned in these pages, this volume is not an exhaustive treatise on ethnology, geography, monarchy, the papacy, literature, law, religion, the arts, numismatics, cuisine, the aristocracy, localities, or orders of knighthood. There are other works on these subjects.

Cinzia Recca has written about Queen Maria Carolina and Jacqueline Alio has written about Queen Maria Sophia, who died in exile, while Lucy Riall has written about certain aspects of the Italian unification movement. Jordan Lancaster wrote an engaging cultural history of the city of Naples.

The kingdom itself is more than a place, a backdrop. Its monarchy is a silent, omnipresent character in our saga, even if our story might be equally interesting were the Two Sicilies a republic.

Because it deals with a subject about which rather little has been written in English, and since it may contradict some of what was published into the latter decades of the twentieth century, this volume necessarily considers historiography to a slightly greater degree than what one finds in the typical general history, but the focus of the main text in the numbered chapters is chronological history.

The two most notable works of literature that depict the Two Sicilies during the unification war and its aftermath are *The Viceroys* by Federico De Roberto, first published in 1894, and *The Leopard* by Giuseppe Tomasi di Lampedusa, published in 1958. The former did not appear in English translation until 1962, following the success of the latter. Though *The Leopard* was made into a film starring Burt Lancaster, little else of Italian cinema dealing with Italy's nineteenth century has made its way into English, a fact that says much about the general lack of foreign interest in that era of the country's history.

Without sacrificing objectivity, this history, contemplated for three decades, reflects long-held authorial interests, though it is not an elegy. While some scholars write about a chosen subject xenocentrically (one imagines a Frenchman passionate about China), cultivating interests which typically begin during their university years, those having a longer personal familiarity with a place and its history can contribute much to a field. There is no substitute for a historian knowing a culture and its language beginning at a young age.

This "inside" knowledge may yield a narrative that differs slightly from what is reflected in histories penned by foreigners lacking those connections because it brings a personally insightful element to the work beyond the documentary record. The information presented in the Prologue is an obvious example.

Cyril Toumanoff and Brenda Meehan, with whom the author discussed the similarities between Charles III as King of Naples and Peter I as Tsar of Russia, were both superlative professors of Russian tsarist history, but the former, an aristocrat born in Saint Petersburg, actually lived through the nation's Revolution of 1917 and knew princes of the imperial family. Princess Urraca of the Two Sicilies was a living link to the kingdom's last queen, whom she knew. James Risk was a witness to irregularities in Italy's referendum of 1946 (described in note 8).

None of this is to imply that a Siculophile historian whose roots and education are elsewhere cannot write an accurate history of the Kingdom of the Two Sicilies. However, a sound knowledge of the place and its people is a distinct advantage if we are to achieve anything approaching understanding, which sometimes proves to be elusive even under the best of circumstances.

Here one is reminded of the Englishman, a professor of

modern Italian history, who tried to convince his students that the Mafia was largely imaginary, or another Englishman, a medievalist, who claimed that it originated amongst the Arabs of Palermo in the twelfth century.

Harold Acton's rare insight into the realities of our Siculo-Neapolitan monarchy was owed less to his being a Briton than to the fact of his being a Neapolitan whose family played a role in great events. Those upon whom destiny has deigned to bequeath a personal knowledge of this kind are morally obligated to make it available to those who seek it. Often, this is a question of an older generation transmitting information to a younger one.

Every source should be considered. When scholars refer to the writing of history as "multidisciplinary," what is usually intended is an incorporation of modern analytical principles such as those present in the fields of anthropology and sociology.

Why are you reading these words? Why do we contemplate history?

Is it to learn? Is it to confirm our perceptions, or perhaps to correct them? Is it to appease our teachers? Do we read history simply to aggrandize our own egos, to claim a recondite knowledge superior to that of others, or do we turn its pages out of genuine curiosity, in our quest for intellectual edification?

"Nescire autem quid ante quam natus sis acciderit, id est semper esse puerum," said Cicero, whose words are just as resonant in plain English: "One who is ignorant of what happened before his birth will always be a child."

Many of us read history to know more tomorrow than we knew yesterday.

History is not hagiography. It is not a refuge or safe space. It can make for uncomfortable reading. The facts speak for themselves.

This work is not a panegyric for the Kingdom of the Two

Sicilies or an obloquy against the state that succeeded it. It does not offer the reader the force of revelation. It is simply an attempt to present information that is not readily available elsewhere in English. While it may find particular interest among those having roots in southern Italy, this volume is intended as an introduction and reference for anybody curious about the region's history after 1700.

In these pages the only "agenda" is historical accuracy based on sound epistemology. Anything less would insult the reader's intelligence. It is only through an *accurate* reading of history that we can learn anything from the past.

This book, which should have been published at least fifty years ago, is not the "last word" on the history of the kingdom. On the contrary, it is a foundational work upon which future efforts may be built.

Some generalities are considered in the Introduction, while historiography is examined in Appendix 7. For now, it should be noted that this book, written from a centrist's perspective, does not advance a specific political view, such as secessionism (the separation of Sicily or other regions from the Italian Republic) or monarchism (the restoration of the Bourbons to a throne in Italy), nor does it advocate any "regional" nationalist or independence movement in Italy comparable to those present in Navarre, Catalonia or Scotland. The author is not affiliated with any political party or movement in Italy, and has never been employed by, or received funding from, any organization or government. He does not represent (or speak on behalf of) any association, institution or dynasty. In spite of his being educated by Jesuits, he is critical of their exploits during the Inquisition. Despite knowing a few Bourbons and Savoys, he is objectively critical of the behavior of some of their forebears, and of his own.

Our story ends in 1861 except for the *coda* of a few pertinent facts, such as the deaths of the last king and queen (in

1894 and 1925), and some events and conditions which occurred subsequently that influenced historiography. For reference, several specialized topics related to the monarchy and its government as an institution are addressed in a concise manner in the appendices.

Contrary to popular belief, the Kingdom of the Two Sicilies is still relevant to Italian law in tangible ways. For example, legal cases involving land ownership sometimes require the consultation of records emanating from official sources before 1860.

At the beginning of *The Last Bourbons of Naples,* Sir Harold Acton (1904-1994), echoing the sentiments of another historian, Denis Mack Smith (1920-2017), observed that after 1860 there was a tendency in the new unitary state "to justify the victors and to damn or forget the defeated." He went on to say that, "I have tried to restore the balance." That is the immediate objective of this work, but our ambition transcends the study of a dynasty. We wish to discover the history of a people.

Along the way, we'll seek to reveal something of the human spirit.

Buon viaggio.

CONTENTS

Prologue	v
Preface	ix
Introduction	1
Maps and Tables	29
1. Prelude	37
2. Charles III	71
3. Ferdinand I	109
4. Interlude	135
5. Francis I	149
6. Ferdinand II	153
7. Francis II	175
8. Postlude	187
Epilogue	201
Timeline	203
Appendix 1: Pragmatic of 1759	211
Appendix 2: Knighthood	221
Appendix 3: Nobility	239
Appendix 4: Heraldry	251
Appendix 5: Coinage	259
Appendix 6: Milestones	263
Appendix 7: Historiography	265
Notes	275
Sources and Bibliography	309
Acknowledgments	329
Index	333

THE KINGDOM OF THE TWO SICILIES

LA SCIENZA
DELLA
LEGISLAZIONE
LIBRO IV,

Delle leggi, che riguardano l'educazione, i costumi, e l'istruzione pubblica.

PARTE II.
Delle leggi, che riguardano i costumi.

CAPO XXXIV.

Scopo di questa parte della scienza legislativa.

' Uomo non può esser felice, senza esser libero: tutti ne convengono. L' uomo non può esser felice, senza convivere co' suoi simili: tutti lo sentono. L' uomo non può convivere co' suoi simili, senza una forma di governo, e senza leggi: tutti lo concepiscono. L' uomo

Tom. VII.   A   dun-

This treatise on law and individual rights published by Gaetano Filangieri in Naples in 1780 is thought to have inspired some of the principles that his friend, Benjamin Franklin, incorporated into the Constitution of the United States of America.

INTRODUCTION

The study of the Kingdom of the Two Sicilies, like the study of any nation's history, brings us a number of themes and a few complexities. Some of these are unique to the region. This book does not presuppose a prior knowledge of these topics by the reader.

In reading about the past, we can choose to dwell on history for its own sake, or we can seek to learn something from it. In striving for the pragmatic over the pedantic or semantic, historians must seek to present the most neutral, unbiased view humanly possible, in the least ambiguous way.

No history is perfect. None ever has been. Deciding what to include or exclude from a historical overview of this kind presents a perpetual challenge to scholars, and every solution is flawed. While the historian need not entertain pretensions to plenitude, it is important to seek accuracy.

Epistemology is vitally important. History is not religion. History has knowledgeable experts but no immutable authorities. No historian has the right to impose his dogmatism on others. History is best approached with the same rigor as science. A work of this kind is not the place for clichés, self-interest, ethnocentrism or fanciful theories.

Bias, either *pro* or *contro*, may be natural, for each historian brings unique experience to the field, but we must seek impartiality and objectivity at every turn.

History bequeaths pride and glory but also pain and infamy. Facts are not always pretty. History is based on what actually happened, not on what we wish had happened. Unpeeling history's layers can reveal sobering facts that temper edifying platitudes.

The study of history is bittersweet. It is not history's responsibility to make us feel good. Facts can't be shaped to accommodate our every sensibility, and in the study of history anything other than fact is fiction, or at best hypothesis. It falls to historians to separate one from the other, even if it takes a few hundred pages (or years) to do so. We look to historians to provide us with accurate information, and we feel betrayed when that sacred trust is violated. Reading inaccurate history is like opening a gift wrapped in beautiful paper to discover that the box is empty. The emptiness disappoints.

To paraphrase a familiar adage: Historians are entitled to their own opinions but not their own facts.

In the course of our discovery, we'll broach a few topics that many Italians are loath to discuss openly, especially with foreigners, perhaps even to the point of denial, as if Italy were never anything but the charming land of Renaissance art, sunny shores, tasty food and high fashion that we see today. Sadly, even many people born, raised and educated here in southern Italy know rather little about the Kingdom of the Two Sicilies. Not every detail in the candid commentary of this Introduction is suitable for the faint of heart. It shall be blunt, undiplomatic, devoid of subtlety. Anything else would be an exercise in deception.

Sadly, most of the history of Italy of the last hundred years is largely ignored in Italian school curricula, leaving the majority of citizens woefully ignorant about the recent past of their own nation. Few Italians know, for example, that Italy was the first country ever condemned by the United Nations for crimes against humanity. Instruction about the history before 1920 is not much better. Having read this book, the reader will know more about Italian history as it has actually transpired since 1800 than most of those educated here in Italy.

The numbered chapters that follow deal specifically with chronological history and Appendix 7 offers information on historiography and its evolution regarding scholarly views of the *Risorgimento* and its myth. The endnotes and bibliography list works further elucidating certain topics. These prefatory pages examine the identity of a people and the story behind the emergent curiosity about the Kingdom of the Two Sicilies.

Identity

In our age, "self-identity" is not uncommon, and it need not coincide with what one has inherited. Heredity is not destiny. Religions, philosophies and ideologies are sampled, adopted, cultivated and abandoned at will.

Certain personal identities, conversely, are closely linked to specific places and cultures, and are more readily inherited than adopted. They are not matters of choice, for we do not choose our ancestors.

Anthropologists define an *ethnie,* from the Greek *ethnos* meaning "nation," very broadly as an identifiable population, known by a gentilic, whose members share a common origin myth and history rooted in the same geographic place. This rudimentary definition shall suffice for our purposes. Several additional characteristics may further identify an ethnie.

Typically, an ethnie accrues its own language, literature and cuisine, though that is not always the case. Normally, an ethnie writes its own history.[1] To some extent, there may be a sense of solidarity or "belonging" among those in the ethnie, even if this happens to occur solely within its more elite social or intellectual classes as the keepers or protectors of tradition. In other words, an ethnie may be a community or society. An ethnie usually develops over time based on the shared experience of those within it rather than an arbitrary inception based on formal planning; one does not "invent" an ethnie. There may be intellectual or localized subcultures within an ethnie, and perhaps more than one language.

Beyond these generalities are highly individualized factors. For example, a person descended from more than one ethnie can identify with each of them or, conversely, favor one over the others. A "diasporic" ethnie exists outside its place of origin.

The concepts of ethnic and "national" identity subsist best when they occur naturally, without being thrust upon us.[2] They may be the product of a certain instinctive mythos, perhaps even something found in psychology.

They are usually unconscious, fruit of the simple realization that people live in societies and that every "ethnic" society is in some ways unique. The typical person does not awaken every morning thinking "I'm Russian" or "I'm Chinese."

Yet, whatever our collective identity, we are all individuals. There are no universal norms to determine what it is that makes one an "ideal" or "prototypical" Calabrian, Catalan or Bavarian. It is not a matter of religion, language or physical appearance. More than anything else, it is a common past and collective culture shared over time long before we were born.

Let us not confuse this with citizenship, from the Latin *civitas* (city), which is essentially a modern legal concept, even though it was known, in a simpler form, to the Greeks and Romans of antiquity. Ethnic groups can exist without governing actual nations. Kurdistan and Hawaii are not countries, yet Kurds and Hawaiians are identifiably "ethnic." Nation states can include members of more than one ethnie; here Canada and the United States are modern examples.

Admittedly, the concept of ethnicity was less "fluid" or variable in centuries past when most people traveled (or migrated) less and were therefore likely to live in the same nation or region where their ancestors had lived. The genealogical records available in Sicily are the best in the world; the combination of well-conserved parochial registers and *riveli* (the tax census) permit the construction of many lineages into the fifteenth century, even for ordinary families.[3] They reveal that during the era leading to the establishment of the Kingdom of the Two Sicilies most Sicilians married other Sicilians. The same endogamy prevailed in Calabria and other regions.

Whether or not somebody wishes to identify with an ethnie is a personal prerogative, but being part of one is an inherent birthright that transcends rules and laws. Amalgamation and assimilation are means to "joining" an ethnie, yet most sociologists would probably agree that a foreigner who obtains Italian citizenship, marries an Italian and takes up residence in Palermo does not "become" Sicilian any more than an Italian who obtains British citizenship and lives in London becomes English or Welsh.

On the other hand, a foreign child adopted by a Sicilian couple and raised in Sicily will be Sicilian socially and culturally. In Naples and Palermo, one encounters the children of immigrants from Africa and Asia born in these two cities who actually speak the local languages, while many grandchildren of Neapolitans and Palermitans born in Chicago and Toronto do not.

Those are deeper waters than we need wade into. Here we are not interested in self-identity, migration, diasporas or "identity politics" for their own sake. This is about inheritance.[4]

More pertinent to our conversation is the simple fact that much survives in the social fabric of southern Italy, the former Two Sicilies, that existed before 1860, including the Neapolitan and Sicilian languages already mentioned.

Did the Kingdom of the Two Sicilies as a polity under the Bourbons reflect the unity of its people as one ethnie or perhaps several that were closely allied to each other? Was the island of Sicily, whose language, government and even architecture were notably influenced by Catalonia (rather than Italy) for centuries, the locus of a distinct ethnie? Are the Italians, whose modern nation includes German-speaking South Tyrol, French-speaking Aosta, some Slovenian speakers in Friuli and other areas around Trieste, a few Albanian speakers descended from refugees who arrived in the south during the fifteenth century, and many observable cultural differences between certain regions, a true ethnie?

While Spain and France, and arguably even Germany, have existed as countries for many centuries, that is not the case of Italy, whose unification is, by comparison, a very recent construct, and even Spain shows signs of disunity if its Catalans and Basques are taken into account, with Navarre sometimes promoting itself as the *Reyno de Navarra* as if it were still a sovereign kingdom.[5] In assembling a nation state, has Italy succeeded in forging a true ethnic identity to accompany her aspirations to greatness?

For an example of Sicilian as it was spoken by 1290, we look to the *Rebellamentu di Sichilia contra Re Carlu*, the memoir of the Salernitan diplomat and physician John of Procida, a onetime advisor of Frederick II and later a proponent of the War of the Vespers.[6] This is one of the languages that was effectively outlawed in Italy in public life until the end of the Second World War (the translation follows).

Quandu lu re di aragona audiu quisti palorj, sì appj grandi dubitanza, audendu chi lu re carlu avia tantu putirj. Et incontinenti mandau currerj per l'isula di sichilia, chi si re carlu vinissi inver palermu. Et in quilla nocti vinni unu notaru inbaxaturi di parti di lu comunj di missina, e quillu missaiu dissi a lu re di aragona comu in missina non avia vidanda exceptu per octu iornj et non per chuj e kj "vuj nj dijati dari ayutu e ssiccursu di gentj e di victuagli, chi per nixunu modu nuj non putimu pluj resistirj dananti di lu re carlu, sì kj nuj nj rindirimu ad ipsu, kj nuj non putimu altru farj."

Hearing these comments about the potentially great battlefield strength of his adversary raised grave doubts in King Peter's mind. Considering that his opponent might be emboldened enough to march on Palermo, Peter sent couriers around the island to keep watch on the situation. That night, a notary arrived who was acting as an emissary on the part of the besieged city of Messina. He told King Peter how that city had victuals enough for eight days and no more, saying that, "You must help and succor us by sending men and food, for there is no way we can continue to resist against King Charles. Otherwise we shall have no choice but to surrender."

With the demise of the Italian monarchy in 1946, the new democracy permitted the revival of such pursuits as the publication of studies of Sicilian, Neapolitan, Friulian and other "unofficial" languages by academics.

In the former Two Sicilies, the evidence of a distinctive social culture is ubiquitous.

The religious feasts preserve the essential elements that characterized them in times past. The passion processions of Good Friday have changed little, and the *Befana* still makes her appearance on the Epiphany.

Many motifs in the majolica art one finds at Vietri sul Mare and Santo Stefano di Camastra are similar to styles that have existed for centuries, ever since the craft was brought from Spain.

The Baroque architecture is eternal. What exists was designed long before 1860. This includes, of course, the *Reggia* at Caserta, the largest royal palace in Italy (according to one method of measurement it is the largest in Europe). The former Two Sicilies boasts what may be the two oldest mikvehs in Europe.

The cuisine is glorious. Pizza was invented in Naples and the first European spaghetti was made around Palermo. Italy's first chocolate was made in Modica. Rice was grown in Sicily long before it was introduced in Piedmont. Its testament is the *arancina,* or rice ball.

A few social practices involving family life have remained quite traditional. For better or worse, weddings are still lavish affairs, and while many couples north of Rome raise children outside marriage, that practice is less common south of the capital.[7]

A certain social conservatism, even conformity, prevails. Fascism and communism never made great inroads in the south, where the Americans who arrived in 1943 were welcomed as liberators and the institutional referendum of 1946 saw marginally more votes cast for the monarchy than the republic.[8] In the former Two Sicilies, families are still infinitely more important than political ideologies.

The political climate in the former Two Sicilies is characterized by apathy, stoicism and a touch of cynicism. As one may infer from the general lack of enthusiasm for national holidays, nationalism is a rarity anywhere in Italy, but in the south it is an anomaly. Indifference has had some unintended yet positive effects, such as there generally being more acceptance of immigrants from Africa and Asia in Naples and Palermo than what one typically encounters in Turin and Milan.

In Palermo — where the author lives — neighborhoods like Ballarò, site of Europe's oldest street market (founded as a souk by the Aghlabids in the ninth century), are legitimately multiethnic and quite safe.

It is generally believed that subtle social differences still apparent between Italy's north and south originated not in the distinctions between societies *per se* so much as the subtle differences one encounters between medieval populations ruled by centralized monarchies, like the Kingdom of Sicily, versus those governed locally by cities such as *communes* like Milan and Florence. Whereas the subjects of kings considered themselves residents of a state, the citizens of a *commune* viewed their city as their own. An oft-cited effect is that the Florentine kept his city tidy while the typical Salernitan, regarding the street as the property of the king, was less likely to do so.

If, in our times, Bergamo and Brescia seem more orderly, perhaps even cleaner, than Cosenza and Caltanissetta, this difference in mentality may account for it, at least partially.

Italians have debated the phenomenon of "civic culture" for centuries, but especially since unification. Regional differences are somewhat less pronounced than they used to be, and they have been colored since 1860 by national developments affecting Italy as a whole.[9]

Kings and Countries

It is no secret that various political systems based on republicanism, as opposed to monarchism, have changed the face of society in recent centuries. As of this writing, there are still ten hereditary monarchies in Europe. Several, such as Monaco, Liechtenstein and Luxembourg, are rather small. Others, notably Spain and Britain, are quite important globally. Even the smaller states have constitutions and legal codes.

Most of the medieval societies from which major nations evolved were hereditary monarchies of one kind or another, most having some form of hereditary aristocracy and a dominant faith, which was usually that of its leaders.

Whether monarchy, being based on the concept of the family, should be considered the most organic or "natural" form of government is a debate best left to another day. An ethnie, if organized into a nation, may be represented by a monarch.[10]

The dynasty that ruled the Two Sicilies identified itself with the people. Its kings spoke Neapolitan and advocated for the local culture at every turn. The passion of Francis II for a local food, lasagna, was the source of his nickname, *Lasa,* and he was even referred to as "the Lasagna King." It was mostly after the unification of Italy that the Neapolitan Bourbons were identified as "Spanish," in order that they might be branded as foreigners. This was ironic if one considers that a kindred dynasty, the House of Anjou, had ruled the Kingdom of Naples from 1266 to 1442, while the Savoys, who take their name from a region in what is now France, had never ruled much of "Italy" except for Piedmont, some bordering territories in Aosta and Liguria, and eventually the island of Sardinia.

True, the Bourbon dynasty originated in France with Hugh Capet, and was more recently descended from Louis XIV and his grandson, Philip V of Spain, but in recent times most royal houses, through centuries of marriage into other families of their class, constituted a special caste that in many ways transcended the modern concept of nationality. Not for nothing was Britain's Queen Victoria called "the Grandmother of Europe." Other dynasties ruling parts of Italy, such as the Savoys, were no different from the Bourbons in this regard; indeed, the mother of Francis II was a Savoy.

A national identity had flourished long before the arrival of the Bourbons, but it is clear that the dynasty, by residing in the kingdom, did much to cultivate it compared to monarchs of the immediately preceding centuries, who ruled from afar. For the underpinnings of the monarchy that became the Two Sicilies, we look to our medieval Norman kings.

Nevertheless, the rebirth of general interest in the Two Sicilies and its dynasty was the result of cataclysmic events that occurred long after its denouement, and during the twenty-first century it was to receive a boost from a new means of electronic communication that facilitated networking among people of like mind.

The New Nationalism

In much the same way that Russians and Ukrainians became "Soviets" in 1922, the people of the Two Sicilies, along with the Piedmontese, Sardinians, Tuscans and Lombards, were expected to become "Italians" in 1860. Before the unification, there were no northerners or southerners, for there was no "Italy" to have a north or south. Henceforth, everybody was officially "Italian."

With unification accomplished, it became expedient, even necessary, to convince the people of the former Two Sicilies that there had been some kind of unseen "flaw" woven into the fabric of a kingdom that had survived, in some form, since the twelfth century, and that the newly-unified Italy offered something demonstrably better. The most convenient tactic was to cast aspersions on the Kingdom of the Two Sicilies and its dynasty. This was achieved through the use of blatant lies.

Seeking the pseudo-credibility conferred by historical precedent, unitarians proclaimed that "Italy" had been united by the Romans when, in fact, Sicily, like Gaul, was a foreign province of Rome. They further claimed that the Longobards had united medieval "Italy" under the Iron Crown when, in reality, Sicily was conquered not by the Lombards but by the Byzantines and then the Aghlabids, while parts of Puglia and Calabria remained Greek. They claimed that a referendum had confirmed the unification with an astounding majority of ninety-eight percent when, in fact, the faux figures they cited exceeded the number of eligible voters. They claimed literacy figures based on a census supported by data which conveniently disappeared, while ignoring more reliable records. They claimed that Sicilian was a "dialect" of Tuscan when, in fact, it was spoken and written before that tongue, in the early years of the thirteenth century. This tendency to misrepresent facts worsened with the passing of time, as the propagandists blamed a regicide on an "American" anarchist born and raised in Tuscany while claiming that another Tuscan invented the telephone.

Italy's surreal social environment discouraged intellectual dissent while maintaining a fair degree of control over the diffusion of information. The distribution of foreign newspapers was extremely limited, and in any case very few Italians were proficient enough in English or French to read what was published. Any foreign book or magazine that happened to mention an unflattering fact about Italy could easily be made to disappear from places in Rome where it was sold. Developments such as the British and American movements to achieve universal adult suffrage were barely reported in Italy. (As recently as 2020, an Italian citizen had to be at least twenty-five years old to vote in elections for senators.)

It took a few decades for there to emerge anything like an "Italian" identity as we understand it today, and in some ways it is still somewhat tenuous. "We have made Italy," declared Massimo Taparelli d'Azeglio. "Now we must make the Italians." To foreigners, these famous words, albeit translated rather loosely from the Italian, had the resonance of a noble idea.

In reality, however, the unified Italy was never very united; many believe it still isn't. Whatever its unitarian founders envisaged, the social conditions that emerged fostered an institutionalized depravity that privileged some regions over others. Meritocracy was rarely recognized or rewarded; many believe it still isn't. The new state's hallmarks were widespread poverty, repressive censorship and a general lack of opportunity that provoked mass emigration. This bred acrimony.

Military adventures were used as a means of attempting to

inculcate a sense of patriotism in the people. Yet the army was routed at Adwa in 1896, earning it scorn across Europe, and during the trench warfare of 1917 *carabinieri* units were posted a hundred meters behind the lines to shoot deserters. Ineptitude prevailed.

Finally, Italy's overzealous efforts to create a novel, overarching ethnic identity based on nationalist ideologies culminated in calamity, taking the monarchy with it. Among innumerable incidents one could cite is a sordid spectacle witnessed by American troops in the Sicilian town of Licata during the Second World War, when local women on balconies launched rubbish onto the heads of Italian prisoners marched down the narrow streets by the victors, something difficult to imagine occurring in Japan. If few of the Americans could understand the insults hurled by the women at the hapless prisoners in Sicilian, their intent was clear enough.

Death and destruction needed no interpreter, no accounting, no analysis. The propaganda spewed for decades by Benedetto Croce, Giovanni Gentile and others of their ilk was insufficient to offset the laconic language of reality.

Italy's ephemeral nationalist folly ended with the king abandoning his capital and Italian women selling themselves to American soldiers. At the demise of the tattered nation, women still were not allowed to vote. Divorce was outlawed. Rape was considered little more than a minor offense "against public decency," as if it were pornography; only in 1996 did Italian law classify the heinous crime as a felonious form of assault.[11]

Be it agreed that life in the Kingdom of the Two Sicilies was far from idyllic, nothing perpetrated in the name of its king ever compared to the mass atrocities inflicted upon the people under the state and the dynasty that followed. Soldiers of the Two Sicilies never committed war crimes so heinous as the raping and pillaging of entire towns as the Piedmontese troops did at Pontelandolfo and Casalduni in 1861.[12] They did not use illegal poison gas to kill Ethiopians. In fact, the Two Sicilies never sponsored the invasion of any country. Its citizens were not massacred in carpet bombings like the one that stole the lives of nearly a hundred civilians near Palermo's Piazza Magione in 1943 and another two hundred when a makeshift bomb shelter behind the city's cathedral collapsed during an aerial assault (the corpses from the latter attack were never excavated from beneath the rubble).

Meanwhile, in a prisoner-of-war camp in the United States, illiterate Italian soldiers were being taught to read and write the Italian language.

Were this a book of theories, one might be tempted to argue, based on an optimistic hypothesis of "what might have happened" in other circumstances, that the rueful abominations mentioned here were not necessarily the effects of unification *per se*. In theory, Italy might well have been unified in a way that did not lead to a modern police state forever defined by its genocide, racism, sexism, press censorship, unwarranted wars, incompetent attempts at greatness through inept colonialism, and failures to embrace fundamental principles of democracy. The fallacy in that mode of thinking reveals itself when one tries to imagine a state having the size, population and industrial capacity of Piedmont or Tuscany (or even the Two Sicilies) declaring war against a power endowed with the awesome military might of the United States of America, for the Second World War, like the global conflict that preceded it, was fought by coalitions of great powers; Italy's participation in these wars was based on the nation's size and misplaced ambition, direct results of unification. History is based on what happens, not what might have been.

Sadly, soberly, unequivocally, very little of good can be said about the Kingdom of Italy, a sullen land of grave character flaws and missed opportunities where the tears of the apologist form a puddle of misery. The chronicle of its foibles and failures reads like a litany of lunacy.

One of the purported advantages of a monarchy is that the monarch, being above politics, represents all of the people. Italy's penultimate king, Victor Emmanuel III, citing constitutional constraints, signed a law against the nation's Jews and declared war against countries with which he had been allied in an earlier conflict. Sagacity was never his strong suit. Japan's monarchy, conversely, managed to survive the war, albeit in a largely symbolic way, partly because the emperor was at least seen as a true embodiment of the people, the ethnie; unlike the Emperor of Japan, the King of Italy was not a living deity.

In its death throes, we find the decrepit Kingdom of Italy a nation run by leaders reluctant to believe in the efficacy of radar and sonar, thus leaving ships full of young Italian men to be torpedoed at will, while admirals supplied the ground troops with tankers departing Taranto for Egypt full of water instead of fuel. We find Italian women sympathetic to a nasty regime captured, stripped naked, their heads shaven and inked with the word *spia* (spy), paraded down city streets to hisses of scorn.

In the wake of the Fascist military debacle, with countless Italian mothers receiving telegrams notifying them of their sons' deaths in foreign lands, tragedies spawned by the blind ambitions of a tinpot dictator, termagantic *Italia* evoked little sympathy from her daughters.

The men were equally embittered. Returning from imprisonment following the lost war, they found the cost of room and board deducted from their military pay. The warped rationale for this affront was that those costs had been defrayed by the Allies running the prison camps in the United States and India, as if soldiers were expected to pay for food and lodging while on duty. Yet these men were the fortunate ones; those held prisoner in the Soviet Union were not repatriated until a decade following the end of the war, many having died in captivity. These broken men, who had been sent to Stalingrad lacking winter clothing, were all but forgotten by their own country.

Many civilians in Sicily harbored a particular antipathy because they had seen the Italian army flee *en masse* across the Strait of Messina, abandoning national territory, despite the pompous proclamations of its generals during the preceding years.[13] But the people of every region of the country had experienced unnecessary hardship.

As if personal suffering were not enough, the united Italy found herself the first nation in history to be officially, formally censured for crimes against humanity by the United Nations. Preoccupied with their immediate concerns, most citizens were indifferent about Italy's genocidal mischief in Libya and Ethiopia, which anyway had never been thoroughly reported in the censored press. As we have said, most Italians are blissfully unaware of it even today, having been fed the self-serving canard of *Italiani brava gente,* "Italians are good people."

Fascism extracted a terrible intellectual toll, forcing the brightest lights out of the benighted country; among its casualties were Maria Montessori, Emilio Segré, Enrico Fermi, Umberto Nobile and Arturo Toscanini.

The tragic postwar situation did not immediately foster nostalgia for the Kingdom of the Two Sicilies, which was largely forgotten, but it provoked the kind of mass disillusion that erodes confidence in a nation.

By early 1945, there were protests in Sicily against the military conscription of young men sought by the provisional government installed by the Allies, along with calls for Sicilian sovereignty.

In May 1946, the burgeoning separatist movement was upended by the last grandiose gesture of the defeated Kingdom of Italy when the island of Sicily was granted political autonomy as the largest of the nation's "regions." This effectively reneged on the ideals of unification espoused by proponents of the *Risorgimento* during the nineteenth century. Soon four other regions were granted such autonomy: Sardinia, Valle d'Aosta, Friuli-Venezia Giulia, Trentino-Alto Adige (South Tyrol).

Sicilians' views about unification, regionalism, nationalism and autonomy were informed as much by the actions of General Giuseppe Garibaldi invading the island in 1860 as by General Alfredo Guzzoni abandoning it in 1943, and everything in-between. In a nation generally devoid of nationalism, Sicily is one of the least nationalist places, trailed closely by Aosta, Friuli and South Tyrol, each lying at the extreme edges of Italy and each endowed with its own distinctive culture. The postwar factionalism reflected in this regional autonomy is the truest token of the failure of Italian unification.

In June 1946, as soon as the monarchy was abolished, a law was passed making it impossible to prosecute citizens for war crimes in the new republic. This meant that Fascists, and a few partisans, who had perpetrated atrocities against their fellow citizens could never be held accountable for their actions. For many families this was a further cause for embitterment.

Two national holidays were instituted based on the bittersweet events of this era, namely the end of the Second World War and the referendum establishing the republic. Despite a few symbolic observances in Rome, scarcely anybody actually celebrates Liberation Day (25 April) or the less important Republic Day (2 June). The indifference is rooted in ambivalence; by the end of the war, with Italy having changed its alliance in September 1943 and its army dissolving except for what was retained in a Nazi puppet state in the north, the hapless Italians were left to speculate about their nation's place in the global conflict and in the world. How was history to be written? Was Italy Allied, Axis or both?[14]

In an attempt to "Italianize" the victory over Fascism, most of today's politicians minimize or even negate the role of the American Fifth Army in defeating a nasty regime, instead giving most of the credit to bands of undisciplined partisans armed by the United States.[15] An examination of the tactical details of the ugly "civil war" fought between partisans and Fascists in northern Italy while the Allies battled their way up the peninsula against German troops at places like Anzio lies beyond the scope of this exposition, but it will suffice to say that the Second World War was hardly as unifying an experience for the Italian nation as it was for the Allied nations.

Unlike Russia, emasculated Italy had no "Great Patriotic War," only humiliation. Italy has no annual "Unification Day" and nothing so patriotic as Memorial Day, a national holiday in the United States marked by local parades in memory of military personnel killed in combat. Italy's surviving veterans of the Second World War are not openly disparaged, but neither are they, to use an American term, "The Greatest Generation" in the eyes of most Italians, who are anything but nationalists.

To most Italians, Liberation Day serves as nothing more than a liberation from work so the family can have a picnic, while Republic Day finds banks and schools closed but most stores and restaurants open.[16]

Instead, the greatest public festivities are reserved for local patrons who gaze down upon the populace from Heaven: Saint Januarius in Naples, Saint Rosalie in Palermo, Saint Ambrose in Milan, Saint Agatha in Catania, Saint Nicholas in Bari. In the subtle yet eternal Italian rivalry between church and state, the church usually wins.

The first mass exodus from the former Two Sicilies was prompted by the economic ruin caused by unification during the nineteenth century. Beginning in 1949, a second wave of emigrés in search of a decent life found their way to countries against which they had recently been at war: Canada, Britain, the United States, France. (To this day, many Italians, from both north and south, abandon Italy in search of greater opportunities abroad.)

Films like *La Ciociara* ("Two Women") and *Napoli Milionaria* ("Side Street Story") chronicled wartime misfortunes. *Riso Amaro* ("Bitter Rice") depicted Piedmontese women, *mondine*, planting rice manually in the nation's most industrialized region years after the war ended. *Divorzio all'Italiana* ("Divorce Italian Style") parodied the bizarre predicament of miserable spouses living in a country where divorce was illegal. Incredibly, there was still censorship; foreign films dealing explicitly with Italian war crimes and genocide were banned in Italy.[17]

With war resulting in a sour defeat, the triumphalist tropes of unification were gone forever. What followed were decades of divisive squabbling between political parties, as if the successors of the Fascists and partisans were eternally trapped in a time bubble that kept them in the year 1945. Now the country was not only divided between north and south, but a deep chasm separated the left from the right. Antagonism was the norm. The visceral hatred sometimes led to fistfights in parliament.

At the sesquicentennial of unification in 2011, scarcely anybody in Italy celebrated despite many organized events, for the dearth of unity, and the lingering lack of economic progress in the south, made a mockery of any talk of the supposed advantages of a unitary Italian state. People still spoke of the *divario* between north and south.

For every book published heralding the praises of unification, another was released revealing its grave defects.[18] The criticism permeated the nation's academic establishment. On March thirty-first 2011, your author attended a conference, *Il Risorgimento e il suo Revisionismo,* at the University of Palermo, an institution operated by the Italian state, openly challenging the concept of the unification, something virtually inconceivable just a few decades earlier; included on the panel of experts was a representative of the Royal House of the Two Sicilies.

The years following that underwhelming attempt to celebrate Italian nationhood witnessed the further erosion of *Italianità,* the cultural concept of being Italian, in industry and commerce as Fiat, the nation's largest automaker, left the country, leaving a few factories in Italy but incorporating in the Netherlands and establishing a tax domicile in the United Kingdom. At the same time, there were debates about whether an Armani suit manufactured abroad except for its buttons being attached in a factory outside Milan was truly "Made in Italy." The flight of Italian industry to eastern Asia and eastern Europe has come as a blow to Milan and Turin. Italy has long been relegated economically to the European Union's "second tier" along with Spain, Portugal and Greece.

In the kind of commentary that, mercifully, does not usually make its way to foreign ears, one sometimes hears frustrated Italians speaking among themselves refer to their country in the kind of unflattering terms that one only rarely encounters in other countries (see note 37).

As a nation, Italy is perhaps more divided socially today than it was at the end of the Second World War, though the divisions are more subtle. Italians only seem truly united when the national football (soccer) team plays another country's national team. There are not many other occasions when Italians fly the flag.

Into the first two decades of the twenty-first century, would the Kingdom of the Two Sicilies have ever launched its own astronauts into space, built a bridge across the Strait of Messina, spared its people the need to emigrate in search of careers, freed itself from the need for European Union subsidies or resisted economic conquests by the United States and China? Would the brown bear of the Abruzzo region thrive beyond the verge of extinction?

Probably not, but the unified Italy has achieved none of these counterfactual objectives. During the pandemic of 2020, beleaguered *Italia* could not even manufacture ventilators to save the lives of her own people, although the United Kingdom, a European country of comparable size, managed to do so; indeed, Italy had to borrow money from Germany and France to keep its economy afloat. California, with half the population of Italy, has a larger economy than this G-7 nation.

The main reason it has proven extremely difficult to defeat the phenomenon of organized crime in southern Italy is that the ordinary citizen is extremely suspicious and distrustful of the state, which is viewed as incompetent or even corrupt, to protect the populace. This situation, which reflects the attitude of many people not thinking themselves to be truly part of a nation, worsened during the last decades of the nineteenth century and is still with us today.

Silence does not constitute assent. In daily life, most Italians have more immediate concerns than engaging in impromptu discourses about the merits of unification. Very little is stated very openly about the subject to foreigners with whom Italians are unfamiliar, but the general opinions are perfectly obvious to anybody who has lived here (in southern Italy) for more than a decade. The mere mention of Giuseppe Garibaldi or the Savoy kings is likely to be met with bemusement, if not ridicule.

Italy's contemporary jeremiad, about which entire volumes have been written, is germane to our study only for the sake of comparisons.

The Old Nationalism

Uncomfortable questions were being asked long before the twenty-first century, with some Italians looking to the past, even to the Middle Ages, for political models that they viewed as the antithesis of a chronically broken paradigm.

By 1990, as the inevitable passing of Italy's "First Republic" loomed following the end of the Cold War that had propped it up for four decades, growing movements garnered increasing support among those seeking a reassessment of the history of the unification as it had been taught in schools. This gave birth to regionalist political parties in "Padania" (its name based on the Po River), particularly in Lombardy, Piedmont, Liguria and Veneto, where proponents looked to the early-medieval Lombard Kingdom for symbolic inspiration, lamenting what they viewed as the corruption endemic to Rome and the regions to its south.[19] Never mind that the medieval Lombards had been subdued by Charlemagne, who integrated them into his European empire, with some of those who had settled south of Rome later amalgamated into the Normans' Sicilian kingdom, the new parties found enough adherents to become a force in national politics.[20] Some even hankered for the secession of the northern third of Italy from the rest of the country; at the very least, they sought a "federalism" not unlike what once existed in northern Italy under the Holy Roman Empire.

In the south the regionalism took a different form, one that was generally more intellectual than political, and some of its activists looked to the Two Sicilies as a point of reference. Though some early "Neo-Bourbonist," or *Duosiciliano,* proponents were monarchists, many simply advocated a socio-economic resurgence of the Italian south without endorsing a specific political party.[21] Not only did the emergence of the Neo-Bourbonists encourage many southerners to think about our history as it existed prior to 1860, it undermined what little was left of the esoteric Italian (Savoyard) monarchist movement in southern Italy. In effect, some activists swapped their support of one dynasty for advocacy of another. If the Neo-

Bourbon movement has survived longer than most of Italy's sundry political parties, that is because it represents something beyond politics, reflecting vaguely ethnic and "regionalist" ideologies rather than a firm manifesto. Neo-Bourbonism promotes an accurate reading of history and the corrective revision of what is typically taught in schools about the Kingdom of the Two Sicilies. Being a loose but effective "coalition" of individuals and organizations rather than a monolithic movement, it can consolidate its supporters at any time without having to register them formally as members. Most Neo-Bourbonists are not extremists; they are well-educated, politically-centrist citizens.

The internet made accurate information about Italian history more accessible than ever. Until its advent, any Italian curious about the historical "facts" taught in schools or presented on the state television networks would encounter difficulty searching for accurate information. But the Italian state could not control the world wide web, or the encyclopedia-type websites indicating that Alexander Graham Bell (and not an Italian) invented the telephone.

Movements and trends aside, certain historical facts were overlooked for a long time.

In 1831, the Kingdom of the Two Sicilies instituted a system of public assistance payments for citizens living in poverty. Except for an inadequate program intended for mothers with young children, Italy offered nothing of the kind until the arrival of the *reddito di cittadinanza* in 2019.

In the unified Kingdom of Italy, where "selective morality" was ubiquitous, an effort was made by apologists to justify the unification by citing incidents such as the occasional suppression of riots in the Two Sicilies whilst overlooking cases such as the Savoys' massacre of Waldensians in Piedmont in 1686 and the Bava-Beccaris massacre in Milan in 1898, long before such tactics could be blamed on Fascism.

Italian nationalists were wont to paint Piedmont and Sardinia, whose dynasty founded the new Kingdom of Italy, as more socially "progressive" than the Two Sicilies, yet the Sardinian penal code of 1859 is strikingly similar to the comparable sections of the code of the Two Sicilies of 1848, right down to the wording of many important statutes, as if influenced by it. Interestingly, the civil code of the Two Sicilies made provision for divorce, something that did not exist in the united Italy until 1974 (see note 11). We find the Kingdom of Sicily instituting a modern constitution in 1812, thirty-six years before the Kingdom of Sardinia, and the Kingdom of the Two Sicilies enacting the first truly modern code of civil law in Italy, in 1819.

Would that the anti-southern bias had ended with the liberation of Italy in 1945 or that its only target were Bourbon rule from 1734 until 1860. In our times, we still hear about the "first paper mill in Italy" being established during the thirteenth century when, in fact, paper was being made in Sicily in the eleventh, if not earlier; a charter written on paper in Sicily in 1109 is shown at the end of Chapter 1, and in 1231 Frederick II mentioned paper in his legal code. For a long time, we were told that Marco Polo introduced spaghetti in Italy in 1295, though *itria* was seen being made at Trabia, in Sicily, where it was described by the geographer Muhammed al Idrisi, before 1154.

A significant phenomenon has brought wider attention to the history and culture of the Two Sicilies and its medieval precursor, the Norman-Swabian Kingdom of Sicily. Not only did the introduction of democracy in 1945 permit further research in Italy by foreign historians like Sir Steven Runciman, Denis Mack Smith, Sir Harold Acton and John Julius Norwich, it facilitated the eventual development of international tourism for the benefit of those curious about the place and its people.

The Baroque grandeur of Naples was generally overlooked by outsiders when Italy was a monarchical dictatorship, while the great Norman-Arab monuments of Palermo were visited only by a few foreign scholars. The royal palace at Caserta is, by far, Italy's largest. The Byzantine mosaics of Monreale cover an area thirty percent more extensive than those of Saint Mark's in Venice.

It is no longer possible to "conceal" these treasures from the world, as if only a few Italian cities were worth discovering.

The Journey

The typical general history assumes the form of an explanatory, or narrative, chronology. This one conforms to that traditional paradigm but for a solitary distinction, namely its occasional forays into social history, and this merits explanation. A prevailing school of thought posits that there are now two principal approaches to the study of history. In simplest terms, the "political" most often deals with great events and famous figures while the "social" considers society at large, the phenomena that shape it, and the everyday lives of the majority of the population, the "common folk." At work in these pages are elements of both. As a *caveat,* it must be observed that the line defining each approach is not always very finely drawn.

In seeking accuracy over allegory, our journey is one of essential history without complex verbiage, pedagogy or deconstructionism. This history is neither "conventional" nor postmodernist. It is simply factual, without excessive hypotheses or analyses. Its emphasis is necessarily one of precision, with a focus on a specific time and place. While developments such as the French Revolution and the rise of the Spanish Empire are peripherally relevant, having influenced events in the Two Sicilies, there is insufficient space in this volume to consider these at great length, for which the reader is referred to other works.

None of this is to suggest that our trek will be prosaic or superficial, but its purpose is to be informative.

Instead of mentioning *every* work consulted by the author, whether useful or not, the bibliography includes only those of immediate relevance or benefit. No effort was made to list every book or paper ever written about the kingdoms of Naples and Sicily, or every opinion ever published on related subjects. It is not the purpose of this work to rebut various theories, however novel or creative.

Beyond "secondary literature" such as Luigi del Pozzo's detailed *Cronaca Civile e Militare delle Due Sicilie sotto la Dinastia Borbonica dall'Anno 1734 in Poi* (1857), which is actually an official publication, and Michelangelo Schipa's *Il Regno di Napoli al Tempo di Carlo di Borbone* (1904), complemented by such documentation as the surviving letters of Charles III and Bernardo Tanucci, many original sources were consulted. These range from royal decrees and legal codes to vital statistics records and newspaper reports, as well as official publications like the *Giornale del Regno delle Due Sicilie*. At all events, most of the information in the numbered chapters and appendices was drawn, ultimately, from *contemporary* sources rather than histories and analyses published long after the fall of the kingdom, such as the work of Santi Correnti or the infamous Benedetto Croce, though such material was reviewed.

Anglice names are generally used for more important proper nouns: *Ferdinand* for *Ferdinando* and *Francis* for *Francesco*, and of course *Naples* for *Napoli*. However, this depends largely on general usage and some Italian forms are retained, hence *Maria Carolina* and *Giuseppe Garibaldi*. Certain usages depend on context: *Basilicata* was anciently *Lucania* and medieval *Puglia* was *Apulia*. The English *Syracuse* refers to the ancient city, the Italian *Siracusa* to the modern one. Most English spellings are American rather than British, and most Italian spellings are modern, hence *Napoletano* instead of *Napolitano*.

Unless it is indicated otherwise, any opinions expressed in this volume, and all of the unattributed translations, are those of the author.

Lu dì... miser palmeri abbati et dissi signuri. Re laudatu sia deu et ben chi esti vinutu effactu nta intendimentu p[er] nostra bontati e quilla di miser iohanni di prochita sipo v[e]l plaza di quista cosa a s[s]a bon mezu eboniu fini. Si comu avimu bonu incomezamentu ma beni viria ki omi fussimu vinutu cum phi genti ch[i] silu Re carlu dixindi p[er] tucta la ysola di sichilia, luquali ami ben qu[i]ndichi milia homini accavallu, siki nui avirrimu troppu affari accumbacti, cum ipsu; et sipero mi pari ki penzamu da[v]anitri phi agenti di quali partikamitri sindi putassi sipo eu cogu ki mi s[i]ma sia p[er] dita tantu ora ristricta et in succurri di vidanda.

Quandu lu Re di aragona audiu q[ue]sti paroli si appi grandi dubitanza audiendu ch[i] lu Re carlu avia tantu putiri et incontineti mandau diceri per li sula di sichilia ch[i] si Re carlu vinissi

Courtesy Biblioteca Centrale della Regione Siciliana

Page from the Spinelli Codex *of the* Rebellamentu di Sichilia *written in Middle Sicilian, the oldest surviving Italian prose*

Death of Nationalism: This column behind Palermo's cathedral marks the place where some 200 civilians in a makeshift bomb shelter were killed by a rather large American bomb in 1943, their corpses left under the rubble. The building in the background was a military school of the Kingdom of the Two Sicilies.

MAPS and TABLES

THE KINGDOM OF THE TWO SICILIES

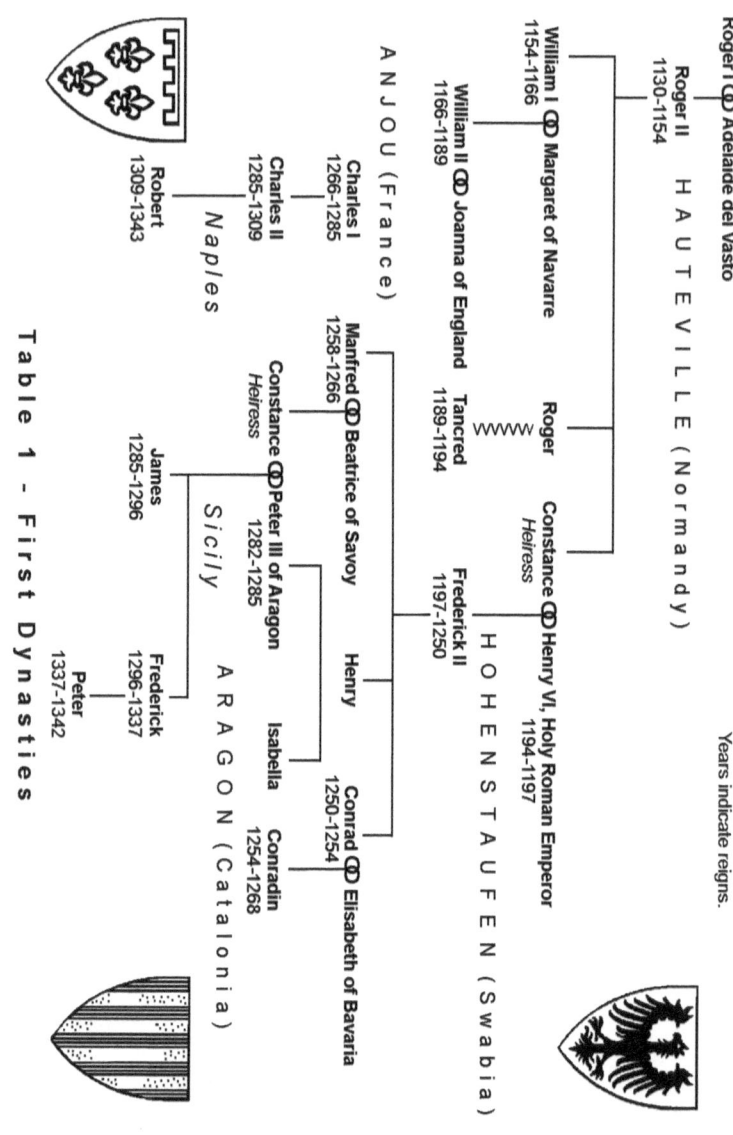

Table 1 - First Dynasties

MAPS AND TABLES

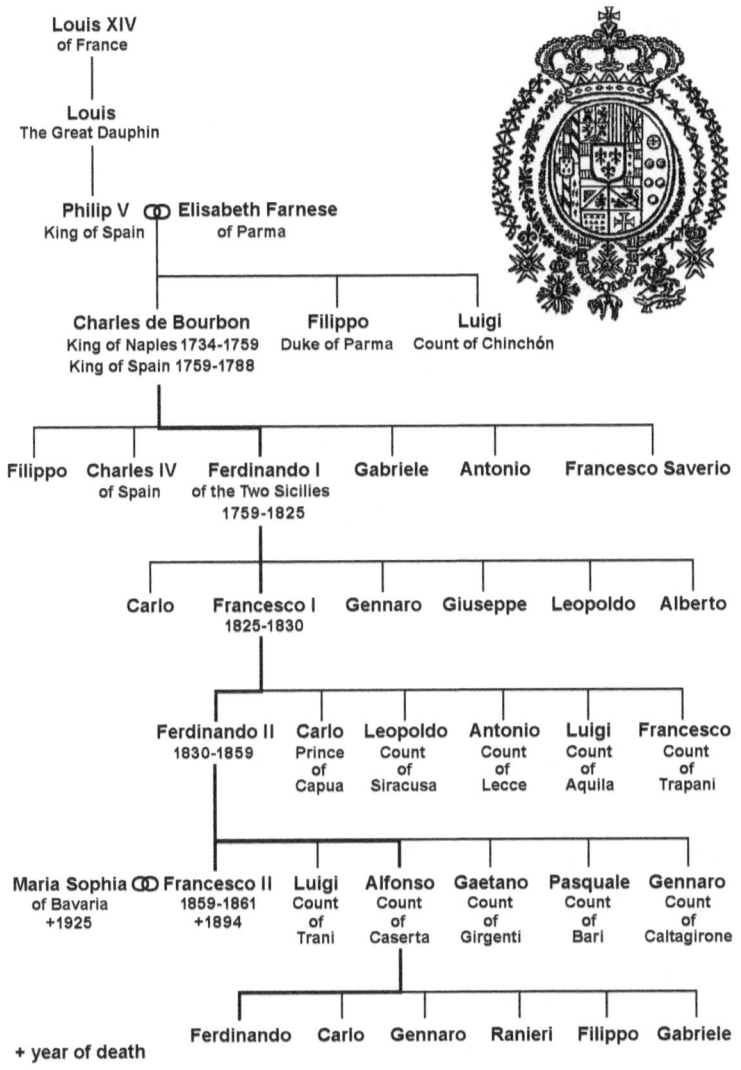

Table 2 - Bourbon Dynasty

THE KINGDOM OF THE TWO SICILIES

Regnum Siciliae: The Norman-Swabian Kingdom of Sicily

THE KINGDOM OF THE TWO SICILIES

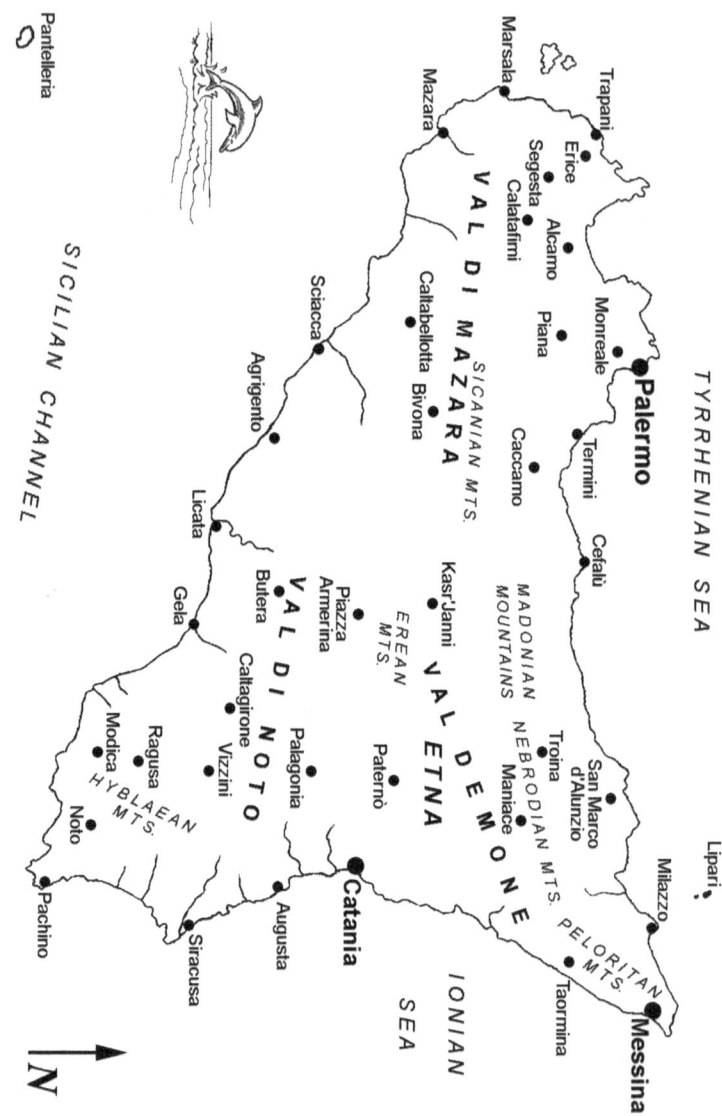

MAPS AND TABLES

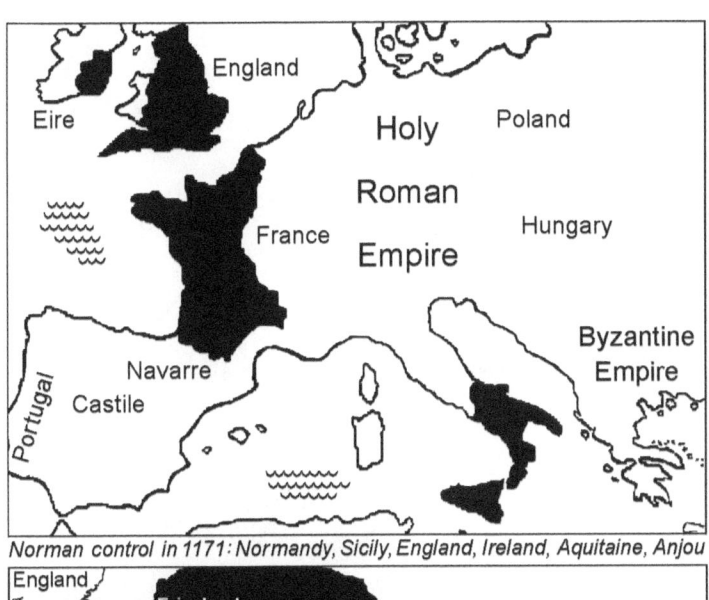

Norman control in 1171: Normandy, Sicily, England, Ireland, Aquitaine, Anjou

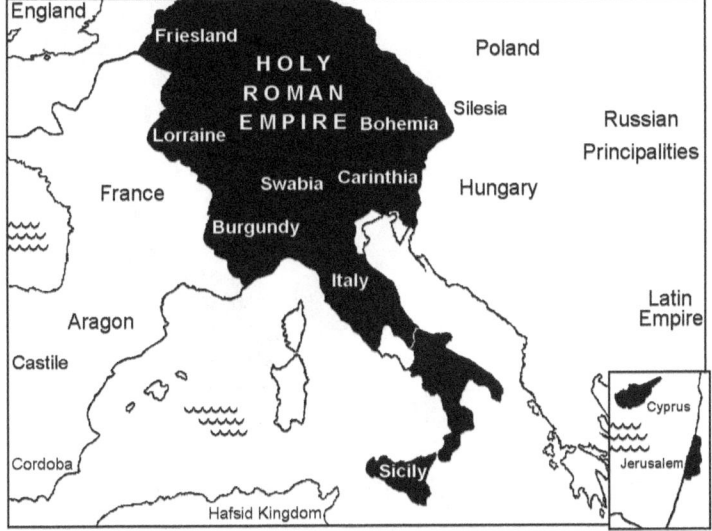

Greatest extent of Hohenstaufen dominion under Frederick II - 1229

Italian states in 1859: The Kingdom of the Two Sicilies was annexed to Italy in 1860

Chapter 1
PRELUDE

The patina of the ages has not obscured the lustre of the place and its people. Its heritage is timeless. Weather changes from day to day; climate evolves over many centuries.

If we seek to identify the earliest historical reality to unite the people of southern Italy into a cohesive societal culture, perhaps even an *ethnie,* it was the arrival of the Greeks *en masse* beginning around 700 BC (BCE). Whereas in earlier times the Greek settlements in Italy were little more than coastal villages, such as Thapsos, which was populated by Mycenaeans, this new wave was nothing less than a mass colonization by people armed with a sophisticated culture, some domesticated olive cultivars, the alphabet crafted by the Phoenicians, and the fork.

Amongst the first Greek colonies in Italy were the cities of Cumae near Naples and Naxos near Taormina.

Slowly but deliberately, Greek culture subsumed existing civilizations, such as those of the Sicanians and Lucanians, amalgamating these societies into something greater.

Our excursus into the ancient and medieval environments that formed the fundaments of the society of the Kingdom of the Two Sicilies shall be one of succinct generalities.

A New World

In the "new world" to their west the Greeks found rivals, most notably the Phoenicians in Sicily and northern Africa and the Italic peoples to the north of the place that became known as *Magna Graecia,* or "Greater Greece," which the Greeks themselves called *Megara Hellas.* In 474 BC, a navy sent from Syracuse handily defeated the ambitious Etruscans in the Bay of Naples. The pugnacious Punics to the south proved more difficult to restrain, and they controlled much of western Sicily.

Southern Italy is full of Greek temples and theatres. The most complete standing temples are those at Segesta (shown at the end of this chapter), Agrigento and Paestum.

Many rivals of the Greeks were other Greeks, for each city was independent. *Megara Hellas* was never anything that most of us would regard as a nation. What united the Greeks culturally sometimes divided them politically.

Nevertheless, the people of *Megara Hellas* shared a common culture consisting of the same societal norms, language, mythology, art, architecture, literature, philosophy, folk customs and cuisine. They were part of a wider Greek ethnie.

In the end, the greatest threat to the Greeks of Italy would come not from the south or even from within, but from the north.

The Romans made conformity to central rule a cornerstone of their expansionist policy. Provinces were permitted a limited degree of self-government but less latitude for dissent. The Romans, their distinctive Latin culture and language colored by those of the Etruscans, Samnites and other "Italic" peoples who gradually assimilated with them, united the Greeks of southern Italy politically while suppressing antagonists like the Carthaginians, the Phoenicians' descendants, in Sicily and northern Africa. Roman victory in the Punic Wars led to the first phase of a Mediterranean conquest destined to shape western civilization for millennia.

The mainland part of *Magna Graecia* became part of Rome's home territory, sometimes known as the "Province of Rome," marked by the Rubicon in the north and the tip of Calabria in the south. In Latin, this came to be called *Italia,* from a word the Greeks had once used for the areas extending up the peninsula from Calabria northward, derived from *Ouitoulia* for the cult of the bulls prevalent in this region. Sicily became Rome's first foreign province.

The Romans adopted much from the Greeks, everything from mythology to architecture. While tongues like Oscan disappeared, Greek, an important literary language, survived and flourished alongside Latin, and it was even studied as a second language among the patricians of the city of Rome. In Sicily, Calabria and Apulia (Puglia), it was used in liturgy and spoken in some families into the twelfth century.

Lasting from 27 BC until AD 180, the *Pax Romana* was a welcome interlude, yet it saw Jesus put to death in a localized disturbance around AD 33.

They have earned justified opprobrium for their brutal executions and their gladiatorial entertainment, but the Romans achieved much even as their imperfect society fostered myriad contradictions. The evil institution of slavery existed, yet the blight of racial bigotry was largely banished. Peoples from around the vast empire could become Roman citizens and many did. Rome brought writing to places lacking it. United by a common language, the inhabitants of disparate regions preserved a few of their own local customs while embracing Rome's system of government and law. Over time, there were emperors from Iberia, Africa and Asia Minor. The Romans' accommodation of this multiethnic panoply is something many modern nations would envy.

Ancient Rome thrived as a polity, in one form or another, for a millennium. The vestiges of her culture survive in Neo-Classical architecture, some traditions of the Roman Catholic

Church, a few juridical principles, and the Roman alphabet of western European languages.

Uninvited Guests

The gradual fall of Rome's mighty empire coincided with the rise of Christianity, which was finally legalized by Constantine the Great with his Edict of Milan in 313. Within a century this religion, once viewed as an eccentric sect of Judaism, was dominant throughout the European regions of the empire and adopted by some peoples beyond its borders.

The change was neither seamless nor painless, but in the end the transition was effected with minimal detriment to the pre-existing social fabric of society. At Syracuse, the greatest city of *Magna Graecia,* the magnificent Greek temple dedicated to the virgin goddess Athena was re-dedicated as a church to the *Theotokos,* the virgin mother of God. The church was literally built around the temple, whose massive columns form the structure. This pattern was typical, leading to the Romanesque style of ecclesial architecture based on Greek temples and Roman basilicas. The title of *pontifex maximus* reserved to the high priest of Rome was assumed by that city's bishops, the popes. In Sicily and much of southern Italy, as we have seen, Greek continued to be spoken, though many also mastered Latin.

In 378, a Roman army was defeated at the Battle of Adrianople, now Edirne in European Turkey, by the ravenous Goths, a Germanic people forced into Roman territory by the migrating Huns. Clearly, circumstances were changing, even if bureaucrats in Constantinople and Rome were initially reluctant to acknowledge the political implications of the debacle that took place at this outpost.

The cause for Rome's ugly decline is the subject of much debate, and the cliché that it destroyed itself from within is not entirely unsubstantiated. The more recent consensus is that the vast empire was torn asunder by too many simultaneous invasions in too many of its remote corners, culminating in the successive mass invasions of the Province of Rome, namely Italy, itself.

Some semblance of Rome's erstwhile grandeur survived in the east, the empire having first been divided in 285. In 395, following the death of Theodosius I, the Roman Empire definitively split into Western ("Latin") and Eastern ("Byzantine") administrations. The splendid Byzantine city of Constantinople eventually became the capital of the Eastern Roman Empire, destined to survive in some form for many centuries.

When the Vandals, Sueves, Burgundians and other tribes crossed the Rhine in 406, the "Great Invasion" had well and truly begun. Alaric's Visigoths, or "Western Goths," sacked Rome four years later, though by then the capital was Ravenna.

Most of the "barbarians" who invaded the empire as it crumbled during the fifth and sixth centuries were Christians. Indeed, some of their leaders had served in the Roman army. The very gentilics of the Vandals and Goths have become quasi-legendary.

The fall of the Western Roman Empire is usually dated to the deposition of its last emperor by Odoacer in 476. Thus began the Dark Ages, the first centuries of the medieval period. Significantly, some Italian localities gravitated politically to the Byzantine east. Venice and Ravenna emerged as important outposts of eastern influence.

The next wave of invaders came from northern Europe, arriving in Italy in 569. Coming to be known as *Lombards,* these Longobards gave their name to a region, Lombardy. They conquered much of the peninsula, introducing something vaguely similar to rudimentary feudalism. In 728, their Donation of Sutri granted the papacy sovereignty over what came to be called the "Papal States," a territory bordering the northern frontier of what had once been *Magna Graecia*. Like the Eastern Roman ("Byzantine") Empire, this polity would survive for many centuries. The Lombards retained pockets of power for centuries after Charlemagne subdued their Lombard "Kingdom of Italy" in 774. In southern Italy their effective capital was Salerno, but many Lombard towns were far removed from the coast, founded in such regions as Lucania (Basilicata).

Other parts of the southern half of the Apennine Peninsula, particularly in Calabria and Apulia (Puglia), were still controlled by the Byzantine Greeks, whose unofficial southern-Italian capital was Bari. The Byzantines handily defeated the Vandals of Sicily in 535, and by 554 they had ousted the Ostrogoths. Their presence in Italy was accepted as natural, for they were the Romans' true successors.

Whatever their differences, the Lombards and Byzantines were Christians who at times achieved a fragile peace. Beginning in 827, the Muslim Arabs conquered Sicily in a series of local conquests by the Aghlabids of northern Africa as part of the expansion of Islam. They introduced irrigation and many new crops and foods, along with the art of silk making. They brought paper making from China and a superior system of numeration from India. Their heirs, the Fatimids and Kalbids, established an emirate based in Bal'harm (Palermo), which they made into a magnificent metropolis.

A few incursions into the mainland followed eventually, but none resulted in permanent settlements. In 915, the pope rallied Lombards and Byzantines in a tenuous alliance to suppress an Arab trading settlement near the mouth of the Gagliano River after the settlers had raided some towns in the region.

It was these three polities — Lombard, Byzantine, Arab — that some Norman adventurers found when they arrived in southern Italy around 1016. Whether the first Norman knights in Italy were pilgrims or mercenaries, or both, depends on which theory one accepts.[22]

Ethnicity was a complex milieu. Over the centuries, the Lombards had intermarried with the local population they found in Italy. Many of the Byzantines were Greek in little more than liturgical practice and the vernacular they spoke. In Sicily, some communities of the west were predominantly Arab while many in the east were largely Byzantine and many were mixed. There were also Berbers. The Muslims were Sunni or Shia depending largely on the dynasty that ruled them, and there was an Ibadi community at Kasr'Janni (Enna). Seeded among these Christian and Muslim populations were Jews. The differences between the Christians of east and west were not yet so great as they would become, but those of Calabria, Apulia and Sicily were in the ecclesiastical jurisdiction of the Patriarch of Constantinople and their liturgy was celebrated in Greek. The Lombard clergy were under the Patriarch of Rome and their liturgical practices were essentially Latin.

Although certain genetic haplogroups are more frequent among specific populations, there was no such thing as a "genetic" Lombard, Greek, Arab or Jew.

Regnum Siciliae

Following early victories as mercenaries in conflicts between Lombards and Byzantines that sometimes pitted one Norman against another, the Normans established their own power base at Melfi in Lucania (Basilicata) and Mileto in Calabria under a family from Hauteville in Normandy. In 1038, they were enlisted to serve in an attempted Byzantine conquest, or reconquest, of Fatimid Sicily by George Maniakes. The incursion ultimately failed but it revealed to the Hautevilles what might be theirs if only they could muster sufficient resources for their own invasion of Sicily.

In 1061, with Rome's blessing, they began this conquest by taking Messina from the Fatimids, exploiting the division that existed among several jealous emirs that now ruled a barely-united island as suzerains of the Fatimids who had moved their capital to Cairo.[23] The Muslim Arabs did not welcome the invaders but neither did the Byzantine Greeks, who justifiably feared the wholesale latinization of their faith in view of the recent schism that formally, if not definitively, separated the patriarchs of Constantinople and Rome in 1054.[24] The Normans were, in effect, Latinizers.

Only in 1071, after a decade of difficult conquests, did the Hautevilles and their Lombard allies reach Palermo. In the meantime, some of their number fought at the Battle of Hastings which led to the comparatively facile conquest of England by Normandy's ruling dynasty.

What they found in Palermo was impressive in every way. Beyond its wealth and opulence, the city boasted a highly-literate, well-educated, multiethnic population. Though chiefly Muslim, it had many Greek Christians and a significant number of Jews. No city in Italy was more populous or prosperous. Robert Hauteville left his younger brother, Roger, in charge of Sicily. Roger himself rarely stayed in Palermo, preferring Messina, Mileto and his castle at San Marco d'Alunzio, but the *diwan,* the treasury, was in good hands with the Arabs, and a steady stream of Normans began immigrating to northwestern Sicily. For the most part, these were men who wed Arab or Greek women and introduced manorialism (feudalism).

At the death of Roger's elder sibling, Robert "Guiscard" (the Crafty), in 1085 while occupying part of Greece, the Hautevilles' conquest of southern Italy was nearly complete. Even so, there was occasional resistance from the Byzantine Bariots. The Lombard Salernitans, for their part, had largely accepted the reality of Norman rule, sealed by such gestures as the marriage of Robert to Sichelgaita of Salerno, even if some of them still resented the Hautevilles.

Like Bari, Salerno was an important center of learning. It was renowned for the medical school where Sichelgaita, a remarkable woman who commanded troops in battle, was educated. Naples was yet to emerge as a great city.

A few Sicilian towns still in Muslim hands were soon subdued.

For now, the Norman territories remained divided between Robert's heirs, who held Apulia, Lucania and other parts of the mainland, and Roger, whose fiefs were Sicily and Calabria. The First Crusade saw some Hautevilles seeking their fortunes in the Holy Land.

In 1098, the papacy granted Roger the "apostolic legateship," effectively the right to approve the choice of the papal appointment of any bishop to a diocese in Sicily. That this later came to be called the *Monarchia Sicula* ("Sicilian monarchy") was a sign of its importance.

At Roger's death in 1101, he was succeeded by a young son, Simon, who died in childhood in 1105. Simon's younger brother, Roger II, thus inherited Sicily and Calabria under the regency of his mother, Adelaide del Vasto. A letter issued by her in 1109 in Greek and Arabic is the oldest known paper document in Italy.[25]

With the death of the heir of his uncle, Robert Guiscard, Roger II inherited the Hauteville dominions of southern Italy. He united the Duchy of Apulia and the County of Sicily as a kingdom with himself as king and Palermo as the royal capital. His coronation in 1130 marked the beginning of the Kingdom of Sicily. It is here that we find the rudiments of the monarchy, its foundational traditions and symbols, the elements which, considered together, made Sicily's kingdom distinctly Sicilian, and later Neapolitan.

The rite of coronation was based on the "Roman-German Pontifical" that was then used in western Europe. Certain elements of this, including parts of its text, were later used in the Two Sicilies and are still used, albeit in English rather than

Latin, in crowning the kings and queens of England. In its original form, it included the oath, investiture, anointing, crowning and enthronement.[26]

A mosaic in Palermo's Martorana church (shown at the end of this chapter) depicts Roger II crowned by Christ Himself. Roger's crown, like those of his son and grandson seen in mosaics and coinage, was of Byzantine design. The oldest crown of the kingdom that actually survives *in toto,* the "kamelaukion" worn by Constance of Aragon, the first wife of Frederick II, was likewise manufactured in Palermo by Greek artisans. The silk "coronation mantle" of Roger II conserved at the Kaiserliche Schatzkammer in Vienna was, in fact, made by Arab weavers a few years after the coronation. As regards regalia fashioned of metal, there is no trace of *Mikalis,* a sword claimed by later historians to be the mystical "Excalibur" of the House of Hauteville, or the anointing spoon used at coronations, which was probably similar to the gold spoon in the collection of crown jewels in the Tower of London. However, several jeweled rings of Constance of Aragon are preserved.

The earliest surviving jewelry known with certainty to have been worn by a king or queen of Sicily is a gold pendant given to Margaret of Navarre, consort of William I, when her son, William II, wed Joanna of England; now conserved in the collection of the Metropolitan Museum of Art in New York, this held relics of Thomas Becket. (The pendant and spoon are shown at the end of this chapter.)

Under Roger II, polycultural Palermo emerged as one of the most cosmopolitan cities in Europe and the Mediterranean and one of the most populous, with as many as two hundred thousand residents. This "New York on the Tyrrhenian" had no official language. Among those in use were Norman French, Siculo Arabic, Byzantine Greek, Medieval Latin, and Judeo Arabic. The king welcomed learned visitors to the court, which became the most sophisticated of Europe.

The kingdom's literacy rate was exceptionally high, especially in Sicily. The use of paper made it easier than ever for children, girls as well as boys, to learn how to read and write. Hindu-Arabic numerals simplified mathematics. These innovations from China and India placed Sicilian society into a wider world beyond most of Europe. Precise figures do not exist, but it is possible that literacy in twelfth-century Sicily exceeded fifty percent, exceeding the levels claimed for Italy in the decades immediately following unification.

Roger's reign saw the completion of a splendid royal palace on high ground in Palermo. This was erected on the site of an Arab citadel, in turn built upon a Punic structure. In the center of the photograph accompanying this chapter is the Pisan Tower, the oldest surviving section of this imposing edifice. The Palatine Chapel, with its Byzantine mosaics and Fatimid muqarnas ceiling, was the site of several royal weddings.

The Norman-Arab-Byzantine churches and palaces of Sicily represent a syncretic form of art and architecture that Roger II fostered during his reign. The kingdom's multicultural golden age, reflected in such jewels as the cathedral of Monreale with its Byzantine mosaics and splendid cloister, did not end with Roger and his immediate heirs. Indeed, it continued in some form into the next century. This distinctive movement was not the only identifying characteristic of the new kingdom.

Roger's first wife, the first Queen of Sicily, was Elvira of Castile, a princess of the House of Jiménez, a dynasty which ruled most of northern Spain; this greatly enhanced the status of the upstart House of Hauteville.

The Archbishop of Palermo became Primate of Sicily, the highest-ranking prelate of the realm, making him the most important cleric south of Rome. In keeping with the apostolic legateship granted to Roger's father, the king could approve this appointment. This was the kind of prerogative that other monarchs, such as Henry II of England, could only envy. The title of primate, but not the special ecclesiastical authority that went with it, survives to this day.

Roger II had to spend the first few years of his reign on the mainland reining in rebellious barons, incidentally rescuing his sister from an abusive husband in the environs of Salerno. At Naples, he ordered the construction of Castel dell'Ovo, a coastal fortress on the site of an older castle.

In 1140, the king promulgated his Assizes of Ariano. Based on the Code of Justinian, it brought order to law through its uniform norms.[27] This, the first formal legal code of the Kingdom of Sicily, was consistent with what we know about Roger's point of view and his appreciation of pragmatic solutions to what lesser monarchs perceived as insurmountable challenges.

A new coin, the *ducat,* reflected Roger's royal authority over the *duchy* of Apulia, hence its name. Here the king was depicted in a manner similar to the image of him in the mosaic in the Martorana, wearing a Byzantine crown and typically eastern robes. Much imitated, the ducat (shown at the end of this chapter) survived as a unit of measurement for coinage throughout the existence of the kingdom, into the nineteenth century. Initially unpopular, the silver coin facilitated trade and commerce.

From commerce was born prosperity, and we find among the Arabs of Norman Sicily the application of an early form of common law, which soon vanished in Italy but survived in England. This likely reflects the influence of Maliki traditions.[28]

Although the kingdom's essential ecclesiastical point of reference was invariably Roman Catholic, Nilos Doxopatrios, a Greek Orthodox cleric who arrived at Palermo around 1142, wrote a convincing theological treatise expounding upon the traditions and prerogatives of the eastern church. There is very little to suggest that the King of Sicily seriously considered undermining papal power, but there were still many Orthodox clergy in the realm, especially at small monasteries around Bari, throughout Calabria and in northeastern Sicily.

Throughout the Norman era, the culture of the kingdom was at once Norman, Arab and Byzantine. In addition to the Latin Christians, there were still many Greek Christians, Muslims and Jews. Visiting Sicily, the traveler bin Jubayr noted that many Christian women dressed in the Muslim style.

When the Second Crusade began in 1147, Roger exploited the moment to send an expedition to attack the lands of the Byzantine Empire. This campaign was successful in bringing some Aegean territories under Sicilian rule. It was followed by conquests on the African coast in what are now Tunisia and Libya, not Roger's first incursion into that region.

King Roger's death in 1154 marked the end of an era.

By the end of his reign, we find Roger's kingdom as the largest, most powerful state in what is now Italy, the same status it was destined to enjoy seven centuries later. Its glory might wane over time, but here was the essential monarchy that constituted the foundation of a Siculo-Neapolitan ethnie.

Roger's son, William I, was by most accounts an unremarkable monarch. Following William's death in 1166 his young son, also William, succeeded him.

For the next five years, the regent for young William II was his mother, Margaret of Navarre, probably the greatest queen of the medieval Kingdom of Sicily.

Stupor Mundi

Following the reigns of three successive kings — William I, William II, Tancred — Roger's posthumous daughter, Constance, became queen regnant in 1194. Wed to the Holy Roman Emperor Henry VI, she gave birth to a son, Frederick, destined to inherit both crowns.

Like Margaret of Navarre, who may have been her role

model, Constance was a highly competent queen, but her regency for her young son, following Henry's death in 1197, did not last long; she died the next year.

As a young child, Frederick II thus lost both his parents. As an adult, he emerged as one of the greatest European rulers of his era. This history of southern Italy during the first half of the thirteenth century is largely the history of Frederick Hohenstaufen.[29]

A series of popes vilified him, for his Sicilian and imperial dominions surrounded the papal lands, constituting what the pontiffs perceived as a perpetual threat. Excommunication failed to intimidate him.

In 1224, he founded the *Studium* of Naples, generally considered Europe's first "secular" university. Although there were clergy among the teachers, many instructors were drawn from the laity. The same was true of Salerno's medical school, an older, more specialized institution.

Fluent in several languages, including Arabic, Frederick conducted a pacific crusade to the Holy Land in 1228 and promulgated a new legal code at Melfi in 1231.[30] He composed poetry as a patron of the Sicilian School, the first literary movement of note to make use of an Italian vernacular other than Latin. He wrote a treatise on falconry that dealt with nature and the care of wildlife.[31] His legal code addressed the need to protect the environment, particularly rivers and streams.

Upon hearing of Frederick's death in 1250, an English chronicler, Matthew Paris, coined the fitting epitaph *Stupor Mundi,* "Wonder of the World."

He was not without his flaws, yet Frederick Hohenstaufen was one of the greatest European monarchs of the thirteenth century.

Frederick's successive heirs — Conrad, Manfred, Conrad the Younger — lacked Frederick's political acumen. Manfred, Frederick's favorite son, suffered a fatal defeat to Angevin forces at Benevento in 1266, and Conradin (Conrad the Younger), the son of Conrad, was routed at Tagliacozzo two years later.

Later historians were inclined to refer to some of the early kings, especially Roger II and Frederick II with their harems, Fatimid dress and Islamic luxuries, as "baptized sultans." Nobody described the Angevins that way. They were austere by comparison.

A Tale of Two Sicilies

This defeat of the last Staufens left Charles of Anjou as King of Sicily. He was not nature's choice but the papacy's. Charles was the less pious younger brother of the French king, Louis IX, and it was Rome's machinations that had put him on the throne, for here was a papal ally whose power, unlike that of the Hohenstaufens, did not extend to the imperial communes of northern Italy. With Charles the popes could relax knowing they shared one border with him, not two.

While Louis was destined for sainthood, Charles was marked for infamy. That would come soon enough.

For now, Charles transferred the capital of the Kingdom of Sicily from Palermo to Naples, where he could be nearer his papal master.

He began to suppress the few Muslim communities remaining in places like Lucera in Apulia, imposing a Latin monoculture in his dominions. He increased taxation while granting lands to his coterie of French knights. Not surprisingly, Charles was rather unpopular, especially in Sicily, but his focus on the city of Naples earned him support there.

His achievements were real. He developed Naples into a truly royal metropolis, where previously Salerno and papal Benevento were more populous and certainly more important than this ancient city.[32]

He could be said to have been ambitious. Among his objectives was the conquest of the Byzantine Empire, which was again under Greek control following its rule by a series of Frankish (Latin) sovereigns.

This ambition was thwarted in 1282 when the Sicilians rebelled against Charles in what has come to be called the "War of the Vespers," offering the crown to Peter III of Aragon on the basis of his consort, Constance, being the legitimate heiress to the Kingdom of Sicily as the daughter of Manfred, whom Charles had defeated at Benevento sixteen years earlier. While Sicily itself fell into Aragonese hands, the peninsular part of the kingdom remained under the control of Charles. With each monarch claiming the Kingdom of Sicily, which was now divided, there were now two "Sicilies," hence the oxymoronic name for the twin realms.

Whether the Vespers uprising was the result of a baronial conspiracy is much debated, but unrest among the Sicilian populace was hardly a secret. The rebellion shocked the monarchs of Europe.[33]

Charles was succeeded by his son, Charles II, sometimes "Charles the Lame," who commissioned the building of a large royal castle, Castel Nuovo, in Naples. Neapolitans sometimes refer to it as the *Maschio Angioino,* or "Angevin Keep." Completed in just five years, it supplanted the "Capuan Castle" as the king's residence.

A treaty signed at the Sicilian town of Caltabellotta in 1302, the year of Constance's death, brought an "official" end to the war but not the rival claims. Even marriages between the dynasties could not resolve the predicament. Except for the coincidence that found the same Spanish monarchs ruling both kingdoms in a "personal union," five centuries were to pass before the realm known to the Norman and Swabian kings was reunited.

A treaty signed at Catania in 1347 was no more successful

than the Peace of Caltabellotta; the state of war truly ended only with a subsequent treaty negotiated under papal auspices in 1372.

By then, Neapolitan and Sicilian were the chief spoken languages of the twin kingdoms. Their basic structure has changed very little since the fourteenth century except for some Tuscanization and the obvious use of modern words like *telefono* and *computer*. Neapolitan is generally nearer to Latin, while Sicilian has more words from Arabic and Greek, and its pronunciation sounds rather like Catalan, which has influenced it.

The essentially Latin, or "Italian," linguistic and social culture we identify with southern Italy was firmly in place. The church was thoroughly westernized and the beginning of folk traditions now associated with it were beginning to emerge.

Some of the larger churches being erected were of a peculiar "Gothic Romanesque" style similar to those of many Franciscan abbeys built in Italy. Good examples are Saint Matthew in Naples and Saint Francis in Palermo, though the former better emulates the true Gothic.

Much of the cuisine would be familiar to people living today. Cannoli, sfince and zeppole existed, along with rice balls and pasta (see note 35). Despite the quaint legend about Marco Polo bringing it from China, spaghetti was mentioned by Muhammed al Idrisi, the court geographer of Roger II. The Neapolitans formed pasta into various shapes they called *maccheroni*.

To somebody in England, such delights as almonds and sugar might be viewed as delicacies, but not here. Introduced by the Arabs, whose *kanats* transported water, rice was grown in southern Italy long before it was cultivated along the Po. Ports like Taranto, Bari and Messina enjoyed commerce with lands to the east. Unfortunately, shipping also facilitated the arrival of the bubonic plague at Messina in 1347, and it rapidly spread across Europe, claiming millions of lives.

The plague resulted in more power for serfs because, in its wake, there were fewer people to work the large feudal estates. This signalled the end of serfdom. By this time, institutionalized slavery was essentially extinct in southern Italy, though it continued in some form in northern cities like Venice and Florence, where many servants were from the Balkans or other regions to the east.

For now, the kingdoms of Naples and Sicily still had extensive forests where deer and boar roamed. There were rivers full of trout. Among livestock unique to the region were the buffalo of the Salerno area and the Girgento sheep of Agrigento. The twin kingdoms even had their own breeds of dog, the stout Neapolitan mastiff and the slender Sicilian hound, or *cirneco*.

The climate was noticeably cooler, partly due to the "Little Ice Age" but also because there was no modern global warming.

The Long Sleep

Following the War of the Vespers, the Kingdom of Sicily, the island itself, was initially ruled from Palermo by the heirs of Peter and Constance, although some of these kings chose to live at Catania on the Ionian coast. By the early decades of the fifteenth century, in view of a dearth of male dynasts in Sicily, the King of Aragon, based in Zaragoza (and sometimes resident in Barcelona), was also King of Sicily. The island was considered part of the loose thalassocracy known as the "Crown of Aragon."

The Kingdom of Naples, as it was called beginning in the fifteenth century, was ruled by descendants of Charles and his Anjou dynasty, thus cultivating close ties to France. Apart from these kings, two queens stand out, Joanna I (1327-1382) and Joanna II (1371-1435).

The reign of Alfonso the Magnanimous from 1442 to 1458

saw the two kingdoms united under one monarch of Aragon's Trastámara dynasty. Alfonso died at Castel dell'Ovo, an imposing fortress that still guards the coast of Naples. It was during his reign that phrases came into use referring to the dominions "on this side of the lighthouse," *al di qua del faro* (referring to the peninsula), and "beyond the lighthouse," *al di là del faro* (the island). The former sometimes became *citra* and the latter *ultra*. When the two kingdoms were eventually united again, this antonomasia was used in royal decrees right up until the fall of the Two Sicilies. The Latin *pharus* comes to us from the Egyptian lighthouse at Pharos.

In 1453, the fall of Constantinople and what remained of her Byzantine Empire precipitated the migration of thousands of Albanian Christians to towns in Puglia, Basilicata, Calabria and Sicily. They were permitted to keep their traditional Greek liturgy but forced to accept papal authority.

What we find in both kingdoms during the centuries following the Middle Ages are epidemics, famines, earthquakes and general exploitation. The Inquisition persecuted Jews, eventually banishing their faith altogether, while prosecuting Christian "heretics" whose devotion was, quite arbitrarily, deemed insufficient — or whose neighbors denounced them as a pretext for confiscating their land. The Renaissance arrived not in the fullness of its glory but through its artistic movements, and then only belatedly. Taxation was oppressive. The general distrust of the crown was somewhat greater in Sicily than on the mainland, but no state in Italy could be said to be truly enlightened or progressive. Revolts and public protests were frequent.

Lying to the immediate south of the Papal State, the Kingdom of Naples sometimes seemed to be an extension of both its territory and its mentality. Many Jews left the twin kingdoms. Those who remained became *anusim,* reluctant converts to Christianity, known as *conversos* in Spain and *neofiti* in Italy. They were definitively cast out or converted in 1493 in the

Kingdom of Sicily and in 1541 in the Kingdom of Naples. This followed the expulsions from Spain in 1492. In Sicily, the expulsions of the Jews were delayed for a year to permit the crown to levy one last tax upon them.[34] Paradoxically, the Jews were tolerated in the papal lands to the north, though rarely treated very well.

In widowhood, the aristocrat Maria Lorenza Longo, who was Catalan by birth, founded a hospital for the poor of Naples operated by her order, the Capuchin Poor Clares. This *Ospedale degli Incurabili,* which still exists, is regarded by some historians as the first "public" hospital in that city.

Meanwhile, the arrival of Europeans in the Americas brought changes in the decades following the landing of Christopher Columbus. Cuisine evolved as new crops like tomatoes, potatoes and peppers were introduced, along with the preparation of chocolate and the cultivation of tobacco.[35] Sicily lost its sugar cane industry to the plantations of the Caribbean.

The importance of the twin kingdoms, especially Sicily, began to diminish as Europeans, and particularly the Spanish kings who ruled southern Italy, forged new empires in a new world. Yet the Ottoman Empire still constituted a power center in the Mediterranean. During the sixteenth century, the Holy Roman Emperor Charles V, a Hapsburg who ruled Spain, Naples, Sicily, Germany and other pieces of western Europe, prosecuted a war in Tunisia and ceded Malta as a fief to the Knights Hospitaller as a bulwark against Muslim influence.

Baroque Paladins

The Reformation made precious few inroads into the twin kingdoms, where the zealous Jesuits, aided by the Inquisition, advocated the vengeful spirit of the Counter Reformation. Like much of Catholic Europe, Naples and Sicily had, in effect, papal "shadow" governments against which no monarch could rebel. We find Neapolitans and Sicilians pressed into service to fight Protestants in foreign wars of religion.

Medicine was primitive and epidemics were lethal. One of the few people who understood such things was the physician Giovanni Filippo Ingrassia. A student of Vesalius, Ingrassia taught anatomy and medicine at the distinguished University of Naples. In 1563 he was appointed *Protomedico* of Sicily, effectively the chief administrator of hospitals. Published in 1576, his book *Informatione del Pestifero et Contagioso Morbo* described the bubonic plague in detail, outlining the development of its recent outbreak. It is the first known work ever to recommend effective countermeasures such as physical isolation to prevent the spread of such diseases. Two years later, he wrote *Methodus dandi Relationes pro Mutilatis Torquendis,* an analysis of the torture methods used by the Inquisition. This, of course, was banned, to be published only much later.[36]

The twin kingdoms were not ignored by the rest of Europe. Shakespeare's Latin inspiration didn't come only from the north of Italy. *The Winter's Tale* is set in Sicily.

There were occasional revolts. Depending on which accounts and interpretations we accept, these were either instigated by the aristocracy or motivated by desperation among the populace.

Except for 1647, when Henry of Guise briefly seized control of Naples, the twin kingdoms were ruled from Spain by Charles V and then his descendants from 1516 until 1700. This led to occasional immigration from Spain, especially when the crown wanted to settle certain abandoned agricultural areas.

Administration was undertaken by viceroys sent from Madrid, though trusted local men sometimes occupied this position. Cartographers and even some diplomats sometimes used the phrase "Kingdom of Naples and Sicily" in referring to the two states, despite there being two separate crowns.

Naturally, there was trade and contact with other parts of Italy, but the kingdoms of Naples and Sicily were quite Hispanicized, and neither enjoyed rule by a resident monarch. Preoccupied with expanding their empire, the Spanish kings had no time to visit. Yet the name "Two Sicilies" again became a convenient shorthand.

It is not difficult to understand the people feeling themselves to be the taxable subjects of a distant king, for such they were. Military conscription, when it occurred, only made matters worse. Ever distrustful of the state, the common folk looked to their families for a sense of identity and solace in an indifferent world. The greatest feasts were those of patron saints: Januarius (Gennaro) in Naples, Rosalie in Palermo, Nicholas in Bari, Agatha in Catania. One of these festivals, a rare respite from a dreary daily existence, might last for days.

Absolutism ruled supreme. Neither of the twin kingdoms was a constitutional state. Centuries of complex and confused administration had left the legal codes an eclectic morass of cryptic legislation. There was no "common law" in the English sense, and judges often invented or reinvented the law as they went along, ruling without taking much account of statutes or precedents except in the most abstract, perfunctory manner.

Sentences were prescribed for some crimes but application of the law was capricious at best. In fact, laws were not applied in any semblance of consistency or uniformity throughout either kingdom. Courts of appeal were essentially dysfunctional and rarely available as a means of recourse. In theory, the laws of the twin kingdoms were rooted in the Code of Justinian, manifested in Roger's Assizes of Ariano and Frederick's Constitutions of Melfi, but centuries of papal meddling, most obviously through the zealous use of the Inquisition, had all but eliminated such fundamental rights as divorce. The monarchs were Catholic, Spain's infamously so.

Personal rights were all but unknown. Rape was rarely prosecuted; it was difficult to know if it were even to be considered a serious crime. Yet a man or woman suspected of an offense against the crown could be arrested on the slightest pretext, then tossed into a jail cell and left to rot there until the authorities decided to level formal charges. The wealthy could purchase justice as necessary.

In criminal cases, the burden of proof was ridiculously high except when either church or state undertook to exercise its own interest under its own authority.

If law was chaotic, administration was oppressive, notably efficient only when the crown was collecting money. There were, of course, the usual taxes on staples, like the *macinato* imposed on flour. During the sixteenth and seventeenth centuries, the state could levy property taxes such as the *donativo* at whim whenever the budget required more funds, a practice that survives in today's Italy.[37] In 1638, the crown levied a head tax to defray the cost of the Thirty Years' War.[38] Here was a typical example of Spain dragging the kingdoms of Naples and Sicily into its own folly. Even the landscape of the Two Sicilies suffered as timber was harvested to build Spanish warships but trees were rarely planted.

Religious freedom was little more than a fantasy. Catholicism's tentacles reached out from Rome to touch every facet of private and public life. There was no freedom of the press to speak of. Censorship was the norm. The papal index of prohibited books was widely published and scrupulously enforced. Semi-legendary, secretive sects like Palermo's *Beati Paoli* seem to have been composed of intellectuals sympathetic to the ideas of the Enlightenment, but far too little is known about them to draw firm conclusions (see note 48). The mere possession of a forbidden book could land its owner in jail.

Books, of course, were a vehicle for learning, but even the University of Naples, founded by Frederick II as a secular school, was not immune to coercion by the Catholic establishment.

Parliaments were controlled by aristocrats and overseen by viceroys. Some viceroys were exceptionally ethical but most were self-interested and corrupt.

In 1656, a particularly grave episode of plague struck the Kingdom of Naples, claiming many lives in the capital.

All was not gloomy. Alessandro Scarlatti, born in Sicily in 1660, founded what became the Neapolitan School of Opera.

The capital cities, Naples and Palermo, boasted some impressive Baroque splendor. They produced their share of artists, architects, sculptors and composers, but this belied the fact that intellectual life was generally stagnant.

None of this is to suggest that the average person in Florence or Milan was better off than a Neapolitan or Palermitan. The level of illiteracy and poverty was generally constant throughout what is now Italy. Most people lived beyond the big cities, and few were educated formally beyond the age of twelve or thirteen, if that. Families were large and life expectancy was short. These conditions were uniform across Europe.

If the people were to be ruled by an autocrat, they wanted it to be their own.

PRELUDE

Ancient and medieval roots of the people of the Two Sicilies: Greek temple (Segesta) and Norman castle (Erice)

This charter issued by Adelaide in 1109 in Greek and Arabic is the oldest surviving paper document in Italy and one of the oldest in Europe (only Spain has earlier exemplars). The damaged seal may be Adelaide's.

PRELUDE

Ducat shows a similar crown and vestments

Roger II, depicted as a Byzantine basileus, crowned by Christ in engraving based on mosaic in Palermo's Martorana church

Worn by Constance of Aragon, queen consort of Frederick II, this is the oldest surviving crown of the Kingdom of Sicily

Little jewelry or regalia in precious metal survives from the kingdom's Norman era. This gold pendant, which held relics of Saint Thomas Becket, was given to Queen Margaret of Sicily by King Henry II of England when his daughter, Joanna, wed her son, William II, in 1177. It was buried with her in Monreale's cathedral.

At coronations, Sicily's kings and queens were anointed with a spoon similar to this gold Norman exemplar preserved in England, the oldest of the Crown Jewels.

The first royal palace of the Kingdom of Sicily, in Palermo

PRELUDE

Apse and cupola of the Palatine Chapel

Fatimid fountain in the cloister of Monreale

Castel dell'Ovo was built in Naples by King Roger II on the site of an older fortress. Charles II of Anjou erected Castel Nuovo.

Castel Nuovo, erected in Naples on the orders of Charles II of Anjou

Chapter 2
CHARLES III

A transition of sorts arrived with the new century. King Charles II of Spain was in fragile health, and when he died in 1700 the Spanish branch of the Hapsburg dynasty died with him. In the end, his relations with other monarchs were cordial. Three years earlier, Spain was a signatory to the Treaty of Ryswick, by which France ended its Nine Years' War against the Grand Alliance (the Dutch, English, Spanish and Germans). Yet some of these Allied leaders were concerned about who would eventually succeed the sickly, childless Spanish king. Hoping to resolve this potential problem, Charles willed the crown to his grandnephew Philip, grandson of his half-sister Maria Theresa, who was the first wife of Louis XIV of France. This extended kinship network was typical of its era, manifesting itself in dynastic complexities.

As always, there were dissatisfied factions among the populace, but a half-hearted revolt by Neapolitan barons in 1701 was no more successful than the occasional protests of the past.

Spanish Succession

Reigning as Philip V of Spain, the new king was the son of

King Louis' son, "Louis, the Grand Dauphin," so-called for being the French heir apparent for many years until his long-reigning father survived him (see the second genealogical table).

This dynastic choice was not so clear as it might seem, for there were other eligible candidates. Charles' sister, Margaret, had married a cousin, Leopold I of Austria, who also claimed a place in the succession as a grandson of King Philip III of Spain (who had died in 1621). Leopold himself had a son and heir, the future Charles VI of Austria. It was not only Spain, Naples and Sicily that interested the Hapsburgs, but the vast Spanish Empire that now existed.

The genealogical nexus of this dispute between descendants of Philip III was that Philip V (a Bourbon) and Charles VI (a Hapsburg) were second cousins one generation removed, and obviously not "kissing" cousins. Further afield, other descendants claiming dynastic rights through the Spanish Hapsburgs included Joseph Ferdinand of Bavaria and Vittorio Amedeo II of Savoy.

As a condition of his succession to the Spanish throne, young Philip V renounced any claims to become King of France. Despite this, King Louis left his young grandson in the French line of succession, something which could someday leave Philip V ruling much of Europe as well as vast colonial territories abroad. Having reneged on certain terms of the Treaty of Ryswick, Louis came to be viewed — or at least characterized — by the powers of the Grand Alliance as duplicitous. There were already grave misgivings about too much power falling into the hands of a single monarch, and these now bubbled to the surface.

What ensued in 1702 was the War of the Spanish Succession.[39] Here the twin kingdoms of Naples and Sicily found themselves caught in the middle of a conflict involving most of western Europe, with their fate hanging in the balance in a wider war that reached as far as the Americas.

Supporting Charles VI of Austria, a new Grand Alliance of Germany, England and the Netherlands fought against France and Spain. In 1707, Austrian troops invaded and conquered the Kingdom of Naples. They would prove less successful in Spain, where Charles briefly occupied Catalonia, while Sicily proved elusive despite a standoff at the Strait of Messina.

The war ended in 1713 with the Treaty of Utrecht. Restoring what was perceived as Europe's "balance of power," this agreement gave Sicily to Vittorio Amedeo of Savoy, who happened to be the father-in-law of Philip V of Spain. Sardinia, another of Philip's dominions, was given to Charles of Austria. Among the sundry territories ceded to Britain was Gibraltar, which an Anglo-Dutch force had captured in the name of Austria during an earlier war.

The peninsular Kingdom of Naples went to Charles VI of Austria. Hardly comparable to the vast Spanish Empire he coveted, it nevertheless augmented his territories in the Balkans and northeastern Italy.

The Austrians' rule of the Kingdom of Naples cannot be said to be much better or worse than their rule of these other regions. There was taxation but a tenuous stability. To the ordinary person the changes probably seemed minimal. The more obvious problems were in Sicily.

As Duke of Savoy, Vittorio Amedeo II ruled Piedmont, Savoy and some adjoining territories from Turin, his capital. Sicily was potentially wealthier than these regions. In late 1713 he arrived on the island with an English fleet. Now he was a king. With him were six thousand northern Italian soldiers to replace the Spanish garrisons. He remained on the island for a year, reopening the University of Catania and attempting to improve general and local administration.

As the Spanish had depleted the treasury, the new monarch's first decision was to levy taxes on the Sicilians, including a *donativo,* a periodic wealth tax imposed directly on citizens based on the value of their assets, in 1714, and to seize what little gold was left in the kingdom's reserves.[40]

Vittorio Amedeo II is sometimes depicted in modern Italian history as efficient and austere. He was also bloodthirsty. In 1686, as a young monarch acting on the advice of reckless ministers, he ordered a ruthless suppression of Waldensians that led to thousands of deaths, either directly or through imposed starvation in Savoyard prisons. In Sicily, he ensured that the censorship of "forbidden" books was more avidly enforced than it had been under Spanish rule.

Nevertheless, sincere efforts were made to improve the government's efficiency while discouraging bribery and embezzlement. Part of the solution was the appointment of Piedmontese officials. Excise taxes on tobacco, salt and other products were increased. Laws against murder and manslaughter were rewritten and enforced.

A strange case involving the Bishop of Lipari tested the traditional "legatine" rights of the King of Sicily (see Chapter 1). In 1711, the bishop had excommunicated several officials who erroneously taxed some produce destined for the church. This was clearly overzealous. When the excommunications were lifted by a royal office claiming to represent the crown's apostolic authority, the bishop sought recourse with the pope. This jurisdictional conflict was not of Vittorio Amedeo's making; he had inherited it from his predecessor, Philip, whose viceroy was seeking to apply an obsolete medieval law to modern circumstances.

In response, the papacy formally revoked the apostolic legateship in 1715.[41] For good measure, to show that popes still had teeth with which to bite insolent kings, Rome absolved Sicily's clerics from paying the most recent *donativo*. In response, many were arrested, and there was a dearth of priests to celebrate mass in parish churches. This discord probably delighted Philip, who was doubtless monitoring developments from Madrid, even though it was he who had instigated the dispute over the legateship four years earlier.

Philip was already plotting to reclaim Sicily even as he expressed public support for Vittorio Amedeo. His wife, Vittorio Amedeo's sister Maria Luisa, was now deceased. In 1714, Philip had wed Isabella (Elisabeth) Farnese, of the family of the Dukes of Parma. He need no longer feel bound to Vittorio Amedeo of Savoy by the strictures of genealogical affinity. Indeed, his ambitious second wife was encouraging him to reclaim Sicily and much more.

Many in Europe already suspected the machinations of Philip, his ministers and his avaricious Italian wife. When King Louis XIV died in 1715, his only legal heir was his infant great-grandson, Louis XV. Philip made it known that he would reclaim a place in the French succession, an assertion that didn't set well with the French. In early 1717, they joined the Dutch and the British in a Triple Alliance intended to thwart Spanish ambitions in France and Italy. They didn't have to wait long for Philip to make the first move.

In August, the Spanish invaded Sardinia while the Austrians were occupied with a war against the Turks in the Balkans. That island was completely conquered by November. By then, the Austrians had decided to join France, Britain and the Netherlands to form the Quadruple Alliance. By now, Philip's intentions should have been obvious.

In July 1718, a large Spanish fleet appeared off the Sicilian coast. Lacking baronial support, the Piedmontese viceroy eventually departed in the face of a landing by more than twenty thousand troops. The developing predicament was bigger than anything he was prepared to confront.

Vittorio Amedeo appealed to Europe to restore his rights in Sicily since his own Piedmontese navy was not sufficient to engage the Spanish. At the same time, he made it clear that he would accept another island, Sardinia, in exchange for Sicily if it would permit him to retain the title of king. His wish was granted with the Treaty of London.[42] Though smaller than Sicily, and far less affluent, Sardinia was nearer Turin and its comparatively docile population was easier to rule.

Sicily was given to Charles of Austria, who was already King of Naples, but he would have to work to possess it.

The first Mediterranean encounter leading up to this War of the Quadruple Alliance occurred in August when a British fleet defeated the Spanish at the Battle of Cape Passaro involving some sixty vessels, threatening Philip's ability to reinforce his troops in Sicily. In December, France, Britain and Austria declared war on Spain; the Netherlands joined them the next year.

In depriving the Spanish of their control over Sicily's eastern coasts, the British victory at Cape Passaro cleared the way for the Austrians to land. Crossing the Strait of Messina from Calabria, they attacked Spanish positions in a series of battles between Messina and Catania. The key to their success was that they were supplied by their British allies with armaments and victuals, while the Spanish began to run low on both.

In October, a large battle was fought at coastal Milazzo. The Austrians numbered about six thousand, the Spanish three thousand more. This was a Spanish victory in as much as the Austrians had to retreat. What was important was that they would live to fight another day.

There were battles around western Europe. In Scotland, the Spanish supported an ill-fated Jacobite rising at the Battle of Glen Shiel in June 1719.

Later that month, the next major ground engagement in Sicily was the Battle of Francavilla, thought to be the largest battle on Sicilian soil since antiquity. Here, with a total of some fifty thousand men on the field, the Austrians and Spanish met head-on in a large plain along the Alcantara River. Spanish artillery won the day, but a series of smaller battles followed around Messina, which the Austrians occupied following numerous attacks.

A Tale of Two Cities

The war ended with the Treaty of the Hague in February 1720, and Sicily came under Austrian rule, making Charles VI of Austria the king of the "Two Sicilies."

By this time, most people had ceased to care who ruled them from afar. Whether the viceroy spoke Spanish, French or German made little difference. The church was the same. Social networks were built around families. Everybody else was an outsider.

Like his predecessor, Charles VI sought to bring some order to the twin kingdoms, and, like him, he found many obstacles. To placate some obstinate nobles, he created them Princes of the Holy Roman Empire, as if there were not already a glut of exalted titles of nobility in use. He imposed a number of localized taxes over the next few years. Soon it was clear that much of this money was not actually being received from the nobles who had collected it from the people in their districts.

The Anglo-Spanish War (1727-1729), which involved Spain's efforts to retake Gibraltar, did not touch Italy. The Treaty of Seville officially ended the hostilities, but it hardly represented a bond of eternal amity between the British and the Spanish, and the dispute over Gibraltar continued to fester.

Charles VI curried favor with the church, and in 1728 a new pontiff, Benedict XIII, granted a pared-down version of the papal legateship that had been rescinded in 1715.

The Inquisition (now the Holy Office) continued unabated, but 1732 was the last year to see a Sicilian burned alive in a public spectacle.

In the Kingdom of Naples, and especially around the capital, the monarch's viceroys unexpectedly encountered the concept of the "Neapolitan Nation" that had begun to evolve in earnest when the kingdom was ruled from Madrid. This was a sense of national identity that transcended the influence of any single dynasty or even the church.[43] The idea itself was not implicitly favorable to Charles and the Austrians, though care may have been taken to make it appear so. Remarkably, it was not linked to a king or, for that matter, a republic, nor was it analogous to the communes (city states) of northern Italy.

Indeed, it reflected what has come to be viewed as the perception of a metropolis so large and important that it dominates an entire country as both its capital and economic center, as if there were a Madrid without a Barcelona, or a Rome without a Milan. The contemporary comparisons, as we shall see, were, and still are, London and Paris.

Naples attracted people from around its kingdom. Eventually, a crude concept of "citizenship" (residency) distinguished the natives from everybody else for the purpose of taxation. By 1700 great prestige was attached to being Neapolitan rather than Salernitan or Capuan. During the next century, with the introduction of civil (publicly-registered) birth records, this obsession reached the point of affluent pregnant women going to the capital to give birth so that their children would be "Neapolitan."

Whereas Palermo experienced occasional competition from Messina, and more recently Catania, in the mainland kingdom the city of Naples completely overshadowed the social and economic landscape, leaving Salerno, Bari, Brindisi and Taranto mere geographical stopovers. It isn't possible to date the inception of this phenomenon precisely, but it was clearly evident by the sixteenth century. By then, Naples was already the largest city in Italy.

In a land of duchies, it was the capital of an eponymous kingdom. There was, after all, no "Kingdom of Palermo."

However we define it, the *Nazione Napoletana* was one of

those socially, and potentially political, notions that might manifest itself in sudden explosions of ethnic or nationalist feeling not unlike what emerged from time to time in other European countries, such as Ireland, long ruled by foreign sovereigns.

At the dawn of the eighteenth century, the population of Naples and its immediate environs is estimated at nearly a half-million. In Europe, only London and Paris were more populous. The next largest Italian cities were Rome and Palermo. These demographic trends continued until the end of the Two Sicilies, although by then Milan eclipsed Rome in population.

No other city in Italy was more important, influential or powerful, either politically or economically.

Its sheer population made the city formidable, for it meant that there were more than enough Neapolitans to form a militia on short notice without the need to muster troops in the hinterland. All that was needed were a few thousand locally-manufactured rifles to distribute to men who knew how to use them. This was rare because protection was normally provided by the police and regular army. The city had a competent navy with additional ships along the coast, at bases like Gaeta and Salerno. Any major revolt in Naples would be difficult to subdue. In recent centuries, the only time the city was actually conquered outright was when it was abandoned by its leaders, most recently in 1860 and 1944.

The city's greatest asset was her large, busy port. A naval blockade might hinder trade, but Naples, unlike Genoa or Venice, had a vast, productive territory at its disposal, and a fairly good system of roads.

The House of Bourbon

In Spain, King Philip's immediate heirs were his two elder sons by his first wife. This left no obvious Spanish patrimony for his sons by his second wife, the ambitious Elisabeth Farnese. With the death of her uncle, Antonio, Duke of Parma, in 1731, Elisabeth became the universal heiress of that small Italian state, already acknowledged as the birthright of her eldest son, Charles.

The young prince might have been content with this modest inheritance, but a greater opportunity presented itself in 1731 when the Treaty of Vienna brought about the end of a tenuous Anglo-French Alliance forged a few years earlier. It marked the birth of a new Anglo-Austrian Alliance. Spain and France were again united, while Austria found herself comparatively isolated in the power structure of western continental Europe. Significantly in the fickle politics of northern Italy, Piedmont was also allied with the Spanish and the French.

The recent treaties confirmed the international recognition of Charles' right to rule Parma, a tiny duchy of little concern to the great powers. Before long, he was on his way to Italy. He was fifteen.

In 1733, the War of the Polish Succession tested the military alliance between Spain and France. The Treaty of the Escorial between Philip V of Spain and his nephew Louis XV of France formed part of the Bourbons' first *Pacte de Famille*, agreements that would remain in effect for decades.

Exploiting Austrian vulnerability in southern Italy, Charles marched with an army of some forty thousand across papal territory to Perugia and then into the Kingdom of Naples, where he encountered minimal opposition. To allay chronic European fears of the concentration of power in a single monarch, Philip V ceded his claims in Italy to his adventuresome son, who was proclaimed king at Naples in 1734. A coronation followed at Palermo the next year.

The change could have made little immediate difference to the ordinary subject or even to the ordinary aristocrat. Charles Hapsburg was replaced by Charles Bourbon.

With the Peace of Vienna of 1738, the European powers

permitted the latter to keep Naples and Sicily while renouncing Parma and Piacenza, though he continued to use those titles. The young king had to give up his claim to Tuscany, which he had been willed by the enlightened but childless Gian Gastone de Medici, his distant kinsman. This treaty iterated the principle that Charles, in the event of succession to the Spanish Throne, would have to abdicate the crowns of Naples and Sicily in favor of one of his sons (see Appendix 1).

Despite its impact throughout Italy, the war had been initiated on the pretext of a disputed succession to the throne of Poland. In its aftermath, Augustus III was recognized as King of Poland, and his daughter, young Maria Amalia, was betrothed to the new King of Naples and Sicily.

Progress and Prosperity

The new leadership provided the impetus and inertia for development and advancement in many fields, ranging from government and law to industry and agriculture. Education, medicine and architecture were supported. There were even a few early attempts at progressive populism and proto-feminism.

It was significant that Charles de Bourbon lived in the sovereign state he ruled, establishing his residence at Naples. For too long had the twin kingdoms of Naples and Sicily been ruled by absentee monarchs. Naturally, King Charles couldn't be in Palermo and Naples at the same time; some tasks in Sicily would always have to be handled by delegates, be they called "lieutenants" or "viceroys."

In Naples, the new monarch established a royal court complete with a council of ministers (cabinet), accredited foreign ambassadors from the great powers and, perhaps most importantly, an efficient treasury that could retain national assets instead of sending money to Spain or Austria. From among the aristocracy and military corps he appointed over a hundred gentlemen-in-waiting to whom he granted access to much of the palace.

His justice minister, a Tuscan named Bernardo Tanucci, quickly made a name for himself by prosecuting and convicting corrupt officials, thus sending a clear message to the judiciary and the bureaucracy that abuses would not be tolerated. A consummate politician, Tanucci was destined to rise through the ranks to greater heights.[44] For now, he was content to curb the ambitions of zealous nobles and ban the books of enlightened authors like Voltaire. The reign of an earlier Charles, Charles of Anjou, may have been long ago, but the Kingdom of Naples was still linked very closely to the papacy, perhaps, given its history and proximity, more so than any other state in Europe.

Despite being resented by Tanucci and others, the trade minister, an austere Sicilian named Leopoldo de Gregorio, undertook reforms to encourage commerce and industry by streamlining the bureaucracy and decreasing taxes. Later, he accompanied Charles to Spain to effect similar measures there.

Though young, Charles was anything but a poseur, and his ministers were not merely "mandarins" who viewed change as anathema. Stagnancy was their nemesis.

The young king's attempt at meritocracy, part of an effort to appoint competent officials, contrasted sharply with the habits of his immediate predecessors and their viceroys to fill these posts based on clientelism, "networking," nepotism or preferments. This new efficiency paid off.

The lack of a resident monarch for so long had permitted the aristocrats of the twin kingdoms to manipulate viceroys and abuse power, often taking justice into their own hands. Unfortunately, this endemic problem persisted in Sicily even as it was curtailed somewhat in Naples.

As a royal expression of the identity of the Neapolitan Nation, and to mark his recent marriage, the new king founded an order of chivalry dedicated to Januarius (Gennaro), the patron saint of Naples. Reserved to the important nobles of the kingdom, this encouraged a certain loyalty to the crown. Until now, the kingdoms of Naples and Sicily, lacking their own dynasties, did not have their own orders of knighthood (see Appendix 2). Kings who ruled the kingdoms normally bestowed their own dynastic or national orders, and so we find knights of Santiago (Spain) and Saints Maurice and Lazarus (Savoy). Another order conferred by Charles, dedicated to Saint George, was inherited from the Farnese dynasty through his mother.

In Palermo, Sicily's parliament had never ceased to exist, but now it would meet more frequently; it might even be more accountable than in the past.

In Naples, the populace was happy to finally have its own resident king to respond to its needs. The Neapolitan Nation was no longer a mere hypothesis.

Charles immediately set about revising the legal and bureaucratic organs of his twin kingdoms while encouraging economic growth through trade and industry.

The king also began to focus his attention on the material development of the kingdoms. He ordered construction of the Teatro San Carlo, an opera house dedicated to his patron saint. It opened in Naples in November 1737 under the direction of Pietro Metastasio. The construction had taken just two years to complete. This structure was largely rebuilt following a fire during the next century.

Among his more monumental construction projects would be the royal palace, the *Reggia,* at Caserta, "the Italian Versailles," and smaller palaces at Portici and Capodimonte, but these were simply the most prominent of many undertakings. Many of the most impressive Baroque churches and aristocratic residences we see in Naples, Palermo and other large cities, as well as smaller localities, were erected during the eighteenth century. This reflected a certain affluence, at least in ecclesiastical and aristocratic quarters. Unfortunately, the prosperity sometimes precipitated the defacement or destruction of splendid medieval churches and castles, which found themselves replaced by "modern" Baroque monstrosities.

Some public projects stand out for being developed at the vanguard of engineering, a few designed by the inspired architect Luigi Vanvitelli, whose crowning achievement is Caserta. The aqueducts built to supply water to the Caserta area were remarkable.

An extension of the water lines stretched to San Leucio, a planned community conceived as public housing (completed during the reign of Ferdinand I). San Leucio was initially intended as a communal town employing principles of what today would be termed "socialism."

Another planned community of this kind was Mongiana, in Calabria, where advanced principles were used in mining iron and other minerals. Though mining towns were infamously squalid, this one took account of the health of the miners and their families.

The porcelain works instituted at Capodimonte, overlooking Naples, in 1743 utilized a novel form of ceramic production suited to industries other than decorative art. An astronomical observatory was also built at Capodimonte; in connection with this, departments were instituted at the University of Naples dedicated to astronomy and nautical science under Pietro De Martino.

In the city below, the Foro Carlino and the Palazzo dell'Immacolatella were particularly ambitious. The cemetery of Santa Maria del Popolo was designed to minimize the effects of contagions spread through epidemics. The hospital of the same name boasted a pharmacy, the so-called "Farmacia degli Incurabili," having a sophisticated laboratory.

Following a highly-destructive eruption of Mount Vesuvius in 1737, the king ordered the establishment of a scientific committee to study and measure volcanic phenomena; a seismic-volcanic observatory was eventually developed a century later.

The vast naval yards at Castellammare di Stabia, which saw completion during the reign of Ferdinand I, facilitated the building of large vessels in the kingdom.

The children of Charles and Maria Amalia seem to have spoken Neapolitan as if it were their mother tongue, but they were tutored in Italian, French, Spanish and German. French, of course, was the language of international diplomacy, while some scholarly texts were still published in Latin. The church clung to Latin in liturgy, but many everyday prayers were learned by the common folk in Italian, Neapolitan or Sicilian. The use of the local languages was not discouraged.

If Charles was progressive, it is clear that most of his aristocratic subjects were reactionary by comparison.

In 1740, he decreed that Jews would again be permitted to live and work in his kingdoms, but bishops and nobles alike protested against this and the legislation had to be repealed a few years later.

A series of minor disputes with the papacy was resolved with a concordat signed in 1741. This permitted taxation of some ecclesiastical estates, limited the number of clergy in the Kingdom of Naples and reduced the extent of ecclesiastical jurisdiction. Printed for the royal household by Francesco Ricciardo, the published record of this *Trattato di Accomodamento* referred to Carlo as *King of the Two Sicilies*.

The new pope, Benedict XIV, appreciated the arts and sciences. His pontificate was a reasonably progressive one compared to those of most of his predecessors. One of his first acts was to formally condemn the enslavement of indigenous peoples around the world. He spoke against the Latinization of Byzantine Catholics, numerous in the Albanian communities of Sicily, Puglia and Calabria. He issued an encyclical in defense of the Jews in Poland.

Though devoutly Catholic, and inclined to condone the church's censorship of "dangerous" books, Charles seems to have been no slave to the principle of rule by divine right. Indeed, he has come to be identified with a form of what is now called "enlightened absolutism." In this he is sometimes compared to his contemporary, Frederick the Great of Prussia, another enlightened despot.

Naples and Sicily each retained their own institutions and laws. Between parliamentary sessions, which were called every three or four years, Sicily's government was administered by the *Deputazione del Regno di Sicilia* based at Palermo. Baronial interests formed the basis of its activity.

On the mainland, however, Charles issued a pragmatic sanction in 1738 representing an early attempt to restrict feudal power.

Charles granted permission for the archeological excavations at recently-discovered Herculaneum in 1738, and at Pompeii a decade later. Indeed, the work at these sites marked the beginning of the development of the modern approach to studying ancient archeology, utilizing methods that soon became the norm across Europe. The Naples archeological museum and numerous institutions of higher learning were founded on Charles' initiative.

Important as archeological studies were, another example of an innovative effort in the field of education was the first school for Chinese studies in Europe, founded by Matteo Ripa, a priest who had lived at the imperial court for some years. Established by Ripa and four young Chinese in 1724, it received papal support, eventually being integrated into the University of Naples.

Charles' reign was nothing less than a mini-renaissance. His popularity in Naples soared. Whether he could boast the same popularity in Palermo is open to question. His greatest achievements, and his greatest reforms, took place on the mainland.

Yet some policies and programs improved the situation of both kingdoms, Sicily as well as Naples. In this regard, better trade with other nations was a constant objective. This included a series of navigation and trade agreements in 1740 with the Ottoman Empire, implying that Charles was not the isolationist that some have suggested, at least not where commerce was involved.

Nature conservancy was an important concern. Charles approved legislation to protect forests and lakes.

In 1742, an academy of medicine was established in Palermo. This proved opportune, for the next year saw a horrific outbreak of bubonic plague at Messina. Arriving on a small vessel returning from Greece, the contagion is estimated to have killed more than half of the city's population. Horrendous as this epidemic was, it might have been worse were it not for the efforts of Pietro Polacco, an enlightened Venetian physician who encouraged physical isolation of patients whenever possible.

Another important thinker of this era was Giambattista Vico, author of *Principi di Una Scienza Nuova,* published in Naples in 1725. Part of a wider treatise on natural (or universal) rights, a concept consistent with the Enlightenment ideas Vico espoused, *The New Science* was influential on the philosophy of history, laying the foundations of constructivist epistemology by advocating a novel, systematic approach to the study of the humanities.

While Messina was suffering catastrophic depopulation, the prosperous capital of Naples was becoming a magnet for people throughout central and southern Italy, and it boasted a growing international community.

Foreign and Domestic Affairs

The young king initially sought to stay out of the War of the Austrian Succession that erupted in 1740 upon the death of Charles VI of Austria. His decision was poorly received in

Paris and Madrid. Fate forced the issue with advancement of an Austrian army down the Italian peninsula in spring 1744. From Abruzzo, Charles personally led an army of twenty thousand men. On August eleventh, a combined Neapolitan-Spanish force defeated the invaders at the Battle of Velletri in the Alban Hills outside Rome, a victory commemorated in Giuseppe Verdi's *La Forza del Destino.*

Apart from its strategic and political significance, this earned Charles a certain respect in the eyes of other European monarchs. He was equally popular in Naples, where he released the political prisoners of the former regime from hellish jails.

Serious efforts were made to care for the poor. The *Albergo dei Poveri,* a large hospice, was begun in Palermo in 1746, thanks in part to the efforts of the Prince of Palagonia years earlier. In 1751, work began on an even larger hospice of the same name in Naples. (Due to the discovery of traces of Carthaginian civilization at the Palermo site, the hospice in that city was completed only in 1772.)

The king and queen underwrote much of the cost of the hospice in Naples, a project estimated to have cost a million ducats, through the sale of the greater part of some of the crown jewels. Additional revenue was raised through a monthly lottery, which, it was hoped, might discourage private betting.

As always, medical research was encouraged. In 1753, Carlo Curzio authored the first published description of scleroderma, a group of autoimmune disorders whose precise causes are still not known.

Poverty and healthcare were not the only needs to be addressed. Charles drew a firm line at reintroducing the Holy Office when an overzealous Archbishop of Naples attempted this in 1746.[45] Here the sovereign was responding to the will of the Neapolitans, who vociferously protested against the machinations of unpopular Cardinal Spinelli. Nevertheless, the Inquisition continued to exist in Sicily as a formal institution, a vestige of Spanish rule.

The king's response to Cardinal Spinelli was part of a more general effort to curtail the entrenched power of the church and the nobility. Feudal (manorial) rights, for example, made it virtually impossible for ordinary farmers to challenge the authority of major landholders. This disparity of justice was now addressed in the Kingdom of Naples, though not yet in Sicily, which had its own legal code.

Not for nothing did some contemporary historians credit this singular sovereign with bringing an end to the Middle Ages in this part of Italy. Beginning in 1735, the organization of the law courts was reformed. A new legal code, the *Codice Carolino*, was formulated in 1739 and partially published two years later, though it would not be entirely implemented for a half-century.[46]

Nevertheless, the government of Charles III achieved something of a symbiosis between several centuries of stagnant historical law that he found and something more modern that he introduced. If not revolutionary, this was reasonably efficacious in melding the *status quo ante* to some slightly updated approaches. At the very least, the new laws did not exacerbate the pre-existing conditions that facilitated the rampant, overzealous power of the church and the aristocracy, factors which had impeded social and economic development for centuries. This accomplishment by a young man and his well-chosen advisors was remarkable by any measure.

In 1739, the combined population of the twin kingdoms of Naples and Sicily was slightly over six million. This was comparable to the population of Great Britain.

On the mainland, the *catasto onciario*, a tax census, was instituted in 1740. Intended to be more equitable than previous wealth/income taxes and the *donativo* of Sicily, it was criticized by the kingdom's economists for its inefficiency. Nevertheless, like the *donativo*, it served as a *de facto* census of the population.

By 1750, Charles had balanced the budgets of both his

kingdoms, and that year he renounced collection of another *donativo* in Sicily, the last one having been imposed just two years earlier (and still not entirely collected). The surplus in the treasury would be put to good use.

During the early years of his reign, he managed to bring food prices under control, with annual fluctuations of ten percent or less, something that his immediate predecessors had failed to accomplish.[47]

In 1751, he formally outlawed freemasonry, forcing it underground. This legislation has usually been viewed as repressive, particularly by foreign historians whose perceptions have been colored by comparisons to the benign freemasonry that existed in Britain and its American colonies. In Italy, however, there was the possibility of freemasonry being used to facilitate a covert network that might garner enough power to subvert institutional authority. Unlike localized entities such as the *maestranze* (guilds), freemasonry, which in Italy was secretive, had the potential to become the largest lay organization in the twin kingdoms. Whereas the guilds had churches and saintly patrons (an example is Saint Joseph as the patron of carpenters), freemasonry was essentially secular. Its adherents were highly-literate; among them were aristocrats, businessmen and intellectuals. The British solution was to place freemasonry under the umbrella of royal patronage. This was impractical in Catholic countries because of a papal proscription on freemasonry since 1738.[48]

In Italy the freemasons seem to have questioned the right of the Holy Office, and hence, by way of implication, the church to exercise authority over the private lives of ordinary people. In Palermo, the *Beati Paoli,* about whom virtually nothing is known (their very name is apocryphal), may have done the same.[49]

In contrast to the freemasons, loose networks of merchants, tradesmen and bandits did not pose an ideological threat, while the Camorra and the Mafia (discussed later), being somewhat localized, did not yet exist as the large organizations they would later become; indeed, the words *camorra* and *mafia* did not always connote their later usage.

It could be argued that the Jesuits, who vehemently opposed the freemasons, were themselves a dangerous organization. Charles would confront this question eventually.

For now, his efforts were more constructive. If, in view of papal constraints, he could not support the Enlightenment directly, he would do so by fostering higher education.

A bizarre territorial and jurisdictional dispute emerged in 1753. Seeking to exercise, or perhaps merely test, the crown's presumed right to appoint or approve bishops in the Kingdom of Sicily, Charles sent a prelate to Malta. The apostolic legateship was thought to have been abolished decades earlier (see note 41), but the greater conundrum was territorial.

When Charles V ceded Malta and Gozo to the Order of the Hospital during the sixteenth century, it was understood that these knights of Saint John would remit the annual feudal rent of a falcon to the King of Sicily. Now their grand master, Manuel Pinto de Fonseca, claimed the order's absolute sovereignty over the islands, without the need for recourse to the King of Sicily. It was true enough that the Maltese themselves had grown to despise the autocratic grand masters and their arrogant knights, but the kings of Sicily had refused to intervene in the internal affairs of the order, which had proven itself a worthy adversary of Ottoman navies and Barbary pirates.

Responding to Fonseca, Charles confiscated the powerful religious order's various properties in Sicily; most of these were in the southeast of the island. The dispute was provisorily resolved in late 1754, with the Sicilian commanderies returned to the order, though the juridical debate continued unofficially.

In the same year, the king established the first university department in Italy dedicated to the study of economics as a science, where the brilliant economist Antonio Genovesi lectured in Italian instead of the traditional Latin. A proto-socialist, Genovesi suggested the reform of agriculture and the redistribution of wealth, particularly in the form of land. Charles protected the professor's right to advocate such views.

The university curricula were updated. Apart from economics, fundamental principles of the new science of electricity advanced by Jean-Antoine Nollet (who pioneered endosmosis) were taught. Departments in botany, chemistry, physics (originally a sub-field of chemistry) and astronomy were established or expanded, and these studies encouraged. The state's promotion of fields of study like jurisprudence and scholastic theology, formerly favored by the lion's share of students, was cut back.

The great majority of university students were men, but women were not absent from the intellectual elite of Naples. Maria Angela Ardinghelli maintained a running correspondence with Nollet on electrical theory and translated the works of Stephen Hales into Italian. Giuseppa Barbapicciola, a student of Giambattista Vico, translated Descartes' *Principles of Philosophy* into Italian.

Though modern feminism had yet to arrive, certain long-standing laws protected some female rights, such as the ownership of property. The most obvious example of this was the "Sicilian Succession," the right of a noblewoman to succeed her father, brother or male cousin to a feudal estate, such as a county or barony, in the absence of male heirs. This principle had existed since the time of Frederick II.

Apart from the sciences and humanities, the study of engineering was encouraged. Here an innovation was an academy of military engineering instituted in 1754.

Charles proved that a devout Catholic need not fear a few novel ideas; Pope Benedict proved that a universal church could embrace them.

In this golden age, benefactors were inspired by their king's example. One nobleman opened his personal library to the general public, another established a public museum dedicated to numismatics and archeological finds from ancient Greek and Roman sites.

The phrase *Two Sicilies* came back into vogue. People spoke with pride of its "thousand cities." When referring to the Kingdom of Naples, they began to speak simply of *il Regno,* "the Kingdom."

Thanks largely to the efforts of King Charles, wondrous Pompeii, Paestum and Naples became stops on the "grand tour" that formed part of the foundation of the cultural education of affluent and aristocratic Europeans. The itinerary eventually reached across the Strait of Messina to Sicily, of which Johann Wolfgang von Goethe wrote in his *Italienische Reise,* "To have seen Italy without having seen Sicily is to not have seen Italy at all, for Sicily is the key to everything."

Charles was highly adept at delegating authority. This left him more time to indulge his passion for hunting at reserves like Carditello, near Caserta. While many kings spent as much time bedding mistresses as bagging prey, Charles seems to have been faithful to Maria Amalia, who bore him thirteen children.

The exceptional king had an exceptional queen. Maria Amalia, who was born and raised in Dresden as a princess of Saxony's House of Wettin, found time to oversee construction of the palace at Caserta, begun in 1752. She served on the council of state. It is said that she convinced Charles to stay neutral at the outset of the War of the Austrian Succession, which Naples was eventually forced to enter.

Although the details of the king's daily efforts were overseen by ministers and other officials, or bureaucrats, many were brought to his personal attention, if only for his approval and signature. In practice, it might take little more than ten minutes to read a simple directive and have the monarch sign it; the charter would then be countersigned and sealed in duplicate or triplicate. The original document signed by the king under the royal seal would be retained in the royal chancery, with a duplicate in the archive of the relevant ministry or tribunal. The interested parties who were the object of the decree would receive copies, which were not always sealed.

Wax seals were reserved for the most important charters; many documents were sealed by "blind" embossing (without ink).

The king himself did not actually sign every decree, rescript or directive issued in his name.

Since the Middle Ages, it had fallen to the crown to address many matters which, one way or another, did not fall directly under the authority of one ministry or another. The crown was the authority of last resort. Thus we find the king signing an order in 1752 freeing sugar cane and sardines from a local tax in the Sicilian coastal town of Sciacca. Many orders of this kind would be issued in the course of a year.

Even a citizen's change of surname required royal sanction. Once or twice each year, a decree listing dozens of names was issued indicating original and revised forms. These minutiae were not, for the most part, name changes based on such facts as a man recognizing his paternity of a child born outside marriage, which could be dealt with through a notarial act presented to a district tribunal, but alterations of embarrassing surnames. *Cane* (dog) might become *Canè*, while *Puzzo* (stench) might become *Pizzo*. This did not become very rigorous until the early years of the nineteenth century, when civil vital statistics registries were instituted. Until then, a citizen might still be able to alter his surname slightly without legal censure. Often, we find surnames such as *Esposito,* typically given to foundlings, changed upon adoption or when the individual reached adulthood.

In a practice that exists in Italy to this day, a woman retained her "maiden" surname after marriage. Pity the young woman named *Immacolata Porca* ("Immaculate Pig") who could not change her surname on her wedding day.

In an age of petty territorial wars and colonial adventures, Naples and Sicily were spared the addictive vice of expansionism. "We have no ambitions," was how Charles expressed this in 1756. By then, he had transformed a languishing metropolis into a splendid royal capital.

Vedi Napoli e poi muori, said the city's foreign visitors. "See Naples and die."

"I devote all my attention to improving the welfare of my subjects," Charles famously said, "since I wish to save my soul and go to Heaven."

When his elder half-brother, King Ferdinand VI of Spain, died in August 1759, Charles succeeded him as Charles III of Spain. This meant abdicating the twin thrones of Naples and Sicily in favor of one of his sons.

Philip, the eldest, born in 1747, was excluded from the succession for his diminished mental ability. Charles, the next oldest, born in 1748, would accompany his father to Madrid as heir apparent to the crown of Spain. This would leave young Ferdinand, born in 1751, as King of Naples and Sicily.

Certain problems were endemic. Long before Charles had arrived, much land had been deforested to raise grain and livestock. Apart from the economic reliance on cereals, particularly wheat, this had destroyed much of the environment, affecting the water supply in some areas. The situation was generally more serious in Sicily than on the mainland, though it could be seen in some parts of Puglia, Calabria and Basilicata. Yet Naples had to be fed, the staples being bread and pasta.

Agricultural improvements were slow to be introduced. The European famine of 1740 was followed a decade later by a notoriously poor harvest; both were acutely felt in the Two Sicilies, though Lombardy was hit harder by the event of 1750. However, food prices remained affordable (see note 46).

During this era the chief crops were wheat, barley, rice,

beans (including chickpeas), switchgrass, olives, almonds and sugar cane. Cotton was also cultivated. This, of course, reflects but a fraction of the diversity of the agriculture of the twin kingdoms.

Among the agricultural incentives was the permission given to farmers to cultivate public land, particularly open areas such as pastures.

Unfortunately, the king's ethos, his singular perseverance of effort, would not always be shared by his successors. The grit of a man who must forge a great enterprise, be it a business, a university or a nation, is not always inherited by his children, privileged to live off the fat of the land.

The Seven Years' War, which ended up involving many countries and their territories on several continents (to Americans it was the "French and Indian War"), began toward the end of Charles' reign in Naples. Although he managed to keep Naples and Sicily out of this conflict, it was something that awaited him in Madrid. For Spain and her empire, it was unavoidable. In the years to come, Charles attempted to maintain Spain's influence in the face of encroachment by other colonial powers. His efforts were generally successful, and he is credited with preserving the Spanish Empire in a minor resurgence.

Charles was as autocratic as any absolute monarch of his age, but he made absolutism palatable.[50]

The Pragmatic of 1759 (Appendix 1), essentially an act of cession, laid the groundwork for the foundation of the Kingdom of the Two Sicilies which would be chartered later, in Ferdinand's long reign. More immediately, it reinforced a national sovereignty which, on paper, had never ceased to exist since 1130. In practice, as we have seen, this sovereignty was sometimes attenuated by the complexities of rule from abroad by monarchs who were also kings of Spain or other nations but rarely set foot in Naples or Sicily.

The Pragmatic also established the Bourbons of Naples

and Sicily as a dynasty juridically separate from the royal houses of Bourbon in Spain and France. This dynastic principle was perhaps more subtle than the obvious matter of political independence, yet inextricably connected to it, for it meant that the crowns of Sicily and Spain were not to be borne by the same monarch.

Viva o' Re, cheered the Neapolitans to welcome the reign of the boy king. They could not know that the end of Charles' reign signalled the end of an age.

As King of Spain, he was one of the first monarchs to recognize the fledgling United States of America, where he sponsored the construction of New York's first Roman Catholic church.

We should resist the temptation to ignore Charles III of Spain after 1759, for he was to be the invisible hand in the life of his young son living in Naples, who would not reach the age of majority until 1767. The visible hand would be Bernardo Tanucci, who became head of the council of regency.

It will be recalled that Charles had brought Tanucci with him to Naples from Tuscany. In the ensuing years, the king appointed him to a succession of posts. Like Charles, the man now acting as regent advocated what later came to be called "enlightened despotism." Indeed, he had been instrumental in bringing about many of the changes Charles implemented during his Italian reign.

There were occasional differences. In 1762, during the Seven Years' War, the Kingdom of Naples, intimidated by the arrival of a British fleet at the capital, declared neutrality despite a pact signed with Spain and France, the other Bourbon kingdoms, the previous year. The Treaty of Paris of 1763 ended this war but not the longstanding antipathy between European powers.

Some adversaries were more tenacious than others. An epidemic of typhus, a so-called "putrid fever," struck Naples in

1764. One of the first physicians to respond to the crisis was Michele Sarcone, from Puglia. Known to posterity as a leading epidemiologist of his time, he wrote a lengthy report on this outbreak of disease and later conducted further research on it. Two of his colleagues, Michele Troia and Domenico Cotugno, were also from Puglia. The work of these three thinkers, and others, represented one of the first serious efforts in Italy to treat epidemics scientifically. In this they followed in the footsteps of earlier trailblazers like Giovanni Filippo Ingrassia and, more recently Carlo Curzio.

Another noteworthy physician of Sarcone's era was Francesco Serao, who served in the government of Ferdinand I. Amongst other efforts, Serao translated into Italian the work of Sir John Pringle.

Double Standard

The twin kingdoms were separated by nothing more than the Strait of Messina, but they were worlds apart in terms of administration, especially after the departure of King Charles.

The basic economy of Sicily was overwhelmingly dependent on exports of grain, a commodity whose price was increasingly influenced by greedy brokers and fickle factors in the market. By 1760, just a few brokers from Genoa seemed to be controlling the entire export market for the Sicilian supply. Price fixing and corruption were rife. Smuggling wheat shipments out of Sicily as contraband was a normal practice.

The harvest of 1763 was disastrous, leading to what can only be described as a famine. The next year's harvest was better, and this brought about a decrease in the domestic prices of wheat and flour for use in Sicily. The harvest of 1765 was still more bountiful, even though growers and export agents attempting to fix grain prices initially sought to convince everybody that it wasn't.

In another detrimental trend, Sicily's hard wheat was falling out of fashion abroad, where easily-milled soft wheat was preferred, but for now it still had buyers in the Ottoman and British empires.

Unfortunately, taxes, transportation (roads in Basilicata, Calabria and Sicily were terrible), bribes and other costs kept the price of the Sicilian product high, making the international market for the island's wheat extremely vulnerable to foreign competition. An unforeseen blow came in the form of Ukrainian grain when Russian ships were permitted passage through the Bosporus and the Dardanelles into the Mediterranean beginning in 1774.

In a bizarre twist, Sicily began regularly importing wheat from the Russian Empire. While the effect of this development should not be exaggerated, it represented an economic turn for the worse. Sicily might still be able to feed her people, but corruption, bad public policy and poor management were destroying the island's economy. There were early signs of the advent of the Industrial Revolution on the mainland around Naples and Salerno, but not in Sicily.

Criminality

Sicily may have been exporting less grain, but she managed to export the charlatan Giuseppe Balsamo, known as "Cagliostro," an occultist and swindler whose travels took him across Europe. Goethe wrote a comedy based on his life. Balsamo, who died in a papal prison, is little more than a colorful footnote to history, but his fame exemplifies the enduring fascination with charlatanry and the social craft of *furbizia*, slyness.

In the countryside, the most *furbi* Sicilians were the *gabellotti*, estate agents hired by absentee landlords. By the end of the eighteenth century they formed part of the corrupt socio-economic milieu that nourished widespread criminality. A greedy mayor might conspire with a *gabellotto* to control the local water supply or to impose illegal "tolls" on the farmer who had to cart his produce down a local road.

Complicit in this phenomenon was a widespread distrust of authority, which the ordinary person saw embodied in the local baron and his *gabellotto*. As often as not, the police colluded with the landholders. The police were more interested in maintaining order, keeping the masses under control, than enforcing the law, which anyway favored the rich.

The scales of justice were generally stacked against the poor. It became expedient for a cattle rustler to steal a flock of sheep in the dead of night and demand a ransom for it from the shepherd the next day. On top of this, the thief might require payment, "protection money," to guarantee that the flock would be safe from theft in the future. To whom could the victim turn? Even if the police investigated, the entire case was based on the victim's word against that of the thieves.

A reliance on whatever local power structure existed was only natural. Some people sought relief from prominent local men rather than the ineffective police or the absent landholders. Most of these local "men of honor" were themselves criminals; some were *gabellotti*. Here were the insidious seeds of organized crime, the Mafia, which would reach fruition during the following century.

This originated in western and central Sicily. Eventually, however, Campania, Calabria and Puglia fell prey to the same phenomenon. We find the Camorra in Naples and the Ndrangheta in Calabria. Over time, these organizations varied in structure based on local norms. The Ndrangheta, for example, had clans based chiefly on kinship, while the Mafia was initially more territorial than hereditary, leading one to refer to the clans of Corleone or Caccamo (towns in Sicily). Only later were they organized into anything having a hierarchy or network. Money and wealth were always the chief objectives. The murders, vendettas and feuds were incidental evils. While the authorities might successfully prosecute an individual *mafioso* for a specific crime, such as a murder, it was difficult to attack a covert activity that could barely be identified. Contrary to popular belief, there was never a single "head" of the Mafia or Camorra, though there might be informal "commissions" or committees linking families, clans or localities.

The historic origins of these organizations are much debated. The fact that most of their activities were conducted in the shadows, without written records of any kind, led certain officials to question their very existence.

Other organizations made easier targets. One of these was a powerful religious order in possession of numerous edifices, a seemingly endless patrimony of rural estates, plenty of gold and an international network spanning the Spanish Empire, much of Europe and part of Asia.

The Society of Jesus, or Jesuits, were a highly influential institution that might arguably be described as corrupt. The order, which had emerged as a tool of the Counter Reformation, owed its very existence to the Spanish crown. Enjoying the support of the state, they worked in tandem with the Inquisition until its belated abolition.

Many had grown suspicious of the order's excessive influence in the church. In Madrid, the ministers of Charles III came to view the order's power as dangerous. Like the medieval Templars, the Jesuit order had become, in effect, a state within a state, virtually a law unto itself. This intolerable condition led Portugal and France to take measures against them. Now Charles would follow suit, imitating the methods employed to suppress the Templars centuries earlier.

In 1767, the order was suddenly and unequivocally suppressed in the Bourbon kingdoms of Spain, Naples and Sicily (along with Malta), where a single day saw the arrest and deportation of thousands of Jesuits and many of their retainers. It was an exercise in efficiency, with local officials opening sealed orders on a designated day. With the expulsions came the confiscation of Jesuit property. This left the Dominicans as the largest, most powerful religious order in the twin kingdoms but there were many others.

Some Jesuit property was granted to other religious orders but the lion's share was simply appropriated by the state for public use. In Palermo, for example, a monastic school behind the cathedral was turned into a military school for the sons of poor aristocrats.

How enlightened was Charles III? Although he contemplated the abolition of slavery in his American dominions, he never achieved that noble objective. He suppressed the troublesome Jesuits but condoned the banning of "subversive" books.

Nevertheless, he sought to bring Jews back to Naples, pursued great building projects and encouraged education, industry and the arts. He reduced wealth taxes and updated the eclectic legal code. In these respects he was a true leader. By any balanced measure, viewed as a man of his time, Charles was a good ruler.[51]

The prosperity of the Two Sicilies during his reign is difficult to gauge precisely because we lack statistics and figures sufficient to quantify much beyond a few generalities regarding tax revenue and food prices. This was true in many nations during the eighteenth century.

It would be overzealous, indeed anachronistic, to characterize Charles de Bourbon as a latter-day Frederick II, yet his social and economic accomplishments in the kingdoms of Naples and Sicily represented a marked improvement over the administration of the three preceding centuries. If there was a contemporary influence on King Charles III, it may have been Tsar Peter I "the Great" of Russia, who ruled until death in 1725 and likewise undertook ambitious building projects and sweeping reforms in a successful attempt to modernize his country. Like Charles, Peter was still quite young when he realized these achievements.

THE KINGDOM OF THE TWO SICILIES

Charles III crowned in 1735 in Palermo Cathedral

ROYAL GIFT, AND THE KNIGHT OF MALTA, two valuable JACK ASSES,

WILL cover Mares and Jennies at MOUNT-VERNON, this Spring, for Five Guineas the Seaſon.

The firſt, is of the moſt valuable Race in the Kingdom of Spain.—The other, lately imported from Malta, by the Way of Paris, is not inferior.——ROYAL GIFT, (now 5 Years old) has increaſed remarkably in Size ſince he covered laſt Year—and not a Jenney, and ſcarcely a Mare to which he went, miſſ d.——THE KNIGHT OF MALTA will be 3 Years old this Spring—is near 14 Hands high—moſt beautifully formed for an Aſs—and extremely light, active and ſprightly.—Comparatively ſpeaking, he reſembles a fine Courſer.

Theſe two JACKS ſeem as if deſigned for different Purpoſes equally valuable.—The firſt, by his Weight and great Strength, to get Mules for the ſlow and heavy Draught.—The other, by his Activity and Sprightlineſs, for quicker Movements on the Road.—The Value of Mules, on account of their Longevity, Strength, Hardineſs and cheap keeping, is too well known to need Deſcription.

M A G N O L I O

Stands at the ſame Place, for FOUR POUNDS the Seaſon.—The Money, in every Caſe, is to be paid at the Stable, before the Mares or Jennies are taken away.----No Accounts will be kept.----Good Paſture, well encloſed, will be provided, at Half a Dollar per Week, for the Convenience of thoſe who incline to leave their Mares, and every reaſonable Care will be taken of them; but they will not be enſured againſt Theft or Accidents.

JOHN FAIRFAX, OVERSEER.

Mount-Vernon, March 12, 1787.

Advertisement for services of donkeys given to George Washington by King Charles III and by Emmanuel de Rohan-Polduc, Grand Master of the Order of Malta

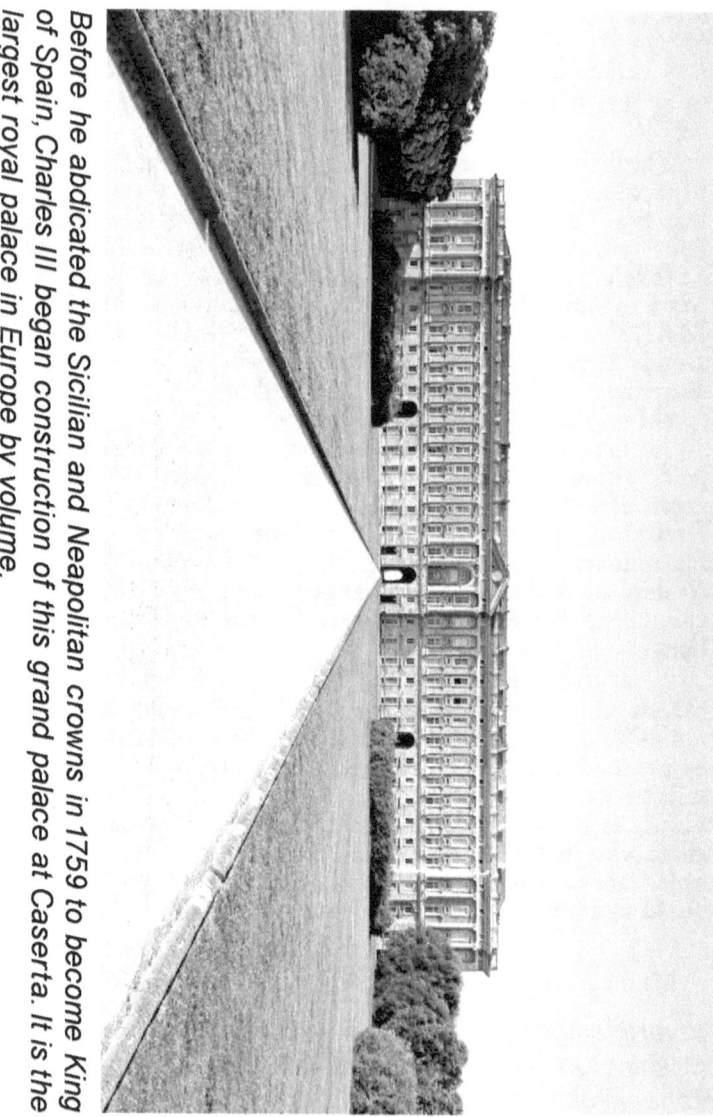

Before he abdicated the Sicilian and Neapolitan crowns in 1759 to become King of Spain, Charles III began construction of this grand palace at Caserta. It is the largest royal palace in Europe by volume.

In 1785, Charles III, King of Spain, formerly King of Naples and Sicily, sponsored the first Catholic parish of New York. Saint Peter's church, in Manhattan, was rebuilt in 1840.

THE KINGDOM OF THE TWO SICILIES

TRATTATO
DI ACCOMODAMENTO
TRA
LA SANTA SEDE
E
LA CORTE DI NAPOLI

CONCHIUSO IN ROMA

Tra i Plenipotenziarj della Santità di Papa BENEDETTO XIV., e della Maeſtà di CARLO, Infante di Spagna, Re delle due Sicilie, di Geruſalemme, &c.

Approvato e ratificato dalla Maeſtà Sua ſotto il dì 8. di Giugno M. DCC. XLI.
E dalla Santità Sua a' 13. dello ſteſſo meſe, ed anno.

Accord signed with the Holy See in 1741

Chapter 3
FERDINAND I

In the same year that saw the Jesuits expelled, Ferdinand (for the first part of his reign he was Ferdinand IV of Naples and Ferdinand III of Sicily) reached the age of majority. While he was not lacking in intelligence, he seems not to have absorbed much of the wisdom of his mentor, Tanucci, or perhaps he simply rebelled against what the regent occasionally tried to instill in him. It is thought that the overbearing Tanucci gave in to a dark side, indulging the young king's idleness and hedonism while ignoring his education. Moreover, the regent was becoming more cautious, even reactionary, in his approach to government. The results of this could not be good, either for the young king or for the populace.

For eight years, Tanucci, as regent, had exercised an undue influence not only over Ferdinand but over the two kingdoms. Charles III was too far away to play a role in daily affairs.

Yet Tanucci and the other caretakers made an effort to afford the kingdom safety and security. There were, for example, initiatives to repopulate the islands of Ustica and Lampedusa to avoid these outposts falling into the hands of Barbary pirates. The navy was developed and enlarged, and subsidies established for the orphaned children of military personnel.

Ferdinand's first important act as king was the expulsion of the Jesuits (described in the last chapter), something his father and others had been planning for some time. His marriage to Maria Carolina of Austria had also been planned.

Realpolitik

True to her parentage, Maria Carolina, who was guaranteed a place in the council of state, advocated for Austrian interests over those of Spain. When Tanucci protested this, he was summarily retired. By now, Ferdinand didn't seem worried at being distanced from the father he barely knew, whether that distance was based on geography or politics.

What emerged from this political metamorphosis was a rapprochement with Great Britain and Austria. Naples and Sicily, to paraphrase Charles III, had no political ambitions in either the Old World or the Americas, so Ferdinand's accommodation of foreign interests was not a matter of great international importance, nor was it a surprise.

That, however, did not mean that the kingdoms of Naples and Sicily were devoid of all significance.

There could be no doubt that Ferdinand's Siculo-Neapolitan dominions stood to be exploited by Britain and Austria, both imperial powers. On the other hand, one could just as easily argue that Sicily, in particular, had long been exploited by Spain, which took the island for granted.

Despite its slow economic decline over the last few centuries, Sicily had much to offer, some of it from the land itself.

Sulfur, the Biblical brimstone, was an essential element in gunpowder long before 1777, when Antoine Lavoisier convinced the world that it was an element rather than a chemical compound. However one defined it, sulfur was needed for

Britain's burgeoning Industrial Revolution. The golden mineral was abundant in Sicily, where it was more easily mined than elsewhere. Before long, Great Britain enjoyed a virtual monopoly on Sicilian sulfur, which at first was extracted from open pits.

Visiting western Sicily in 1773, John Woodhouse, an English merchant, immediately realized that the grapes and climate were similar to those of Portugal and Spain. Here he could produce a fortified wine similar to Port, Madeira and Sherry, for which there was an unslakeable demand in Britain. Moreover, the British did not wish to rely on their fragile relationship with Spain for their supply of fortified wine; these concerns were substantiated a few years later by the outbreak of the "Anglo-Spanish War," part of a wider conflict, the American Revolutionary War.

Before long, Marsala was being shipped as far as the United States, where it was served in the White House by President Thomas Jefferson. Competition eventually arrived from Benjamin Ingham and his nephew, Joseph Whitaker.

Sicily also provided Britain a convenient base for its Mediterranean naval operations, and here Ferdinand's amenability facilitated the negotiation of several military agreements. An Englishman, John Acton, was enlisted to reorganize the navy and the army. These efforts met with mixed success, but Acton eventually rose to the rank of prime minister.

While Woodhouse was enjoying the sunshine of rural Sicily, and perhaps a pleasant sip or two of his wine, Palermo suffered a long revolt that began as a food riot but quickly turned into a rebellion against an unpopular viceroy (or "lieutenant") who had increased local sales taxes. Most of Ferdinand's ministers, unfortunately, seemed to learn very little from this experience. They tended to regard Sicily as a mere appanage and appendage of the Kingdom of Naples, whose capital was as large and affluent as ever.

A noteworthy exception to this way of thinking was the jurist, philosopher and sometime minister Gaetano Filangieri, who wrote a sophisticated treatise on efficient law with an emphasis on the rights of the individual. Reflecting Enlightenment principles and common sense, Filangieri's work, *La Scienza della Legislazione,* published in installments beginning in 1780, criticized the Catholic church, which consequently placed it in the index of forbidden books.

Apart from his direct criticism of a church that had long permitted the Inquisition and discouraged social progress, it is easy to see how certain aspects of Filangieri's doctrine, influenced as it was by that of Montesquieu, offended the papacy, for he strongly advocated the idea that citizens were entitled to a happy life free from excessive interference by either the church or the state, institutions which he believed should be entirely separate from each other.

Luigi Pio, the secretary of the Two Sicilies delegation in Paris, gave a copy of Filangieri's work to the American polymath, publisher and diplomat Benjamin Franklin. This led to a correspondence between the two thinkers. Some of Filangieri's ideas may well have inspired his American counterpart to enshrine certain principles in the constitution of the United States ratified in September 1787. In the autumn of that year, the Neapolitan aristocrat received a copy of this along with Franklin's request for eight more copies of the *Scienza,* which was also being published in other languages. Filangieri died the next year; his ideas did not die with him.

A public stock exchange was founded in 1778. Based in Naples, this supplanted "informal" trading, which had existed for centuries, and brought regulation to the activity. It reflected the growing importance of the twin kingdoms and facilitated foreign investment in Neapolitan industries. A mercantile and commodities exchange would be established much later.

Reflecting plans put into motion by Charles III, in 1778 Italy's first public housing estate, San Leucio, was built near Caserta. This became the cornerstone of an industrial town dedicated to the silk trade. One of the advisors on this project was Domenico Caracciolo, who had lived as a diplomat in London and Paris, where he assimilated some principles of the Enlightenment.

The very antithesis of his reprobate predecessors, Caracciolo became Sicily's viceroy in 1781. His first major act was to suppress the Inquisition the following year. It was good to finally be rid of the "Holy Office." An inspired reformer, Caracciolo attempted to enforce laws and curtail baronial privileges. The barons' displeasure can be imagined. Accustomed to purchasing justice, they resented being called to book for their crimes and corruption.

One of Caracciolo's greatest humanitarian challenges was responding to the Messina earthquake of 1783.

In 1785, he anonymously published a treatise on the Sicilian economy and its failing agricultural policy in response to widespread malnutrition during a famine the previous year. Some years earlier, he had written about water management in Sicily.

At least a few changes survived the end of his term, which came in 1786. The following year, a school of agricultural science named for the gifted Paolo Balsamo, who advocated many practical reforms in his field, was established at Palermo's Royal Academy of Studies, precursor of the university. In connection with this, a department of botany was set up, complete with a botanical garden (the larger public gardens would open later). An attempt was made to introduce agricultural ideas from England. Some concepts, such as crop rotation, were rudimentary, but the stagnant mentality of the major landholders impeded significant progress.

Elsewhere, seeds were sprouting with uncommon alacrity. They were seeds of revolution.

The French and the British

The French Revolution broke out in 1789. Not without reason, monarchs across Europe watched in fear as events unfolded.[52]

Ferdinand, of course, was a cousin of King Louis XVI. Queen Maria Carolina was the sister of his wife, Marie Antoinette. The French king and queen were executed in 1793. By then, Ferdinand had joined the many nations of the First Coalition arrayed against France and her expansionism. The queen was likely one of the influences upon his decision, though as a Bourbon monarch his position was, to use a French term, a *fait accompli*.[53]

On the domestic front, Ferdinand's advisors suggested that he curtail reforms of the kind advocated by Caracciolo.

The republican animus reached Sicily in a series of revolts, but even the largest, led by Francesco di Blasi in Palermo in 1795, was underwhelming. The response to this revolutionary riot, with its treasonous overtures, was uncompromising; its leader was tried and executed as surely as the French had beheaded *citoyen* Louis Capet.

As the revolutionary spirit, which the *ancien régime* viewed as a lethal virus, spread across Europe, anything seemed possible. At the very least, serious reforms might be demanded. Ever reactionary, Ferdinand and Maria Carolina were resolute in their opposition to political change in any form. It would be conceded only over their dead bodies. Some in the kingdom might think that a suitable solution.

Ferdinand chose this ungodly moment to recognize another nation founded in revolution, the United States of America, whose president, George Washington, sent a consular agent to Naples in 1796. Here there were no diplomatic intricacies; quite simply, Ferdinand acted only after his British ally, King George III, approved "Jay's Treaty," which the United States Senate had ratified the preceding year. Although President

Thomas Jefferson sent a consular agent to Palermo in 1802, the kingdom's full diplomatic relations with the young nation across the ocean would be established only much later.[54]

In 1795, Ferdinand founded Palermo's *Orto Botanico*, the first public botanical gardens in Italy, associated with the local university. These gardens and the adjacent public park still exist near the shore.

Popular revolts were not the only outgrowth of France's revolution. Before long, the rise of a faction led by charismatic Napoleon Bonaparte was exporting its ideas by force. Like the Punic Wars of yore, the incessant Napoleonic Wars spawned myriad complexities, constantly reshaping alliances and borders.[55]

Over the next two decades, most European rulers were dragged into this quagmire. The King of Naples became one of them. A factor that made matters worse for Naples was that Ferdinand was more easily manipulated than his counterparts who ruled other nations, and by his own wife, who had come to despise the French.

Notwithstanding that Ferdinand had made peace with the current French government, the Directory, two years earlier, Napoleon Bonaparte seized Malta *en route* to Egypt in June 1798, evicting the Knights Hospitaller from the fief they held from the Sicilian crown. It is quite possible that the French (like many in Europe) inferred that the Hospitallers' possession of Malta and Gozo was tantamount to sovereignty, without realizing that both were legally part of the Kingdom of Sicily. At all events, the islands now joined Napoleon's rapidly-expanding empire.

In August the British defeated the French at the Battle of the Nile. Within weeks, Britain commenced a blockade and siege of Malta.

Ferdinand was more immediately alarmed by events transpiring to the north of Naples. The French had already occupied most of northern Italy.

In November, acting impetuously instead of waiting for promised support from his Austrian allies, Ferdinand marched on Rome, where his army was handily defeated by the French forces. Following this debacle, he retreated to Naples, where he and his family boarded a British warship for Palermo. The French, meanwhile, made their way southward.

In January 1799, the French marched on the city of Naples which, despite fierce resistance from the loyalist faction, fell to the invaders, who established the Parthenopean Republic on behalf of some local revolutionaries, stationing a French garrison there. That this new republican state was a French puppet did not seem to bother its Neapolitan founders, who claimed the Enlightenment doctrine of Gaetano Filangieri as one of their inspirations.

Ferdinand's rashness had cost him one of his kingdoms, at least for the moment. He retreated to Palermo.

Before long, the greater part of the overextended French army was recalled to northern Italy. This offered Neapolitan troops, led by the intrepid Fabrizio Ruffo — aristocrat, politician and cardinal — the chance to take back the Kingdom of Naples. In June his army reached the city of Naples, where it was aided by Horatio Nelson's formidable naval forces. Deprived of French military support, the Parthenopean Republic crumbled. Unfortunately, it took some eight thousand Neapolitan lives with it.

Although Ferdinand returned to Naples on a British warship for a symbolic re-entry, he did not immediately take up residence in the city, choosing to wait until the revolutionary dust settled. Some of the revolution's leaders were tried but most were eventually granted amnesty.

In September 1800, the French garrison at Valletta capitulated. By now, the Maltese were disillusioned, having come to view the French troops as arrogant, but Napoleon Bonaparte, the modern Caesar, had brought more than an army to Malta.

The French freed slaves and political prisoners, abolished the rights of the nobility and introduced democratic principles. All Maltese were to be equal before the law, and the few Jews were given permission to erect a synagogue. It was enough to make despotic kings tremble in trepidation.

The British retained most of these reforms but refused to restore the Maltese islands to the King of Sicily, who likely would have suppressed the islanders and reinstalled the nasty knights. Malta, the Diego Garcia of the Mediterranean, would make a useful base of military operations. Unlike Sicily, where Britain's Royal Navy enjoyed specific port privileges accorded it by treaty, this became a British possession. Ferdinand's strenuous objections fell on deaf ears.

In 1802, the Peace of Amiens brought a brief respite from French expansionism. Before leaving Palermo for Naples, Ferdinand sought to put Sicily's affairs in order. He called a parliament where Gaetano Cottone, a nobleman, adamantly urged the adoption of a constitution. This proposal was ignored.

Cottone wasn't the island's only intellectual to support reforms. Another was Giuseppe Piazzi, an astronomer who discovered the first known dwarf planet, Ceres, in 1801, based on observations made from atop the Norman Palace in Palermo.

Back in Naples, the government imposed austerity measures in view of a national budget saddled with extraordinary deficits resulting from the French occupation that bolstered the republican revolutionaries. Compounding the crisis, a bad harvest necessitated the importation of grain from abroad. In March 1803 there was a run on the Neapolitan banks, a serious matter in an age when currency was backed by precious metal.

French power in the region may have dissipated, but it had not disappeared. Indeed, the French encamped some troops in coastal regions of the Kingdom of Naples after being ejected from Malta by the British and Corfu by the Russians.

Ferdinand now sought to avoid involvement by keeping his kingdoms neutral.

In 1804 the papacy permitted the return of the Jesuits in the kingdoms of Naples and Sicily, an action that antedated by a decade their general restoration around Europe. The order's influence in the twin kingdoms, where the Society of Jesus reacquired only a fraction of their former property, was to be muted.

In late 1805, the bloody Battle of Austerlitz resulted in a French victory over Russia and the German states. This "Battle of the Three Emperors" precipitated the dissolution of the Holy Roman Empire while effectively ending the Third Coalition uniting Britain, Russia and Sweden.

Having consolidated his position to the north of the Alps, Napoleon dispatched an army to conquer the Kingdom of Naples despite having recognized its neutrality.

In advance of the arrival of the French, Ferdinand again left Naples, which the invaders occupied following token resistance in February 1806. For the second time, he found himself in Palermo. This sojourn would be longer than the first one.

This time he already had a place to stay. The Ficuzza Hunting Lodge was located amidst a woods in the Sicanian Mountains near Corleone. On the edge of Palermo, in the *Favorita* hunting reserve, was the Chinese Villa. Both were built in 1799 to designs by Giuseppe Venanzio Marvuglia.

Napoleon also had designs on Sicily — military ones. As the island kingdom's army and navy were underdeveloped, there was no choice except for the British to defend the region.

For the most part, Ferdinand stayed at Ficuzza with his courtiers and his mistresses, while Maria Carolina preferred Palermo, where she could intrigue against the British, who she regarded as natural enemies.

A ray of sunlight came with the marriage of her daughter, Maria Cristina, to Carlo Felice of Savoy in the Palatine Chapel of Palermo's Norman Palace in March 1807. Maria Cristina became Queen Consort of Sardinia when Carlo Felice was crowned in 1821; she lived until 1849 surviving her husband by eighteen years.

In Naples, the French were laying serious plans to invade Sicily. Appointed king by his brother, Joseph Bonaparte amassed a large army but lacked enough suitable ships to effect a safe crossing to Messina, where the British beat back an attempted landing by a small contingent.

In 1808, Napoleon replaced Joseph with Joachim Murat, who was married to his sister, Caroline Bonaparte. An able administrator, Murat instituted civil vital statistics records and undertook a number of measures to curtail the influence of the church in daily life. That Murat's government was an efficient one is confirmed by statistical surveys undertaken by 1811 covering everything from industry to agriculture.

If there were ever any doubt in the past, by now it was becoming painfully obvious to the British in Sicily that Ferdinand was not especially competent as a ruler. Whenever it was possible, they preferred dealing with his son and heir apparent, Francis. In January 1810, Francis' wife gave birth to a son, christened Ferdinand Charles. He was to be the last King of Sicily born on the island.

The British were loath to interfere in local politics, but Ferdinand left them little choice. When parliament rejected the crown's request for a *donativo* that was viewed as an excessive imposition, the compromise was a fixed-rate tax of one percent on certain financial transactions. In July 1811, William Bentinck, an experienced governor, arrived to take command of the British forces and he effectively took control of Sicily.

The intrigues of Queen Maria Carolina had not ceased. She continued to cultivate a keen interest in statecraft, becoming infamous for her machinations.

At Bentinck's urging, Ferdinand named Francis his "Prince Vicar," or regent for Sicily, in January 1812. Great changes were in the offing.

Even so, if either Ferdinand or Maria Carolina had ever entertained socially progressive ideas akin to those espoused by Charles III, the French Revolution and the Napoleonic wars soured their attitudes to the point of abandoning any pretensions to change.

Evolution and Constitution

While the Kingdom of Naples under French occupation had undergone some republican evolution, the Kingdom of Sicily under British protection was influenced by British ideals of constitutional monarchy. Both would make their mark in tangible ways but neither would result in anything like a sea change, a shift in the political paradigm.

Bentinck proposed a constitution loosely based on the British model. Ratified in July 1812, it had several significant effects, the greatest being the modernization of government based on democratic principles. It sought to bring Sicily out of the social morass of the Middle Ages, in the process stemming the tide of revolution.

It established that only parliament, consisting of two chambers as in England, was to propose laws and levy taxes. The infamous *donativo,* a wealth tax imposed upon personal property at royal whim, was categorically abolished. Parliament was to be called at least once each year.

Here the *vox populi* came to life in a constitution for the people. Freedom of speech and freedom of the press were formally recognized, even though restrictions were placed on direct criticism of church and crown. Torture was abolished, and citizens were to enjoy equal rights before the law. Nobody would be denied due process, or detained without being charged. The principle of *habeas corpus* thus became a reality.

The ephemeral Sicilian constitution was the first constitution chartered in Italy during the nineteenth century. What follows is a concise summary of the preamble and some other sections.

The state religion is Roman Catholicism, and a sovereign who professes any other faith is *ipso facto* deposed.

Legislative power is vested exclusively in parliament, with laws effected upon royal approval. Laws may be proposed only by parliament, not by the executive.

The sovereign may approve or veto, but not alter, the bills submitted for his approval, though executive power is vested exclusively in the crown.

Juridical authority is distinct and independent of executive and legislative power. There shall be a judiciary composed of justices and magistrates, subject to review by the two legislative chambers, namely the House of Commons and the House of Lords (Chamber of Peers).

The person of the sovereign is sacred and inviolable.

Royal ministers shall be subject to the review and approval of parliament, and may be tried by parliament for crimes, including abuse of office in the exercise of their duties.

As peers, eligible titled nobles will have one vote each. The High Notary of the Kingdom (effectively the chancellor) shall publish the roll of nobiliary and ecclesiastical peers. The sovereign shall enjoy the exclusive prerogative of calling or dissolving parliament, but he shall be obligated to convoke a session at least once per year, even if by proxy.

No Sicilian citizen may be arrested, exiled or in any way deprived of his rights except according to the new legal code.

Peers will enjoy privileges similar to those in England, to be established by statute. Feudalism is abolished (see the next section).

All laws must pass through both chambers of parliament as their only venue, but citizens may propose bills through the appropriate channels. Every citizen has the right to defend himself legally against any person, including magistrates.

Under *Libertà, Dritti e Doveri del Cittadino* (Freedoms, Rights and Duties of Citizens), freedom of speech is established. Any citizen may express any political opinion, without fear of harassment by the authorities. Sedition is outlawed.

No citizen may hold more than two paid positions in the public sector.

Nobody can be charged with an offense that was not part of the legal code at the time the offense was allegedly committed. That is to say, retroactive prosecution is proscribed.

Hunting is permitted on private property for deer, boar and other game in compliance with the relevant code. Specific hunting seasons are established, and trespassing on private property prohibited.

No person, community or ecclesiastical organization may claim financial compensation for losses incurred as a result of the abolition of feudalism, but specific cases may be addressed by the law courts. The state may not confiscate property without due legal process. A new financial code would address these matters in detail.

The rights of Sicilian citizens, not referred to as *subjects,* are governed exclusively by the laws of the Kingdom of Sicily.

The constitution shall be published, to be disseminated in localities, universities and schools.

By 1830, no citizen was to be permitted to vote who could not read.

No citizen may refuse to testify in a court of law unless (in a criminal trial) he is related to the accused.

No citizen may serve another national government without royal assent, and at all events may not take up arms against the Kingdom of Sicily.

Under *Libertà della Stampa* (Freedom of the Press), every citizen may print and publish his ideas without need of permission or censorship.

However, published criticism of the Catholic church, its dogmas and interpretations of Biblical scripture, is subject to censorship and prosecution.

Moreover, the sovereign and the royal family may not be criticized explicitly in the press.

Statements that incite readers to commit crimes or disobey orders executed by judges are illegal.

Libel is outlawed. It is illegal to publish defamatory personal (private) information regarding spouses and families. The publication of affronts to public decency is illegal.

Journalistic material must be signed by the author before two witnesses prior to its publication. The year and place of publication must be indicated. Religious material must have episcopal approval prior to publication.

The British themselves viewed this new constitution as unrealistically ambitious. On the mainland, Murat soon instituted a constitution of his own.[56] The constitution drafted in Bologna in 1796 was of French inspiration, and so was the tricolor (green, white and red) flag popularized in Italy in the decades to come.

End of Feudalism

In a separate law incorporated into the Sicilian constitution, feudalism (manorialism) was abolished. In its stead, the feudatories whose estates had the highest tax base were accorded seats in a Chamber of Peers similar to Britain's House of Lords. The abolition of feudalism is usually cited as the most significant element for several reasons, not the least being that it was one of the few reforms to survive the constitution's suppression a few years later. In practice, it meant that any vestige of feudal privilege vanished overnight. Anachronistic rights of local taxation and control over forests, streams and lakes were abolished. (The Napoleonic government had likewise abolished feudalism on the mainland a few years earlier.)

Land holdings large and small became "freehold" properties for which only the owners or the state could claim rights to water and minerals. Now the owner of a sulfur pit or salt mine located on heretofore manorial land became its absolute proprietor.

Because the largest estates, the *latifondi,* remained in existence, the major landholders still wielded power, but certain areas used by the general public, such as major roads, became the property of the state. No longer was it possible for a baron to literally own an entire town.

While the social order did not change immediately, the status of the nobility itself evolved. Until now, most nobiliary titles were feudal. Purchase of (for example) a county brought with it feudal rights and also the title of count. By 1800, Sicily's largest manorial estates were princedoms and dukedoms. Many *gabellotti* (estate agents) purchased baronies, which typically were smaller than marquisates and counties, in the decades immediately before 1812, and this explains a certain snobbery toward barons on the part of Sicily's princes, dukes, marquesses and counts. Since the new peerages were based on revenue rather than title, a few wealthier barons obtained parliamentary seats.

In view of feudalism's abolition, titles of nobility became personal, to be inherited based on blood rights, with no connection to feudal tenure. Dukes and counts could, in theory, be landless, and in time more than a few eventually ended up that way.

With the help of the astronomer Giuseppe Piazzi, twenty-three administrative districts analogous to provinces were established in Sicily based on topography, and some local officials would be elected. Initially, only literate landholding males were eligible to vote.

Some constitutional principles deal with dynastic law. In the absence of male heirs among descendants and collaterals, a woman can succeed to the Sicilian throne. If there are no heirs whatsoever, parliament may elect to nominate a King of Sicily from a reigning European house, and not necessarily from one of the houses of Bourbon.

Alas, the life of Sicily's constitution was not destined to be a long one. Palermo would never be Westminster or Washington, but a sincere attempt had been made to achieve what existed beyond Italy's reactionary shores.

Two Crowns in One

The death of Maria Carolina coincided with the beginning of the Congress of Vienna. With France's defeat, Europe sought to restore some semblance of the *status quo ante bellum* to the continent while laying the foundations of a cohesive policy that might prevent the likelihood of a major war breaking out again in the near future. This met with success if we consider that Europe enjoyed a respite from an extensive, multinational conflict for a solid century. Conversely, the Congress failed to address most of the underlying social problems that existed *within* the signatory nations, things that nourished a general discontent among citizens.

German unity of a kind was recognized in the form of the German Confederation. Italy, which Metternich famously described as being little more than "a geographical expression," remained a checkerboard of monarchies ruled by the papacy, the Bourbons and the Savoys, with Lombardy and Venetia under Austrian control. Here the boundaries were nearly identical to what they were before the beginning of the Napoleonic Wars years earlier.

Ferdinand was now free to decamp to Naples, which he much preferred to Palermo. Aside from an attempted invasion during the brief "Neapolitan War" by Murat, who was executed in Calabria in May 1815 by the people he sought to liberate, Ferdinand found himself unchallenged.

Others found him unintelligent, unschooled and uninspired. Retaining his tenacious grip on power, he had become a true reactionary, an opponent of social change, growing more cynical with every passing day. In 1816, he abolished the Sicilian constitution of 1812, justifying this by uniting the states of Naples and Sicily that had been institutionally separate since the War of the Vespers. This new state would need a new constitution, but Ferdinand had no immediate intention of granting one.

The neoteric Kingdom of the Two Sicilies, the largest of the Italian states, owed its name to the Angevins and Aragonese, and its territorial legacy to the Greeks and Normans, but it was far from a merely nostalgic restoration. Uniting Naples and Sicily may be seen as part of a European trend, resulting from the recent wars and the Congress of Vienna, of smaller countries seeking to become larger, and hence more powerful. The reconstituted kingdom, whose borders were essentially similar to those of 1282, was the largest and wealthiest state in Italy.

Yet the unification had the unintended consequence of fostering a subtle division, for the Sicilians, deprived of their parliament and other national institutions, found themselves more firmly than ever under Neapolitan control. Until now, Palermo had been a royal capital. Henceforth, the Two Sicilies would have but one capital city. Aristocrats and bureaucrats felt this change most acutely.

The Jesuits' general restoration in 1814 alarmed many, and not only in Europe. Across the ocean, John Adams wrote to American President Thomas Jefferson in 1816 that they "merited damnation."

While his counterparts around Europe were scrambling to institute reforms of some kind and accommodate popular demands, reactionary Ferdinand resumed the role of doctrinaire despot, his soul hardened by recent experience. Feudalism, however, was not restored, and a few laws established by the French on the mainland were retained.

The ephemeral constitution was not the only attempt at implementing new laws.

New Laws

A development generally ignored by historians is the legal code enacted in 1819. Though it lacked the support of a constitution, it governed most aspects of law. In some respects, it may even be considered an improvement over the legal code of Charles III. At the very least, it brought uniform standards to jurisprudence throughout the Two Sicilies while making clear just what, exactly, the laws were.

In practice, law in the Two Sicilies marched in step with what existed elsewhere in Italy and most of western continental Europe, with the obvious exception of France. There was nothing like England's *Magna Carta* or common law, nor the progressive Bill of Rights of the United States of America. Though the practical application of certain principles enshrined in those laws could well be questioned (in the United States slavery still existed), their constitutional basis facilitated a means for amending some ideas while introducing others; parliamentary representation and legislation were concrete realities.

Ferdinand's legal code governed much in everyday life, ranging from rights within families to commercial transactions. Like the codes in force in Italy to this day, it was based on "Roman" law, and in that sense it was not unlike the earliest statutes of the kingdom, embodied in the Assizes of Ariano and the Constitutions of Melfi, in turn influenced by the Code of Justinian.

There was no "common law" in which court rulings established precedent. (This still does not exist in Italy, though a barrister or judge may cite earlier decisions in similar cases.) Means of appeal were limited.

Although parliament could propose laws, the procedure for this was not always very consistent. Most often, a committee of jurists submitted its suggestions to the crown for approval.

This was more efficient, perhaps even more just, than might be imagined. For example, the kings commuted sentences and released convicts rather often. Although raucous revolts were suppressed, sometimes with military force, even the most violent rioters were rarely detained for very long. Judges were reasonably consistent in decisions, verdicts and sentencing.

Pretensions to the belief that there was generally equal justice would be fallacious, but efforts were made to consider the rights of ordinary citizens. Although aristocrats might seek to "purchase" justice in civil cases, a judge could well render a decision in favor of a common man.

The greatest challenge was localized power. Many towns were remote, more so in the mountainous regions that comprised most of the kingdom. Though the typical family owned its own home and perhaps a parcel of land, the large estates were still under the control of a tiny class. Exploitation was normal in the Two Sicilies, as it was in most of Europe.

The state existed in tandem with the church, which sometimes sided with the common folk against the aristocracy. The clergy was a powerful force, often for good. Yet true democracy was long in coming.

The *Codice per lo Regno delle Due Sicilie* of 1819 was divided into five parts, actually being several codes in one. The first part, civil law, governed matters such as trade, commerce, finance, possession of property, and even marriage and the rights of children. The second part, penal law, dealt with criminal offenses and the statutory sentences for specific crimes.

The third part, a supplement to the first, established juridical procedures for civil cases. The fourth part, a supplement to the second, set forth procedures for the trial and treatment of criminal suspects. The fifth part was a compendium of statutes addressing specific aspects of commercial law.

As the preamble states, these codes supplant those formulated more than a decade earlier, published in a decree of 1808 when the king was in Sicily.

An attempt is made to render justice efficient and discourage abuses of authority. Citizens, not described as *subjects,* have the right to file complaints, *querele,* though not anonymously. Police are allowed to arrest a citizen seen to be committing a crime. Statutes address procedures such as the examination of witnesses. As in Italy today, the suspect is presumed innocent, and provided an attorney for his defense, though in most criminal cases the prosecutor is also, in effect, the judge.

Many aspects of Ferdinand's *Codice* are strikingly similar to what was eventually enacted elsewhere in Italy, particularly in the Kingdom of Sardinia ruled by the Savoys. This is remarkable because the Sardinian code formed the essential basis for what later became the legal codes of the Kingdom of Italy, whose essential criminal procedures are those of today's Italian Republic.

This observation is fodder for analysis and debate since none of these legal codes was notably originative, but there were clearly broad similarities in the laws of the two most important pre-unitary Italian states during the first half of the nineteenth century, leaving aside the Papal State where, as one may imagine, we see some obvious shadows cast by ecclesiastical law.

Very little in the *Codice* implies special authority or privilege being vested in the church except in areas such as marriage. It establishes that weddings should be celebrated civilly as well as ecclesiastically. Spousal separation exists, and the church may annul marriages. Divorce, which the French permitted during the occupation of Naples, was outlawed by a royal decree in 1816. Yet the civil "separation" outlined in the code seems to be divorce in everything but name (see note 11).

Catholic institutions such as the religious orders still owned much land and operated many schools, indeed most of the schools in Ferdinand's dominions and throughout Italy.

In examining the *corpus* of law, it should be remembered that numerous decrees, rescripts and circulars were issued after 1819. Ferdinand's *Codice* was not the last word.

We shall return to the matter of law because a revised legal code, the one that survived until the end of the kingdom, was published three decades later.[57]

In response to continued demands for a constitution, the parliament instituted in the new state worked with Francis, the heir apparent, to draft a detailed series of directives defining such matters as citizenship and nationality, with statutes governing parliamentary rules and legislation, local election procedures, the authority of the crown and royal succession, the cabinet, the courts, the armed forces, the national guard, and the public school system. Arguably, this *Costituzione Politica,* drafted in 1820 and published early in 1821, was not exactly the constitution that some people wanted. It was loosely modelled on the Spanish constitution of 1812, not the more liberal Sicilian constitution of that year; the more progressive principles found in Murat's constitution of 1815 were ignored. Nevertheless, it guaranteed freedom of expression.

In many respects, it was no more than a charter intended to "constitute" the kingdom's sovereignty, religion (Roman Catholicism), tax policies, and the organs of government already mentioned. In fact, many of these details had already been formulated and decreed in the years immediately preceding 1820.

For example, the constitution reorganized provincial boundaries in view of a decree of 1817. On the mainland were: Naples (the city and its environs), Campania (Terra di Lavoro), Marsia (part of Abruzzo), Pretuziana (part of Abruzzo), Frentania (part of Abruzzo), Sannio (Molise), Daunia (Capitanata), Peucezia (Terra di Bari), Salento (Terra d'Otranto), Lucania Orientale (Basilicata), Irpino (part of Principato), Lucania Occidentale (part of Principato), Calabria Cosentina (the Cosenza area), Calabria Brezia, Calabria Reggina (the Reggio area). In Sicily: Palermo, Catania, Messina, Siracusa, Girgenti (Agrigento), Trapani, Caltanissetta.

There were later alterations. For example, the province of Siracusa became the province of Noto. That Noto, an inland city of little consequence, would be made the administrative seat irritated the proud Syracusans, whose city, where Paul of Tarsus preached, was once the most important center of *Megara Hellas*. The province of Girgenti was eventually abolished and then restored. Some of the new provinces' names, such as those for Abruzzo and Molise, were unpopular. Benevento was a papal territory.

The government soon settled on the following provinces with essentially the same borders: Naples, Terra di Lavoro, Principato Citeriore, Principato Ulteriore, Basilicata, Capitanata, Terra di Bari, Terra d'Otranto, Calabria Citeriore, Calabria Ulteriore I, Calabria Ulteriore II, Molise, Abruzzo Citeriore, Abruzzo Ulteriore I, Abruzzo Ulteriore II, Palermo, Catania, Messina, Noto, Girgenti, Caltanissetta.

Campania, Puglia, Abruzzi, Molise, Basilicata, Calabria and Sicily are now *regions,* each consisting of provinces. A northern part of what was formerly Campania is in the Lazio region.

Although the constitution itself was not destined for a long life, some of its laws survived through subsequent legislation, a few enacted by royal decrees.

Nature and Technology

Some crop failures led to what could be described as a minor famine in Europe in 1816, "the year without a summer."

Affecting the northern hemisphere generally, it resulted from the major eruption of Mount Tambora, in Indonesia, the previous year. This was the largest volcanic eruption of the Holocene geological epoch and recorded history.

In 1818, the *Ferdinando I,* constructed at Naples, became the first steamship in the Mediterranean. This vessel was thirty-eight meters long. Several similar steamships followed over the next few years. Indeed, the building of ever larger steamships was destined to become a major industry in Naples and Palermo in the decades to follow, leading this activity in Italy.

Carbonari

Over the next few years, a liberal movement gained steam around Italy. To describe this as a "grass roots" effort would be imprecise. Like some recent European uprisings, it was essentially a bourgeoisie movement supported by intellectuals, even if it had its "populist" faction of tradesmen and farmers. It did not have a very specific political agenda beyond the dream of democracy and the implementation of some progressive principles. It did, however, enjoy exceptionally wide support, and many of its proponents advocated a republic over a monarchy. Some desired a unitary Italian state. Clearly inspired by the French Revolution, one of these loose-knit organizations emerged in southern Italy.

The *Carbonari* (literally "coal burners") formed a secret network whose *modus vivendi* of covert activity was probably patterned after certain practices common in Italian freemasonry.[58] With its membership rites and code of conduct, it had all the trappings of a sect. As a first step toward greater reforms and perhaps a republic, many of its members were willing to accept a constitutional monarchy.

By 1820, the insurgents had gained enough support to foment open revolts in Naples and other cities, compelling King

Ferdinand to call a parliament and begin formulating a constitution for the recently-chartered Kingdom of the Two Sicilies. The result was the *Costituzione Politica* described earlier. Palermo saw months of violent protests as the Sicilian peers sought to restore the Sicilian constitution of 1812. This they achieved, but only until the crown suppressed their efforts.

If not allied formally with the *Carbonari,* some of the protesters certainly shared a few of their objectives. This time, however, the ringleaders were aristocrats acting in their own interests rather than those of the general population.

The Kingdom of the Two Sicilies was not the only locus of this discontent; the next year, the *Carbonari* marched on Turin.

In February 1821, the Holy Alliance, a military coalition of Russia, Prussia and Austria, sent troops to help crush the uprisings in southern Italy. They also crushed the recently-promulgated constitution.

With the Austrians came Carl Mayer von Rothschild, who set up a bank in Naples, which he perceived as economically stable despite the occasional civil unrest.[59]

Meanwhile, in Piedmont, Victor Emmanuel I abdicated in favor of his brother Carlo Felice, who sought and received Austrian military intervention to suppress the riots. This ended *Carbonari* activity for the time being. It didn't take long for Pope Pius VII to condemn the *Carbonari* as a masonic secret society, imposing excommunication on its members, who in any case rarely revealed their identities to the general public.[60]

The Italian kings weren't the only monarchs drawn into this chaotic vortex. Spain was equally unsettled. The epoch of absolutism was nearing its end, but its demise would be a slow one.

At his death following a hunt in the first days of 1825, Ferdinand I had reigned sixty-six years. By most accounts, his intellect and capacity were abysmal, with tragic results for the people he ruled. Despite a few moments of inspiration, his reign was the antithesis of social progress. Ferdinand rarely missed the opportunity to miss an opportunity. Nary a tear was shed for the crowned nemesis of constitutions. Once, responding to his subjects' request for one, he cynically replied that, "Yes, my children, I shall give you a constitution. I shall even give you two."

By this time, in view of the changes sweeping across Europe, King Ferdinand I of the Two Sicilies was little more than an anachronism.

Viewed from that perspective, it is remarkable that the kingdom thrived despite some of his ideas, thanks in no small measure to the policies of inspired ministers like Domenico Caracciolo and John Acton. In retrospect, it may be seen that the national economy and the lives of the ordinary people might have fared worse.

Chapter 4
INTERLUDE

By 1825, life in the Kingdom of the Two Sicilies was essentially comparable to life elsewhere in Europe, and certainly in Italy, and not necessarily much better or worse. Nevertheless, it was distinctive in certain respects. The vibrant social culture of the city of Naples itself has been the subject of much study.[61] Let's cast a glance over a few of the kingdom's social realities during the first half of the nineteenth century.

Faith

By this time there were virtually no Jews or Protestants in the twin kingdoms. Though a few Jewish religious, culinary and linguistic traditions had survived in some rural localities during the last three centuries, the eccentric theory that there were actual "Crypto Jews," those who practiced their faith secretly over the course of many generations in regions such as Calabria, is by no means conclusive.

Most of the Protestants present in Naples and Palermo were British or German diplomats and merchants. There were not many Orthodox Christians except for Russian diplomats.

The Byzantine Rite churches associated with Albanian descendants who had fled Ottoman expansionism in the Balkans during the fifteenth century found themselves under Rome's ecclesiastical jurisdiction.

The greater number of citizens were "practicing" Catholics. Yet witchcraft was practiced as well; every town had its resident witch, usually an older woman who offered other women, especially younger ones, spells and potions to control their husbands (this should not be confused with astrology). However, the penal code of 1819 expressly proscribed the distribution or sale of harmful potions.

Non-believers and simple deists constituted only a tiny segment of the population.

In many ways, the church, not the state, was the constant in the lives of most people. The Catholic church was, in effect, a state within a state; this is still true in Italian law today.[62] Although the vital statistics laws enacted in the legal code of 1819 required the civil registration of marriages, the acts in the registers had a section for a notation indicating the parish where the wedding was celebrated. Officially, the age of majority for males was twenty-one, yet parental consent was required even for couples beyond that age to marry unless one of the spouses was widowed.

Decisions regarding matters such as close consanguinity between the betrothed spouses being an impediment to marriage were left to the church. Not until 1865 would other regions of Italy institute vital statistics records of this kind.[63]

Each town, city and *borgo* (district) had its patron saint. Most public holidays were religious festivals, and to the mind of the ordinary citizen the church was infinitely more significant than the state.

Cuisine

Certain foods were associated with some of these feasts.

There were the *sfince* and *zeppole* of Saint Joseph's Day and the hard biscuits and fortified wines of Saint Martin's Day. In Catania, a certain pastry was made to resemble the breasts of Saint Agatha. In Siracusa, *cuccìa* (wheat berry pudding) is associated with the feast of Saint Lucy.

A major feast like that of Saint Januarius (San Gennaro) in Naples or Saint Rosalie in Palermo would occasion the preparation of all manner of seasonal foods.

The seasons were the basis for *sagre* that celebrated local cuisines. Some were harvest festivals. One town might celebrate artichokes, another almonds or olives. Products like *ricotta* would be celebrated during the early spring when the sheep grazed in green pastures.

Oenicultural festivals were rarer. Sicily's wine country (which is still Italy's largest contiguous viticultural area) straddles a series of graceful hills between Salemi and Marsala. Following in the footsteps of John Woodhouse, the Inghams and Whitakers greatly augmented the scale of Marsala wine production. Until then, the principal crop in that part of Sicily was wheat.

It wasn't long before various dessert wines, such as Passito, were becoming popular in the Two Sicilies, especially among the aristocracy.

Food is inextricably linked to culture. Most of what we now associate with the cuisine of southern Italy already existed by the third decade of the nineteenth century. Coffee made its way into Europe when it became known to the knights on Malta via the Turks they imprisoned during the siege of the island in 1565. Ice cream was known to the ancient Greeks and Romans of Sicily, who made it from the snows of Mount Etna.

Pizza and lasagna were made in Naples long before the eighteenth century, and, as we have seen, spaghetti was known in Sicily during the reign of Roger II. The traditional Palermitan "pizza" is *sfincione*, a thick, spongy crust topped with tomatoes, onions, anchovies and grated cheese.

The Sicilian *arancina,* or fried rice ball, was not the only popular rice food. There was also the *timballo,* rice baked in a deep tray with meat and vegetables, which around Naples sometimes became the more sophisticated *sartù* popularized at court during the Bourbon period. The *gattò,* from the French *gâteau,* is a potato tort.

During this era, beginning with the reign of Ferdinand I and the influence of his wife, Maria Carolina, aristocratic cuisine underwent a certain "fusion" as French flourishes were added to it. A few wealthy aristocrats in Naples and Palermo even hired French chefs for their households. The Neapolitan *monsù* and Sicilian *monzù,* from the French *monsieur,* came to refer to these chefs, whether they were French or not. Words like *crocchè* (potato fritters), *ragù* (chopped meat stewed with tomatoes) and *supplì* (a variation of the larger arancina) assumed French names even though the recipes themselves were already part of the cuisine of southern Italy and differed greatly from their French counterparts.

The former Two Sicilies has a rich culinary tradition.[64]

The climate and geography of the kingdom permitted the cultivation of a great diversity of fruits and vegetables, from dates to potatoes. Growing seasons extended from early March into October. Some regions had two annual harvests.

Livestock was a staple in the hinterland. It was more ovine than bovine, and in many regions during this period there were probably more sheep than pigs. In coastal areas seafood dishes were greatly varied, ranging from squid to urchins. In Sicily tuna were captured in the *mattanza,* an Arab method of trapping the large fish in giant nets.

By tradition, the midday meal was the most substantial, particularly on Sundays. Despite the perception of Italians having nothing more than a sparse "continental breakfast," the first meal of the day might be sizeable.

The *cuccagna* was a large public banquet occasionally held at

Naples and Palermo into the eighteenth century. Taking various forms, it involved the placement of a huge quantity of food on large tables in a large city square as a sign of royal largesse. It might be accompanied by music. Such an event drew thousands of attendees.

Women

The state might create institutions, even constitutions, but the one most citizens knew best was the family.

Until very recent times the few Neapolitan or Sicilian women known to us as anything more than names were abbesses and aristocrats. As we have seen, there were intellectuals, such as the women who studied at the University of Naples, but these black swans were a rare breed.

Most Italian marriages in the nineteenth century were arranged by the spouses' parents, or in any case contracted only with parental consent, just as they had been since medieval times. The new vital statistics laws formalized the betrothal process.

Two customary practices among common folk represented opposite approaches to betrothal. Being *fidanzati in casa* was an engagement, sometimes before the future bride had reached the age of majority, where the parents of the future spouses would formally agree to the marriage.

Conversely, in Sicily and Calabria the *fuitina* was essentially an elopement in cases where the young woman's parents did not approve of the marriage, or perhaps could not afford to defray the cost of the wedding and therefore chose to tacitly condone the elopement. More precisely, in the *fuitina,* from the Sicilian word for "fleeing," the couple "escaped" together for a few days, and upon their return an immediate "reparative" marriage was deemed necessary to avoid further scandal because the young woman was presumed to have "lost her honor" during the sojourn. Practices similar to the *fuitina* existed elsewhere in Italy.

Apart from these perennial practices, courtship, such as it was, might entail chaperones to ensure that the couple was never alone. On average, husbands were around eight years older than their young brides. Dowries and other details could make betrothals quite complicated.

The generic description of such a social hierarchy as "matriarchal" is specious at best. Nevertheless, the salient role of Italian women as wives, and especially as mothers, must not be overlooked. Into the early decades of the twentieth century, the ordinary Italian mother raised a large family — five or six children on average — on meager means in what was essentially an agrarian society all but ignored by the Industrial Revolution.

Ordinary mothers were not the only women of fortitude. By 1812, Queen Maria Carolina had become famous, or infamous, in British circles for her outspoken opinions and endless intrigues. This led to her "self-exile" to Austria. In Vienna in early 1814, she met with Klemens von Metternich and her nephew, Francis I of Austria, to discuss the details of the royal family's restoration in Naples in view of Napoleon's recent defeat at Leipzig. Her death in September ended those negotiations but not the restoration.

As we have seen, the legal code enacted in 1819 addressed the rights of women to some degree by permitting a form of divorce, or at least separation. Abortion was explicitly outlawed. Contrary to what seems to be a popular belief, a husband was not exonerated from the crime of murder (or manslaughter) for killing his wife if he found her committing adultery *in flagrante* by having sex with another man. Likewise, parents who discovered their unwed daughter having sex with a man in their home, whether the act was consensual or not, had no right to commit homicide, even if rape were involved.

Women could not vote but neither could most men, and elections were very rare, even for local officials. We find a modicum of democracy within such institutions as the trade guilds and local civic councils, whose jurats (aldermen) were appointees.

Children

The legal code of 1819 had several statutes regarding the parental care of children, some more efficacious than others. These addressed the fundamental rights of pre-teen children to be housed, fed and clothed, and protected from the worst domestic violence. The potential shortcoming in this kind of law, something which still persists in our world today, was that it was predicated on the abuse or neglect being reported.

While a woman abused by her husband might take her children into her own care and custody in the event of a separation, such separations were, in fact, extremely rare. In practice, though the state could intervene in the case of a severely abused child, this occurred only infrequently.

There were provisions for adoption and a very simple form of foster care. Orphanages were many and orphans were myriad.

Some of these children were the sons and daughters of unwed mothers. Others were abandoned by parents who, already having many children, could not support still another young child. Entire volumes of vital statistics records of *proietti* confirm the great number of infants abandoned in this way, typically to the care of nuns who then left them in orphanages.

However, the penal code of 1819 forbade the abandonment of children under the age of seven. Moreover, the law prescribed that any abandoned child of this age, once found, had to be granted a surname and registered with the local vital statistics office. In effect, the state assumed a duty that formerly had been undertaken by the church.

Most orphanages, like most schools, were operated by the religious orders. Typically, orphanages for girls were operated by nuns, while those for boys were run by priests. Here was an example of the longstanding synergy between church and state.

In 1768, Ferdinand decreed that at least one public school be established in each town of the Kingdom of Naples, with a similar plan for the Kingdom of Sicily; these schools were for both boys and girls. This meant that, in principle, essential elementary education was now obligatory.

In practice, however, that was not always the case. Unfortunately, the planning and construction of the public schools was not implemented with much alacrity. Two decades later, they were present only in cities and some larger towns. Fortunately, there was another solution.

The religious orders were required to educate children free of tuition. By the beginning of the nineteenth century, there were more than enough schools, the great majority operated by religious orders like the Dominicans. The problem was that attendance was not actually mandatory, and would be difficult to enforce even if it were. Rather few children attended school beyond the age of twelve, and some parents viewed this kind of formal education as being less necessary for daughters than sons. Moreover, the curricula were rather uneven.

In connection with the lack of schools and schooling, it should be remembered that this problem persisted throughout Italy into the first decades of the unification period. This is reflected in literature. Set in Tuscany, Carlo (Lorenzini) Collodi's *Pinocchio,* first published in 1881, depicts an environment where young boys, instead of attending lessons, wander the streets in search of adventure.

Into the twentieth century, most orphanages in Italy were still operated by the Catholic church.

INTERLUDE

Aristocrats

True, the typical family owned their own home and a small plot of land. There were even agriculturalists, gentlemen farmers, who accumulated rural estates of considerable size. However, despite the abolition of feudalism, most of the kingdom's larger estates, and hence the local politics, were still controlled by the aristocracy.

Apologists for hereditary privilege are inclined to cite the examples of the productive bureaucrats and intellectuals in this social class, yet these affirmations overlook the fact that a greater number of ordinary people might well have achieved much were more opportunities available to them.

The aristocracy is a subtext, a leitmotif, that runs through the annals of the history of the Kingdom of the Two Sicilies and the state that succeeded it.

The problem transcended simple, if significant, questions of wealth. For example, admission to some of the kingdom's better military schools was reserved to the nobility. This was the incentive for many citizens to seek to prove descent from noblemen (some specific laws are listed in Appendix 3).

While England had a large *untitled* aristocracy, the landed gentry, most of the aristocrats in the Two Sicilies bore titles such as *count* or *baron,* or were born into families where an uncle or elder cousin held such a title. Service in certain high offices conferred untitled nobility.

On the continent, the reforms of republican France had the effect of diminishing aristocratic privilege in a very obvious way. Some countries were more retrograde than others; in the Russian Empire a form of serfdom still existed.

By now, most of the wealthier aristocrats had palaces, or "town houses," in major cities as well as the rural townships where their estates were located.[65] On the peninsula, Naples, now the capital of the entire Kingdom of the Two Sicilies, reigned supreme, though a noble family holding its lands further afield would choose a city nearer their interests, such as Bari, Taranto or even Brindisi. In Sicily, the three major urban orbits were Palermo, Messina and Catania, though smaller cities like Siracusa and Trapani had their share of *palazzi*.

With the civil and penal codes of 1819, the nobility lost any vestigial legal privileges that might have existed since the Middle Ages. In a court of law, for example, the rights of an aristocrat were now equal to those of any other citizen. A count or baron could be arrested, jailed and charged with a felony such as murder, just like anybody else in the kingdom. Except for a few perquisites, such as the preferences in admissions to military schools (already mentioned), there were no tangible benefits in law attached exclusively to the fact of having inherited a title of nobility.

None of this is to suggest that the disproportionate influence of the aristocracy disappeared. Aristocrats still occupied many important positions in government, and the largest landed estates.

Arts, Science, Commerce

The arts flourished. Composer Vincenzo Bellini (1801-1835) was known for his *bravura* works during opera's *Bel Canto* era. Later, Giuseppe Verdi (1813-1901) composed *I Vespri Siciliani* about the War of the Vespers.

His contemporary, Richard Wagner, composed *Parsifal,* his last opera, during a sojourn in Palermo. In folk art, crafts such as marionettes were inspired by the same medieval culture.

The kingdom had scientists besides the astronomer Giuseppe Piazzi, whom we met earlier. In a later generation, Stanislao Cannizzaro (1826-1910) was a chemist whose work took him to the vanguard of the new field of physics, which he taught at the University of Genoa as "theoretical chemistry." He was one of the first scientists to clearly distinguish between atoms and molecules and define valence. His work led to the development of the periodic table of elements.

Chroniclers of cultural history usually focus their attention on such arts as painting and sculpture in public places like churches. Here the opera houses and Baroque palaces of the Two Sicilies are supreme examples. There was no dearth of musicians, composers, writers and poets. However, despite the growth of Naples, the great majority of the kingdom's population was mostly rural, living in small cities or towns, the "thousand cities." These citizens were exposed more to folk arts and such things as plays performed locally in Neapolitan or Sicilian than opera sung in Italian.

A few entrepreneurs stood out from the crowd. Apart from vintners, one of the first food exporters was the innovative Vincenzo Florio (1799-1868), who sold tuna in jars. This Calabrian gentleman founded a small steamship line.

John Goodwin, a British consul who reported on the social and economic situation in the Two Sicilies in the years leading up to 1840, was reasonably optimistic:

It appears, therefore, that in 1826 about three-fourths of the male population were variously employed, and the remaining fourth was unemployed. The proportion borne by the latter class to the whole population is undoubtedly large, but to him who bears in mind that this fourth includes the very young and the very old, with all those incapacitated by physical or other causes, it will not appear excessive. It is smaller than the reports of travellers, which represent the Neapolitans as a nation of idlers, might have led us to expect.[66]

We may speculate that life was better in the country than in the cities. Italy, where the effects of the Industrial Revolution were minimal compared to Britain, has nothing comparable to eloquent critiques like those of Friedrich Engels, who wrote *The Condition of the Working Class in England* in 1845.

The "idlers" mentioned by Goodwin are not necessarily the infamous *lazzaroni* of Naples. More often, foreigners from northern Europe were surprised that a lunch break could last for two or three hours, or that schools, offices and stores might be closed for much of the afternoon. Although this has changed somewhat, visitors regard its pace of life as one of Italy's more appealing traits.

The regulation of the professions was based on what were then continental European norms. There were few formal law schools but an examination existed to license the practice of law, and a registry of barristers had been in place since 1780. The practice of medicine necessitated a degree and certification, but dentistry did not; there is much truth to the old trope about barbers extracting teeth. Babies were delivered by midwives.

At the same time, the government sponsored industrial projects that placed the Two Sicilies at the vanguard of the day's technology. This trend saw, for example, the first catenary suspension bridge in Italy, completed in 1832, span the Gagliano River. It was designed by the gifted engineer Luigi Giura (1795-1865). The first railway in Italy, connecting Naples and Portici, was completed in 1839. These projects were undertaken at the direction of the Corps of Bridges and Roads, precursor of the Civil Engineering Corps. Components were manufactured at the Mongiana works in Calabria.

Telegraphic connections were developed between Naples and Palermo. Amongst other innovations were Italy's first glass recycling program, in 1832, and first gas-fueled public lighting system, in 1839.

By 1838, Raffaele Piria was studying the effects of salicylic acid, which is an active metabolite of aspirin. Today, it is used in skincare medications.

In 1842, Biagio Miraglia, a psychiatrist from Cosenza, began publishing the first journal in Italian dedicated to this field. He conducted research and cured patients at the psychiatric hospital in Aversa, one of the few in Italy.

Social Justice

The legal code of 1819 went far in bringing some semblance of equal justice to the kingdom. While this did not satisfy those who desired an actual constitution, it represented a step toward ensuring fair law enforcement, prosecutions and trials.

In the interest of public health, a commission for vaccinations was set up in 1818; there was already an office charged with overseeing treatments.

The same year saw establishment of the commission for public instruction and education, which supplanted the general deputation of studies set up in 1778 to administer policies and curricula regarding the public schools that were being opened.[67]

In our times it is taken for granted that communication is essential to social evolution. In 1819, a new agency, the *Amministrazione Generale Poste e Procacci,* replaced an existing agency that provided postal services. (Until 1786, postal services were assigned to private contractors; in that year these were then entrusted to a public agency until 1813.)

The constitution enacted and suppressed in 1821 was gone but not forgotten.

In 1831, as we shall see (in Chapter 6), a plan was established to financially assist the poorest citizens of the kingdom, those having no form of income.

Of course, there were still great disparities between the very wealthy and the poor. This was true throughout Italy and most of Europe.

(N.° 130.) *Decreto affin di autorizzare il comune di Ostuni in Terra d'Otranto a censire in beneficio di* Vito Porcelli *un piccolo tratto di suolo pubblico sito nel borgo detto* Demaschino, *della estensione di un terzo di stoppello, ad oggetto di farvi un orto botanico, per l'annuo canone lordo di grana 62 e cavalli 6.* (Napoli, 24 Gennajo 1831.)

(N.° 131.) *Regolamento per la real Commessione di beneficenza creata da S. M. con decreto de' 4 di gennajo 1831.*

De' 24 di Gennajo 1831.

CAPITOLO I.

Degl' indigenti e de' sussidj.

Art. 1. La beneficenza reale reputa veri indigenti e degni di soccorso tutti coloro i quali non possono assolutamente col proprio travaglio sostentare se médesimi, o le di loro famiglie, purchè aggiungano a tal requisito una condotta intemerata per morale e per religione.

2. Chiunque si ritrovi in tale condizione potrà domandare soccorso alla real Commessione di beneficenza. Rimane espressamente vietato il presentar petizioni direttamente a' membri della Commessione o a' suoi uffiziali. Le suppliche dovranno esser poste da' richiedenti nel cassettino, che sarà sempre alla porta del locale addetto alla real Commessione.

Potranno farsi in qualunque carta; ed il richiedente vi noterà, oltre il suo nome e casato, la strada ed il numero della sua abitazione, la parrocchia cui appartiene, e se sia solo o con famiglia; aggiugnen—

Chapter 5
FRANCIS I

Francis I seemed to be a slight improvement over his father. Nearing fifty at the time of his accession, he understood the importance of science and industry, and even founded an order of knighthood to recognize these efforts, but in other ways his government was just as stagnant as his father's had been. Some of the most disturbing social practices known in his time are still with us in Italy today.[68]

The coronation itself was quite austere, devoid of much of the pomp that characterized the ceremony in Palermo for his grandfather, Charles III, nearly a century earlier. Having served as Ferdinand's vicar, or regent, in Sicily, the new monarch was familiar with government. Beyond his service in Palermo, the precise degree to which he influenced affairs during the last decades of his father's reign cannot be known with much certainty.

Given his age and experience, Francis should have been prepared to reign. Perhaps he was. He was endowed with an inclination toward scientific reasoning.[69] Yet, so far as we can tell, the shadow of dilemma never crossed his mind.

By contrast, the nation he inherited was full of unresolved

conflicts and unrealized ambitions. Few knew precisely what these were. Fewer seemed to care. Daily life was challenging enough. The rebels were a small but vocal minority.

Austrian troops were still present. Not only was this costly, it made the kingdom seem like an occupied nation. Francis wanted order to be maintained by national forces, so the Austrians left in 1827.

Reform Movements

The new king granted a general amnesty for those involved in the recent revolts. This facilitated the return of political exiles.

Unfortunately, he made no effort to restore the constitution of 1821 which he had helped to draft.

Inspired by a French organization of the Napoleonic era, a group called the *Filadelfi* was revived in 1828 beyond the largest cities, especially in the Cilento region (around Salerno). These revolutionaries sought the restoration of the constitution enacted in 1820, which was based on the Spanish model. Like the *Carbonari,* who they predated, the *Filadelfi* had a masonic type of hierarchy. These revolts were suppressed, some ruthlessly, by Neapolitan forces. Dissension seemed dead.

Yet there are signs that Francis was more progressive than his father. His knightly Order of Francis I was founded to reward merit in industry and the arts, something none of his predecessors had done quite so overtly.

Francis was dead by the end of 1830, succeeded by his Sicilian-born, son, Ferdinand II.

Revolution was still in the air, its winds blowing across the Alps from France. The July Revolution of 1830 blew another gust of dissent into Italy.

Despite some renewed activity in central Italy around that time by the *Carbonari* or allied groups sharing their sympathies, the *Carbonari* movement itself was destined to dissolve into the ether because, realistically, it would always lack the means to bring about change by force. Something less "militant" might be more effective, even preferred, at least for the time being. In northern Italy, Giuseppe Mazzini, a young Genoan intellectual who advocated Italian unification under a republic where papal power would be marginalized, organized *Giovane Italia*. Some former *Carbonari* eventually joined this new organization. As one can imagine, Mazzini was no more beloved by the Savoys in Turin than by the Bourbons in Naples. At first, he would prove a thorn in the side of the Piedmontese. While the survival of *Giovane Italia* depended on secrecy or at least discretion, it was not, strictly speaking, a sect or "secret society."

Most of the changes implemented by Francis I during his brief reign were symbolic at best. The existing legal code may have been sufficient but this was an age of constitutions, and for now the kingdom lacked one. The idea of a monarch commuting prison sentences by royal grace was perfectly acceptable, but the application of sound constitutional law would be better.

The kingdom never lacked great humanists. Giambattista Vico was such a man. So was Gaetano Filangieri. But both were long gone. In 1830, the Enlightenment was still elusive.

This distance marker erected outside Palermo's royal palace by King Francis I is one of the few surviving vestiges of his brief reign.

Chapter 6
FERDINAND II

One of the first acts of young King Ferdinand II of the Two Sicilies was a proclamation promising to guarantee justice to all citizens. He made an early attempt to root out corruption while encouraging fresh ideas by replacing jaded bureaucrats and aged personnel. In the end, this was only partly successful. However, cutting expenditures while encouraging commerce led to a reduction of the national debt.

The first years of his reign revealed Ferdinand II to be what today might be called a progressive. Compared to his grandfather and namesake, he was something of a reformer, at least during the first years of his reign.

For the moment, the frequent protests, though a matter of grave concern, were hardly tantamount to general civil strife. The economy of the Two Sicilies made it the most prosperous state in Italy. (In fairness, it must be observed that it was also the largest and most populous.) According to a royal decree issued in January 1831, the balance of the state's assets was substantial enough to justify reduction of certain taxes, such as those on flour.

Social Programs

To direct tangible assistance to the poor while instituting safeguards to prevent these funds ending up in the pockets of corrupt bureaucrats, Ferdinand established the Royal Charity Commission, the *Real Commissione di Beneficenza*.[70] Supplanting the role of the *Comitato Centrale di Beneficenza*, this program was one of the first European examples of a public welfare agency to provide subsidies to indigent citizens. This social welfare program should be distinguished from the large "poor houses," or *alberghi dei poveri*, in Naples and Palermo, intended for those who would otherwise be homeless.

There existed no infrastructure for granting the subsidies. Therefore, local administration, and the preliminary selection of appropriate recipients for this assistance, was entrusted to Catholic pastors, the nearest thing to a network of social workers that existed in the kingdom. Here was yet another case of church and state working in tandem.

The procedure for obtaining this assistance was remarkably simple compared to what came later, and the onerous "investigation" required for obtaining the *reddito di cittadinanza* today.[71] The request was made in writing but there was no printed form or prescribed text required for it. Only one adult per household could request the financial assistance, either indefinitely or temporarily.

The statute states that the first recipients to be considered are young adults lacking parents (having been orphaned or abandoned in childhood), and widows having children of a young age. Among those eligible for indefinite assistance (the statute uses the term "perpetual") are aged persons, those having grave physical disabilities, the blind, those having chronic illnesses, and the like. The text uses the phrase *i vecchi, gli storpj, i ciechi, i cronici, ed altri simili*.

Finally, those to be considered last were persons living

alone, perhaps lacking the support of kin, who over time might improve their conditions. This included those who were temporarily unemployed. The subsidies were based on a schedule of monthly payments, with a minimum of one ducat, according to the number of persons in the recipient's household.[72]

A specific regulation required confidentiality to avoid embarrassing the recipients of the subsidies.

The commission had a reserve fund of five hundred ducats per month for emergencies, unforeseen cases of extreme poverty.

Care was taken to avoid redundant payments from the state. A citizen receiving any other payment or subsidy was not eligible to receive this one.

There was a limit to the number of subsidies that could be paid. In the case of similar conditions or circumstances affecting two or more petitioners, the one who petitioned first would take precedence. Otherwise, an aged petitioner would be assisted before a younger one.

The commission issued the payments as checks on the last business day of each month, and no later than the eighth day of the next month.

There were other agencies for the public benefit. The office of surgeon general, or *Protomedico Generale,* had existed in Sicily for four centuries. Now there was an agency for public health in the Two Sicilies, the *Soprintendenza Generale di Salute Pubblica.* It will be remembered that Ferdinand I had instituted a commission for vaccinations.

These various agencies and commissions were reasonably efficient.[73]

Affairs of the Kingdom

The brief emergence of Ferdinandea, a volcanic islet in international waters in the Sicilian Channel between Sciacca and the island of Pantelleria, incited a minor diplomatic row. Surveyed by the British, who named it "Graham Island" and claimed it for themselves, it submerged early in 1832, to arise again briefly in 1846. It is part of an active submarine volcano.

Turning to address concerns expressed by privileged citizens on dry land, Ferdinand established a Commission for Titles of Nobility. This was not as superficial or elitist as it might seem, for it curtailed the avaricious claims still entertained by some aristocrats long after the abolition of feudalism, all the while discouraging the ambitions of a new class of social climbers.

Ferdinand wed Maria Cristina of Savoy in 1832. The youngest daughter of King Victor Emmanuel I of Sardinia was a kind, devout girl. She was pretty and shy. Maria Cristina may have found Naples and its court more stifling than the austere ambience she knew in Turin, but here, despite her natural modesty, she was a queen.

It is worth noting a fact conveniently overlooked by Italian-born historians writing after 1860, namely that for many years the Bourbons in Naples had cordial relations with the Savoys in Turin. Indeed, both Italian dynasties shared a sense of solidarity in confronting the revolutionary spirit that threatened to topple them from their lofty perches.

The year he was married, Ferdinand proposed a "League of Italian States," a federalist union that would include the Two Sicilies, the Papal States, Piedmont, Liguria and Tuscany. This was anathema to the Austrians, Germans and Russians, who saw in it a violation of the terms of the Congress of Vienna and the potential foundation of a new power. Leopold II in Florence seemed indecisive while Carlo Alberto in Turin was evasive, perhaps viewing it as a reflection of Ferdinand's personal ambition to rule the whole of Italy.

Pope Gregory XVI objected pre-emptively. This may have seemed unreasonable but it was not surprising. Gregory was a rabid reactionary who feared that the introduction of such inventions as railways and gas lighting in the Papal States might promote commerce and therefore empower the bourgeoisie. More immediately, he wanted to retain his grip on a third of the Italian peninsula.

In Naples, Queen Maria Cristina urged that offerings be made to the poor in lieu of nuptial festivities to be held around the country to mark her wedding. Unwavering in her religious devotion, she influenced Ferdinand to release inmates from the debtors' prisons, to forgive debts of less than twenty ducats, and to grant amnesty to convicts serving terms for lesser crimes. The municipal pawn brokerages in Naples and Palermo were ordered to return to the owners items having a pawn value of six ducats or less.

Young, sweet, innocent Maria Cristina of Savoy, Queen Consort of the Two Sicilies, would be Italy's last fairy-tale princess.

She died in 1836 shortly after giving birth to a son, Francis. She was twenty-three years old. The death of the saintly Maria Cristina (she was beatified in 2014) seems to have had a profound effect on Ferdinand, who was just two years her senior. A king's personality change, if such it was, might not be a determining factor in the running of a constitutional monarchy, but it might well exert an adverse impact on a state ruled by an absolute monarch. A nation that was soon to face great challenges.

The fairy tale was over.

In 1837, a terrible cholera epidemic struck Sicily and part of the peninsula, leading to the deaths of thousands. The larger cities were hit especially hard. Revolts erupted at Siracusa and Catania. Although these were not initially political, they were exploited by revolutionary elements. In the face of widespread suffering and death, the insurgents diffused the notion that the cholera was in some way the fault of King Ferdinand. The idea was popularized that a poison was somehow responsible for the epidemic.

Along the way, the crown was enjoined to invoke the lost constitution. The entreaties were ignored. Ferdinand II may have begun his reign as a progressive but this was changing.

Unprepared, the local authorities found it difficult to suppress violent uprisings fed by rumors and conspiracy theories, and now political demands. At first, the worst violence was seen in Catania, where troops sent from Naples put down the rebels with the same overzealous brutality they had used against the *Filadelfi*.

This period is sometimes cited as a turning point in public policy. Theretofore, Ferdinand II had been viewed as a reformer, perhaps a liberal.

During a visit to Sicily in 1838, the king granted amnesty to a number of prisoners, as he did occasionally.

He also conceded the major part of Sicily's sulfur mining licenses to a French firm. As Sicily provided around eighty percent of the world's sulfur, this did not set well with the British. Indeed, it conditioned Britain's attitude toward Ferdinand over the next two decades and would have major consequences.

More immediately, the British threatened a blockade of the Sicilian ports that exported most of the sulfur, along with the confiscation of ships carrying it. In 1840, following a protracted series of diplomatic maneuvers, the crown annulled the sulfur monopoly granted to the French. This pecuniary benefit placated the British for a time.

At the same time, the Pietrarsa metal and engineering works near Naples employed over a thousand men.

To outside observers, it seemed that Ferdinand was using one hand to introduce industry through innovations like the railroad, and the other to slap down the population. Perhaps he contemplated using technology to subdue the people, said the conspiracy theorists.

The next few years were comparatively serene, but the pot of discontent continued to simmer. It wasn't very appetizing.

The people wanted a constitution. Thus far, Ferdinand had failed to give them one.

Winds of Change

In 1844 around a hundred armed rioters sympathetic to the ideas of Mazzini were arrested in Cosenza, in Calabria. A number were tried and a few executed, but some of the sentences were commuted.

The following year, Ferdinand hosted a major scientific congress in Naples. Like similar congresses held in other cities, this one had its political side.

If Ferdinand lacked encouragement of his suspicions about social progress, it arrived in Palermo in the person of Tsar Nicholas I of Russia, the quintessential autocrat. Here was Ferdinand's kindred soul, an equally conservative monarch equally willing to quash dissent. The tsar was impressed by Pietrarsa, which became the model for a similar plant he built in his own country.

Apart from its excellent commercial relations with Russia, the Two Sicilies negotiated sound trade treaties with Britain, France and the United States. These treaties, which were essentially similar to each other, governed such commerce for the duration of the life of the kingdom.

Commerce itself may have been good, but agriculture was as fickle as ever, and governments were rarely prepared for nature's caprices. The terrible potato blight that struck Europe was unforeseen. While its effects in Italy were minimal, Ireland, which depended on this crop, was hit hard. The result was a lethal famine that decimated the population.

Sicily depended as much on grain as Ireland depended on potatoes, and a Europe-wide drought lasting several years resulted in a critical reduction of wheat supplies. The very definition of the word *drought* varied from one region to the next;

in comparatively arid Sicily a drought was worse than what the term implied in Germany.

Acting on sound advice, Ferdinand ordered a general ban on grain exports and began a tour around the country to ensure that starvation might be avoided. Arriving unannounced in the various provincial capitals, he and his suite of officials conducted inspections to uncover any cases of hoarding. In a land where price fixing and speculation were normal, corruption might, in theory, be punished when exposed in this manner. Nevertheless, the sovereign still found himself in the crosshairs of domestic critics, such as Luigi Settembrini, who penned an anonymous tract against the crown.

To the *popolino,* the common folk, Ferdinand II came to be known for *feste, forche e farina* (festivals, gallows and flour).

The climate, both literally and figuratively, was perfect for another round of protests. The first was at Messina in 1847. This was planned some months in advance, and it coincided with similar insurrections in Reggio across the Strait of Messina. The use of artillery to bring the rioters under control earned Ferdinand the enduring nickname *Re Bomba,* "King Bomb." Despite this distinction, he was not the only monarch to use such tactics during this era.[74]

The bomb of popular discontent was not going to be contained, restricted to just one city. On January twenty-fourth of 1848 it exploded in Palermo.

There were several underlying causes for these protests. The paucity of grain was an obvious catalyst; food shortages and high prices made it easy to enlist the support of the common people, who suffered the most during such a crisis.

In Sicily, a subtle independence movement was also at work; this reflected the desire for a constitution, and perhaps a separate king, for the island. Presumably, this revived "Kingdom of Sicily" would be governed separately from the mainland. This minority view by the intellectual elite probably belied the more banal grievances of the general populace, more immediately concerned with bread and taxes.

As usual, the list of demands was soon amended. A republic was placed on the agenda and a few prominent aristocrats jumped on board. These developments were perhaps predictable, or at least conceivable, but the Palermitans' rabid fervor portended incidents far beyond Sicilian shores.

The mini-revolution at Palermo has been painted as the determining spark that ignited a series of revolts around Europe, as if this were a simple chain reaction. The decisive impetus was the revolt that began in Paris a month later. Europe's "hungry years" of high food prices and an industrial downturn made revolution seem attractive to a new generation.[75]

Even before the Sicilian riots, several revolutionary movements of a similar kind were in the planning stages across the continent. It was only a matter of time before they became open insurrections. Nevertheless, there were French and British diplomats and merchants in Naples and Palermo to encourage the revolts on behalf of their fellow citizens back home, while reporting to Paris and London.

This time there was a new element in the revolutionary mix. It would change the world forever. The telegraph, a novel technology zealously promoted by the Neapolitan government, provided the network. It made possible fast communication between cities, and between the allied revolutionaries in those cities. Their *lingua franca,* the language of diplomacy, the second tongue of aristocrats and intellectuals, was French. Railroads made travel between European capitals easier than ever. Europe's autocrats had underestimated the power bestowed upon the citizenry by telecommunications and the steam engine.[76]

Viewed as a trend, the scattered European protests defy simple description. One might loosely describe many as "nationalist" or "liberal." Some political theorists even characterize them as "proto-socialist." Apart from such labels, each assumed a local flavor. Their common element was a neglected population in search of change and a greater voice in government, things that might lead to more prosperity for all.

This had festered ever since the Congress of Vienna, for which many Europeans entertained high hopes, restored the social order to what it had been before the Napoleonic Wars. True, the borders drawn by the delegates to Vienna kept the peace among nations, but socially the Congress left a tattered legacy of unresolved issues because the nations themselves did not move with the times. This wave of popular dissent was the price to be paid on a continent where, for the ordinary person, little had changed in fifty years. If monarchy were to continue, it would have to be constitutional, granting citizens a larger role in government. Nobody but a few selfish aristocrats, reactionaries and religious zealots wanted an absolute monarchy.

Alexis de Tocqueville saw "a world divided between those who had nothing joined in common envy against those who had everything joined in common terror."

Yet each regional protest had its peculiarities. In the German states, national unity was a key factor. In Poland, the rebellion was characterized by calls for independence. In Switzerland, the cantons sought and achieved greater autonomy. In Austria, many of the first protesters were students, while in allied Hungary the protests evolved into a call for independence from Austria. Romania also saw riots.

Unlike earlier revolutions, this one would not be quelled by tossing the peasants a few loaves of stale bread. In Denmark, where a new king granted a liberal constitution, real social change was coming. That was the exception in what has come to be called the "Springtime of Peoples."

In Lombardy, the initial lament seems to have been about tax increases imposed by the Austrians. In Piedmont, the revolt was an effort by the bourgeoisie to obtain a constitution.

Newly-elected Pope Pius IX was forced to flee Rome. He left as a reformer, he returned a reactionary.

Almost immediately, Ferdinand's response was to grant a constitution. This was not based on his grandfather's constitution of 1820 but on the French constitution ratified ten years later, which many viewed as less progressive.

In Turin, King Carlo Alberto followed suit, promulgating his *Statuto*. This became a point of divergence between the two Italian kingdoms, for the lasting changes effected by Carlo Alberto would elude Ferdinand.

Following the revolts of 1848, the *Statuto* enacted in the Kingdom of Sardinia remained in force, even if its principles were not always applied with rigor. The one in the Two Sicilies was suppressed as soon as the protesters were brought under control. This earned King Ferdinand II the ire of many in Europe, especially in Britain. In the Two Sicilies, his obstinacy played into the hands of detractors seeking the alternative model of a comparatively liberal — or in any case constitutional — monarchy elsewhere in Italy.

Unwittingly, Ferdinand and his Piedmontese counterpart Carlo Alberto set the stage for an Italian dichotomy, a rivalry, even a regionalist antipathy, the infamous *divario* that taints Italy to this day, pitting Turin and Milan against Naples and Palermo, northerners against southerners. Although it was soon to be repressed in favor of a national unification movement, Sicily's aspirations to independence would resurface from time to time, notably in 1866 and again in 1945.

Ferdinand was demonized in the most emphatic terms. William Gladstone described his sclerotic policies as "the negation of God erected into a system of government."

Such sentiments were doubtless sincere, but more broadly the political relationship with Britain was still complicated by such concerns as the sulfur industry. By 1850, this was a *sine qua non* of the rapport between the two nations. The lust for the yellow mineral vexed Britain just as major nations (in later centuries) resented less important states controlling the petroleum supply.

It was not only British ideas that Ferdinand wanted to hold in check, but Britain's economic and military influence in the Kingdom of the Two Sicilies.

Here was the consummate pragmatist, the inveterate survivor. The king who began his reign as something of a progressive was now a full-fledged, autocratic reactionary. This prompted a number of citizens to leave the Two Sicilies for self-imposed exile in northern Italy.

In 1856, the Congress of Paris was held to formally end the Crimean War. The Two Sicilies had nothing to do with this but Piedmont did. The Piedmontese representative, Camillo Benso di Cavour, exploited this opportunity to disparage Ferdinand's government in the south. By diplomatic standards, it was an underhanded tactic, especially if one considers that there was no Neapolitan representative present to defend Ferdinand. The same year, the French and the British recalled their ambassadors from Naples.

The next few years saw an effort by external forces to curtail Ferdinand's international influence, but isolating Italy's largest state would not be easy. For now, Ferdinand's detractors in Paris, London and Turin could only await his death, all the while thinking and planning.[77]

In the *Regno,* the revolutionaries were always a minority of the population. The majority of the citizens were unsupportive of radical change. In 1857, when Carlo Pisacane, an exiled Neapolitan aristocrat, landed with some rebels at Sapri, a town in the Cilento region south of Salerno, his effort to gain local control met with failure. Indeed, the local residents opposed him. To later Italian historians, however, he has come to be known as Italy's first non-Marxist socialist.

Unification

The *Risorgimento,* or "resurgence," was an intellectual movement that began long before the middle years of the nineteenth century. Indeed, early concepts of it had already been formulated, in a very general way, by a few writers before 1800. It was not born as an explicitly political effort to unify the Italian states but, for better or worse, that is how it has come to be identified in the popular mind. One could even say, with only the slightest hyperbole, that the movement, along with its name, was "hijacked" by opportunistic politicians, so that what began as the humanistic *Risorgimento* evolved into the movement toward political unification.[78]

Although the idea had been broached decades earlier, Giuseppe Mazzini's *Giovane Italia,* the organization that enlisted some of the disenchanted *Carbonari,* was the first major political movement to advocate a unitary Italian state. Its leaders wanted a republic where papal influence would be marginalized. It was largely covert, even conspiratorial, its members identifying themselves in correspondence by nicknames. No state in Italy would tolerate such a movement. In 1833, some members plotting a revolt in Piedmont were arrested and summarily put to death.

Each passing year after the tumultuous revolts of 1848 saw a wider advocacy of Italian unification. Naturally, the greatest support for this came from the political elite of the smaller northern states, who were most likely to benefit from a united Italy. For the most part, this was the aristocracy and the middle class. It seems that most people were indifferent to the idea, or perhaps simply outwardly stoic, but we have no opinion surveys to tell us what most people thought. Expressing certain ideas could be dangerous.

The revolts of 1848 left Austria weakened. Seeking to exploit this, Carlo Alberto of Savoy invaded the Austrian-occupied Italian regions bordering Piedmont in an attempt to expand his realm. This ambitious effort met with failure. Following his defeat by Austrian forces in 1849, Carlo Alberto abdicated in favor of his son, who ruled as Victor Emmanuel II.

As a monarch, Ferdinand II of the Two Sicilies may have been no worse than his Piedmontese counterparts. The problem is that he wasn't much better, either.

Despite the obvious setbacks, Italian unification, in some form, was inevitable. What shape would it assume? A republic, a confederation of states, or a monolithic monarchy? Each concept of nationhood had its proponents.

Giuseppe Mazzini's anticlerical republican faction was the most "radical" element. Camillo Benso di Cavour, the Piedmontese cabinet minister and nobleman we met earlier, led another faction — initially defined as "liberal" — which sought to coexist with the established monarchical order; in time, the liberals came to embrace the "moderates" of the bourgeoisie, such as bankers and industrialists, who wanted political continuity but a free-market economy. It was these moderates and liberals, enjoying a certain degree of sympathy from the British, who would plot the course of Italian unification. To that singular end, Cavour was tireless in his backstage machinations.

The role of freemasonry, though real, was never more than peripheral. Freemasonry, of course, was condemned by the papacy. The secretive nature of *Giovane Italia* and the clandestine methods of many unificationist proponents were probably inspired by freemasonry.

Apart from the diminution of Catholic influence in public affairs, the "anticlerical" facet of the unification movement as it manifested itself around 1860 was never quite so liberal or secular as its most vocal apologists subsequently claimed. It certainly was not atheistic, nor much inspired by the Enlightenment.

Although a number of disaffected southerners joined its ranks, the movement's founding leadership was northern; Mazzini was from Genoa, Cavour from Turin. Few of the northerners had spent much time south of Rome. To some extent, this influenced certain unificationist views of Italy's southern regions.

Nevertheless, as the movement gained ground, Ferdinand's cousin in Turin offered him the crown of Italy if only he would agree to a federalist union, something vaguely conceived along the lines of the Holy Roman Empire and already proposed in 1832. This Ferdinand declined despite his earlier advocacy of the same idea, explaining that he had no wish to infringe the rights, and the territory, of the pope, who would never willingly relinquish Rome.

Foreigners, with Britons leading the charge, generally directed their criticism at the Two Sicilies as Italy's largest, wealthiest state, and the one that, at least superficially, seemed to suffer the most from outmoded laws and an entrenched, unenlightened ruling class. These criticisms of an obsolete ethos chained to the church were not without merit. However, they must be considered in the context of the times.[79]

Closely allied with the Two Sicilies, the Papal State garnered its share of opprobrium, much of it deserved. The church, of course, was a perennial target of Europe's more strident Protestants, but never more so than during the pontificate of sanctimonious Pius IX.

A case could be made that some states in pre-unitary Italy were at least marginally more socially progressive than others. Tuscany first abolished the death penalty in 1786 (only to re-institute it four years later) and, as we have seen, Piedmont's *Statuto* of 1848 proved to be more enduring than the constitutions enacted in the Two Sicilies, however lofty their aspirations.

In such an environment, it was easy enough to paint the Two Sicilies as being somewhat more repressive than the comparatively "liberal" mini-nations of northern Italy.

But didn't the revolts of 1848 touch Turin as well as Palermo? Wasn't Roman Catholicism the official religion of the "anticlerical" Kingdom of Sardinia? Wasn't the Shroud of Turin venerated just as fervidly as the blood of Saint Januarius and the bones of Saint Rosalie, its provenance equally dubious? Was there not press censorship in Piedmont? Would a recalcitrant journalist in Turin go unpunished if, in his reckless *lèse-majesté,* he wrote an article calling for the deposition of the reigning Savoy?

It would be ridiculous to conclude that life in the Two Sicilies was any better than life in Piedmont, but ludicrous to imagine that it was any worse, or that Palermo was in some way backward compared to Turin. There are no precise figures for annual household income outside the aristocracy, but in Sicily proper the *riveli,* referred to elsewhere, provide a general indication of taxation based on familial assets to pay the *donativi.* The Two Sicilies had a high number of students enrolled in universities compared to other parts of Italy.[80]

Sicilian political dissentients went to Piedmont. Where were the Piedmontese dissidents? Where did *they* go?

To America, of course.

The first major wave of Italian immigrants to make their way across the ocean were Piedmontese and Genoans.

While few of these emigrés were political exiles *per se,* it is obvious that they made the long journey to a strange land for a reason. Even if their motivations were purely economic, that begs a number of questions about life in "Savoy Land" where, to read the writings of some apologists — Italians and Britons alike — everyday existence was one giant, continuous bacchanal of Barolo consumed with bresaola, risotto and truffles.

A transitory expatriate was sometime general Giuseppe Garibaldi, a native of Nice (under Savoy rule since 1814) who had fallen out of favor in Turin but would live to play a pivotal role in Italy's unification. Arriving in New York in 1850, he befriended Antonio Meucci, a Tuscan inventor best known today for his rudimentary experiments in the field of voice transmission via electrical signals over wires.[81]

The truth is that until unification, and indeed for some years thereafter, the greater part of Italy's emigration came from the regions to the north of Rome, not from the south.

Statistically speaking, the people living in Piedmont, Lombardy, Liguria, Venetia and Tuscany were every bit as impoverished and illiterate as those in Abruzzi, Calabria and Sicily. In rural Piedmont, rice had been planted and harvested the same miserable way for centuries, by women wading through the water, all the while being harassed by the merciless mosquitoes.

Some unification apologists chose to focus on the movement's "political philosophy." But what was actually promoted to the majority of people in the middle years of the nineteenth century had very little to do with political theory as such. It was all about the purported benefits of unification.

Were the "ideological" issues in Italy any more complex than the contemporary questions of serfdom in Russia or slavery in the United States?

Among political theorists, Karl Marx was especially critical of the movement after it transpired because it did not represent, in his view, a step forward. If one were to create a new nation, why a monarchy? Why not a republic like France or even the United States? In the end, Marx was as critical of some of the men who forged the new state as he was of the unitary kingdom they erected upon the embers of the monarchies of the Two Sicilies, Tuscany, Parma and Modena. They were a disappointment. To be fair, Marx in his later years was critical of almost everybody, but many commentators came to agree with his sentiments about Italian unification.

The road to Hell is paved with good intentions, says an old aphorism. Mazzini and Cavour entertained some good ideas about great things the "New Italy" was going to do but, in the end, never achieved. The former was cast aside, and the latter died soon after the Kingdom of Italy was proclaimed. Deprived of the guidance of such intellectuals, the nation floundered along a self-destructive path these thinkers never foresaw.

Once the united Italy became a reality, many of the ideas espoused by the unification movement's intellectuals were ignored, even disparaged. Its pseudo-democracy never fostered the freedom one found in France, Britain or the United States. (A few foibles and fiascoes of the Kingdom of Italy are mentioned in later chapters.)

However noble its ideals may have been in the beginning, the unification effort, like many political movements, took on a life of its own with the passage of time. By 1860 it would be something slightly different from what it was ten years earlier.

While the Two Sicilies didn't need Piedmont, it is clear that Piedmont needed the Two Sicilies, or at least its gold reserves. Based on this measure alone, the wealth of the southern kingdom eclipsed that of all the other Italian states combined, while its national debt was a mere fraction of Piedmont's. This was a matter of public record. Somebody in Turin wanted the gold in Naples. And they were willing to kill for it.[82]

Ferdinand's refusal to accept the Italian crown left a Savoy as the next logical candidate. For the moment, Ferdinand was an implacable roadblock. He commanded Italy's largest standing army. More importantly, he was willing to use it, to lead it himself if needs must, even — as he had already shown — against his own people. Of course, redoubtable Ferdinand wouldn't live forever.

On the wider stage, the one that counted internationally, stringing together a few Italian monarchies was never a matter of global import. It was, at its best, a sideshow. True, commingling yet another major state with the existing European potpourri could alter the balance of power, as the united Germany eventually did, but Italy never had the population or industrial might of the *Reich,* and nothing that happened anyplace in Italy during the nineteenth century had global consequences, despite what a few rabid Italian nationalists would have us believe. Russia and the United States spanned entire continents, while Britain's empire linked one sea to another in a chain encircling the globe. Whatever pretensions she eventually entertained, and at whatever cost, little Italy was not destined to be the mouse that roared, or the tail that wagged the dog.[83]

Technology and Industry

During this era, much of the leading research on seismic and volcanic phenomena was conducted in the Two Sicilies.

In 1855, Luigi Palmieri, a professor of physics and geology at the University of Naples, invented the mercury seismometer, a precursor of the modern seismograph. His invention was put into continuous use at Vesuvius, where he was director of the seismic observatory.

It has been stated elsewhere that the individual wealth and education of most people throughout what is now Italy was essentially uniform. Nevertheless, certain industries in the Two Sicilies stood out. Here obvious examples were shipbuilding in Naples and Palermo, and the metal works at Pietrarsa. Porcelain, for industrial as well as ornamental purposes, was another prosperous industry. Much glass was produced and, since 1832, also recycled.

Yet another important sector of the manufacturing economy was textiles, not only in the production of fabric but items made from it. By 1850, the Two Sicilies was producing about half a million pairs of woolen, cotton, silk and leather gloves per year. A decade later, the figure was nearer seven hundred thousand pairs, more than almost any other European nation.

Most of these gloves were exported to other European countries and to the Americas. Indeed, the Two Sicilies dominated the international glove market.

Although this was, in part, a "cottage industry" much like linen embroidery or (in Scotland) the weaving of Harris tweed, most of the gloves were manufactured in factories in and around Naples. The city's Sanità district was full of glove factories. Glovers performed much hand stitching since very few of the sewing machines becoming available were suitable to such delicate work.

Much like Italian high fashion today, the product enjoyed a certain demand and prestige abroad. Naples was, in fact, one of the fashion capitals of Europe.

In 1859, a public mercantile and commodities exchange, the first of its kind in Italy, was established in Naples. The kingdom's public stock exchange, as we have seen, was chartered in 1778; this was reorganized and expanded in 1860.

The Legal Code of 1848

Though the constitution of 1848 was soon abrogated, the tumults of the era inspired a revision of the legal code of 1819. It is to the updated code of 1848 that most historians refer when considering the status of law in the Two Sicilies on the eve of Italian unification. Most of the statutes of 1819, such as the laws governing marital separation, are retained; some are expanded. Only a few were deleted outright.

Like the earlier code, that of 1848 covers all aspects of law. As a publication, it runs to more than nine hundred pages.

The statutes governing parenthood and marriage are numerous.[84] A procedure exists for a father to recognize his child born outside marriage; a distinction is drawn between recognition and legitimization.

Juridical procedures are set forth for penal cases. Sentence terms are prescribed, but so are principles such as prosecutorial and judicial discretion.

Statutes govern the comportment of soldiers, sailors and police. Finance and commerce are considered; contracts, accounting, international letters of credit and bankruptcy (and bankruptcy fraud) are addressed in detail.

In the event of a business failure, the rights of a debtor's wife to be indemnified against liability are considered. Here the principle of separating marital assets (prior to marriage) appears; this is still part of Italian law, where this is indicated on the marriage license form.

The Two Sicilies code of 1848 was as complete and sophisticated as any in Europe. Indeed, it may have influenced that of the Kingdom of Sardinia issued a decade later.

ATTO DI NASCITA	Indicazione del giorno, in cui è stato amministrato il Sagramento del Battesimo.
Numero d'ordine *cinquantidueiennove* L'anno *milleottocentotrentasei* il dì *quattordici* del mese di *Novembre* alle ore *ventidue* avanti di Noi *Cav. D'Andreani* *Senatore* ed Uffiziale dello Stato Civile del Comune di Palermo, Distretto di Palermo, Valle di Palermo è comparso *Antonino Arena* di anni *trentasette* di professione *Cuciniere* domiciliato *Casa nuova al Borgo* il quale ci ha presentato un *maschio* secondochè abbiamo ocularmente riconosciuto, ed ha dichiarato che lo stesso è nato da *Ma-* *ria Lofammarano jugi* di anni *trentasei* domiciliata *ivi* E da *lui dichiarante* di anni *..........* di professione *..........* domiciliato *ivi* nel giorno *tredici* del mese di *so-* *pra* anno milleottocento *trentasei* alle ore *ventidue* nella casa *seguente* Lo stesso ha inoltre dichiarato di dare al *lo stesso* il nome di *Alfonso*	Numero d'ordine *cinquantidue* L'anno milleottocento *trentasei* il dì *quindici* del mese di *Novembre* Il Parroco di *..........* ci ha restituito nel dì *suddetto* del mese di *sopra*, anno milleot- tocento *trentasei* il notamento che noi gli abbiamo rimesso nel giorno *quattordici* del mese di *sopra* anno milleottocento *trentasei* del controscritto atto di na- scita, in piè del quale ha in- dicato, che il Sagramento del Battesimo è stato amministra- to a *Alfonso* nel giorno *quattordici* In vista di un tale nota- mento, dopo di averlo cifrato, abbiamo disposto che fosse conservato nel volume dei documenti al foglio *1037* Abbiamo inoltre accusato

Civil birth registration in the Kingdom of the Two Sicilies in 1836 when very few nations had vital statistics records of this kind

Chapter 7
FRANCIS II

Ferdinand II died in May 1859. Francis II, the son of Ferdinand's first wife, saintly Maria Cristina of Savoy, was a very devout young man. That would be his undoing.

The young king lived under the spell of dogmatic, intransigent Pope Pius IX. Zealous Pius was a pontiff given to pontificating. Too much of it, in fact. Not enough has been written about the influence on Italian unification by the most pertinacious man since 1800 to occupy the See of Saint Peter. If Cavour and his confederates orchestrated the unification, it was Pius IX who provided its instruments, setting the stage for a pathetic performance.

Pius wasn't always opposed to Italian unification; early in his pontificate, during his ephemeral liberal phase, he was willing to accept an Italy united under the papal tiara. The obvious defect in such a proposal is that no king with any knowledge of history was ever going to accept it.

A true reactionary, Pius came to defy social progress in all its forms. For the times in which he faced adversity, Francis could not have chosen a worst mentor.

In some countries today we find military chaplains holding

officer rank. Even in the Middle Ages, there were bishops and imams who commanded armies, but they were the exception rather than the rule. For most men, the path that leads to soldiery is not the one that leads to priesthood. A good king must be a good leader, and that sometimes means spilling blood in defense of his subjects' lives. This is never pretty, but it's a fact of life — or death. Such a terrible task, undertaken only after the most judicious consideration, may spell the difference between a people's survival or its subjugation. Francis' fatal flaw was a conflict between competing vocations. Heaven might welcome him, but posterity would curse him.

The young man's coronation greeted him with subtle political complexities regarding the great powers. A few months before his death, Ferdinand II had granted certain mining concessions to the French firm operated by the Bérard family for a term of five years. That this effectively reinstated the basic conditions of a contract signed decades earlier was mentioned in the decree. While it did not compromise the existing, if arguably fragile, trade agreement with Britain signed in 1845, the new accord gave the outward appearance that infringing upon rights to the sulfur claimed by the British was within the realm of possibility. Nevertheless, Francis could not easily extricate the Two Sicilies from the recent agreement without provoking a diplomatic incident with France. For Britain, the immediate concern was not the availability of the sulfur, since the monopoly was still in place, but the mineral's quantity and price.

The Undeclared War

In Turin, the Savoys knew that their newly-crowned Neapolitan cousin was unlikely to be as ferocious as his father, and they knew something of his piety. Nevertheless, it would be imprudent to risk a major military invasion against a state boasting the largest army on the Italian peninsula. A few zealous Neapolitan generals might actually annihilate a Piedmontese regiment or two. Initially, therefore, support was sought from within the Kingdom of the Two Sicilies. The most efficacious tools were old-fashioned bribery, treason and sedition.

It was never difficult, anywhere in Italy, to find a few disgruntled generals. This discontent was not, for the most part, political so much as personal. Perhaps it was born of an Italianate apathy in response to too many conquests. Whatever their root cause, the lamentations were many, reflecting a lack of *esprit de corps* that would plague the armies of the Kingdom of Italy for the whole of the monarchy's existence. In the decades to come, Italian generals prosecuting campaigns from Africa to Austria regularly blamed their failures on their troops rather than themselves; military training of conscripts was rarely more than mediocre, and a lack of morale came to define the downtrodden, often indolent, Italian soldier, making him the object of condescension.

Apart from their more obvious efforts to sow the seeds of sedition among the populace, Piedmontese agents had sought to incite treason among Neapolitan generals for some years, ever since Ferdinand II rejected the Italian crown.

The extent to which they succeeded is a matter of historical debate because supporting documents and reliable accounts are scarce. Be that as it may, the fact that a tendency toward indifference prevailed by 1860 is beyond disputation. Equally indisputable was Britain's support for the unification. This would come in handy.

As early as the Plombières Agreement of 1858, Cavour was sounding out the French and the British about cooperating in a hypothetical invasion of the Two Sicilies he knew Piedmont couldn't achieve on its own.

The crown of the Two Sicilies was never Victor Emmanuel's to win, it was Francis' to lose.

Yet the Piedmontese ministers didn't want to risk their own

troops, and they didn't want to be accused of starting an unprovoked war even though, like other European sovereigns, the Savoys had participated in quite a few. The solution arrived in the person of Giuseppe Garibaldi, a sometime general and occasional mercenary with a checkered past who was willing to fight such a war. As it was known that Garibaldi had not always enjoyed the good graces of his Savoy masters, he could be supported tacitly, surreptitiously, and in the event of either a military or diplomatic disaster Cavour could simply deny having ever authorized an attack by a man who didn't even hold an active, formal commission as a Piedmontese general. This meant that Garibaldi and his assemblage of ragtag volunteers were expendable. Whatever the outcome of an invasion, Piedmont's ignoble "plausible deniability" would be a useful political tool where Piedmont lacked a clear justification, a legal *casus belli*.

Cavour wanted unification but he wanted it on his terms, not Mazzini's, and he was suspicious of Garibaldi.

"War is merely the continuation of policy by other means," said Carl von Clausewitz. The first order of business was the occupation of the tiny duchies of Parma and Modena, along with the larger Grand Duchy of Tuscany in early 1860. Here there was little resistance to the overwhelming numerical superiority of the Savoyard forces. Sicily would be left to Garibaldi, with Turin's tacit approval.[85]

In late April, the military command at Messina received news of Garibaldi's impending arrival someplace in Sicily. Further intelligence referred to the transportation of armaments and additional troops, possibly with British logistical support. Acting on these reports and others, Paolo Ruffo, the Lieutenant of the Realm for Sicily, alerted some port officials in the major cities. Cavour ensured that Garibaldi's ships were shadowed along most of the route to Sicily by Piedmontese warships; in effect, they had an "unofficial" military escort.

On the eleventh of May, Garibaldi's two large vessels landed at Marsala while the commanders of the two British warships stationed there stood by and watched. Indeed, it appears that the British may have actually assisted the landings of the "red-shirts" directly, probably by maneuvering into position between them and the Two Sicilies forces, but this is not known with certainty. In the confusion that followed, overpowering Marsala's garrison was not extremely difficult, and naval relief for the Sicilian troops arrived too late to save the day. The city's British wine merchants raised the Union Jack.

Four days later, the garrison at Calatafimi surrendered following what some have described as token resistance. Several "political" prisoners, mostly aristocrats, were released from the local prison. Here is where wholesale desertion began, swelling the ranks of Garibaldi's army. Before long, Salemi, Alcamo, Partinico and other towns had fallen to the invaders.

Garibaldi's force enlisted more men *en route* to Palermo, where a bloody battle raged in the streets for days. Here the hostilities continued until early June. Traditional unificationist accounts paint the picture of a popular insurrection leading to an "easy" victory over the "cowardly" Sicilian troops who "abandoned" the city. The real pictures, the photographs, tell the story of a highly destructive series of bloody engagements similar to urban guerrilla warfare, their death toll surpassed only by the aerial bombings of the Second World War.

The defenders did not lack the courage to fight; what they lacked was courage of conviction. They did not abandon king and country; they were abandoned by generals who failed to act in unison against a common enemy.

Rationalists are wary of conspiracy theories (and none shall be advanced here), but there are a few details of the Palermo campaign that are likely to spark suspicion in the mind of any scientific, critical thinker. The events suggest, at the very least, covert planning if not a wider cast of international players lurking offstage just beyond view. In early April, weeks before Garibaldi's landings, there was an attempted revolt by insurgents, amply supplied with guns and ammunition, at the Gancia monastery. Francesco Crispi, a dissident, is thought to have masterminded this.

Loquacious Giuseppe Garibaldi was the darling of the foreign press, especially fawning Britons, some of whom still pen whimsical narratives of the invasion. A few foreign journalists even met him at Palermo. It was in Sicily that Garibaldi's apotheosis began.

Whether General Ferdinando Lanza's surrender was the result of something other than a looming military defeat is still hotly debated; following a brief truce arranged with Garibaldi on a British ship, Lanza's army resumed fighting for a few days before suddenly capitulating. Less polemical is the fact that in June, following the Battle of Palermo, British ships sent from Malta supplied rifles, and American ships arrived full of arms and northern Italian troops. That the war soon assumed the character of a multinational invasion bolstered by foreign navies is beyond cavil.

Garibaldi had taken to wearing a Piedmontese general's uniform when it suited him, especially when meeting with high-ranking officers of the Two Sicilies or Britain. While in Palermo, the general found time to be promoted to the thirty-third degree of freemasonry during a ceremony at the home of Count Federico.

In Naples, King Francis, encouraged by his wife and the prime minister, Carlo Filangieri, resurrected the short-lived constitution of 1848. As ever, there were intrigues at court. The king's stepmother, his father's second wife Maria Teresa of Austria, wanted to see one of her own sons on the throne.

Meanwhile, the war continued eastward across Sicily. During the torrid summer, the troops of the infamous Nino Bixio executed some rebels at Bronte, a town of little strategic importance associated with the Nelson family, which had asked that it be protected.[86] By the end of August, Garibaldi's troops had crossed over to Calabria. It wasn't long before the growing force was making its way toward Naples.

Wishing to avoid a civilian slaughter, Francis and Maria Sophia left the capital in favor of the coastal stronghold at Gaeta to the north. This was a strategic error, and Garibaldi entered Naples in early September. British warships anchored in the Bay of Naples stood by, just in case Garibaldi's troops needed assistance.

The Battle of Volturno, a series of engagements into early October, some led by Francis' younger brother, Alfonso, made it clear that there were still people willing to defend the realm.

The royal family left behind all its personal assets, including accounts in the Bank of Naples. All were confiscated by the occupiers.

On October twenty-sixth, Giuseppe Garibaldi met King Victor Emmanuel II at Teano, between Naples and Gaeta, formally recognizing him as the ruler of the conquered territories. The old state was gone, the new one stillborn.

Appearances aren't everything, but both king and general were short and stout, so depicting them with any verisimilitude proved challenging for painters, sculptors and photo retouchers seeking a heroic national archetype.

The withdrawal of French ships anchored in the Gulf of Gaeta made it possible for the exigent Piedmontese to bombard the fortress from the sea, and Francis surrendered it on February thirteenth of 1861. The anschluss was complete, even though a piece of Sicily fought on for another month. Messina's massive citadel held out until March thirteenth, when it surrendered to the Piedmontese army. In Abruzzi, Civitella del Tronto surrendered on the twentieth.

The Italians, for such they became, finally got their unitary monarchy and the British would have their Sicilian sulfur.

Southern money and new industries would enable Milan and Turin to overtake Naples and Palermo economically. Nobody in Britain could contemplate a war against a future Victor Emmanuel forcing a stalwart, half-American, cigar-chomping prime minister to dismember the Empire to secure a new alliance that might defeat an axis of evil.

Francis II, the last King of the Two Sicilies, before succeeding to the throne in 1859

Maria Sophia of Bavaria, the last Queen of the Two Sicilies, died in exile in 1925

Barricades near Palermo Cathedral during the campaign of 1860

Little remains of Palermo's seaside castle, largely destroyed by invading troops in 1860. The stout round tower is Arab. The gatehouse is Aragonese.

Chapter 8
POSTLUDE

Would that we could revel in the advent of the Kingdom of Italy. In vain do we search for its virtues. The Kingdom of the Two Sicilies was far from perfect, but for the great majority of people life in the unitary state that succeeded it was nothing less than tragic. Now, more than ever, poverty and suffering were to be the order of the day. Very little that is edifying can be said about the Kingdom of Italy. Its history makes for uncomfortable reading; this exposé shall be mercifully succinct.

Elections and Insurrections

A plebiscite held in the invasion's aftermath — but before the besieged fortress of Messina surrendered — allegedly confirmed Savoy rule with an astounding ninety-eight percent of eligible voters favorable to the new regime. Were this a legitimate balloting, its results would be studied around the world as a rare electoral phenomenon, for how many elections are ever won with such a majority?

Of course, the referendum of 1860 was fraudulent. Only the most inscient among us would claim otherwise. Even though the paper ballots were ostensibly "secret," the election officials, who already saw the fall of the Two Sicilies as a *fait accompli*, would know who the local dissenters were most likely to be. In the event, such evidence as exists suggests that the officials simply "corrected" any dissenting ballots to reflect approval. The only eligible voters were literate males of at least twenty-five years of age who declared a certain taxable income, and this was but a fraction of the adult male population; the literacy rate was twenty percent at best.

The best-known example of this electoral fraud is Sicily, where the result most often cited is approximately 432,050 votes favorable to annexation and a mere 667 in opposition, in a general population (including men under twenty-five, women and children) estimated at approximately 2,232,000. Moreover, the figure (equal to some twenty-five percent of the *total* adult population, including men under twenty-five years of age *not* entitled to vote) suggests a far higher level of literacy and taxable personal income than there actually was, rendering voting by any more than 300,000 literate, taxable men over the age of twenty-five mathematically impossible. That there might be so many eligible voters is altogether untenable in view of the most rudimentary statistical analysis.

Throughout Italy, region after region confirmed the annexation in referenda resulting in majorities invariably comparable to that claimed for Sicily. Not everybody was taken in by this ruse. Massimo Taparelli d'Azeglio, formerly prime minister of Piedmont, observed:

"At Naples we overthrew a sovereign in order to set up a government based on universal suffrage. Yet we still today need sixty battalions of soldiers to hold the people down, or even more, since these are not enough, whereas in other provinces of Italy nothing of the sort is necessary. One must therefore conclude that there was some mistake about the plebiscite. We must ask the Neapolitans once again whether they want the Piedmontese or not."[87]

Naturally, no such query was ever posed to the populace, at least not officially. The unification was a misconceived amalgam. What emerged in the new Italy was an ingrained disdain for southerners.

The former Two Sicilies was an occupied country in everything but name. Atrocities were not unknown. In August 1861, two southern towns, Pontelandolfo and Casalduni, suffered murder, rape and destruction at the hands of Piedmontese troops for two long days (see note 12). This was far worse than the war crimes Nino Bixio's troops had committed at Bronte.

Other occurrences during this period were equally surreal, if less violent, and a particularly sobering incident said much about the credibility of the new Italian state in the eyes of the world. In November 1861, a Marseille court upheld King Francis' earlier sale of two Neapolitan ships despite a vociferous protest from the hubristic Italian ambassador, who claimed that the vessels belonged to Italy. The splenetic reasoning advanced for this idea was that Francis was no longer a reigning monarch when the ships were sold, and his former kingdom was by then part of the Kingdom of Italy. (History would repeat itself nine decades later when Great Britain refused to relinquish to the Italian Republic several million pounds that the "patriotic" Savoy kings had stashed in British banks.)

Following the fall of Gaeta, Francis and Maria Sophia resided in the family's Farnese Palace in Rome until that city's occupation by Italian forces a decade later. It was there that their only child, a daughter, was born. She died in infancy. Francis' dynastic heirs are descended from his younger half-brother, Alfonso, Count of Caserta.

In the wake of the lost war, a number of military officers who had loyally fought against the Piedmontese invasion in mainland Italy, particularly around Gaeta, found themselves incarcerated, along with numerous partisans — often branded as "brigands" by the new government — who continued an armed resistance in the countryside. Most were from Naples and such regions as Calabria and Basilicata. Fenestrelle, an Alpine fortress converted into a prison, thus became Italy's first concentration camp in 1862, eventually housing some three hundred political prisoners. In most cases, their only "crime" was to have supported the crown and country they were sworn to defend. Others, tried as "war criminals" by the new regime, were pardoned or received suspended sentences.

Some veterans made their way to the recently-disunited United States of America, where a bloody civil war raged. So embittering was the Italian "civil war" of 1860 and the defamatory propaganda of the new regime that these men went to New Orleans, a largely Catholic city, to enlist in the Confederate army to fight against their nemesis, Giuseppe Garibaldi, who led troops in the Union army. This choice was not ideological in nature; the men from the Two Sicilies did not condone slavery, even if many of them probably supported secession. Their motivation was a very simple reaction to the conquest of their homeland by invaders in an undeclared war. Here was an expression of the timeless principle that "the enemy of my enemy is my friend."

Before long, a series of "extraordinary" taxes were levied on the residents of the former Two Sicilies to defray the cost of the invasion of 1860. Naturally, the treasury, holding more gold that what was held by all the other pre-unitary states combined, had already been pillaged.

The Rothschilds were forced to close their bank in Naples in view of the precipitous decline in the economy following the annexation. (Historian Cyril Toumanoff used to infer the prosperity, or at least the wealth, of the Two Sicilies from the fact that the Rothschilds operated a bank there; many shared his view.)

In a sense, the pro-Bourbon revolt that broke out in Palermo in September 1866 was not unlike the pro-Hohenstaufen rebellion, the Vespers, six centuries earlier, except that Charles of Anjou never claimed to have been "elected" king. Leading to martial law and suppression by Piedmontese troops, the riots prompted many in Turin besides Massimo d'Azeglio (quoted above) to question how such a protest was possible in view of the Savoys' phenomenally high "approval rating" a few years earlier. Tellingly, some leading the revolts, which broke out in a number of towns around Palermo as well as the city itself, were aristocrats and public officials.[88]

Life in the New State

Attempts to disparage the exiled Bourbons were undertaken with uncommon zeal. All manner of defamatory material was published, from cynical caricatures of the "foreign tyrants" to retouched photographs depicting a nude, "promiscuous" Maria Sophia. Every effort was made to discredit the dynasty and the kingdom in the popular mind. Such revisionism, or "historical denial," was part and parcel of the new state, which advocated a feeble *Italia über alles* nationalism.

There was never any grand conspiracy, for such planning requires concerted effort and courage of conviction. There was no coherent philosophy, no apologetics, indeed nothing more than a vague proclivity for expedience. In the Kingdom of Italy, propaganda was never much more than the pernicious result of improvised censorship supported by politicians and their shills. Like the spoiled boy caught with his hand in the cookie jar, unable to remove his chubby paw, they tried to deny what they had done, but never very convincingly. Destroying evidence while concealing facts was their *modus operandi,* but some *biscotti* crumbs always remained: witnesses, bodies, documents, foreign newspaper reports, a few collective memories passed from one generation to the next.

A new coinage, the *lira*, was introduced, and the metric system replaced the historical system of measurements. The ducat, as we have seen, had existed since 1140, being created in the *Regnum* and soon imitated elsewhere. The ducat, *piastra* and *tornese* (see Appendix 5) were as much part of Siculo-Neapolitan culture as the pound sterling in the United Kingdom and the dollar in the United States.

There were units of measurement like the *tumolo* and *carozzo*, as well as the *cantaro* and *rotolo*. The *oncia* (ounce) was of medieval origin, associated with coinage as well as weight measurement.

Most of these words eventually disappeared from common use but we occasionally, if rarely, hear the terms *salma* and *tumolo*, especially in rural areas, where they are still favored by a few vintners and olive growers. Both measure volume as well as area. A *salma* is seventy-five liters or, as a land measurement, about a hectare. A *tumolo* is fifty-five liters; in area it is approximately sixty-five percent of a hectare. (Units such as the *tumolo*, or *tomolo*, were so widely used into the present century that a law was passed in 2009 to prohibit their use in official records.) In length measurements, the *palmo* is twenty-six centimeters and the *canna* is slightly over two meters.

These terms were also used by the church. In 1869, a great deal of church property was confiscated. For the most part, these were monastic estates. Many included schools, and as these schools operated by the religious orders had been the chief means of educating young children, the south's literacy rate actually declined somewhat over the next decade. Compulsory public instruction for children in primary grades was instituted in 1877 (mandatory education to the age of fourteen years was made law in 1962), but very few public (state) schools were built in the south before 1890 or even 1900. The first state schools established by this law opened in Tuscany, Piedmont and other regions north of Rome.

A few monastic schools survived the divestiture of church property. The Dominicans were especially resilient. In rural monastic schools, far from the censors of the cities, the boys were taught two versions of history — the "official" one in the authorized textbooks and the traditional (oral) one which explained the facts of Bourbon rule and the invasion of 1860 in blunt terms. Such lessons became rarer as time passed and the Bourbons were all but forgotten.

The school history texts were bereft of all rhyme or reason. Every shortcoming of the Two Sicilies was starkly highlighted while none of Piedmont's were even mentioned. A glaring omission was the infamous Piedmont Easter Massacre, which saw over a thousand Waldensians slaughtered by Savoyard troops in 1655, followed by another bloody suppression in 1686.

Deception of this kind might have been dismissed as risible were there not millions of Italian lives involved. Based on the *Statuto,* Carlo Alberto's "Albertine Statute" of 1848, the new state's constitution was trumpeted as an achievement comparable to the drafting of England's *Magna Carta* and the American Bill of Rights. In a land where few were conversant with traditions beyond their own borders, or even their own localities, such sleight of hand was quite credible, even convincing, but foreigners didn't take it too seriously.

There were obvious physical scars. Although Naples was largely spared, the invasion of 1860 led to the destruction of most of Palermo's medieval seaside castle, with its round tower that had been erected during the Arab era. In the years to follow, no effort was made to preserve what little was left of this architectural treasure, and most of the castle's massive stone blocks were used in the construction of buildings nearby. What could have been a tourist site of inestimable historic value was reduced to a few walls standing in an empty field strewn with rubble.

Unfortunately, like many other regions, beginning around 1880, southern Italy was attacked by the phylloxera louse and many vines were destroyed. This affected viticulture as new grape varieties were introduced. The government failed to respond to this economic crisis in a serious way.

In 1882 the first deep sulfur mines opened in Sicily. These were tunnels and shafts, as opposed to the open-pit "strip" mines that had been used previously. Too often, children were pressed into labor as miners because few adults were skinny enough to get through the narrow passages. What resulted can only be described as slavery, but the government made little effort to prevent it. Although other reasons were cited as a pretext, Philip Carroll, the United States consul in Palermo, was expelled from Italy in 1890 for exposing these inhumane conditions in a detailed report written two years earlier on Sicilian sulfur mining.[89]

Italians

The surfeit of Italy's grandiose political propaganda did nothing to change reality, for the people of the former Two Sicilies were now "southerners" from a place called the *Mezzogiorno* or the *Meridione*.

By the last decade of the nineteenth century, most Italians were virtually destitute. Some emigrated, typically identifying themselves firstly as Neapolitans, Sicilians or Calabrians, and only secondly as "Italians." Until now, most Italian emigration was from the north, not the south. It is true enough that poverty existed elsewhere in Europe, but Italy's level of indigence, coupled with illiteracy, was not commensurate with the population in what was ostensibly an industrialized society, or even a sophisticated agrarian economy. Around the country, pellagra and goiter were as frequent as ever, and perhaps increasing. The childhood of Angelo Roncalli, the future Pope

John XXIII, is instructive; he was born and raised near Bergamo, in the heart of Lombardy, on a diet of potatoes, polenta and an occasional portion of meat.

Francesco Crispi, a bigamist, became Italy's first Sicilian prime minister in 1887, but this did not help his fellow Sicilians.

In 1894, during Crispi's second term in office, the *Fasci Siciliani*, a rural workers' movement, was brutally suppressed, resulting in lengthy prison sentences for the leaders. Nevertheless, Crispi and others acknowledged that problems existed in farming and mining. Prison terms were commuted but political attempts at reform failed.

The same year, King Francis II died at Arco in Trent, which was then part of Austria, and Federico De Roberto's novel, *The Viceroys*, chronicling the life of a Sicilian family in the years immediately following unification, was published.[90]

Two years later, the Crispi government fell when Italian forces were defeated at Adwa, in Ethiopia, during an ill-fated, imperialist campaign. The diplomatic chicanery that led to this fiasco was typical of what passed for foreign policy in the Kingdom of Italy.[91]

In the event, the unforeseen thrashing of Italian troops led the nation's army to be ridiculed internationally for generations. Yet it was domestic incidents that earned the Royal Italian Army the enmity of Italians.

In early May 1898, a series of mass protests broke out around the country over the scarcity and high price of bread amidst what was rapidly becoming a full-fledged famine. Even before the food shortages, many Italians lived in conditions bordering on debt peonage. In Milan, over a hundred demonstrators were killed by the army in the infamous Bava-Beccaris Massacre. Italians grew indignant when King Umberto I knighted the general responsible for this bloodbath.

The ever-present propaganda was ridiculously transparent. "Outside elements" were a frequent scapegoat. Born and raised in Tuscany, and then resident in the United States for just six years, Gaetano Bresci, the anarchist who assassinated King Umberto in retribution for the carnage that took place in Milan, was portrayed as "an American," as if New Jersey were a breeding ground for regicidists.

Despite having a constitution and parliament to lend it the outward appearance of democracy, the Kingdom of Italy was in almost every way a police state. Besides the widespread poverty, the lack of freedom prompted many citizens to emigrate. Often, this was simply the freedom to dream of a better life.

Oddly enough, certain Neapolitan traditions survived better *outside* Italy, in the "diaspora" of emigrés, than in Italy itself. This was true even in the culinary sphere. *Spumoni,* an ice cream flavor (layers of cherry, pistachio and chocolate), became very rare in Naples but quite popular in New York.

In Italy, a fundamental defect, and one thus far explored only superficially by historians, was the suppression of personal individuality in a nation based not on the lofty principles of the Enlightenment seen in the United States, or even the enlightened constitutional monarchy in the United Kingdom, but a warped expediency that valued the survival of an intrinsically corrupt state over the life of the individual citizen. Sadly, though perhaps unsurprisingly, this extended to the teaching of children, whose desks, known as *banchi a doppio posto,* were each constructed to accommodate a pair of students, depriving the youngest Italians of a sense of individuality. This bleak setting, where a student, even as a teenager, wasn't entitled to so much as her own desk, did little to cultivate a love of learning, and even less to encourage an affinity for her social environment.

At least one Italian challenged this uninspired approach to education. Maria Montessori's teaching methods were based on her scientific observations that children learn best when they are comfortable in their surroundings and permitted to express themselves as individuals. This makes learning natural and enjoyable. Self-confidence and independence are the results.[92]

Independence of thought was the last thing *Italia* wanted to see in her citizens, and little effort was made to adopt any of Montessori's ideas in public schools.

The New Century

With the arrival of a new century and, as fate would have it, a new sovereign, King Victor Emmanuel III, it was clear that little had changed over the years, at least not for the better. In this sisyphean setting, opportunities were ever in sight and always missed. Some kind of land reform was necessary to wrest control of the Sicilian *latifondi* from the nobility, but these were effected only later, in 1949, after the monarchy was abolished. Matters weren't much better on the mainland.

Rome responded inadequately to the catastrophic earthquake at Messina in 1908, the first major natural disaster to confront the Kingdom of Italy and an event that revealed the country's woeful state. To her credit, Queen Elena accompanied her husband to the city to do what she could. Montenegrin by birth and upbringing, she was the only queen consort of Italy who could be said to have found favor among the common people.

The lives of the common people were miserable. Following a visit in 1910, Booker T. Washington, an American scientist born into slavery, wrote that, "the condition of the colored farmer in the most backward parts of the southern states in America, even where he has the least education and the least encouragement, is incomparably better than the condition and opportunities of the agricultural population in Sicily."

Although their precise evolution is difficult to track, criminal organizations such as the Mafia and Camorra gained power and influence in a society where most ordinary citizens were suspicious of the government and the state it represented, and hence reluctant to report incidents of extortion or robbery to the police. While police agencies might suppress movements such as the *Fasci,* they were generally indifferent to the activities of *mafiosi* and *camorristi.*

With the dismemberment of the Ottoman Empire, Italy occupied Libya in 1911. This is where the nation's worst war crimes began, as indiscriminate massacres in small villages. As the Ottomans retreated, the Italians also seized the island of Rhodes. Like its domestic policy, Italy's imperial policy was based on ineptitude.

Although Italy found herself on the winning side in the First World War, which she entered belatedly in 1915, the cost in Italian lives was high. A disproportionate number of draftees were from the south; many northerners obtained exemptions by working in factories built in the north, often with government support, while the south languished in poverty.

Combat is always hellish, but the morale of the typical Italian conscript was abysmal at best, spawning such sayings as "better a pig than a soldier." Trench warfare on the Austrian front found *carabinieri* snipers a hundred meters behind the Italian lines, posted there to shoot deserters.

South Tyrol was formally, and legally, annexed to Italy in 1920, with the Istrian peninsula annexed less legally four years later. By that time, Italy was governed by a new regime, a genocidal dictatorship masquerading as a constitutional monarchy. Prosperity remained a chimera.

In 1925, Queen Maria Sophia died in her native Bavaria. By then, the erstwhile Kingdom of the Two Sicilies was little more than a faded memory.

In time, however, a few foreign voices rose up to defy conformity. In *The Great Heresies,* published in 1938, Hilaire Belloc wrote that:

There was no united Italy, and such effort as was being made to create one was being made by anti-Catholics. Indeed, it is one of the most amusing ironies of history that the great power which Italy has now become was largely called into being by the sympathy Protestant Europe felt for the original Italian rebellions against the Catholic King of Naples and the authority of the Papal States.

Maria Cristina of Savoy, mother of Francis II

EPILOGUE

In December 1994, the author was present in Palermo and Naples for the observances of the centennial of the death of King Francis II, the last King of the Two Sicilies. Some members of the royal family attended, including Princess Urraca, who as a child had known Maria Sophia, the last queen.

The first occasion, in Palermo, was a somber event marked by a solemn mass at the Magione, a splendid medieval church of the dynasty's Constantinian Order that once belonged to the Teutonic Knights, followed by a dinner at the palatial residence of Count Giuseppe Tasca d'Almerita attended by the flower of the local nobility, around two hundred guests in all.

The scene in Naples a few days later was completely different. The memorial mass at the Basilica of Santa Chiara, where the last king and queen rest, was filled with thousands of congregants. Thousands of sympathizers crowded into the square and streets surrounding the church. The crowd was ecstatic, the royal family received to cheers of *Viva ò Re!*

White flags of the Two Sicilies were flown from balconies. An honor guard consisted of *carabinieri* in formal dress wearing silver helmets. The enthusiasm was palpable. Yet it was a very balanced event. The celebrant, Bishop Karel Kasteel, began his homily by stating: "We are not here as revisionists. We are here to commemorate the life of a good man."

It was as if the collective memory of the kingdom had been resurrected for a day.

We will learn from history as long as we remember it.

TIMELINE

1734 - Prince Charles of Spain becomes King of Naples and Sicily (and Duke of Parma) following invasion; crowned in Palermo in 1735.

1738 - Major eruption of Vesuvius deposits ash in Sarno, Palma, Nola, Avellino, Ariano. Charles marries Maria Amalia of Saxony, construction of palaces begins at Portici and Capodimonte.

1741 - New legal code formulated, partially published but not entirely enacted.

1743 - A major epidemic of bubonic plague strikes Messina. Jurisdictional crisis with Malta.

1745 - Monthly lottery begins at Naples.

1748 - *Donativo* tax levied by King Charles, excavations begin at Pompeii.

1751 - Hospice for poor established in Naples.

1752 - Cornerstone laid for Reggia palace at Caserta.

1754 - Italy's first university chair/department in economics established at Naples.

THE KINGDOM OF THE TWO SICILIES

1759 - Charles becomes Carlos III of Spain. Forever separates Spanish crown from those of Naples and Sicily, ceding Italian dominions to his son, Ferdinand I.

1764 - Famine strikes following bad wheat harvest. Epidemic at Naples.

1767 - Jesuits expelled from kingdoms of Naples and Sicily, King Ferdinand I reaches majority.

1768 - Ferdinand weds Maria Carolina Hapsburg of Austria.

1772 - Hospice for the poor opens in Palermo.

1773 - Revolt against viceroy (lieutenant) in Palermo.

1776 - United States of America declares independence from Great Britain; France and Spain support Americans.

1777 - New, enlarged library and museum open at University of Naples.

1778 - San Leucio (near Caserta) becomes first public housing complex/estate in Italy, college of arts and sciences founded at University of Naples. Public stock exchange founded.

1779 - Precursor of University of Palermo founded as *Regia Accademia degli Studi San Ferdinando*.

1780 - Publication of Filangieri's *Scienza della Legislazione*.

1782 - Spanish Inquisition abolished in Sicily.

1783 - Highly destructive earthquake hits Calabria and eastern Sicily. Peace of Paris treaties signed by Britain, France, Spain and United States end American Revolutionary War.

1785 - Charles III sponsors construction of first Catholic church in New York.

1788 - First public school for the deaf in Italy established in Naples (school founded in Rome in 1784 was private).

TIMELINE

1789 - Legal code of Charles III becomes effective in Kingdom of Naples. French Revolution begins.

1793 - Alliance with Great Britain against French Republic.

1794 - Plot against government uncovered in Naples, eruption of Vesuvius, earthquake in Calabria.

1795 - Victory with Britain against French in naval battles. First public botanical gardens in Italy open in Palermo (others were private or scholastic). Revolt in Palermo suppressed.

1796 - Peace with France. King of Naples and Sicily recognizes the United States of America; full diplomatic relations established in 1832.

1798 - Military alliance with Britain, Austria, Russia and Ottoman Empire against France. Malta, part of the Kingdom of Sicily, occupied by Napoleonic fleet which expels Knights of Saint John. Following Britain's victory over the French, Malta and Gozo become British protectorate in 1800 and are never returned to Sicilian Crown.

1799 - Parthenopean Republic declared in Naples. Ferdinand I resides in Palermo during crisis. Cardinal Ruffo reclaims Naples.

1800 - Neapolitan expedition to Rome.

1801 - Peace treaty negotiated with France. Dwarf planet Ceres discovered based on work at astronomical observatory atop Palermo's Norman Palace.

1802 - Ferdinand I returns to Naples during Peace of Amiens. The future Francis I, presently Viceroy of Sicily, weds Princess Maria Isabella in Madrid.

1803 - Napoleonic Wars begin, end in 1815. Ferdinand I declares neutrality.

1804 - Jesuits restored in Kingdom of Naples.

1805 - Earthquakes in Kingdom of Naples.

THE KINGDOM OF THE TWO SICILIES

1806 - British troops are based in Sicily as bulwark against possible Napoleonic invasion. King Ferdinand I again resident in Palermo. The French abolish feudalism on the mainland.

1810 - Ferdinand II born in Palermo.

1812 - Under British influence, feudalism is abolished in Sicily by new constitution.

1814-1815 - Congress of Vienna.

1814 - General restoration of Jesuits in Europe (rehabilitated in southern Italy in 1804).

1815 - Joachim Murat executed in Calabria following attempted incursion. Unification of Neapolitan and Sicilian crowns is declared following the Congress of Vienna.

1816 - Kingdom of the Two Sicilies is established in December following Ferdinand's return to Naples; Sicilian constitution is suppressed when Neapolitan and Sicilian crowns are formally unified. Minor famine in Europe following Mount Tambora eruption.

1818 - The *Ferdinando I* becomes the first steamship in the Mediterranean.

1819 - Legal code introduced for the Two Sicilies.

1820 - Constitution drafted and ratified. Revolts in Naples and Palermo, suppressed with aid of Austrian troops the following year.

1821 - Constitution published and repealed. Rothschild Bank opens in Naples (closes in 1863 following unification).

1825 - Ferdinand I dies, Francis I becomes king.

1830 - Francis I dies, Ferdinand II crowned.

1832 - First glass recycling program introduced in Two Sicilies. First steel suspension bridge in Italy constructed over Gagliano River.

TIMELINE

1833 - Naval expedition to Tunisia.

1836 - Maria Cristina of Savoy, queen consort, dies; beatified in 2014. Asian cholera epidemic in Naples.

1839 - First railroad in Italy built from Naples to Portici. First gas-fueled public lighting system introduced in Two Sicilies.

1841 - First seismic observatory in the world established at Mount Vesuvius.

1846 - First commercial electric telegraphs introduced in Europe.

1846-1848 - Bad grain harvests in the Two Sicilies and across Europe; Potato Famine worsens in Ireland.

1847 - Revolts in Messina. *Giglio delle Onde* becomes first steamship with screw propulsion in the Mediterranean.

1848 - Revolts begin in Palermo and spread across Europe. New constitution is enacted but soon abolished. Civil legal code is updated.

1849 - Order restored throughout kingdom.

1851 - Earthquake in Basilicata.

1852 - Two Sicilies sets up first functioning electric telegraph in Italy.

1854 - Second outbreak of Asian cholera in Naples. Steamship *Sicilia*, constructed in Palermo, crosses Atlantic and arrives in New York (passengers are Irish).

1855 - Luigi Palmieri invents seismometer.

1856 - Britain and France recall their ambassadors from Naples. Congress of Paris formally ends Crimean War.

1857 - Carlo Pisacane lands at Sapri and is defeated.

1859 - Ferdinand II dies, Francis II becomes King of the Two Sicilies. Mercantile exchange established.

THE KINGDOM OF THE TWO SICILIES

1860 - Northern Italian troops led by Giuseppe Garibaldi (1807-1882) embark in Sicily. At Bronte, Nino Bixio's troops become the first military contingent identified with the united Italy to massacre civilians. Sicily is annexed to the Kingdom of Italy.

1861 - King Francis II of the Two Sicilies surrenders Gaeta north of Naples, exiled. Victor Emmanuel II of Savoy, King of Sardinia, becomes King of Italy.

1862 - Fenestrelle, a "secret" Alpine prison for political detainees (mostly Two-Sicilies loyalists), becomes Italy's first concentration camp.

1866 - Revolt against Piedmontese occupation and annexation in Palermo, protests suppressed by Piedmontese troops.

1869 - Ecclesiastical property confiscated in Sicily, leading to closure of most monastic schools and (in the absence of state schools to substitute these) decrease in general literacy.

1877 - Mandatory public education instituted but few public (state) schools established south of Rome before 1900.

1882 - First major sulfur mines (rather than open pits) excavated in Sicily, resulting in exploitation of child labor.

1887 - Francesco Crispi (1818-1901), a bigamist, becomes prime minister (1887-1891 and 1893-1896).

1894 - *Fasci Siciliani,* a rural labor movement founded in Sicily, suppressed by force and summary trials. Death of King Francis II of the Two Sicilies.

1896 - Italians suffer major defeat by Ethiopians at Battle of Adwa; some 7,000 Italian troops killed and 3,000 taken prisoner. Italy earns disdain of world's great military powers (Russia openly supports Ethiopia politically). Crispi government falls following resulting protests in Rome; Italy, followed by France and the United Kingdom, recognizes Ethiopia in 1897.

1898 - Bava-Beccaris Massacre in Milan.

1900 - King Umberto I of Italy assassinated at Monza.

TIMELINE

1908 - Earthquake and tsunami destroy most of Messina, killing as many as 100,000 in Sicily and Calabria.

1911 - Italy occupies Libya (formerly an Ottoman territory), and many Italians migrate to the new Italian colony despite civil unrest. Rhodes is also occupied.

1915 - Italy enters the First World War.

1920 - Italy formally annexes occupied South Tyrol by terms of treaty ending First World War.

1922 - Fascist government installed; becomes dictatorship by 1924. Rijeka and territories in Istrian peninsula, now Slovenia and Croatia, already occupied (illegally) by Italy, annexed formally in 1924. Fascists institute program to populate this region and South Tyrol (see above) with Italian-speaking settlers; by 1940 Italian is the principal spoken language of Bozen (Bolzano) and remains so today.

1924 - Giacomo Matteotti, member of parliament and outspoken opponent of Fascism, kidnapped and murdered by Fascist secret police; murderers granted amnesty by King Victor Emmanuel III.

1925 - Death of Maria Sophia, last Queen of the Two Sicilies.

RELAZIONE
DELLA
Felicissima esaltazione, e proclamazione al Trono, e Monarchia delle Spagne della Maestà di D. Carlo III.

Circular published in Naples in 1759 when Charles III became King of Spain

Appendix 1
PRAGMATIC OF 1759

All but ignored by historians, this act of cession (as it was described by the historian Luigi del Pozzo in 1857) merits at least passing attention for several reasons. Most obviously, in acceding to the wishes of the European leaders who hoped to avoid confronting the potentially destabilizing concentration of power in a single monarch, it forever separated the kingdoms of Naples and Sicily from rule by the King of Spain.

While the preamble mentions the sovereign's *de jure* dominions (such as Jerusalem) as well as those he actually ruled, it is interesting that the phrase *the Two Sicilies* is used (in the preamble) to describe the kingdoms of Naples and Sicily jointly even though they were not yet united officially or juridically, and the document effectively reiterates the sovereignty of both states, referring to these near its end as *the Kingdoms of the Sicilies*. The three passages referring more generically to *my Italian states* refer to the kingdoms of Naples and Sicily, without Parma (which Charles had renounced); at all events, the succession of young Ferdinand to the Constantinian Order inherited from the Duke of Parma was recognized by a subsequent decree of 16 October 1759 (see Appendix 2).

In connection with the Two Sicilies, it is interesting that Charles was *proclaimed* King of Naples in 1734 but *crowned* king of *both* kingdoms, Naples and Sicily, in a single ceremony at Palermo the following year (see the photograph of the ornate memorial in Palermo Cathedral at the end of Chapter 2). True, the two kingdoms had been united by his recent ancestors in a "personal union," but this dual coronation, though not indicative of an actual political (juridical) union of Naples and Sicily, reflects an effort to unite these nations in the popular mind, almost as a revival of the kingdom founded by Roger II.

The pragmatic sanction sets forth dynastic female succession in the absence of male heirs while offering insight into the approach taken to diagnose mental disabilities in royal families. Establishing laws of succession, this is, in effect, the "foundation charter" of the House of Bourbon of the Two Sicilies as a dynasty separate from the House of Bourbon of Spain and the "act of emancipation" of young Ferdinand. It does, at all events, make provision for a Spanish Bourbon prince to succeed to the throne of the Two Sicilies in the event of the extinction of the dynasty in Naples. (See the second genealogical chart in this volume.)

Not only is the document itself self-explanatory, its effects over the next few generations were self-evident, as the descendants of King Charles in the Two Sicilies became Neapolitan *Borboni* in every respect. Even the distinctive plural *Borboni* reflects traditional Neapolitan onomatology and was used by King Ferdinand II himself; in modern Italian the plural of a surname does not change from its singular form, hence *Borbone*. (We find similar usage with *Bologni* from *Bologna* for the name of an old square in Palermo named for a noble family.)

From Madrid, Charles offered guidance to young Ferdinand long after 1759, but it would emerge that father and son had little in common with regard to their ideas about government and foreign policy; for example, Ferdinand was a staunch ally of Britain while Charles was an early supporter of the United States. In domestic policy, Charles was far more enlightened than Ferdinand. For its era, this singular document is eloquent in its simplicity of language, clarity of expression, and transparent intent. The first-born son excluded from the succession is not mentioned by name in the text; he was Philip (1747-1777).

Regulation of the titles to be used by dynasts of the Kingdom of the Two Sicilies arrived with decree number 594 of 4 January 1817. These are the titles indicated for the sons of Ferdinand II in the genealogical chart mentioned earlier. Laws regarding succession and rights of members of the royal family are listed in articles 167-211 of the short-lived *Costituzione Politica* published in 1821.

Not being a tome on royal history, and seeking to avoid pedantry, this book generally uses the terms *house* and *dynasty* interchangeably. However, some historians and jurists might distinguish between the *house* of Bourbon (descendants of Louis XIV of France reigning in France, Spain, the Two

Sicilies, Parma and later Luxembourg), an individual Bourbon *dynasty* (such as that of the Two Sicilies), and the extended Bourbon *family* (comprising *all* the legitimate descendants of the historical Bourbons). After 1759, Ferdinand I and his successors (Francis I, Ferdinand II, Francis II) were not subject to the authority of other Bourbon sovereigns.

The original Italian text follows the English translation.

WE, Charles III, by the Grace of God King of Castile, Leon, Aragon, the Two Sicilies, Jerusalem, Navarre, Granada, Toledo, Valencia, Galicia, Majorca, Seville, Sardinia, Cordova, Corsica, Murcia, Jaén, Algarve, Alzira, Gibraltar, the Canary Islands, the East and West Indies, the Islands and Continent of the Atlantic Ocean, Archduke of Austria, Duke of Burgundy, Brabant, Milan, Parma, Piacenza and Castro, Hereditary Grand Prince of Tuscany, Count of Hapsburg, Flanders, Tyrol and Barcelona, Lord of Biscay and Molina, et cetera.

Among the grave burdens that the monarchy of the Spanish lands and the Indies, following the death of my beloved brother King Ferdinand VI, have visited upon me, is that of the clear mental incapacity of my firstborn son. Furthermore, the spirit of the treaties of the present century demonstrates the wishes of Europe, to the extent these can be granted justly, to divide the Spanish powers from those in Italy.

Seeing, therefore, the opportunity to appoint a legitimate successor in my Italian states as I depart for Spain, and seeking to choose him from among the many sons that God has given me, it is necessary to decide which of my sons is to be considered my second-born legally for the purpose of succeeding to rule the Italian states and having no union with Spain or the Indies. This act for the tranquility of Europe, which I wish to guarantee to ensure that nobody is alarmed by my indecision in retaining in my person these Spanish and Italian powers together, requires that I now renounce my sovereign authority in Italy.

An important body composed of me and my Councillors of State, of a Castilian cabinet minister present here in Naples, of the Chamber of Santa Chiara, of the Lieutenant of the Cabinet of Naples, and the entire Council of Sicily, assisted by six physicians appointed by me, has determined that, insofar as examinations and observations have been made, the unfortunate prince is unable to reason, converse, or exercise rational judgement, and that his abilities have existed as such since infancy; not only is he presently incapable of morality or reasoning, but there appears to be not the slightest likelihood that he ever will be. Expressing a unanimous decision, this body of experts therefore concludes that he be excluded from consideration, and we shall therefore act as nature, duty and paternal affection dictate.

Therefore, finding myself in this fateful moment for Divine Will, I cede the legal right and capacity of second-born to the Infante don Ferdinando, though my third-born son by nature. Because of his tender age, I have had to consider his tutelage. For my Italian states, as a king and as a father, I have undertaken to provide for this son, that he shall become an Italian sovereign while I am in Spain.

Firstly, I constitute the Infante don Ferdinando, by nature my third-born son, to receive from me the Italian states, undertaking, even if it be unnecessary, to emancipate him by the present act, which I wish to establish as most solemn. With the force of a legitimate act and indeed a law, he shall henceforth be free not only of my parental authority, but from my sovereign royal authority.

Secondly, I establish a Council of Regency for the duration of the minority of my third-born son, which must be sovereign of my states and holder of my Italian assets, acting to administer sovereignty and dominion during his youth and minority according to methods prescribed by me in an order of this day issued by my hand under my signature and seal, witnessed by my Councillor and Secretary of State of the Department of State and the Royal Household, which order shall be integrated into this act, having the same force of law.

Thirdly, I decide, and constitute in immutable and perpetual law of my Italian states and holdings, that the age of majority of those who succeed as sovereigns and rulers and enjoy freedom of administration be the sixteenth year fully computed (seventeenth birthday).

Fourthly, desiring likewise to establish in constant and perpetual law the succession of the Infante don Ferdinando, further enumerating the preceding sections, I establish that the line of succession be ordered according to male primogeniture from male to male.

In the absence of sons in that line of descent, succession devolves to the next male heir in the cadet line with respect to the last regnant dynast, be it a patrilineal uncle, brother or more distant kin, so long as it be the eldest male in the aforementioned line or its direct, patrilineal branch with regard to the Infante don Ferdinando or the last regnant king.

In the case of the absence of male heirs in the line of descent from Infante don Ferdinando, the line of succession shall be transmitted in turn to my other sons, namely Gabriele, Antonio and Francesco Saverio, and henceforth through their sons, in order of seniority of birth.

In the event of extinction of all heirs male descended from me, a female of the blood royal may succeed if she be my daughter or the eldest daughter of a prince in the senior line of descent, nearest in descent from the most recent king or the last, most recently-deceased prince. To wit, the right of succession is traced by primogeniture along the nearest agnate line of descent according to the order set forth above.

In the absence of female as well as male heirs, the succession shall devolve to my brother, the Infante don Filippo, and thence forth to his sons and male successors *ad infinitum*. In the absence of Filippo and his male issue, the succession shall devolve to my brother the Infante don Luigi and thence forth to his sons and male successors *ad infinitum*. In the absence of male posterity in these lines, daughters may succeed according to the prescription mentioned above.

Be it well understood that the order of the line of succession prescribed herein shall never result in the union of the Spanish Monarchy with the sovereignty of the Italian dominions.

In this way, either males or females descended from me as described above shall succeed to the Italian sovereignty, so long as they are not already declared Kings of Spain or Princes of Austria; otherwise they must declare themselves when there are other males to succeed to the Italian states and holdings based on this norm. In the absence of all heirs, the King of Spain, as soon as God graces him with a second-born son, or with a grandson or great-grandson, shall transfer to this heir the Italian states, territories and holdings.

Having established the succession of my posterity to the Italian states and holdings, I humbly commend to God the Infante don Ferdinando, bestowing upon him my paternal blessing and inculcating in him the Roman Catholic religion, and the sense of justice, forbearance, vigilance and love of country which have aided me in faithfully and obediently serving my royal house.

I cede, transfer and give to the same Infante don Ferdinando, my third-born son by nature, the Kingdoms of the Sicilies and my other Italian states, holdings, territories, rights, titles and interests, and I cede to him the fullness of their traditions, so that none of these shall remain in my possession.

He, however, from the moment that I depart this capital, may with the Council of State and Regency administer all that I will have transferred, ceded and given to him. I hope that this my law of emancipation, constitution of age of majority, designation of tutelage and care of the child and minor (adolescent) king, succession to the said Italian states and holdings, transfer and endowment, will abound him with a love for the people, in tranquility with my royal family, finally contributing to the peace of Europe.

The present order shall be signed by me and by my son the Infante don Ferdinando, bearing my seal, witnessed by the aforesaid Councillor and Secretary of State, also acting as Regents and Tutors of the aforementioned Infante don Ferdinando.

Given at Naples this 6th day of October, 1759

Signed: Carlo, Ferdinando

NOI Carlo III, per la grazia di Dio Re di Castiglia, Leone, Aragona, delle Due Sicilie, Gerusalemme, Navarra, Granata, Toledo, Valenza, Galizia, Majorca, Siviglia, Sardegna, Cordova, Corsica, Murcia, Jaen, Algarves, Algezira, Gibilterra, delle Isole Canarie, delle Indie Orientali ed Occidentali, delle Isole e Continente del Mare Oceano; Arciduca d'Austria; Duca di Borgogna, Brabante, Milano, Parma, Piacenza e Castro; Gran Principe Ereditario di Toscana, Conte di Abspurgo, Fiandra, Tirolo e Barcellona; Signore di Bistaglia e Molina, et cetera, et cetera.

Fra le gravi cure, che la Monarchia delle Spagne e delle Indie, dopo la morte dell'amatissimo mio Fratello il Re Cattolico Ferdinando VI, Mi ha recate, è stata quella che è venuta dalla notoria imbecillità della mente del Mio real primogenito. Lo spirito dei trattati di questo secolo mostra, che si desideri dall'Europa, quando si possa eseguire senza opporsi alla giustizia, la divisione della potenza Spagnuola dall'Italiana.

Vedendomi perciò nella convenienza di provveder di legittimo successore i Miei stati italiani nell'atto di passare alla Spagna, e di sceglierlo tra i molti figli, che Dio Mi ha dato, Mi trovo nella urgenza di decidere qual dei Miei figli sia presentemente quel secondogenito atto al governo dei popoli, nel quale ricadano gli Stati Italiani senza l'unione delle Spagne e delle Indie. Questa convenienza per la quiete di Europa, che voglio avere, perché non sia chi si allarmi nel vedermi indeciso continuare nella Mia persona la Potenza Spagnuola ed Italiana, richiede che fin da ora io prenda il Mio partito rispetto all'Italia.

Un Corpo considerabile composto da Me, dei Miei Consiglieri di Stato, di un Camerista di Castiglia che qui si trova, della Camera di Santa Chiara, del Luogotenente della Sommaria di Napoli, e di tutta la giunta di Sicilia, assistito da sei Medici da Me deputati, Mi ha riferito, che per guanti esami, ed esperienze abbia fatto, non ha potuto provare nell'infelice Principe uso di ragione, né principio di discorso, o giudizio umano e che tale essendo stato fin dall'Infanzia, non solamente non è capace né di Religione, né di raziocinio presentemente, ma neppure apparisce ombra di speranza per l'avvenire; conchiudendo questo Corpo il suo parere uniforme, che non si deve di Lui pensare e disporre come alla natura, al dovere, ed all'affetto paterno si converrebbe.

Vendendo Io dunque in questo momento fatale cadere per Divina Volontà, il diritto e la capacità di Secondogenito nel mio Terzogenito per natura l'Infante Don Ferdinando, ed insieme la di Lui età pupillare, a lui, ed alla Lui tutela ho dovuto pensare per la traslazione dei Miei Stati Italiani, come Sovrano e Padre, che non stimo di esercitare la tutela e la cura del Figlio, che divenga Sovrano Italiano, mentre Io sono di Spagna.

Costituito dunque l'Infante Don Ferdinando mio Terzogenito per natura nello stato di ricevere da Me la cessione degli Stati Italiani, passo in primo luogo, ancorché forse senza necessità, ad emanciparlo con questo Presento mio Atto, che Io voglio riputato il più solenne, e con tutto il vigore di Atto legittimo, anzi di Legge e voglio che Egli sia fin da ora libero non solamente della mia Potestà Paterna, ma ancora dalla Somma e Sovrana.

In secondo luogo stabilisco ed ordino il Consiglio di Reggenza per la pupillare e minore età di esso mio Terzogenito, che debbe essere Sovrano dei miei Stati, e padrone dei Miei beni italiani, acciò amministri la Sovranità, ed il Dominio durante l'età pupillare, e minore col metodo da Me prescritto in una ordinazione di questo stesso giorno firmata di Mia mano, suggellata col mio suggello, e referendata dal mio Consigliere e Segretario di Stato del Dipartimento di Stato, e della casa Reale; la quale ordinazione voglio che sia e s'intenda parte integrale di questa, e si riputi in tutto, e per tutto qui ripetuta, acciò abbia la stessa forza di Legge.

In terzo luogo decido, e costituisco per Legge stabile e perpetua dei miei Stati e Beni Italiani, che l'Età maggiore di quelli, che dovranno come Sovrani e Padroni averne la libera amministrazione, sia il decimosesto anno compiuto.

In quarto luogo, voglio egualmente per legge costante e perpetua della successione dell'Infante Don Ferdinando, anche a maggiore spiegazione delle Ordinazioni anteriori, che la successione sia regolata a forma de primogenitura col diritto di rappresentazione nella discendenza mascolina di maschio in maschio.

A quello della linea retta, che manchi senza figli maschi, dovrà succedere il primogenito maschio di maschio della linea prossima all'ultimo regnante, di cui sia zio paterno o fratello od in maggior distanza, purché sia primogenito nella sua linea nella forma già detta, e sia nel ramo, che prossimamente si distacca, o si è distaccato dalla linea retta primogeniale dell'Infante Don Ferdinando, o da quella dell'ultimo regnante.

Lo stesso ordino nel caso di mancare tutti i Maschi di Maschio della Discendenza dell'istesso Infante Don Ferdinando mascolina, e di Maschio di Maschio, rispetto all'Infante Don Gabriele Mio Figlio, al quale dovrà allora passare la Successione, e nei di Lui Discendenti Maschi di Maschio, come sopra. In mancanza di esso Infante Don Gabriele, e dei di Lui discendenti Maschi di Maschio, collo stesso ordine passerà la Successione nell'Infante Don Antonio, e suoi Discendenti Maschi di Maschio come sopra.

Ed in mancanza di questo, e della di Lui Discendenza Mascolina di Maschi di Maschio, la Successione collo stesso ordine passerà all'Infante Don Saverio e dopo Esso e la di Lui Discendenza tale Mascolina, come sopra agli altri Infanti Figli, che Dio mi desse, secondo l'ordine della natura e Loro Discendenze tali Mascoline.

Estinti tutti i Maschi di Maschio, nella Mia Discendenza, dovrà succedere quella femmina del sangue e dell'agnazione, che al tempo della mancanza sia vivente, o sia questa mia Figlia o sia d'altro Principe Maschio di Maschio della mia Discendenza, la quale sia la più prossima all'ultimo Re, ed all'ultimo Maschio dell'agnazione, che manchi, o di altro Principe, che sia prima mancato. Sempre ripetuto, che nella Linea retta sia osservato il diritto di Rappresentazione col quale la prossimità, e la qualità di Primogenitura si misuri, e sia essa dell'Agnazione.

Rispetto a questa ed ai Discendenti Maschi di Maschio di Essa che dovranno succedere, si osservi l'ordine stabilito. Anche questa mancando vada la successione al Mio Fratello Infante Don Filippo, e suoi Discendenti Maschi di Maschio in infinito. E questi ancora mancando, all'altro Mio Fratello Infante Don Luigi, e suoi Discendenti Maschi di Maschio; e dopo mancati questi alla Femmina dell'Agnazione coll'ordine prescritto di sopra.

Ben inteso, che l'ordine di Successione da Me prescritto non mai possa portare l'unione della Monarchia di Spagna colla Sovranità e Domini Italiani.

In guisa che o i Maschi o le Femmine di mia Discendenza di sopra chiamati, siano ammessi alla Sovranità Italiana, sempre che non siano Re di Spagna o Principi di Asturia dichiarati già, o per dichiararsi quando sia altro Maschio, che possa succedere in vigor di questa ordinazione negli Stati e

Beni italiani. Non essendovi, dovrà il Re di Spagna, subito che Dio lo provvegga di un altro Maschio Figlio, o nipote o pronipote, a questo trasferire gli Stati e Beni Italiani.

Stabilita così la Successione della mia Discendenza negli Stati e Beni Italiani, raccomando umilmente a Dio l'Infante Don Ferdinando, e dandogli la mia Paterna Benedizione ed inculcandogli la Religione Santa Cristiana Cattolica, la Giustizia e la Mansuetudine, la Vigilanza, l'Amor dei Popoli, i quali sono, per avermi fedelmente servito ed obbediti benemeriti della mia Casa Reale; cedo, trasferisco e dono all'istesso Infante Don Ferdinando mio figlio Terzogenito per natura, i Regni delle Sicilie, e gli altri miei Stati, e Beni, e la Ragione, e Diritti e Titoli, e le azioni Italiane e cedo all'istesso in questo punto la piena tradizione, sicché in Me non rimanga alcuna parte di essi.

Egli però, sin dal momento, nel quale Io partirò da questa capitale, potrà col Consiglio di Stato e di Reggenza amministrare tutto quel che sarà da Me a Lui trasferito, ceduto e donato. Spero che questa Mia legge di Emancipazione, di Costituzione di Età maggiore, di Destinazione di Tutela, e di Cura del Re pupillo e minore, di Successione, nei detti Stati e Beni Italiani, di cessione e donazione, ridonderà in bene dei Popoli, in tranquillità della Mia Famiglia Reale, finalmente contribuirà al riposo di tutta anche l'Europa.

Sarà la presente Ordinazione sottoscritta da Me, e dal Mio Figlio Infante Don Ferdinando, munita del Mio Suggello, e referendata dagl'infrascritti Consiglieri e Segretari di Stato, anche nella qualità di Reggenti, e Tutori dello istesso Infante Don Ferdinando.

NOI CARLO III.

Per la grazia di Dio Re di Castiglia, Leone, Aragona, delle due Sicilie, Gerusalemme, Navarra, Granata, Toledo, Valenza, Galizia, Majorca, Siviglia, Sardegna, Cordova, Corsica, Murcia, Jaen, Algarves, Algezira, Gibilterra, delle Isole Canarie, delle Indie Orientali ed Occidentali, delle Isole e Continente del Mare Oceano; Arciduca d'Austria; Duca di Borgogna, Brabante, Milano, Parma, Piacenza, e Castro; Gran Principe Ereditario di Toscana; Conte di Abspurg, Fiandra, Tirolo, e Barcellona; Signore di Biscaglia, e Molina, &c. &c.

FRA le gravi cure, che la Monarchia delle Spagne, e delle Indie, dopo la morte dell' amatissimo mio Fratello il Re Cattolico Ferdinando VI. Mi ha recato, è stata quella, che è venuta dalla notoria imbecillità della mente del mio Real Primogenito. Lo Spirito de' Trattati di questo Secolo mostra, che si desideri dall'Europa, quando si possa eseguire senza opporsi alla Giustizia, la divisione della Potenza Spagnuola dall' Italiana. Vedendomi perciò nella convenienza di provveder di legittimo Successore i miei Stati Italiani

Preamble of the Pragmatic of 1759

Appendix 2
KNIGHTHOOD

Several orders of knighthood were bestowed in the Kingdom of the Two Sicilies. In addition to these, the Knights Hospitaller, or Knights of Saint John (Order of Malta) held Malta and Gozo as a fief of the King of Sicily from 1530 until 1798 and had commanderies in the kingdom into the nineteenth century. There were also knights outside these various orders.

What follows is a concise outline of the modern institution of knighthood as it existed in the kingdom into the nineteenth century.

In law, the modern practice of kings dubbing knights is based on the arcane principle of *fons honorum*, literally "fount of honor," by which a monarch and his heirs have the right to bestow honors (knighthoods) and to create or recognize titles of nobility. Neither the last King of the Two Sicilies nor the last King of Italy lost these rights when they were deposed and exiled (in 1861 and 1946 respectively), as neither ever abdicated. Into the thirteenth century, barons and knights could elevate esquires to knighthood, but our focus here shall be the practices that existed from the eighteenth century onward. (Titles of nobility are considered in Appendix 3.)

There are three broad categories of orders of chivalry.

Court orders, or "collar orders," include the Order of Saint Januarius and older institutions such as England's Order of the Garter founded in 1348, the Savoys' Order of the Annunciation founded in 1362, and the Order of the Golden Fleece founded in 1430 (eventually bestowed in both Austria and Spain). King Arthur's legendary Knights of the Round Table were mentioned by Wace in 1144, leading some historians to posit possible literary influences inspiring the development of court orders in subsequent centuries.

Military-religious orders are rooted in the crusading tradition. These included the Hospitallers, Templars, Teutonic Knights and Knights of Saint Lazarus, which were all present in the Kingdom of Sicily during the Middle Ages. These orders were essentially "sovereign" or independent, though the Teutonic Order was sponsored by the Hohenstaufens while Spain's military-monastic orders (Santiago, Alcantara, Calatrava, Montesa) flourished under the protection of specific monarchs. In the Kingdom of the Two Sicilies, the Constantinian Order was part of the military-religious chivalric tradition except for the anomaly of its grand master being a king. In times past, most of the knights in these orders were drawn from the aristocracy. Postulants to the military-religious orders had to be Roman Catholic.

Orders of merit, as their name implies, were founded in modern times to recognize military or civil merit. In the Two Sicilies, the Order of Francis I was in this category, which did not make the conferee's religion a requirement. When one reads a press report about a prominent man or woman being invested in an order by a head of state, this is the form of knighthood that most often comes to mind.

The title *cavaliere ereditario* was a specific hereditary knightly rank just below that of baron, a status loosely comparable to that of a baronet in England. In the kingdoms of Naples and Sicily, this modern title was inspired by the enfeoffed knighthood of the Middle Ages; it also existed in Piedmont.

The simple title of *cavaliere* (outside an order) usually denoted a knight bachelor whose rank could not be transmitted to his son. This title was only rarely bestowed in the kingdoms of Naples and Sicily.

The title of *commendatore* (knight commander) was associated with the orders of chivalry. The Constantinian Order, as we shall see, also had hereditary commanderies.

As a "courtesy title," *cavaliere* was sometimes used to address the younger son or younger brother of a count or baron. This informal usage was more commonplace in the Two Sicilies than in some of the other Italian states.

In the Two Sicilies, a clear distinction was not always drawn between dynastic orders (Saint Januarius) and the orders of merit that elsewhere might appertain to the state rather than the dynasty (Francis I). Although the Constantinian Order was military-religious originally, and transferred from one dynasty to another, it came to be identified as dynastic.

With decree number 718 of 19 May 1817, following the formal unification of the kingdoms of Naples and Sicily, King Ferdinand I prohibited the subjects in his jurisdiction from accepting foreign knighthoods without royal consent. Similar policies also existed in other kingdoms.

Some of the orders guaranteed pensions to conferees.

Decree number 1205 of 8 June 1818 establishes that knights condemned for serious crimes can be divested of their status by being expelled from the orders of chivalry of the kingdom. The law states that this need not be a formal procedure; indeed, it may be automatic once the knight is convicted of a felony. However, a procedure is prescribed by which the man's name is provided to the Secretary of State for the Royal Household, described below.

With decree number 129 of 8 October 1821, Ferdinand I placed all of the orders, even the Constantinian Order (which by tradition was administered quasi-independently), under the authority of the Secretary of State for the Royal Household and the Orders of Knighthood, a position that was later abolished following a reorganization.

On 9 September 1832 (with decree number 1119), administration of the orders of knighthood passed from the royal household, as the office of Secretary of the Royal Household was discontinued, to the office of the Prime Minister, *il Ministero della Presidenza del Consiglio dei Ministri*. Article 5 of this decree is the basis for a commission on nobiliary titles established in 1833, q.v. Appendix 3.

The year 1832 also saw several commanderies (estates) in southeastern Sicily held until recently by the Order of Malta transferred to princes of the royal family. These were not the only landed estates in the kingdom belonging to an order of chivalry.

In view of the revolts in Palermo and then Naples, and the granting of an ephemeral constitution, a decree of Ferdinand II on 11 May 1848 (number 15) somewhat revised the court administration established in 1832 by further streamlining its bureaucracy, yet leaving management of, for example, abeyant ("vacant") hereditary *giuspatronato* commanderies (described below) of the Royal Constantinian Order to civil servants appointed by the office of the Prime Minister.

Ferdinand II occasionally used these "vacant" *giuspatronato* commanderies as a source of income for his children. For example, we find him granting a "trust fund" to his son Gennaro, Count of Caltagirone, born in 1857, with a decree given at Caserta in March of that year.[93] This reflects the monarch's commendable effort to provide for his children with funds other than the kingdom's tax revenue.

Researchers will find much information regarding the activities of the orders of knighthood, and the exercise of royal authority over them, in two compendia published annually in the kingdom by the *Stamperia Reale* (Royal Press), namely the *Collezione delle Leggi e de' Decreti Reali del Regno delle Due Sicili*e (royal decrees) and the *Almanacco Reale del Regno delle Due Sicilie* (the court circular).

Although King Francis II continued to bestow honors in exile, for the essential laws governing the orders we look to decrees, legislation and usage before he left the territory of the kingdom on 14 February in 1861.

The Order of Saint Januarius

In times past, every major dynasty or kingdom had its premier order of chivalry whose knights wore a "collar" formed of links resembling those of a chain. Such an order had a limited number of knights, each of whom swore fealty to the king, who was the order's grand master. Unlike the military-religious orders such as the Hospitallers, whose original knights were men-at-arms skilled in combat techniques, these orders were a means of affiliating a faithful subject, usually a nobleman, with the monarch without the requirement of military service.

The Distinguished Royal Order of Saint Januarius was founded by King Charles of Naples and Sicily in 1738. It received Papal approval from Benedict XIV on 30 June 1741. Its original statutes reflected the times, for example forbidding knights to participate in duels.

The insignia of the order is a white or silver Maltese-style cross having fleurs-de-lis between its four limbs, with the center bearing the image of Januarius as a bishop holding two vials of his blood. On a blue enamel banner beneath this is the motto IN SANGUINE FOEDUS, which may be translated, "Faithful in blood" or "By blood is the covenant sealed."

Its insignia is modelled on those of the French royal orders of Saint Michael and the Holy Spirit. It had a single rank, that of knight, their number limited to sixty. The ribbon of the order is red, representing the saint's blood.

Martyred in 305, Saint Januarius (San Gennaro) is the patron saint of Naples. His solidified blood, kept in two vials in the cathedral that bears his name, liquefies on his annual feast day, September nineteenth. (The author once witnessed this occurrence in the cathedral's sanctuary as a guest of the Archbishop of Naples; the substance, which probably contains blood as well as other compounds, did indeed liquefy when the portable reliquary containing it was slowly rotated by the late Cardinal Giordano.)

This recurring event was mentioned in the *Chronicon Siculum* in 1389, the narrative stating that it had occurred already for a number of years. It may be noted that only one of the two vials is filled with the saint's surviving blood. King Charles extracted half of the substance from the other vial and took it with him to Spain when he departed in 1759 (see Appendix 1).

Charles III also founded the Order of Saint Charles (see below).

The Constantinian Order of Saint George

This is the order having the longest history, surviving today as a charitable institution that functions in much the same way as the Sovereign Military Order of Malta (based in Rome). Unlike the other orders bestowed by the kings of the Two Sicilies, it was not founded by these sovereigns and it was not originally linked to the Neapolitan crown.[94]

The Sacred Military Constantinian Order of Saint George was brought to Naples in 1734 by Charles de Bourbon, who inherited it from his mother's family, the Farnese. Like the Duchy of Parma itself, this institution was considered a patrimony separate from the crowns of Naples and Sicily, though borne by the same monarch.

Although its origins are military, over time it became dynastic in character, and in that respect its history is not unlike that of the Order of Saint Lazarus, which was founded in the Holy Land and eventually obtained the patronage of the House of Savoy.

An apocryphal "history" ascribes the foundation of the Constantinian Order to the Eastern Emperor Isaac II Angelus (1155-1204), who was supposedly inspired by the story of the victory of the Emperor Constantine the Great at the Milvian Bridge in 312. It is said that the night before the battle, Constantine saw the vision of a flaming cross in the sky with the *Chi Rho* monogram of Christ (the first letters of the Greek *Christos* as XP) and the words *In hoc signo vinces* (By this sign you shall conquer). Following his victory, he legalized Christianity across the Roman Empire. The insignia of the order represents this, being a deep red cross *fleury* displaying the XP and the letters IHSV, the decoration's light blue ribbon representing the sky. This Byzantine mythos was suitable to the aspirations, or pretensions, of the family that actually founded the order.

Among a number of ambitious military families struggling for control of the Balkans following the fall of Constantinople to the Turks in 1453 were the Angelus Comnenus, who claimed, with little evidence, to be the lawful pretenders to the Byzantine throne. In this they were supported by the opportunistic Venetians, who feared losing their strategic and lucrative territories around Albania to the invading Turks. This Angelus family, which ended up in Venice, led troops against the Turks even if, in the end, their efforts were no more successful than those of their ally and countryman, George Kastriot Scanderbeg (1405-1468).

Papal bulls confirming pontifical protection to the Angeli grand mastership were issued in 1545 and 1551. These were followed by other bulls, circulars and briefs.

The first members of the family of whom we have a reasonably certain knowledge are Andrew and Jerome (Girolamo), whose grand mastership was recognized by Pope Julius III in 1555. The order's statutes were published in 1573.

By the time Andrew died in 1580, the Constantinian Order had thus obtained papal approval. It was sometimes referred to as the "Constantinian Golden Militia" in imitation of the papal "Golden Militia."

The Angeli base was still Venice. We find a historiography published in 1626 by Majolino Bisaccioni.

Supporting the goals of the Counter Reformation movement, the order's religious model was the Rule of Saint Basil. Remembering its mission against the Turks, the order sent a contingent to fight alongside King John III Sobieski of Poland at Vienna in 1683; he recognized their privileges in his dominions.

By now, Bernardo Giustiniani, a chancellor of the order descended from a distinguished Venetian family, had published its decrees, and the Constantinian Order is the first entry in his exhaustive history of chivalric orders published at Venice in 1692. This attempt to prove its antiquity did not go unchallenged.[95]

In 1697, the last Angelus Comnenus heir, John Andrew II, ceded the hereditary grand mastership of the Constantinian Order to the sovereign Duke of Parma, Francesco Farnese. Pope Innocent XII approved this transfer two years later with his bull *Sincerae Fidei*.

The Farnese family ruled sovereign territory that included not only Parma but nearby Piacenza. They boasted kinship with other important families in northern Italy and abroad.

In 1705, the new grand master issued an effective constitution for the order that has come to be known as the *Farnese Statutes*. It received papal approval and became the governing framework for the order, establishing succession to the grand mastership by the principle of male primogeniture. In the absence of male heirs, the Duchy of Parma could be transmitted through a female. In the same circumstance, the grand mastership of the Constantinian Order would be inherited by an heir appointed by the grand master; otherwise, the knights could elect one from among their number.

On 6 June 1718, Pope Clement XI further confirmed the canonical protection of the order by the Holy See with the lengthy papal bull *Militantis Ecclesiae,* summarizing its history and setting forth its status.[96]

In 1727, Antonio Farnese, the last of his dynasty to rule Parma, lacking male heirs, designated as his universal heir a niece, Elisabeth (Isabella), who was by then married to King Philip V of Spain. Upon Antonio's death in 1731, this succession came to pass.

When Elisabeth's son, Charles, claimed his birthright in Parma before marching on Naples, the Constantinian Order was already part of his inheritance.[97] Most of the knights were in northern and central Italy, and there were a number in Spain.

For a few years after 1759, Charles III administered the order from Madrid on behalf of his young son who was in Naples (see Appendix 1), and he did likewise for the Order of Saint Januarius until 1766.

Two years later, Ferdinand established the ecclesiastical seat of the Constantinian Order at a Neapolitan church dedicated to his patron saint. In 1777, the order was given the small church of Sant'Antonio Abate in Naples as its *de facto* seat. Other churches followed, such as the Magione in Palermo in 1787; once a commandery of the Teutonic Order, this was a royal church as the resting place of King Tancred of Sicily, who died in 1194, though his tomb was eventually removed.

It should be remembered that until 1816 the Two Sicilies was made up of two separate kingdoms (Naples and Sicily) in law. The Magione was significant as the seat of the order in the Kingdom of Sicily.

By the nineteenth century, the Farnese Statutes governing the structure and administration of the Constantinian Order were being interpreted and applied in view of current realities; indeed, they had been revised several times since 1705 (an example of the order's subsequent evolution is that it has admitted women as dames since 1886).

There were a few Constantinian knights from countries beyond Neapolitan borders, an early one being Anthony Plunkett, an Irishman invested in 1789. Contrary to popular belief, not every foreigner invested into the order was Roman Catholic, even though the statutes made Catholicism a requirement for entry.

Toward the end of his long reign, King Ferdinand I sought to "modernize" the administration. In a decree of 8 October 1821 (number 129), he dismisses the present members of the Royal Deputation, the governing body of the "Royal Constantinian Order," appointing in their stead a president and just four deputies. The king reorganizes the order and makes it answerable to the Secretary of State for the Royal Household and the Orders of Knighthood, *il Segretario di Stato di Casa Reale e degli Ordini Cavallereschi* which, as we have seen, was eventually abolished. Until that time, the Constantinian Order usually had been treated as a distinct institution.

This may reflect a more general effort by the king, having returned to Naples and united the crowns of Naples and Sicily, to bring all of the knightly orders more firmly under his control. By this time, his heir, the future Francis I, was increasingly involved in day-to-day administration of the kingdom.

Henceforth, official publications, such as the *Rito e Forma* (rite of investiture) published by the *Stamperia Reale* (Royal Press) at the command of King Francis I in 1826, also refer to the "Royal Constantinian Order of Saint George," which is to say, a dynastic order like the others. In 1832, we find Raffaele Ruo, the order's notary (and an attorney), writing that "the grand mastership is always attached to the crown." Both publications reflect the usage established a few years earlier by Ferdinand I.[98]

The activities of the order were published in the *Almanacco Reale,* the annual court circular, which reports, in one of many pertinent entries made over the years, that in 1841 the government official responsible for administration of all the orders then bestowed in the Kingdom of the Two Sicilies was a court officer.[99]

The order still had nobiliary grades and such ranks as knights commander of *giuspatronato,* who had donated estates to it (and whose descendants would inherit minor nobility). These estates were in the Kingdom of the Two Sicilies.[100]

As grand master, King Francis II took the order with him into exile in 1861.

Today, the Constantinian Order supports several charitable foundations and is recognized by the Italian government, which permits its citizens to use its titles of *commendatore* and *cavaliere* and allows military and diplomatic personnel to wear its decorations.

Its feast days are Saint George's Day on 23 April and the Exaltation of the Holy Cross on 14 September.

It is important to note that the focus of the order's activities is medical relief and other charities directed toward the poor to alleviate human suffering, not "human rights" as a political effort. The order is apolitical.

The Order of Saint Charles

Founded in 1738 to recognize military service rendered during the recent conquest of Naples and Sicily, this may be considered one of Europe's first orders of merit, obviously named for the monarch's patron saint, to whom he dedicated the opera house of Naples. Its cross was based on that of the Constantinian Order, the arms of which coincidentally resembling the Bourbons' fleur de lis. The Order of Saint Charles became inactive when King Charles of Naples and Sicily left Italy in 1759. The insignia of the order of the same name instituted by him as King of Spain in 1771 is of a different design.

The Order of Merit of Saint Ferdinand

This Order was founded in 1800 to recognize individuals who had rendered exceptional service to the crown. This included Neapolitans and Sicilians, as well as some British officers who were based in Sicily when the royal family resided in Palermo while Naples was occupied by republicans.

Despite its dedication to a Catholic saint, the order never had a religious character. It has always been awarded irrespective of the conferee's faith.

It was part of the general trend in orders of knighthood bestowed for merit, mentioned earlier. It provided the king an order he could bestow besides those he already had, which were not suitable to every appropriate candidate.

The Order of Saint George of the Reunion

Founded in 1819, this order for military merit was intended to replace an order bestowed upon citizens of the Kingdom of Naples by the French during the Napoleonic occupation. The "reunion" refers to the peninsular region being reunited with the island of Sicily as the Kingdom of the Two Sicilies.

The Royal Order of Francis I

Francis I of the Two Sicilies instituted this order of merit in 1829 to recognize achievement in the arts, letters and sciences. The decoration, typical of that era, is a white Maltese-style cross bearing four golden fleurs de lis between its limbs; in the center medallion is the king's royal monogram "F.I." The cross pends from a large golden coronet. The ribbon of the order is deep red with a blue edge.

As head of his dynasty and pretender to the Neapolitan throne, Prince Alfonso, Count of Caserta, brother and heir of King Francis II, bestowed the Order in exile into the twentieth century. Alfonso died in 1934.

This was the last order of knighthood founded in the Kingdom of the Two Sicilies. It reflects the esteem in which scientific, industrial and artistic progress were held. The decree of foundation follows.

Decree Founding the Order of Francis I

Francis I, by the Grace of God King of the Kingdom of the Two Sicilies, of Jerusalem, etc., Duke of Parma, Piacenza, Castro, etc., Hereditary Grand Prince of Tuscany, etc.

It being one of our chief interests to promote by all the means at our disposal the zeal of our subjects in the exercise of various civil offices assigned to them by us, and ever desiring to foster advancements in the sciences and the fine arts, as well as in the various aspects of industry, agriculture and commerce upon which the continued prosperity of the kingdom depends; Considering that awards of honor and merit are the most powerful recognition of such virtuous and praiseworthy activities; Having heard our Council of State in Ordinary; We have resolved to sanction, and by these presents do approve the following law.

1. We hereby establish in our Kingdom of the Two Sicilies an order of knighthood, expressly intended to recognize civil merit, which shall bear the name of the *Royal Order of Francis I.*

2. Insofar as this distinguished order of knighthood shall be accorded the dignity of our illustrious and esteemed Crown, we declare ourself and our Royal Person the Sovereign Head and Grand Master of the aforementioned Order, and shall display its decoration and ribbon upon our Royal Person, as well as suspended from the royal coat of arms; and we desire that the Grand Magistry of the said Order shall always be vested in our Royal Crown.

3. The said Order shall have five grades, namely Knight Grand Cross, Knight Commander, Knight, Conferee of the Medal in Gold, and Conferee of the Medal in Silver.

4. Exclusively those our subjects who have rendered to the crown and to the state the most outstanding and loyal service in the exercise of the highest offices in the political, diplomatic, or judicial spheres, or in any branch of administrative or ecclesiastical service, may be decorated with the Grand Cross.

5. Those who have rendered extraordinary service in the exercise of important offices in the political, diplomatic, or judicial spheres, or in any branch of administrative or ecclesiastical service, may be decorated with the rank of Knight Commander.

6. Those who have rendered faithful service in the political, diplomatic or judicial spheres, or in any branch of administrative or ecclesiastical service, as well as those distinguished in scientific fields, writing and publishing, fine arts, or as the authors of great works, may be decorated with the rank of Knight.

7. The Gold Medal may be conferred upon those who have excelled in the abovementioned fields, having rendered important service at an elementary level.

8. The Gold Medal may likewise be conferred upon those who have displayed exceptional merit in the fine arts, and those who have introduced new industrial methods, or have introduced extraordinary procedures in the mechanical arts, or have notably improved the fields of agriculture or animal livestock development, or have promoted industry and commerce.

9. At all events, we reserve to ourselves the right to bestow the rank of Knight in the extraordinary instance of one of our subjects having executed a distinguished public project, or reflecting discoveries in one of the aforementioned fields of study.

10. The Silver Medal may be conferred upon those who, though not meeting all the requirements expressed in the aforementioned articles 7 and 8, have rendered worthy projects in the fields described.

11. Those in the military who have rendered distinguished civil service as described in the preceding articles 4, 5, 6, 7, 8, 9 and 10 may also be decorated in various grades of the Order.

12. The dispositions of the present law do not abrogate or diminish the effect of other sovereign resolutions established to reward merits in the fine arts or manufacturing; on the contrary, those so rewarded may be considered for the Gold or Silver Medal of this Order.

13. The rank of Knight Commander or Knight, as well as the Medal in Gold or Silver, may be bestowed upon worthy individuals according to the level of their service, in recognition of rare and virtuous merits demonstrated toward the Throne and the State.

14. Those Knights who continue to render distinguished service of such importance as to merit further consideration may be rewarded by us with bestowal of the rank of Knight Commander or Knight Grand Cross. On the same basis, those who have been decorated with the Gold Medal may be rewarded with the rank of Knight, and those decorated with the Silver Medal may be rewarded with the Gold Medal.

15. Our Ministerial Secretaries of State, regardless of their department, and our Lieutenant General in Sicily, shall advise us, through our Ministerial Secretary of State for the Royal Household, of the names, qualities and merits of those our subjects who have rendered services which should be recognized by decoration with a grade of the Order, including that of Knight Grand Cross; we shall reserve to ourself the ultimate decision to recognize merits such as are described by the present law.

16. The Knights Grand Cross shall have the privilege of entry into the Throne Room, and may attend Court dinners and royal receptions. They may display the cross of the Order in their places of business and in their coat of arms.

17. The Knights Commander shall have the privilege of attending Court dinners and royal receptions.

18. The Knights may attend royal receptions.

19. We reserve to ourself, according to the circumstances, and according to the nature and importance of services rendered by the individual decorated with the Order, to assign a pension as we see fit. Such pensions shall be paid from the Royal Purse until such time as we decide it opportune to establish a fund for the Order.

20. The insignia of the Order shall be a cross enameled white between four gold fleurs de lis, bearing a center medallion upon which appears our cipher F.I., surmounted by the royal crown, encircled by an oak wreath enameled green, this encircled by a blue band bearing the legend *De Rege optime merito* in gold letters, the medallion bearing on the reverse the inscription *Franciscus Ius instituit MDCCCXXIX,* encircled by an oak wreath enameled green.

21. The decoration of Knight Grand Cross is the cross described herein, surmounted by a gold crown, suspended from the neck by a wide watered (moire) ribbon of deep red bearing at each edge a narrow blue stripe. The insignia of Knight Grand Cross also includes a badge to be worn attached to the left breast of the jacket. The said badge shall consist of the same cross as the neck decoration but of silver rather than white enamel, displaying between its arms four fleurs de lis, bearing at its center a medallion upon which appears our cipher F.I., surmounted by the royal crown, encircled by an oak wreath enameled green, this encircled by a blue band bearing the legend *De Rege optime merito* in gold letters.

22. The decoration of Knight Commander is similar to that described in Article 20, except that it is slightly smaller, surmounted by a gold crown, suspended from the neck by a ribbon slightly narrower than that of the neck decoration of Knight Grand Cross.

23. The decoration of a Knight is similar to that of Knight Commander but slightly smaller, surmounted by a gold crown, suspended from the lapel buttonhole of the jacket by a ribbon slightly narrower than that of the neck decoration of Knight Commander.

24. The Gold and Silver Medals shall bear on the obverse our likeness in profile encircled by an oak wreath, this encircled by the legend *Franciscus I. Reg. utr. Sic. Hier Rex;* bearing on the reverse three fleurs de lis, one in chief and two in base, encircled by an oak wreath encircled by the legend *De Rege optime merito MDCCCXXIX.* The Medal is suspended from the lapel buttonhole by a ribbon slightly narrower than that of the decoration of Knight.

25. The precise measurements of the decorations and ribbons are indicated in a design which accompanies the original document of this decree.

26. The conferral of the aforementioned honors and awards shall be made by effect of royal rescript by our Ministerial Secretary of State for the Royal Household.

27. Our being desirous that no form of endeavor that could benefit the public good in some way be ignored, even if its merits have not been made known to the public, and wishing that such worthy activities which influence society, however indirectly, be recognized by this Order, we have determined that the Medal of Civil Merit instituted 17 December 1827 shall no longer be bestowed for services rendered expressly to the benefit of the King and the State, recognition of such services being addressed instead by the present law.

28. To that end we authorize the competent administrators to make known those deserving recognition with the awards mentioned in Article 27, submitting the relevant proposals and documentation to the office of the Ministerial Secretary of State for the Royal Household or, in Sicily, to the office of the Lieutenant General, who will forward these to the former. The names of those thus honored, as well as the services for which Our Royal Person has determined that they be recognized, shall be published in the official gazette of this Kingdom.

29. The affairs of the Order shall be managed by a Deputation composed of a President (who shall be a Knight Grand Cross), two Knights Commander and two Knights, one of whom shall serve as secretary and archivist. We shall nominate the members of the Deputation on the recommendations of our Ministerial Secretary of State for the Royal Household. Specific regulations shall establish the duties and internal functions of the Deputation.

30. As this Deputation shall depend upon the aforementioned Secretary of the Royal Household, it shall answer directly and exclusively to him.

31. In bestowing the Order, we shall rely upon the advice of the Deputation, whose responsibility it shall be to examine and consider the merits of the worthy services mentioned in Article 27.

32. The expenses of the Delegation, and of certain decorations which it shall please us to bestow, shall be drawn from the funds existing for our royal orders of knighthood under the Royal Secretariat and the Ministerial Secretary of State for the Royal Household. We desire and command that this our law signed by Us and ratified by our Councillor Minister of State and Ministerial Secretary of State of Grace and Justice, given under our great seal, registered and deposited with the Ministry and Royal Secretariat of State of the Presidency of the Council of Ministers, be published in our royal dominions by the competent authorities, who shall ensure accuracy of publication and timeliness in dissemination. Our Councillor Minister of State and President of the Council of Ministers is particularly charged with the duty of its publication.

Given at Naples this 28th day of September 1829

KNIGHTHOOD

Knightly Orders of the Kingdom of the Two Sicilies

St Januarius

Francis I

St Ferdinand

St Charles

Constantinian Order

Engravings from Raffaele Ruo's *Saggio Storico* (1832)

RITO E FORMA

DA PRATICARSI

NELL' ARMARE UNO O PIÙ CAVALIERI

DEL

REAL ORDINE COSTANTINIANO
DI S. GIORGIO

NELLA CAPITALE DI NAPOLI

ESTRATTO

DALLE COSTITUZIONI DELL'ORDINE,

CHE HA COMANDATO OSSERVARSI LA MAESTÀ DEL RE N. S.

FRANCESCO I.

GRAN MAESTRO DEL REAL ORDINE.

NAPOLI, DALLA STAMPERIA REALE.

1826.

Rite of investiture of the Royal Constantinian Order of Saint George published by command of Francis I in Naples in 1826

Constantinian Cross at entrance of the Magione, a medieval commandery of the Teutonic Order

THE KINGDOM OF THE TWO SICILIES

Foundation of a hereditary Constantinian commandery in 1858 signed by the jurist and scholar Raffaele Ruo (see note 100).

Appendix 3
NOBILITY

The nobility was a social class present in most monarchies. What follows here is a very concise survey of a complex topic about which myriad monographs and studies have been published.

Following their arrival in southern Italy around 1016, the Normans gradually introduced their feudal (manorial) system throughout their dominions, eventually displacing the systems of the Lombards and Byzantines. By the time the kingdom was founded in 1130, the transition was nearly complete, having also begun to supplant the system of smallholding known among the Arabs in Sicily. Except for demesnial (royal) localities, whose feudal rights and taxes appertained directly to the crown, most of southern Italy, including Sicily, became a patchwork of towns and large holdings (fiefs or manors) belonging to the companions of the Hautevilles. They held these estates in return for military service, but over the centuries it became common practice for the barons to render a tax (scutage) in lieu of this service.

The first formal codification of Norman law for the entire kingdom arrived with the Assizes of Ariano of Roger II in 1140.

Compiled a decade later, the *Catalogus Baronum,* which is only partly preserved, lists the nobles of peninsular southern Italy and their feudal rights and duties. This is southern Italy's *Domesday Book,* but it deals only with the southern part of the peninsula, not the island of Sicily, whose earliest feudal registry was destroyed during a revolt by disgruntled barons in Palermo in 1161; parts of the *Catalogus* were reconstructed by 1167 during the regency of Queen Margaret. It is clear from the *Catalogus* that the members of the new aristocracy based their surnames on toponyms. In other words, their surnames were in most instances the names of places they held in Italy, rather than Normandy. A typical example:

"Robert of Molinara declares to hold Molinara which is a fief of two knights, and with the tax increase he has offered four knights and two sergeants."

This is why among the Italian aristocracy there are few surnames of Norman derivation. It is obvious that most of these knights, and even the Hauteville dynasty itself, were of minor families of Normandy's nobility. Like some of their Viking forebears, many were simply adventurers in search of fortune. The more important families sent their sons to conquer England, not Italy.

Despite popular misconceptions, in Italian a surname prefix (de or di) does not denote nobility, as does (in most cases) the German *von*. Nor do double surnames indicate aristocratic origins; most often, a dual surname simply indicates that numerous families in the same town bore the same surname and eventually required differentiation to distinguish among themselves.

Frankish succession (inheritance by male primogeniture) became the standard means of transmitting land and titles, though Longobard succession (inheritance by all heirs male) was practiced in certain Lombard families for some time to come and, beginning in 1231, female succession was sometimes permitted, having been legislated by the Constitutions of Melfi.

By the fourteenth century, the titles of baron and count were in wide use, whereas formerly the vassals were either *seigneurs* (manorial lords) or *cavalieri* (enfeoffed knights). Under the Normans, the title *seigneur* was used to refer to most landed nobles, though one referred to the nobility collectively as "the baronage" or simply "the barons." By the nineteenth century, most of the *signori* were designated *baroni* (barons), their holdings baronies.

Into the fourteenth century, it could still be said that a county was likely larger than a barony. This changed over time.

Contrary to popular belief, the title *cavaliere ereditario* (hereditary knight), mentioned in Appendix 2, was a late development, though its name is redolent of the much older title of enfeoffed knight. Not being heirs, the younger sons (as opposed to the eldest sons) of feudatories (vassals) often went off to serve in the military orders, of which the best-known was the

Order of the Hospital, later the Order of Malta. This established the Sicilian practice, which existed into the twentieth century, of referring to a titled nobleman's younger sons as "cavalieri" even if they were not actually knights, something akin to the loose use of "chevalier" in France in times past.

Over the centuries, many prominent noble families were gradually promoted through the aristocratic ranks. By the eighteenth century, the titles of noble prince, duke and marquis were held by many men whose ancestors, just two centuries earlier, had been barons or *signori* of the same feudal manors.

Certain families emerged as simple *nobili* (untitled nobles), a class loosely comparable to England's landed gentry. They had coats of arms, aristocratic homes, and in some cases feudal rights over a single manor. Some attained their status as the noble jurats of demesnial cities or towns. This was a *minor* nobility.

In the Kingdom of Sicily, feudal investiture continued as a formal ceremony, however simple and perfunctory, until 1458. Henceforth, acts certified by a public notary were sufficient proof of the oath of fealty and homage to the sovereign when a feudatory inherited (or purchased) manorial property such as a barony. A similar system was already in place in the Kingdom of Naples (known by that appellation from 1444). By that time, nearly all holders of feudal property in these kingdoms were at least barons. Feudal inheritance occasioned taxation.

Historically, the titles used were: prince, duke, marquis, count, baron, lord, noble (untitled nobleman), hereditary knight. Viscount, a rare title anywhere in Italy, was held by very few in the south, while patrician (patrizio) was known primarily in Italy's northern communes (city-states) though eventually in Naples and Messina.

A few *commendatori* (knights commander) were knights invested into the Constantinian Order (see Appendix 2) in the special category of *giuspatronato*, which meant that they donated substantial estates to the order for its good works. The descendants of these *commendatori* were eventually recognized as minor nobles. The man invested with such a commandery would designate an heir, usually a son or nephew, who would succeed the founder much as if he were inheriting a barony.

Until feudalism was abolished in the nineteenth century (1806 on the mainland, 1812 in Sicily), most titles of nobility from the rank of baron upward were based on feudal tenure. Impersonating an aristocrat was not very easy, but this became problematic in the decades following the abolition of feudalism.

In 1833, the crown instituted a Royal Commission for Titles of Nobility, based at Naples, to oversee nobiliary succession and usage. This consisted of a president and vice president appointed by the king, a committee of seven or more councillors from around the kingdom, and normally four or more supplementary councillors (two from the peninsula and two from Sicily), plus a royal procurator. The committee sometimes reached its decisions by voting, in the manner of a jury. Those appointed to the commission were listed in the *Almanacco Reale* (described below), usually in the section immediately before that dedicated to the orders of knighthood.

The peerage (most recently in Sicily during the revolt of 1848) consisted of wealthier nobles entitled to vote in parliament. Since the appointment to a peerage presupposed a certain taxable income, it was possible for an affluent baron to receive a peerage while a poor marquis was excluded from receiving one.

Titles used within the royal family are listed in the royal decree of January 1817 mentioned in Appendix 1.

Being recognized as a nobleman was more than a question of prestige. The status of nobility sometimes dictated such matters as eligibility for admittance to certain military schools; here was the antithesis of meritocracy. For example, the large school behind Palermo's cathedral was established for the sons of nobles, and especially those lacking the means to defray the tuition at other elite schools. The building itself had been confiscated from the Jesuits.

For decrees, legislation and usage regarding titles and ranks, as well as the recognition of the status of nobility in the Two Sicilies, we look to what existed before the departure of the last king for exile in February 1861. In subsequent decades, the *Consulta Araldica* of the Kingdom of Italy undertook to recognize the titles of nobility borne by persons in the constituent states that existed before unification. Because that effort generally overlooked the status of untitled nobility and even some minor baronies, particularly where barons failed to come forth to petition to have their claims recognized, the records of the Kingdom of Italy should not be considered authoritative regarding the pre-unitary states.

For researchers, the most relevant records for Siculo-Neapolitan titles borne before the abolition of feudalism are acts of manorial succession retained in the state archives of Naples and Palermo (some of these have been published as compilations such as *La Storia dei Feudi* by Francesco San Martino de Spucches), though it must be noted that not every title used before the nineteenth century was linked to feudal tenure. Many (but not all) subsequent ennoblements and recognitions are listed in the *Collezione delle Leggi e de' Decreti Reali del Regno delle Due Sicili*e (royal decrees) and the *Almanacco Reale del Regno delle Due Sicilie* (the court circular), both published by the *Stamperia Reale* (Royal Press) until 1860. The surviving archives of the Order of Saint Januarius and the Constantinian Order of Saint George (see Appendix 2) include some nobiliary records because nobility of birth was usually a requirement for admission, but most of that information is also available in the sources already noted. The *catasti* in Naples and the *riveli* in Palermo make reference to feudal property. Notarial acts, though useful, are unindexed and infamously difficult to research. Parochial and vital statistics acts of events such as marriage recorded in the Kingdom of the Two Sicilies (beginning in 1809 on the mainland and 1820 in Sicily) indicate titles of nobility from the rank of baron upwards.

Principe, Principessa (Prince, Princess). From the Latin *princeps,* meaning first, this is the highest Italian title of nobility, and also the title accorded members of the royal families. Many of Italy's noble princes, particularly in northern regions, are "of the Holy Roman Empire," and some lack territorial designations attached to their titles. A few southern princes, such as the Ruffo, descend from the vassals of medieval kings. In most cases, the holder of a princely title in Italy is the descendant of forebears who in times past were barons or counts, the family and its feudal estate having been "elevated" through the nobiliary ranks over the centuries. Until the unification of Italy, princes were addressed most formally as "Your Excellency," a form of address that may be compared, in this instance, to the British use of "Your Grace" for a duke or duchess. The wife of a prince is a princess. The younger son of a prince, and the heir before succession to the title, is a *nobile dei principi di* (seat), namely a "noble of the princes of" some place. Use of the honorific appellations *don* (lord) and *donna* (lady) for the son and daughter of a prince is obsolete.

Duca, Duchessa (Duke, Duchess). Derived from the Latin *dux,* a military leader, this title originally was reserved to the sovereign rulers of important territories, such as the Duchy of Spoleto. Like princedoms, dukedoms are sometimes borne by nobles whose medieval forebears holding the same feudal estate were barons, enfeoffed knights or other manorial lords. Like princes, dukes were formerly accorded the address "Your Excellency." The younger son of a duke, and the heir before succession to the title, is a *nobile dei duchi di* (seat), namely a "noble of the dukes of" some place.

Marchese, Marchesa (Marquess, Marchioness). The word derives from the Old Italian *marchio,* referring to the man charged with guarding a march, or border territory, and the French *marquis* shares the same origin. The Marches region is so-called because it was once such a territory. Some attribute the origin of this word to the Middle Latin *marchisus,* a prefect. Most marquisates are of modern foundation; one reads of few *marchesi* before the fifteenth century, and the title is quite rare even today. The younger son of a marquess, and the heir before succession to the title, is a *nobile dei marchesi di* (seat), namely a "noble of the marquesses of" some place.

Conte, Contessa (Count, Countess). The word traces its origin from the Latin *comes,* for a military companion. Comital territories were large in the eleventh century, but virtually indistinguishable from baronies by the seventeenth. For purposes of precedence, there is no contemporary distinction between a feudal count and a count palatine; the latter was usually a court officer who lacked a fief or territorial designation attached to his title. It is noteworthy that *conte* is one of the few Italian titles sometimes – though rarely – inherited by all heirs male, depending on the terms set forth in the patent of creation. The younger son of a count who bears a territorial designation, and the heir before succession to the title, is a *nobile dei conti di* (seat), namely a "noble of the counts of" some place.

Visconte, Viscontessa (Viscount, Viscontess). Originally *vice comes,* for the attendant of a count, this is the rarest of the modern Italian nobiliary titles, almost unknown in some regions. The younger son of a viscount, and the heir before succession to the title, is a *nobile dei visconti di* (seat), namely a "noble of the viscounts" of some place.

Barone, Baronessa (Baron, Baroness). The word is Germanic in origin; the title of nobility denoted the holder of a barony. Most smaller seigneuries (see below) were eventually elevated to baronies. The largest medieval baronies were elevated to princedoms or dukedoms by the eighteenth century. Though often employed loosely in the remote past, in modern times the title *barone* was established to be a creation or recognition by royal decree or patent; it was never an honorific privilege to be appropriated at will by any wealthy landholder. A number of Sicilian barons held feudal titles based not on land but on the rights to collect certain taxes such as those levied on anchorage of ships in a port or on the sale of grain in a certain locality. Heraldic regulation in the Kingdom of Italy established that the sons of barons could no longer appropriate *cavaliere* as a courtesy title, though many continued the practice. The younger son of a baron, and the heir before succession to the title, is a *nobile dei baroni di* (seat), namely a "noble of the barons of" some place.

Signore (Seigneur). Originally a manorial lord, the title was introduced into Italy by the Normans. The title is rarely used today because most *signori* bear greater titles by which they are commonly known and because, in common parlance, *signore* has come to mean "Mister." Seigneuries were feudal lands, manors, similar to baronies but typically smaller, appertaining to lesser lords, either as moieties within baronies or, in some cases, feudal tenure depending from the crown directly, so a *signore* might owe fealty to a baron (through subinfeudation) or directly to the king. This is the lowest title which carries a territorial designation or seat, as manors were named in the same style as the baronies which many became. At the abolition of feudalism, there was scholarly debate as to whether *signore* should be considered a title in itself, as not every manor was construed to have become a barony. In Piedmont, however, the analogous title *vassallo* (vassal) was used into the nineteenth century.

Patrizio (Patrician). Rare in the Two Sicilies except for a few families in larger cities like Salerno and Messina, the term obviously derives from that used to describe the aristocratic class of ancient Rome, and identifies the urban patriciate of certain northern Italian cities but also Rome and others. A *patrizio* is said to be "of" a certain place, such as Venice or Florence; patricians were an urban aristocracy recognized in published lists. The rank is normally transmitted to heirs male general. There is no feminine, but the daughter of a *patrizio* might be said to be *dei patrizi* (surname), namely "of the patricians (surname)." *Patrizio* is also the Italian for the name Patrick; *Patrizia* is Patricia but is never used as a title.

Nobile (Untitled Nobleman). In the Dark Ages, local leaders were *nobiliti*, from the Latin *nobilitas*, because they were "known" to the populace. The rank denotes some – though not all – Italian families which legitimately bear historic coats of arms and aristocratic status but lack titles of nobility based on historic feudal tenure or creation by patent. In some ways, this class may be compared, albeit tenuously, to the landed gentry of Great Britain. There are, strictly speaking, two classes of *nobili* — the younger sons or collateral kinsmen of titled nobles such as counts and barons, and males of the aforementioned noble families in which there have never been titles. The last category includes the *giurati nobili* and members of the *mastra nobile* councils of Sicily's demesnial cities, such as Piazza Armerina, and those listed in the *seggi* of cities like Salerno.

Cavaliere Ereditario (Hereditary Knight Bachelor). This rank, usually transmitted by male primogeniture but sometimes to heirs male general, is rather similar to a British baronetcy. However, it does not, as is commonly believed, have any direct connection to the medieval rank of the enfeoffed knight. Most *cavalieri ereditari* descend from the younger sons of nobles or from historically untitled families ennobled with this form of knighthood in the fifteenth or sixteenth centuries in Sicily, Sardinia and some parts of mainland Italy.

Nobiliary Laws 1743-1861

Here are a few laws often cited regarding the status of the nobility of southern Italy during the Bourbon period. Though not complete, this lists the most significant nobiliary legislation of the era.

Decree (dispatch) 16 October 1743: Declaration of nobiliary status for prominent citizens of several cities, particularly Pozzuoli and Bitonto, based on families having lived in a noble manner for at least three generations.

Dispatch 19 January 1751: Governors of certain cities may transmit nobility to their heirs only with royal assent.

Pragmatic 25 January 1756: Identification of several classes of nobility based on long-established norms not satisfactorily codified during the preceding two centuries. Specifically identified are the feudal nobility, nobility by office (judges, generals, et al.), and the civic nobility (patriciate) of royal cities. These distinctions served to differentiate the status of military cadets.

Pragmatic of 6 October 1759: Establishes line of succession in the House of the Two Sicilies.

Dispatch 19 February 1757: Declares that royal assent is needed for appointments to local nobility in cities where there is a *mastra nobile*.

Dispatch 20 June 1763: Clarifies that petitions for recognition of hereditary nobility must be submitted in a specific genealogical format and to a specific office in Naples.

Dispatch 2 December 1770: Declares that hereditary nobility may obtain from feudal tenure or a personal title created by the crown, or from certain ecclesiastical and civil offices.

Dispatch 23 April 1774: Descendants of certain *giurati nobili* (noble jurats) of Siracusa are ennobled.

Decree 24 December 1774: Identification of various professions which might engender nobility.

Dispatch 25 April 1778: Establishes that the legitimate descendants of nobles whose titles were created outside the Kingdom may have such titles recognized with royal assent.

Decree 27 November 1780: Confirms status of nobility to families residing in cities or towns which are now feudal (under a count or baron) but in the past were regarded as royal (demesnial or "free").

Decree 7 May 1795: Guarantees to certain high officials and their children the same privileges as nobles by birth.

Dispatch 27 October 1798: Establishes that certain high-ranking aldermen (jurats) traditionally regarded as nobles may be recognized legally as nobles only with royal assent.

Decree 20 December 1800: Prohibits nobles contracting marriages which are unworthy or indecent, without defining these terms explicitly.

Law 10 August 1812: In keeping with the recent constitution, feudal titles become personal, no longer attached to feudal land tenure. In effect, feudalism is abolished.

Proclamation of 20 May 1815: Consent to recognition of both ancient and modern nobility in the Kingdom of the Two Sicilies (previously the kingdoms of Naples and Sicily) now being constituted; this places descendants of the titular (personal) nobility at parity with those of the previously-feudal nobility.

Dispatch 24 September 1827: Clarifies titular inheritance by male primogeniture and thenceforth to younger sons, brothers, nephews of the deceased, necessitating royal assent for transmission through any other line.

Rescript 4 March 1828: Confirms the longstanding practice of the husband of a lady titled in her own right to make use of his wife's title during the marriage and as a widower.

Decree 23 March 1833 (number 1437): Establishes the *Royal Commission for Titles of Nobility* in view of the abolition of feudalism and the increasing usurpation of nobiliary titles and appellations (refers to article 5 of decree number 1119 of 9 September 1832). States that inheritance and succession of titles is ultimately by royal authority alone.

Ministerial Decree 7 December 1839: Confirms the effect of previous decrees abolishing feudalism regarding the personal, hereditary nature of nobiliary titles apart from land tenure.

Dispatch 6 March 1841: Before a title of nobility may devolve to a cadet, all senior heirs must cede their rights to him formally. This applies, for example, to the fifty year-old son of a ninety year-old man who has inherited a title from a recently-deceased elder brother. A rescript of 5 August 1843 specifies that the cadets referred to must be adults to be able to renounce their hereditary rights.

Rescript 4 March 1843: Any citizen of the Kingdom must obtain royal permission to accept a foreign title of nobility. (In 1817, a similar policy was decreed regarding foreign knighthoods.)

Rescript 2 December 1843: Addressing a circular issued (in error) by the Royal Commission for Titles of Nobility on 28 September in a specific case (a marquisate created in 1829), clarifies that titles so created devolve through male descendants in the direct, agnatic line, not through female collaterals.

Decree 11 May 1848 (number 15): Reorganizes court administration and *Royal Commission for Titles of Nobility* under Prime Minister (President of the Council of Ministers).

NOBILITY

Rescript 20 May 1851: Recognizes ancestral nobility of families of the civic nobility in cities (such as Salerno) where the patriciates of historic jurisdictional districts have been closed to new admissions since 1800.

Rescript 22 September 1852: Sicilian titles of ancient creation pass to direct descendants rather than to collaterals.

Rescript 29 July 1853: Clarifies that, in cases of female succession in the absence of male heirs, devolution is always based on seniority of age, and that the titles devolve to the legitimate heiresses who would have succeeded under the feudal system.

Rescript 10 September 1855: Establishes clearly that adopted children may not succeed to the ranks of nobility of their adoptive parents.

Rescript 11 October 1855: Establishes that in-laws and other kin through marriage (affines) may not succeed to titles of nobility as if they were heirs by blood.

Rescript 13 February 1856: Clarifies that the law abolishing feudalism in the Kingdom of Naples (in 1806 during the Napoleonic occupation) did not apply to the Kingdom of Sicily, where the constitution abolished feudal land tenure in 1812.

Rescript 15 October 1857: Establishes that serving as Justice of the Great Court (a supreme court) does not ennoble *ipso facto*.

Rescript 19 December 1857: Establishes that only the officers of the Royal Secretariat of State and their descendants are to be ennobled *ipso facto*.

Nobiliary Creations January 1861: Patents of nobility issued at Gaeta during the siege were to take effect upon the return of King Francis II to Naples.

CARMINI FIMIANI

IN REG. NEAP. ARCHIGYMNASIO
PRIMAR. ANTECESSOR.

COMMENTARIOLVS
DE SVBFEVDIS
EX IVRE LONGOBARDICO
ET NEAPOLITANO

IN DVAS PARTES TRIBVTVS.

Adneſtitur Catalogus Baronum Regni Neapolitani
fub Gulielmo II. Rege conditus pro expeditione
ad Terram Sanctam, adnotationibus paſſim
inſtructus, quo ſolida iuris feudalis pa-
trii principia confirmantur, dete-
guntur, illuſtrantur.

NEAPOLI MDCCLXXXVII.
EX TYPOGRAPHIA SIMONIANA.

Catalogus Baronum published in Naples in 1787

Appendix 4
HERALDRY

The term *heraldry* originally referred to the various functions of court officers known as *heralds* and particularly the field of *armory*, the study of coats of arms, designs painted on knights' shields.

The field of heraldry is a "science" (methodology) having its own rules and conventions. This is merely an introduction.

Heraldry, as we understand it today, originated with the decoration of shields (escutcheons) around the middle of the twelfth century, when knights, their faces concealed by helmets, sought a means of identifying themselves in combat or during tournaments.

As trusted — and unarmed — officials outside the military hierarchy, medieval heralds were sometimes pressed into service as diplomats or even royal messengers, and in Great Britain they still have ceremonial court functions. Such esteem was not universal; some early records list the names of heralds alongside those of minstrels.

The colorful designs on knights' shields were repeated on embroidered surcoats, hence the term "coat of arms," and by 1200 heraldic signets (seals) bearing these designs were not uncommon. Like surnames (initially an aristocratic perquisite), these "heraldic" designs soon became hereditary, passed from father to son, and this explains the connection of heraldry to genealogy. They became a mark of gentility and nobility, and in time they were regulated by royal authority to prevent abuse and usurpation, though the rulers of Naples and Sicily were more concerned with the abuse of feudal rights than with coats of arms.

In an age of widespread illiteracy, a coat of arms was a personal logo, a kind of hereditary trademark. It was also an ensign of the bearer's social status as well as knighthood past or present. By the end of the Middle Ages, a certain snobbery was attached to the bearing and use of a coat of arms, but this changed when virtually anybody could design his own or appropriate that of somebody else, usually with impunity, a situation commonplace by the end of the nineteenth century. In some countries, such as Switzerland and the Netherlands, burghers eventually assumed coats of arms as familial insignia

Coats of arms appeared widely on coins and seals, as well as architecture. Western European cities are full of heraldry.

There is no known contemporary evidence that the Hautevilles actually used the coat of arms later attributed to them. The first King of Sicily known to use a coat of arms was Henry VI of Hohenstaufen, Holy Roman Emperor.[101]

Heraldic records traditionally took two forms. Rolls of arms were scrolls of vellum or parchment depicting the shields of numerous knights. Armories were written records in which shields were identified in a prescribed language called *blazon*.

Medieval coats of arms were often "canted" for surnames, representing them symbolically as a kind of rebus. The Grifeo family displayed a griffon (figure 5 in the following drawings), the Leone a lion, the Chiaramonte, literally "light mountain," three white mountains (figure 2), Oliveri an olive tree (figure 9). Bearing simple geometric designs such as wide stripes (known as ordinaries), symbols such as stars or animals (called charges) or canting references to surnames, the oldest coats of arms are the simplest and most aesthetic.

The bend (figure 7), a diagonal stripe covering a third of the shield, probably originated as the most elementary form, easily painted with minimal artistic skill. The chevron (figure 8) finds its origin in the tracing of the lines of the shield's reinforcing struts.

Heraldry, of course, has its own rules. There are seven principal colors or tinctures: red (gules in English or *rosso* in Italian), blue (azure, azzurro), black (sable, nero), green (vert, verde), purple (purpure, porpora), gold (or, oro) and silver (argent, argento). The last two, known as "metals," are often rendered (respectively) in yellow ochre or white; the remaining tinctures are sometimes called *colors* or *enamels*. Of these, purpure is rare in Italian heraldry. There are also various *furs,* patterns bearing medieval names, with vair and ermine the most common, while the rarer scaly (representing fish scales rather than animal fur) appears, if rarely, in Italian and French heraldry.

A Rule of Tincture dictates that metal may not be placed on metal or enamel upon enamel, but this does not apply to small details or to objects rendered as "proper" in their natural colors. Hatching, a system of lines and dots, is used to represent tinctures where it is not possible to show color images.

If an armiger inherited coats of arms from more than one ancestor, these might be displayed in "quarters" on the same shield. The coat of arms of the House of the Two Sicilies, which became the insignia of the kingdom, consists of complex "quarterings" that Charles III inherited from various ancestors, and his pretension to certain realms, such as the Kingdom of Jerusalem (claimed by the kings of Naples and Sicily from their medieval predecessor Frederick II). It is shown at the end of this appendix and also on the title page of this book.

Escutcheons

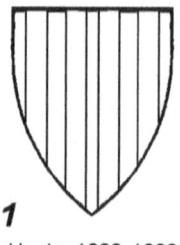

1 Heater 1200-1800 **2** "Sicilian" 1300-1550 **3** Sannitico 1700-1900

Armigerous Families

4 Leone **5** Griffeo **6** Ventimiglia

Blazon and Hatching

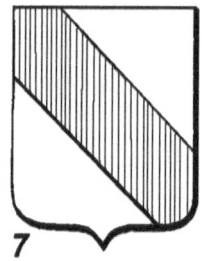

7 Argent a bend gules

8 Azure 3 stars argent between a chevron or

9 Azure an olive tree fructed proper on a chief or an eagle displayed sable

10 Achievement of Arms

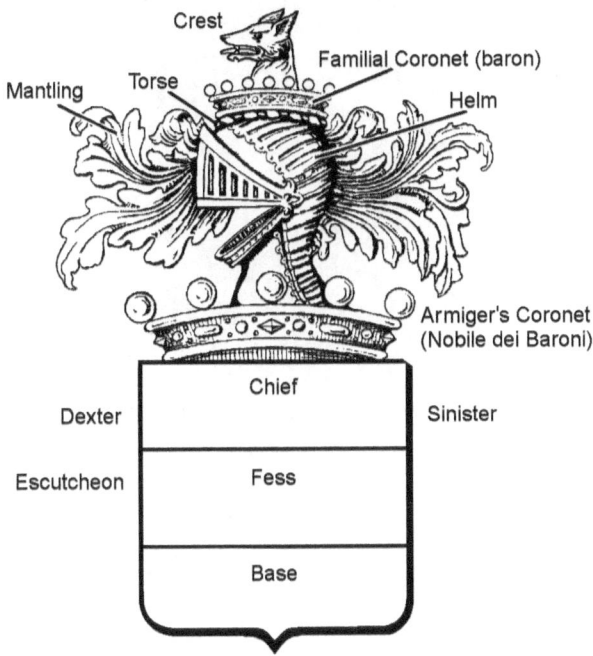

11 Tinctures and Furs

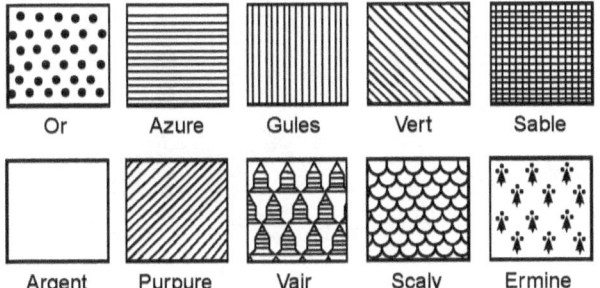

Shields Before Heraldry

Copper follaris of Roger I struck at Messina

Norman knights in a capital in Monreale's cloister

Two Sicilies Coat of Arms
Quarterings and Arms of Pretension

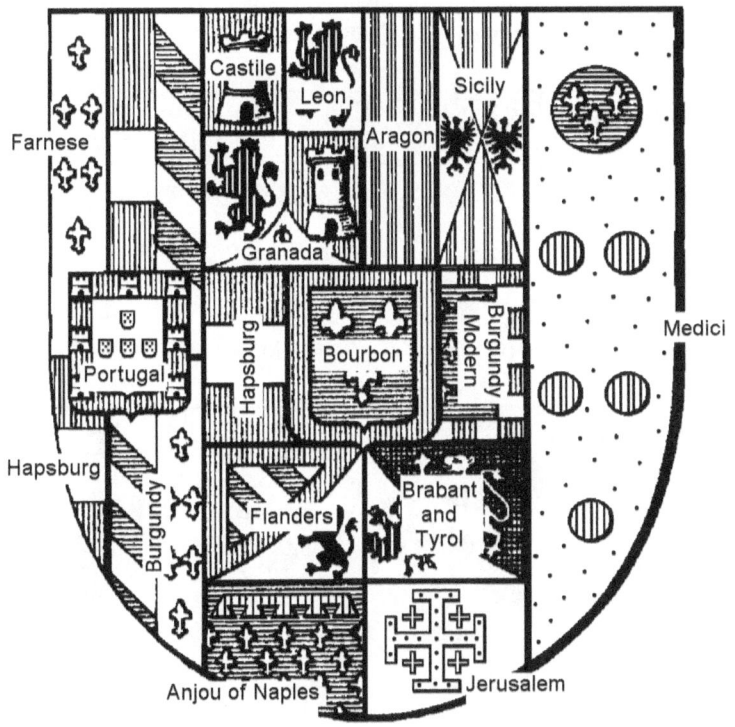

The coat of arms of Naples and Sicily beginning with the reign of Charles de Bourbon (later Charles III of Spain) in 1734. This was the coat of arms used in the Kingdom of the Two Sicilies until its demise in 1861.

THE KINGDOM OF THE TWO SICILIES

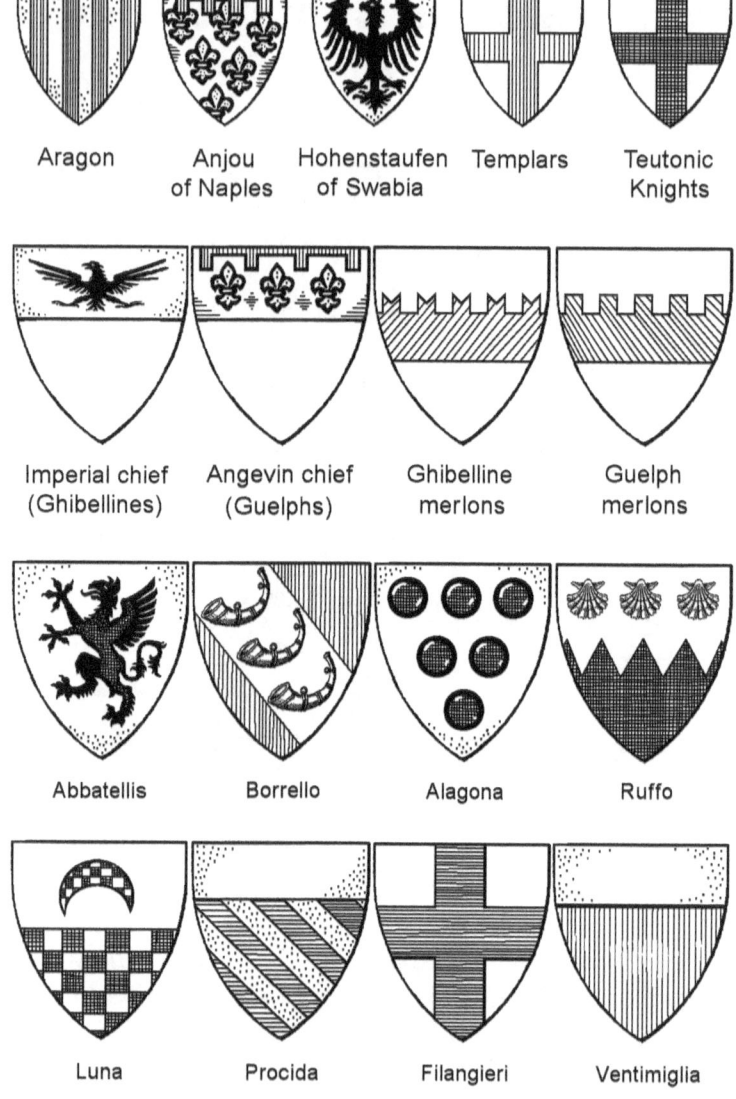

Appendix 5
COINAGE

The coinage of the Kingdom of the Two Sicilies was standardized in 1816 with the unification of the kingdoms of Naples and Sicily. Naturally, the intrinsic value of gold and silver coinage was linked to international trading. Except, arguably, for copper coins, there was no "fiat" currency, and even copper had value as a metal. The kingdom, like other states, used gold and silver as the basis for determining monetary value and wealth. Banknotes, which took many forms (some were issued by private banks), were backed by actual coinage.

Even though some of these coins share the names of those minted in other kingdoms, they are unique to the Two Sicilies and should not be confused with foreign coinage. The monetary system in place in the Two Sicilies cannot be compared directly to what existed elsewhere.

The royal decree establishing the monetary system of the kingdom was issued at Portici on 20 April 1818 (number 1176). Naturally, this set forth standards and tolerances in metal purity and sizes of the various coins. It also clarified the substitution of the coinage of the kingdoms of Naples and Sicily, and the coins minted by the Napoleonic government of Naples during the recent occupation.

The standard unit of measurement was the *ducat*. Although its name was based on that of a silver coin instituted by King Roger II in 1140, the ducat of the Kingdom of the Two Sicilies was never an actual coin but simply a means to gauge the value and quantity of currency in accounting. This replaced the Neapolitan *ducat* and the Sicilian *piastra*.

In the decree of 1818, the ducat was established as a measurement of silver weighing 23 grams, assuming a purity of over 83 percent for coinage.

The notation used in accounting was based on traditional Neapolitan measurements of the ducat, *grana* ("grain") and *cavallo,* sometimes called the *callo.* By way of example, the figure 3:52:6 indicates 3 ducats, 52 grana and 6 cavalli (or calli). Six cavalli were equal to a full *tornese.* The last figure (in this example 6), could only be 3, 6 or 9.

This system was obviously complex because the units of measurement used in accounting and taxation differed somewhat from the actual coinage in circulation. The crown possessed an extensive reserve of gold that was never minted into coinage. In 1860, this gold reserve exceeded that of all the other pre-unitary Italian states combined (even if the exact quantity of the reserves of the Papal State is open to question). Despite its greater wealth, more extensive territory and larger population, the Kingdom of the Two Sicilies does not seem to have had more circulating coinage than the other Italian states, and barter was not uncommon for simple daily transactions.

The tornese was a copper coin roughly comparable to a modern penny or pence, except that it was minted in a range of sizes. It was issued in denominations of one-half, one, one and one-half, two, three, four, five, eight and ten. Two tornesi were equal to one grana. The ten-tornesi coin was 37 millimeters in diameter, while the one-tornese coin was 19 millimeters.

There were several silver coins. The *piastra* (not its official name) was 37 millimeters in diameter in its highest denomination; this was worth 120 grana or 200 tornesi. The *mezza piastra* was worth 60 grana, the *tarì* (its name based on that of a small gold coin used in the Middle Ages) 20 grana, and the *carlino* 10 grana.

The rare gold coins were usually called simply *oro* or even *onze* (here again a medieval term), but sometimes *piastre d'oro.* These were minted in denominations of 30, 15, 6 and 3 ducats.

Among the populace, the 120-grana silver piastra was not widely circulated, nor were the gold coins.

The coat of arms of the Two Sicilies (described at the end of the previous appendix) appeared in a slightly modified form on the reverse of the silver piastra shown here.

The photographs of coins accompanying this text are not shown in their relative scale.

COINAGE

Silver piastra of Ferdinand II in 120 grana

10 tornesi of Francis I   *2 tornesi of Francis II*

Coins are not shown to their actual scale

1½ tornese of Ferdinand II

30 ducat onza (piastra d'oro) of Ferdinand II

THE KINGDOM OF THE TWO SICILIES

"Scyphate" ducat of Roger II

"Lion's face" follaris of William II

Fatimid tarì   Tarì of Roger II

Appendix 6
MILESTONES 1735-1860

The territory of the former Two Sicilies *circa* 1862 had a population of some seven million, with 3,216 students enrolled in its public universities, almost half the Italian national total (excluding the city of Rome) of 7,957. Piedmont-Sardinia, with a population of 4.2 million, had far fewer university students *per capita*.

An interesting list of "firsts" was presented in Michele Vocino's *Primati del Regno di Napoli* (1950).

Herewith, posthumous plaudits to a semi-forgotten country in the form of a list of noteworthy achievements in the Kingdom of the Two Sicilies relative to the other pre-unitary Italian states.

- First pension system in Italy (2 percent deduction from salaries),
- Most printing presses of any Italian city (Naples with 113),
- Lowest commercial and personal taxes in Italy,
- Largest international commercial bank in Italy (de Rothschild in Naples),
- Largest naval yards based on number of employees (1900 in Castellammare di Stabia),
- Largest iron and steel engineering-manufacturing plant in Italy (at Pietrarsa),
- Largest iron casting foundry in Italy (Ferdinandea in Calabria),
- Oldest continuously-active opera house in Europe, the San Carlo in Naples (1737, rebuilt in 1816),
- Largest porcelain factory in Italy (Capodimonte, 1743),

- Largest royal residence in Italy (Caserta, 1752),
- First university chair/department in economics (Antonio Genovesi, Naples, 1754),
- First *public* botanical gardens in Italy (opened in Palermo in 1795); others were private or scholastic,
- Dwarf planet Ceres first observed (Giuseppe Piazzi, Palermo, 1801),
- First modern paved carriageway in Italy (Piana-Palermo, 1810),
- First steamship in the Mediterranean, the Ferdinando I (1818),
- First welfare program for the poor and unemployed (1831),
- First glass recycling program (1832),
- First steel suspension bridge in Italy (Gagliano River in 1832, components from Mongiana Works),
- First gas-fueled public lighting system (1839),
- First railroad in Italy (Naples-Portici, 1839),
- First seismic observatory in the world (Vesuvius 1841),
- First steamboat with screw propulsion in the Mediterranean (the Giglio delle Onde 1847),
- First functioning electric telegraph in Italy (1852),
- Ranked 3rd country in the world for industrial development (1st in Italy) by Paris International Exhibition (1856),
- First adhesive postage stamps in Italy (1857),
- First submarine telegraph in Europe,
- First military steamship in Italy (the Ercole),
- First maritime code in Italy,
- First public housing complex/estate in Italy, 1778 (San Leucio near Caserta),
- Highest per capita number of physicians in Italy (1850-1860),
- First *public* school for the deaf in Italy (Naples, 1788); school founded in Rome in 1784 was private,
- Lowest infant mortality rate in Italy (1850-1860).

Appendix 7
HISTORIOGRAPHY

What researchers usually refer to as *historiography* may be defined loosely as "the history of history." It includes, among other things, the body of research by scholars who have studied sources such as documents contemporary to the events they describe, as well as the work of peers. The *historical method* is based on the scientific method, a reading of *all* the available data, not a selective interpretation of *some* of it. Accurate historical writing relies upon solid epistemology, ontology and evidentiary standards. Unfortunately, these were often absent in Italy after 1860, when officialdom and academia sought to impose certain historical narratives upon the populace in the interest of keeping the country unified.

Most of the original sources for the Two Sicilies and its dynasty are found in Italy, with a few in Spain, particularly at major archives and libraries in Naples, Palermo, Bari, Messina, the Vatican, Parma, Madrid and Simancas. With the exception of very specific information, the most essential facts are readily available or have become part of "common knowledge."

In these pages the author, while acknowledging the contributions of serious scholars, gives pride of place to contemporaneous records rather than "secondary" commentaries written long after the facts they describe.

Despite certain documents "disappearing," a surprising amount of this information was consultable in Italian archives, albeit sometimes in rather biased, intentionally derogatory, accounts such as Vincenzo Maggiorani's description of the Sicilian revolt of 1866 (see note 88). Contemporary accounts of the Siege of Gaeta in 1861 had been recorded and a few, such as those of Pietro Quandel and Charles Garnier, had been published, if not very widely distributed.

Yet very few publishers in Italy were willing to risk censorship by publishing major books on the Two Sicilies until after the fall of the Kingdom of Italy.

The collective attempt to suppress a general diffusion of information regarding the history of the Two Sicilies was never so sophisticated as a "cover-up" or conspiracy, even if it occasionally bore the marks of such phenomena. Here several forces were at work.

Ghibellines and Guelphs

The first blow was delivered during the Middle Ages. The defeat of the last Hohenstaufens, at the battles of Benevento in 1266 and Tagliacozzo in 1268, signalled the end of the multicultural golden age of the Kingdom of Sicily. By 1300, the victorious dynasty, the House of Anjou, which had lost Sicily during the War of the Vespers in 1282, was suppressing Islam at Lucera, the last major Muslim community in Italy.

With the defeat of the Ghibellines who had supported the Hohenstaufens as Holy Roman Emperors, the rival Guelphs of northern Italy redoubled their efforts to denigrate that dynasty, something seen in the work of Dante and Boccaccio. Such tropes became ingrained in Italian literary culture, where they generally went unchallenged. Whereas Sicilian had once been the most important literary language in Italy, Tuscan took its place, eventually making inroads even in Sicily. As the Renaissance enveloped the regions north of Naples, the south embraced this significant movement somewhat belatedly.

Unification

During the nineteenth century, the *Risorgimento,* or "rebirth," sought to rekindle the spirit of the Renaissance. The philosophical facet of these lofty efforts can be traced to 1800, if not earlier, but the chief political objective of the *Risorgimento* was the unification of Italy, a movement with which the word has become synonymous. Its greatest impetus came from proponents in Tuscany and then other regions.

An underlying — if often unstated — aspect of the *Risorgimento,* if not the subsequent political unification movement, was that "Italians" were already "united" culturally. As stated in the Introduction, this presupposition was, at best, only partially correct. Owing to history, the Sicilians, for example, had more in common with the Catalonians than with the Ligurians.

Beyond the essential concept of an ethnie, a cultural identity presupposes a commonality of historical traditions and a vernacular language. Together, these elements and others work to form an individual's self-concept (self-identity).

As we have seen, during the middle of the nineteenth century parts of northern Italy were painted as "progressive" or "liberal" while the Papal State and the Two Sicilies were represented as repressive or reactionary. Following the unification, it was deemed necessary to dispel anything that might challenge this notion, a phenomenon described in this volume's Introduction and in Chapter 8.

The most obvious strategy was simple censorship. While a professor in Italy might publish an article on Frederick II in an academic journal such as the *Archivio Storico Siciliano,* a major biography with wide distribution was out of the question because it would probably remind southerners of our glorious medieval past. Schools taught a revised version of history, both medieval and modern. Very recent history was especially problematic.

The fact that the seeds of Garibaldi's invasion were planted by Piedmont and nurtured by Britain was conveniently omitted from the historical narrative. Despite her kinship to the kings of the new country, saintly Maria Cristina of Savoy, the first wife of Ferdinand II and mother of his deposed son Francis II, was studiously ignored so that less attention might be directed to the Two Sicilies and its dynasty in the popular mind.

The use of "regional" languages like Neapolitan, Sicilian and Friulian was officially discouraged. In a propagandistic claim divorced from reality, such languages were disparaged as "dialects" of Italian, which is essentially a modern form of Tuscan. There are uncanny parallels with fascist Spain, where Catalan and other tongues were suppressed in public life.

Later, the arrival of Fascism saw the teaching of English banned in Italy's public schools, a policy whose dire effects stretched into the last decade of the twentieth century, when the nation still suffered a dearth of English teachers, the education ministry advocating French instead.

Even before the advent of Fascism, the paranoia of the unitary state knew no bounds. Following the death of her husband in 1894, Maria Sophia, the exiled Queen of the Two Sicilies, was said to be recruiting mercenaries and planning a major coup d'état. Misinformation campaigns of this kind were much less successful outside Italy, where the press could publish accurate reports about such events as the humiliating military defeat at Adwa in 1896, a fact that led to the nation's army being ridiculed for the next half-century. Within Italy, failures such as Adwa may have been the motivation for somebody actually believing that even a widow living abroad could muster enough military might to defeat the less-than-competent Italian army.

As we have seen, a number of persistent myths colored certain negative perceptions about southern Italy during and immediately after the Two Sicilies era, to around 1900. Though these clichés did not all emanate explicitly from political propaganda, they were largely a result of life in the united Italy as a certain bias against the south became normal in a state whose leadership class was dominated by northerners. In the wake of the unification war, literacy, at around twenty-five percent, was constant throughout Italy; it was not significantly higher or lower in the south.[102]

It seems that *per capita* income was likewise about equal throughout Italy. (Reliably measuring either statistic is difficult.) Before unification, and for some years afterward, most Italian emigration was from the north, not the south; this changed by around 1880. Organized crime worsened following unification as poverty became more prevalent in the south due to governmental policies that, by comparison, favored the north; at the same time, southerners grew ever more doubtful of the ability of the state and its police to defend them.

Before unification, the Two Sicilies was at least marginally more industrial than Tuscany and Piedmont.

Arguably, the Two Sicilies was no more reactionary, suppressive or censorious than these other states, yet the south came to be identified with every conceivable social ill. As we have seen, the very word "south" is relative, for there was no north or south of Italy (except as a peninsula) until there was an Italy.

In recent decades, Italy's warped historiography has been described by historians, especially foreigners such as Denis Mack Smith (see note 18), infamously despised by the Fascist apologist Renzo De Felice. Due to the government's control of relevant information, this was not possible until the fall of the Kingdom of Italy. Even today, access to certain records regarding, for example, the Italian invasion and occupation of Ethiopia (1936-1941), is restricted. Much documentation has simply disappeared. Italy has nothing like a freedom of information act; in the humanities and social science the Italian academy is characterized by clientelism, favoritism and nepotism, with little transparency or meritocracy (see note 68).

As we have seen, the Italian government censored unflattering depictions of the Fascist regime decades after the end of the Second World War (see note 11).

Disunification

The first official political blow to the concept of a united Italy came in May 1946 when its last king, Umberto II, signed the decree making Sicily an autonomous region. This implicit recognition of the fact that Sicily had once been a sovereign kingdom was instigated by the Americans occupying the country, who were acting not out of Bourbonist sentiment but in response to a growing separatist movement. Despite the liberators' noble intentions, this localized authority eventually added extra *strata* of bureaucracy, expense and inefficiency to the function of government in the largest of Italy's twenty political regions.

The dissolution of the Kingdom of Italy the next month set the stage for democracy and a more balanced examination of national history. Even so, the presence in the academy of formerly-Fascist professors made for a laggard evolution. For example, Francesco Cognasso, a sycophant known for his fawning histories of the House of Savoy, ensured that a Jewish colleague at the University of Turin was not reinstated to his former post as a tenured professor following the war. Such behavior was not unusual, nor was it, by then, characteristic of any single region.

In the wake of the Second World War, Italy found herself as divided as ever, perhaps even more so — north and south, left and right, secular and Catholic, rich and poor. So fragile was the new state politically that the realities of the imminent Cold War discouraged placing the previous few decades, much less the very unification that formed the country, under a magnifying glass that might highlight its shortcomings. There was, after all, the very real possibility of a communist faction gaining enough power to place Italy's support of NATO in jeopardy. Exposing the true evils of Fascism, the lost war, and attendant consequences like the mass rape of southern Italian women by Moroccan troops, might drive otherwise centrist citizens farther to the left. Nobody in the government wanted to admit publicly that these things had occurred, or that the referendum ousting the Savoyard monarchy had most likely been rigged (see note 8).

Fascism, which in the end endorsed the monarchy and of course the nationalist mythos, enhanced the unitarian narrative. For example, the school texts and the *Enciclopedia Italiana,* a tool of Fascism, proclaimed a friend of Giuseppe Garibaldi to be the "true" inventor of the telephone despite dubious historicity and the failure of the kings of Italy to lend much support to the tenuous claim of hapless Antonio Meucci while he was alive.

To this day, Italian schools teach very little about the Second World War or Fascism as part of the official national curriculum (though this is gradually improving as the wartime generation goes to its reward), nor do they confront the misinformation about the national unification movement. They still teach that an Italian invented the telephone.

The apathetic reactions of most Italians to the celebrations marking the sesquicentennial of unification in 2011 are indicative of a wider skepticism about what has been promoted as history.

"In the name of the Italian Republic, I apologize to you for what happened here," said a former prime minister to the people assembled in the town square of Pontelandolfo on August fourteenth of that year. In this town, a hundred and fifty years earlier, the ancestors of these people were subjected to days of rape, pillage and murder by the troops sent from Piedmont to "liberate" the citizens from the Two Sicilies dynasty. The pretext for these atrocities was a reprisal visited upon the townsfolk for allegedly collaborating with "brigands," armed partisans defending the king who had reigned until being deposed in an undeclared war. So atrocious was the Piedmontese attack on unarmed civilians at Pontelandolfo that it was even condemned by some Piedmontese politicians.

Despite being omitted from most history books, it was never entirely forgotten, and these citizens, like many in Italy, had refused to celebrate the unification (see note 12).

Revisionism

The telling of history should be as complete as possible, not merely selective. Confirmation bias should be strenuously avoided.[103]

Work published in Italy about the unification movement and subsequent history is improving in its depth, scholarship and objectivity. Yet in our times we still find that foreign historians, especially those having journalistic or multidisciplinary backgrounds, sometimes seem more willing than Italians to expose the nation's warts. For example, one of the finest studies of the shortcomings of Italian rape law was written by an American legal scholar and published in English, though in recent years Italian women have begun to write about the subject, and about Italian women's issues generally.[104]

Nowadays, the majority of Italy's most rabid unificationist, or anti-

Neapolitan, apologists fall into several broad categories. Most (like your author until the incident recounted in the Prologue) are simply misinformed, perhaps indoctrinated by what they were taught in school. Many, especially Italians raised in the northern part of the country, have fallen prey to credence in stereotypes, clichés, regionalist self-interest or political propaganda.

The achievements of fugitives from Fascism, such as Enrico Fermi, Emilio Segré, Arturo Toscanini, Umberto Nobile and Maria Montessori, are recognized in the national history taught to young Italians, but so are those of Fascists like Guglielmo Marconi, Luigi Pirandello and Italo Balbo.

Some of the facts presented in this book are based on the very simple principle of *res ipsa loquitor* (the facts speak for themselves). This includes, for example, the attitudes, or mentalities, of citizens noted in the Introduction, and the comments about the plebiscite of 1860, which counted more voters than there were.

In the words of Adam Zamoyski:

The stirring myth of the Risorgimento, the rebirth that allegedly brought about the unification of Italy and the creation of the Italian state in the mid-nineteenth century, has been definitively exploded by historians over the past couple of decades.[105]

Not every historian is as astute as Mr Zamoyski, whose family married into the House of the Two Sicilies.[106] As your author has occasionally been called upon by editors to peer review papers and other work intended for publication in academic journals, he has been afforded a close view of the field. To those of us working in the scholarly sphere, it is overwhelmingly obvious that what is published in the academy differs from many "popular" or "trade" publications intended for a general readership. For example, John Julius Norwich's book on the history of Sicily, published in 2015, parrots many clichés about Garibaldi and the unification movement which one is less likely to encounter in the work of specialized academics; indeed, he seems to have ignored much research published in the two decades immediately preceding publication of his work.

Back in the 1980s, the author of the book you are reading was one of just a handful of scholars to challenge the tropes that had tainted the teaching of Italian history for more than a century. It has been gratifying to be joined by others having similar research interests.

That having been said, what emanates from academia is sometimes far from perfect, occasionally given to revisionism for its own sake.[107]

Caveat Lector

The environment of the academy is increasingly competitive, with ever more specialized papers and monographs written by professors, or aspiring professors (the job market for full professorships in social science and humanities is abysmal), zealously seeking to distinguish themselves in extremely crowded disciplines, fields and sub-fields. As a result, "originality" often takes precedence over reality.

Year by year, ever more arcane, subjective, imaginative theories and theses are published about subjects ranging from the Normans in Italy to the poetry of Dante to Italian unification, some being revisionist merely for the sake of revisionism or to draw attention to themselves as originative amongst much competing work.

In the preceding chapters, your author has resisted the temptation to respond to such theories, preferring instead to present essential information on the subject at hand. Though some of it is quite good, the more "analytical" work published during the present century regarding medieval and modern Italy should be viewed with a critical eye, considering its objectives and factors such as its conformity to movements that include, among others, deconstructionism and post-modernism (as explicated by Michel Foucault, Jacques Derrida and scholars of like mind whose principles may be perfectly valid in other contexts).

In many cases, this concerns broad distinctions between "political" and "social" history. Often, however, it reflects little more than what has been noted here.

Broadly speaking, there are two "personal" categories of Italophile scholars who write about the history of the Italian south: the "insiders" privileged with ancestral connections to our kingdoms, perhaps having been raised in southern Italy speaking Neapolitan or Sicilian, and the "outsiders," foreigners who cultivate a xenocentric interest in a place and culture foreign to them and their ancestors. In that context, Lombards or Tuscans having no roots in the former Two Sicilies are "foreigners."

Among the most glaring shortcomings of certain native Italian historians are the extremist politics that often color their views; Benedetto Croce, for example, was a fickle Fascist, and Rosario Villari, who came later, was a rabid communist, though both were southerners. Croce's work was not devoid of merit, but the Italian academy needs more centrists. There is rather little "social" history in the Italian academy.

Beyond Italian borders, a history professor born and educated in Italy may be unwilling, when lecturing non-Italians, to speak ill of the nation of her birth, hence her reluctance to address many shortcomings of recent historiography which might be considered "embarrassing." This can foster ambivalence.

It is also quite possible for a professor born, raised and educated in Lombardy or Piedmont to lack much firsthand knowledge of the regions south of Rome. Whereas Sicilians, out of necessity, speak Italian because it is the national language, very few northerners speak Sicilian (the exceptions being some of those raised in Sicilian families that migrated to Milan or Turin).

Conversely, not every foreign scholar specialized in Italian studies is very objective. Some are indeed quite condescending while others simply don't know Italy, in all its intricacies, well enough to write about it very cogently. Some, having received scholarships, subventions or other largesse to study in what, to them, is a foreign country that welcomes them as guests, may not wish to "offend" their hosts by desecrating the altar of Italian unification, as if the existence of a southern kingdom since 1130 could be defined by a movement born around 1800.

A foreigner's lack of sufficient familiarity with our social culture (i.e. with Italian society itself) can lead to serious misconceptions, as when Christopher Duggan, an Englishman, concluded that the Mafia was an idea but not an organization. Your author was a few blocks away from Judge Paolo Borsellino when that magistrate was killed in Palermo by a huge bomb set off by the Mafia in the summer of 1992; the blast was deafening. It is utterly ridiculous to tell Sicilians that the Mafia is not a form of organized crime or that Garibaldi was a "hero."

Often, non-Italians (and even some Italians) simply fail to grasp Italy's regional differences. Outside Italy, very few academic programs, even at the graduate level, adequately consider "regional" (actually national) cultures pre-1860 except perhaps for those of places such as Tuscany (i.e. Dante, the Renaissance, etc.) although, as stated earlier, there is a growing interest in such topics as the Norman Kingdom of Sicily and Angevin Naples. It was truly bizarre that no book quite like the author's *Sicilian Studies* was published in English until 2018 to aid professors teaching undergraduate courses.

These arcane complexities need not concern the reader at length, but they should be borne in mind when evaluating the quality of the work and the opinions voiced by foreign scholars, and even some Italians.

As we have seen, the history of the Two Sicilies is inextricably linked to the identity of its people, and it is more complex than many imagine.

Rivelo (tax census) of 1756 recorded in Sicilian and Tuscan

NOTES

1. The author refers to the first *major* histories on subjects of significance to the identity of the ethnie when it has a written language. For the people of *Magna Graecia,* the territory destined to become the Kingdom of the Two Sicilies, these were being written even before the time of Diodorus Siculus, a Siceliot historian who died around 30 BC (BCE). By comparison, the lost *Bella Germaniae* of Pliny the Elder and the *Germania* of Tacitus (the latter never set foot in the German lands) were ethnographies written by foreigners. The observation that an ethnie writes its own history is not meant to imply that in our globalized era "outsiders" should be discouraged from writing about subjects that interest them outside their own countries (e.g. the many non-Italian Italophiles who study the work of Dante), but it is natural for the initial work published on a significant historical or cultural topic to be written by somebody *within* the society itself. For example, the first published history of the Kingdom of Sicily was written by Thomas Fazello, a Sicilian, in 1558, long before foreigners began writing about it, while Neapolitans such as Cornelio Vitignano and Angelo di Costanzo wrote about the Kingdom of Naples. The first biography of Elizabeth I of England (1533-1603) was written not by a foreigner but by William Camden, one of her subjects. The first biography of Margaret of Sicily (1135-1183) was written by Jacqueline Alio, a Sicilian descended from the queen's subjects. There are persuasive socio-cultural reasons for people to write their own history; Catholics, Muslims and Jews, for example, may understand certain aspects of their own religious practices better than persons raised in other faiths. Xenocentric scholarship (scholars writing at length about societies that are not their own) sometimes gives rise to complexities when subtleties of the culture being studied are not carefully considered. For an example of a debate see Freeman, Derek, *The Fateful Hoaxing of Margaret Mead: A Historical Analysis of Her Samoan Research* (1999), which was dutifully challenged in Shankman, Paul, *The Trashing of Margaret Mead: Anatomy of an Anthropological Controversy* (2009). For the medieval Kingdom of Sicily see Matthew, Donald, "Modern Study of the Norman Kingdom of Sicily," *Reading Medieval Studies,* volume 18 (1992), pages 34-56 (specifically page 37): "If we became aware of foreign authors regularly selecting a chunk of English history, such as the Civil War, and not bothering with what came before or after, I think we would likely feel entitled to point out the importance of studying problems in their proper context. We might also, as Englishmen, I think, rather wonder at, even resent, perhaps, for-

eigners meddling with our history and wonder about their motives for doing so." For commentary on xenocentrism as a wider phenomenon see Schulman, Sarah, "White Writer," *The New Yorker* (21 October 2016); de Waal, Kit, "Don't dip your pen in someone else's blood: Writers and 'the other,'" *The Irish Times* (30 June 2018); Balakrishnan, Anjana, and Cleveland, Mark, "Appreciating versus Venerating Cultural Outgroups: The Psychology of Cosmopolitanism and Xenocentrism," *International Marketing Review*, volume 36, number 3 (May 2019), pages 416-444; Magner, Denise, "When Whites Teach Black Studies," *The Chronicle of Higher Education* (1 December 1993); Young, James (editor), *The Ethics of Cultural Appropriation* (2012).

2. For an insightful analysis of the concept of a continuum of group identity from the Middle Ages, see Davies, Rees, "Nations and National Identities in the Medieval World: An Apologia," *Belgisch Tijdschrift voor Nieuwste Geschiedenis: Revue belge d'historie contemporaine,* volume 34, number 4 (2004), pages 567-577. See also the introduction and essays in Jensen, Lotte (editor), *The Roots of Nationalism: Identity Formation in Early Modern Europe 1600-1815* (2016). For one of many analyses regarding Italy, see Galasso, Giuseppe, "Appartenenze e identità dagli Stati preunitari alla nuova Italia," *La Nazione tra i Banchi* (2012), pages 24-36.

3. See Mendola, Louis, *Sicilian Genealogy and Heraldry* (2014), pages 204-206.

4. For a theory of Sicilian cultural and historical identity, see Correnti, Santi, *Storia di Sicilia come Storia del Popolo Siciliano* (seventh edition, Catania, 1995). More generally, Grimson, Alejandro, "Culture and Identity: Two Different Notions," *Social Identities,* volume 16, number 1 (2010), pages 61-77. Other relevant studies are Williams, Lynn, "National Identity and the Nation State: Construction, Reconstruction and Contradiction," *National Identity* (1999), pages 7-18; Smith, Anthony, "Chosen Peoples: Why ethnic groups survive," *Ethnic and Racial Studies,* volume 15, number 3 (1992), pages 436-456.

5. See Llobera, Josep, *Foundations of National Identity: From Catalonia to Europe* (2004); Balcells, Albert, *El Nacionalismo Catalán* (1991); Lledó-Guillem, Vicente, *The Making of Catalan Linguistic Identity in Medieval and Early Modern Times* (2018).

6. In English see Mendola, Louis, *Sicily's Rebellion against King Charles: The Story of the Sicilian Vespers* (2015), from which the translation in the Introduction is excerpted.

7. Figures reported by ISTAT, the Italian National Statistics Institute, for *Nati Vivi: Nati dentro e fuori dal matrimonio,* reported in 2018 and available online. In Italy nationally, 32 percent of all births were outside marriage. In selected regions we find Piedmont at 37 percent, Lombardy at 33 percent, Emilia-Romagna at 36 percent, Tuscany at 41 percent, Valle d'Aosta at 39 percent, Umbria at 35 percent, Campania at 22 percent, Puglia at 27 percent, Calabria at 21 percent, Sicily at 23 percent. The last legal distinctions between legitimate and "natural" children (those born outside marriage) were abolished by law number 154 on 28 December 2013, with compliance prescribed in the Italian Civil Code.

8. The referendum of 1946 is full of complexities. In Milan, for example, 68 percent of the vote favored the republic, while in Naples it was 21 percent and Palermo reported 39 percent; in Rome 49 percent chose the republic. The figures have always been dubious in any event. In *The Kingdom of Sicily 1130-1860,* the author reported that there were irregularities in the balloting. As just one example, Lieutenant Commander James C. Risk, an American naval officer stationed as an observer in Rome's Quirinal Palace, witnessed the *pro tempore* justice minister, a communist politician, enter with some armed men in the dead of night to tamper with some national ballot reports. Commander Risk recounted this episode to the author in 1992. No Italian commentator or historian, not even the right-wing (formerly Fascist) journalist Indro Montanelli (1909-2001), has ever written about the incident, which was absolutely unknown to Italians for almost seventy years. The Americans were reluctant to investigate this kind of infraction (reportedly widespread) because to do so might prompt the complete annulment of the referendum, thereby necessitating another balloting in an atmosphere of similar acrimony. The hapless citizenry was already bitterly divided in the war's aftermath; the occupiers wanted to finish the job and go home, and anyway the Americans favored a republic.

9. While the author begs to differ with some of its conclusions, this topic is addressed in Robert Putnam's *Making Democracy Work: Civic Traditions in Modern Italy* (1993). John Dickie's *Darkest Italy: The Nation and Stereotypes of the Mezzogiorno, 1860-1900* (1999) is a fine exposition; another is Nelson Moe's book, *The View from Vesuvius: Italian Culture and the Southern Question* (2002). Nicola Zitara's monograph, *L'Unita d'Italia: Nascita di Una Colonia* (1971), is also informative. *The Pursuit of Italy: A History of a Land, Its Regions, and Their Peoples* (2011), by David Gilmour, is a reasonably objective view

of Italy's regionalism based on centuries of history. See also the works mentioned in note 18.

10. For insightful overviews of formative ethnic identity during the Middle Ages, see Elliott, John, "A Europe of Composite Monarchies," *Past and Present,* volume 137, number 1 (November 1992), pages 48-71; Leyser, Karl, "Concepts of Europe in the Early and High Middle Ages," ibid, pages 25-47; Dunbabin, Jean, *France in the Making 843-1180* (1985, 2009); Ruddick, Andrea, *English Identity and Political Culture in the Fourteenth Century* (2013). Other works of interest are Armstrong, John, *Nations Before Nationalism* (1982); Davies, Norman, *Vanished Kingdoms* (2012).

11. Law number 66 of 15 February 1996. Historically, the rape of nuns and other unmarried women was outlawed in the Kingdom of Sicily by the legal codes of 1140 and 1231 (see notes 27 and 30); for the statute in the Kingdom of the Two Sicilies see *Codice per lo Regno delle Due Sicilie, Parte Seconda, Leggi Penali* (1819), sections 333-345, pages 82-85. Divorce was legalized in Italy only in 1970, and even then the law was contested, necessitating a referendum in 1974. For the simple form of separation (but not called "divorce") permitted until the dissolution of the Kingdom of the Two Sicilies, see *Codice per lo Regno delle Due Sicilie* (1848), pages 27-29. For a contemporary analysis of the statutes in the previous code, see Saverio Cangiano's *Lezioni di Diritto Positivo secondo il Codice per lo Regno delle Due Sicilie* (1841), part 1 (civil law), volume 1, pages 193-212. There was no specific legislation addressing homosexual activity in the Two Sicilies but the Sardinian penal code of 1859, reiterating a statute from 1839, outlawed it, and this made its way into the Italian code of 1889; see *Codice Penale per gli Stati di Sua Maestà il Re di Sardegna* (1859), section 425, pages 133-134. For additional comparisons among the Italian states, see Marco Soresina's *Italy Before Italy: Institutions, Conflicts and Political Hopes in the Italian States 1815-1860* (2020).

12. This is described in Appendix 7. For a contemporary report, see the *Corriere della Sera,* 14 August 2011, page 41, "Pontelandolfo, scuse per un massacro: il ricordo dei civili uccisi come rappresaglia contro i briganti 150 anni fa." See also Fraschetti, Mario, *Pontelandolfo e Casalduni Bruciano Ancora* (2019). The "official" reports compiled by the Piedmontese occupiers list a dozen or so deaths but do not report the rapes, beatings and torture. For crimes against humanity (and war crimes) committed by the Kingdom of Italy, and specifically the Royal Italian Army, in Africa and the Balkans during the twentieth century, see note 17.

13. The Italian army never actually defended the people of Italy. During the First World War, which Italy took months to contemplate entering, abandoning its alliance with Germany and Austria for the promise of territory made at the secret Treaty of London (26 April 1915), the Kingdom of Italy attacked its northern neighbor; though some battles were fought in Italian territory, this was a campaign of aggression. When the Allies invaded Sicily in July 1943, the Italian army offered what could, at best, be described as token resistance, leaving the bulk of the fighting to the Germans; at Santa Croce Camerina, for example, some 500 Italian troops surrendered without a shot being fired. Army and *carabinieri* units made no effort to defend Palermo; the only resistance to General Patton's advance on the largest Italian city south of Naples was made by a small German unit at a pillbox bunker outside Altofonte. Nevertheless, Alfredo Guzzoni's flight from Sicily is the kind of act that lives in infamy. Many books consider the war in Sicily. The best general histories are Carlo D'Este's *Bitter Victory: The Battle for Sicily, 1943* (1988) and Rick Atkinson's more recent entry, *The Day of Battle: The War in Sicily and Italy, 1943-1944* (2007). There are also more specialized studies and memoirs. A noteworthy analysis from the German perspective is *The Battle of Sicily: How the Allies Lost Their Chance for Total Victory* (2007), by Samuel Mitcham and Freidrich von Stauffenberg. Also of value are *Assault on Sicily: Monty and Patton at War* (2007) by Ken Ford, *Drop Zone Sicily* by William Breuer (1997) and *The Liberator: One World War II Soldier's 500-Day Odyssey from the Beaches of Sicily to the Gates of Dachau* (2012) by Alex Kershaw. *A History of Fascism 1914-1945* (1995), by Stanley Payne, is a fine overview. Philip Cannistraro's *Historical Dictionary of Fascist Italy* (1982) is a good reference. Revisionist "historians" writing in Italy have sought to portray the Americans as habitual war criminals based on isolated incidents of prisoners or civilians being shot, seeking to depict the few Italian soldiers who actually fought well as being indicative of the entire Italian army, though they clearly were not. Despite the records being publicly available at archives in the United States, it has even been claimed that the Americans somehow "concealed" information about these few incidents. In contrast, the Italian government has yet to unseal its records regarding many of its military actions in Ethiopia during the Fascist era, and indeed much of this information has been intentionally destroyed; Alcide De Gasperi, prime minister from 1945 to 1953 and a leader of the Christian Democrats, explicitly ordered archivists to refuse requests from Ethiopia for the relevant records on activities connected with Italian crimes against humanity. That is not the only dubious tactic to emanate from Italian offi-

cialdom. In the early years of the present century, Italy's motion in the United Nations to have the *Foibe* killings of Italian civilians in Istria (an occupied territory Italy lost after the war) by Yugoslav partisans from 1943 to 1945 recognized as war crimes was vehemently vetoed by Croatia and Slovenia, receiving no endorsement whatsoever from any permanent member of the Security Council; the Allied Military Government ceded control of Trieste to Italy and Yugoslavia only in 1954, the territorial division being formalized with the Treaty of Osimo in 1975.

14. In English, two sober histories of this period are *Italy and Its Monarchy* (1989) by Denis Mack Smith and *The Fall of the House of Savoy* (1972) by Robert Katz. It is noteworthy that Italy paid war reparations to several nations; the figures (in US dollars) are: $25 million to Ethiopia (principally "in kind" via construction projects), $105 million to Greece, $100 million to the Soviet Union, $5 million to Albania, $125 million to Yugoslavia (not entirely remitted). American aid to Italy (the Marshall Plan) was $1.2 billion by 1952.

15. Again, there are numerous works on this topic. A candid commentary on the ambivalent presentation of history by Italian officialdom following the war is Gianni Oliva's monograph, *L'Alibi della Resistenza* (2003). See also Lorenzo Del Boca's *Italiani, Brava Gente?* (2014) and Filippo Focardi's *Il Cattivo Tedesco e il Bravo Italiano: La rimozione delle colpe della seconda guerra mondiale* (2016). For an apologia for Fascism and the Republic of Salò by a sitting president as recently as 2001, see Guido Panico's *La Storia e il Suo Racconto* (2017), page 16, and note 8 on the same page. It should be noted that the Allied Military Government permitted the Italians to implement certain directives which, in fact, were ordered by the occupiers; in this way, the acting prime minister (who had actually been appointed by the Allies) could state in 1945 that the Italian government decided to give women the right to vote.

16. Some scholars have attempted to rationalize or explain these phenomena through research; see, for example, Bedani, Gino (editor), *The Politics of Italian National Identity* (2000).

17. Most obviously, in 1981 the government, at that time controlled by the Christian Democrats, refused to license the theatrical release of *The Lion of the Desert,* a motion picture (starring Anthony Quinn, Oliver Reed, Rod

Steiger, Irene Papas, John Gielgud and numerous Italians) depicting civilian massacres in Italian-occupied Libya. The film was finally broadcast by Italian satellite television on 11 June 2009. For a contemporary review see "Lion of the Desert: Bedouin vs Mussolini" by Vincent Canby in *The New York Times* (17 April 1981). Published in 2005, Eric Salerno's *Genocidio in Libia* is a rare example of Italian "corrective revisionism" regarding Italy's colonial misadventures. Unfortunately, such works rarely emanate from Italy, the more profound research being conducted by foreigners; see Ali Abdullatif Ahmida's *Genocide in Libya: Shar, A Hidden Colonial History* (2020); Ian Campbell's monograph, *The Addis Ababa Massacre: Italy's National Shame* (2017); and Robert Mallett's *Mussolini in Ethiopia 1919-1935: The Origins of Fascist Italy's African War* (2015). Though generally ignored by Italian school history curricula (hence the widespread ignorance or "denial" of the facts among many Italians educated here in Italy), the numerous crimes against humanity perpetrated by the Royal Italian Army have been extensively documented by scholars and journalists, as well as Allied military intelligence and various international agencies. To cite, *pro forma,* just a few articles: "Italy's Bloody Secret" by Rory Carroll in *The Guardian,* London, 25 June 2001; "Italy: Airbrushing History of Nazi Puppets" by Alfio Bernabei in *Searchlight* magazine (UK), January 2002; "Britain and the 'Hand-over' of Italian War Criminals to Yugoslavia 1945-48" by Effie Pedaliu in *Journal of Contemporary History* (UK, US), October 2004, volume 39, number 4, pages 503-529. A fine documentary film is Michael Palumbo's *Fascist Legacy* (1989), produced by the BBC. The last few years have seen books written by Italians, such as Giacomo Scotti's monograph about the massacres in Yugoslavia in the Sources, whereas in the past these were typically authored by researchers in the countries that were occupied by the Italians or historians from Allied nations such as Britain or the United States.

18. Some historians place the beginning of the ideological *Risorgimento* movement in the eighteenth century; the birth of the political unification effort based on this is often dated to the Congress of Vienna. In common parlance the proper nouns *Unificazione* (unification) and *Risorgimento* (resurgence or "rebirth") are often used interchangeably in Italy. In Italy a number of recent books confront unificationist revisionism (and denialism) and the socio-economic failures of unification itself. One translated into English is Pino Aprile's *Terroni: All that has been done to ensure that the Italians of the South became southerners* (2011). Giordano Bruno Guerri's *Il Sangue del Sud: Antistoria del Risorgimento e del Brigantaggio* (2010) and Gianni Oliva's *Un*

Regno Che è Stato Grande: La Storia Negata dei Borboni di Napoli e Sicilia (2011) consider the revisionism that infected Italy after 1860. See also Silvana Patriarca's *Italian Vices: Nation and Character from the Risorgimento to the Republic* (2010). *Memorie del Sud* (1999), edited by Andrea Orlandi, presents a number of revelatory details regarding the peninsular half of the Two Sicilies and the war of 1860-1861. Other works of note: Michele Topa's *I Briganti di Sua Maestà* (1993); Antonio Ciano's *One Nation Under Blood* (2018); the collection *The Risorgimento Revisited: Nationalism and Culture in Nineteenth-Century Italy* (2012), edited by Silvana Patriarca and Lucy Riall. Also by Lucy Riall are *Under the Volcano: Revolution in a Sicilian Town* (2013) and *Sicily and the Unification of Italy: Liberal Policy and Local Power 1859-1866* (1998). For revisionism based on the intentional concealment of unflattering information by the Italian government after 1860, see Denis Mack Smith's Introduction in *Italy and Its Monarchy* (1989), and his essay, "Documentary Falsification and Italian Biography," in *History and Biography: Essays in Honour of Derek Beales* (Cambridge 1996), pages 173-187. See also note 9.

19. These political parties were eventually consolidated into the center-right *Lega Nord* (Northern League) party.

20. Here reference is made to the "Lombards" present in southern Italy when the Normans arrived *circa* 1016; their chief city was prosperous Salerno, known for its medical school.

21. At times, there have been small political parties advocating for the separation of Sicily from Italy; these should not be confused with the Neo-Bourbon movement. Initially, the effects of the southern movements were covered in the press but not by many scholars; for example, there is no mention of these in Patriarca, Silvana, "Italian neopatriotism: debating national identity in the 1990s," *Modern Italy*, volume 6, number 1 (2001), pages 21-34. For a report published later see Bucher, Michael, "Re-Discovering the Italian Kingdom of the Two Sicilies," *Time* ("Lightbox" section), 25 August 2016.

22. Barbara Kreutz's *Before the Normans: Southern Italy in the Ninth and Tenth Centuries* (1996) addresses this period, with a focus on peninsular Italy. Over the years, two accounts of the Normans' arrival in southern Italy have given rise to two schools of thought, each supporting one "theory" (tradition) or the other. They are not mutually exclusive. In their general

outlines, both descriptions mention Norman knights being in Italy for pilgrimages. Neither tradition seems slavishly faithful to fact, but neither does one contradict the substance of the other. Indeed, there may have been several bands of Norman knights present in Italy by 1016. For the "Gargano" and "Salerno" traditions see Joranson, Einar, "The Inception of the Career of the Normans in Italy: Legend and History," *Speculum*, volume 23, number 3 (July 1948), pages 353-396. For the earliest medieval European civilizations of southern Italy see *People and Identity in Ostrogothic Italy, 489-554* (1997) by Patrick Amory, *The Vandals* (2010) by Andrew Merrills and Richard Miles, *Byzantine Civilisation* (1933, 1969) by Steven Runciman, *Byzantium* (1989) by John Julius Norwich, and *Bizanti e Bizantinismo nella Sicilia Normanna* (1950) by Francesco Giunta. See also *The Arabs* (1976) by Peter Mansfield. *Siculo Arabic* (1996), by Dionisius Agius, is a study of the language spoken by Sicily's Arabs, of which a modern form is Maltese.

23. The best introduction and overview is Chiarelli, Leonard, *A History of Muslim Sicily* (second edition, 2018). Another good reference is *A History of Islamic Sicily* (1975), by Aziz Ahmad. Also useful is *The Muslims of Medieval Italy* (2009), by Alexander Metcalfe. Michele Amari's *Storia dei Musulmani di Sicilia* (1854), traditionally taken as gospel by some Sicilians, should be read very critically because many of its "facts" are uncorroborated by original sources; Amari may be the first modern writer to refer to Roger II as a "baptized sultan." A historical benchmark unfortunately overshadowed by Amari's work is Alfonso Airoldi's *Codice Diplomatico di Sicilia sotto il Governo degli Arabi* published by the *Stamperia Reale* (the royal press) in 1790; this survey was formerly the definitive reference consulted by Sicilian Arabists, along with works by Salvadore Morso, a competent professor of Arabic whose monographs appeared long before Amari's books. For insights into the status of the Jews during this period, see Gil, Moshe, "The Jews in Sicily under Muslim Rule in the Light of Geniza Documents" in *Italia Judaica 1* (1983), pages 87-134; more generally, *Between Scylla and Charybdis: The Jews in Sicily* (2011) by Shlomo Simonsohn.

24. *The Eastern Schism: A Study of the Papacy and the Eastern Churches during the XIth and XIIth Centuries* (1955), by Sir Steven Runciman, approaches its subject with a fair degree of balance. A pragmatic theological treatment of the underlying issues is to be found in John Meyendorff's *Orthodoxy and Catholicity* (1966).

25. See Alio, Jacqueline, *Queens of Sicily 1061-1266* (2018), pages 107-126, and *Sicilian Queenship: Power and Identity in the Kingdom of Sicily 1061-1266,* pages 76-79; also Houben, Hubert, "Adelaide 'del Vasto' nella Storia del Regno di Sicilia," *Itinerari di Ricerca Storica,* number 4 (Lecce 1990), pages 9-40. Despite what has been reported by several scholars, Adelaide's letter is not "the oldest paper document in Europe." At Nájera, in Spain, monks composed the *Missal of Silos,* which antedates it by several decades.

26. For a good biography of Roger II see Houben, Hubert, *Roger II von Sizilien* (1997), also available in an English translation by Graham Loud. For the coronation rite: Elze, Reinhard, "Tre Ordines per l'Incoronazione di un Re e di una Regina del Regno Normanno in Sicilia," *Atti del Congresso Internazionale di Studi sulla Sicilia Normanna* (Palermo 1974), pages 438-459; Elze, Reinhard, "The Ordo for the Coronation of King Roger II of Sicily: An Example of Dating from Internal Evidence," *Coronations: Medieval and Early Modern Monarchic Ritual* (1990), pages 165-178. For a translation and notes on the rite used for queens, see Alio, Jacqueline, *Queens of Sicily 1061-1266* (2018), pages 567-574. Ferdinand Chalandon's *Historie de la Domination Normande en Italie et en Sicile* (1907) was the first major "generalist" work of length about the Normans in Italy. In English, John Julius Norwich followed in this tradition with two books, *The Normans in the South* (1967) and *The Kingdom in the Sun* (1970). A useful introduction is *The Norman Kingdom of Sicily* by Donald Matthew (1992); additional commentary will be found in volume 1 of Rosario Gregorio's *Considerazioni sopra la storia di Sicilia dai tempi normanni sino ai presenti* (reprinted in 1972). Another good entry is Jeremy Johns' *Arabic Administration in Norman Sicily: The Royal Diwan* (2002). Not to be overlooked is Hiroshi Takayama's superlative study, *The Administration of the Norman Kingdom of Sicily* (1993).

27. For both codices of the Assizes of Ariano in the original Latin, see Alio, Jacqueline, *Margaret, Queen of Sicily* (2016), pages 369-386; for an English translation of the older codex with notes, see Loud, Graham, *Roger II and the Creation of the Kingdom of Sicily* (2012), pages 314-328. An early modern analysis is to be found in Hans Niese's *Die Gesetzgebung der Normannischen Dynastie im Regnum Siciliae* (1910). An insightful essay on the legal significance of the *Assizes* is "The Birth of the Ius Commune: King Roger II's Legislation," by Kenneth Pennington, in *Rivista Internazionale del Diritto Comune,* Number 17 (2006). Rape was defined as a form of assault and divorce

was legal; in the united Italy such statutes were not enacted until 1974 (divorce) and 1996 (rape). These rights were addressed more explicitly in the Constitutions of Frederick II q.v. note 30; see also note 11.

28. See Makdisi, John, "The Islamic Origins of the Common Law," *North Carolina Law Review* (June 1999). Among the English institutions thought to have been influenced by Islamic law are the Inns of Court and perpetual endowment. As early as 1955, Henry Cattan noted the striking similarity between the perpetual endowment of a trust and the Muslim principle of *waqf*. A very succinct overview is presented in Chapter 25 of *The Peoples of Sicily: A Multicultural Legacy* (2014).

29. An excellent introduction to Frederick and his times is David Abulafia's *Frederick II: A Medieval Emperor* (1988). Another fine entry is Thomas Curtis Van Cleve's biography, *The Emperor Frederick II of Hohenstaufen, Immutator Mundi* (1972). Ernst Kantorowicz's *Friedrich der Zweite* (1927) is also very good.

30. For an English translation of the Constitutions of Melfi with notes, see Powell, James, *The Liber Augustalis or Constitutions of Melfi* (1971). The first complete transcription was published in Naples in 1773 as *Constitutionum Regni Siciliarum*. Brief commentary on the legal rights of women guaranteed by the *Constitutions* is presented, from the Italian (and male) point of view, in Mazzarese Fardella, Enrico, "La Condizione Giuridica della Donna nel Liber Augustalis" in *Archivio Storico Siciliano*, series 4, volume 21-22 (Palermo 1997), pages 31-44. It should be noted that Frederick II had already instituted the Assizes of Capua in 1220, followed by the Assizes of Messina the following year.

31. For English translations of Frederick's poems see Alio, Jacqueline, *Sicilian Queenship: Power and Identity in the Kingdom of Sicily 1061-1266* (2019), pages 191-216. More generally, see Jensen, Frede, *The Poetry of the Sicilian School* (1986); Langley, Ernest, *The Poetry of Giacomo da Lentini* (1915); Lansing, Richard, *The Complete Poetry of Giacomo da Lentini* (2018); Mallette, Karla, *The Kingdom of Sicily 1100-1250: A Literary History* (2005); Mangieri Cono, Antonio, *Il Contrasto di Cielo d'Alcamo: Introduzione, testo manoscritto e diplomatico, testo critico-congetturale, traduzione e note* (2005); Panvini, Bruno, *Le Rime della Scuola Siciliana*, volume 1 (1962); Di Girolamo, Costanzo, et al., *Poeti della Corte di Federico II*, volume 2 in the series *I Poeti della Scuola Siciliana* (2008).

The *Contrasto* of Cielo of Alcamo, the longest poem of the Sicilian School, appears with an English translation in Alio, Jacqueline, *Queens of Sicily 1061-1266* (2018), pages 549-565. Frederick's *De Arte Venandi cum Avibus* is preserved in manuscript in the Vatican Apostolic Library as *Codex Pal. Lat 1071*. For photography and notes see *Das Falkenbuch Friedrichs II* (2000) by Dorothea Walz and Carl Willemsen. The first English translation was published in the United States in 1943 as *The Art of Falconry*. This was translated by Casey Wood and Marjorie Fyfe. A fine Italian translation by Anna Trombetti Budriesi was published in 1999 as *L'Arte di Cacciare con gli Uccelli*. This is accompanied by a Latin transcription.

32. King Charles I of Naples remains a contentious figure. A departure from the usual demonization of him is to be found in Jean Dunbabin's *Charles I of Anjou: Power, Kingship and State-Making in Thirteenth-Century Europe* (1998). See also Mendola, Louis (translator), *Frederick, Conrad and Manfred of Hohenstaufen, Kings of Sicily: The Chronicle of Nicholas of Jamsilla 1210-1258* (2016). For the suppression of the Muslims of Lucera see Egidi, Pietro. *La Colonia Saracena di Lucera e la Sua Distruzione* (1912), and Taylor, Julie Anne, *Muslims in Medieval Italy: The Colony at Lucera* (2003).

33. See Runciman, Steven, *Sicilian Vespers: A History of the Mediterranean World in the Later Thirteenth Century* (1958); Mendola, Louis, *Sicily's Rebellion against King Charles: The Story of the Sicilian Vespers* (2015); Amari, Michele, *La Guerra del Vespro Siciliano* (1843).

34. See Zeldes, Nadia, *The Former Jews of this Kingdom: Sicilian Converts After the Expulsion 1492-1516* (2003).

35. For the cuisine of southern Italy until this time, including some recipes, see Alio, Jacqueline, *Sicilian Queenship: Power and Identity in the Kingdom of Sicily 1061-1266* (2019), pages 151-190. Despite longstanding beliefs that Cristobal Colon (1451-1506) was Genoan, for which there was never much reliable evidence, he may well have been Catalan, apparently being fluent in speaking and writing a tongue typified by a difficult grammar rarely mastered by foreigners. Indeed, there is virtually nothing in the navigator's life to suggest that he was from Genoa, and early historians may have confused it with Girona or another locality near Barcelona. See Merrill, Charles, *Colom of Catalonia: Origins of Christopher Columbus Revealed* (2008); this corrective thesis was first advanced by Luis Ulloa in 1927.

NOTES

36. Outbreaks of bubonic plague were fairly frequent. A detailed study concerning Sicily is "Due Episodi di Peste in Sicilia, 1526 e 1624" by Calogero Valenti, in *Archivio Storico Siciliano,* series 4, volume 10 (Palermo 1984), pages 5-88.

37. For the *donativi,* resulting in the *riveli* (tax declarations) paid by various communities in Sicily in 1651, 1681, 1714 and 1748, see *La Finanza Locale in Sicilia nel '600 e '700* (1994) by Alfredo Li Vecchi, which presents tables and a concise analysis. Another useful work is the series *Storia Civile e Politica del Regno di Napoli* (1796) by Pietro Giannone and Carlo Pecchia. In English, an interesting study is *The Government of Sicily under Philip II of Spain: A Study in the Practice of Empire* (1951) by Helmut Koenigsberger, who published various papers in this area. For modern population trends, a good overview is *Dinamiche Demografiche nella Sicilia Moderna 1505-1806* (2002) by Domenico Ligresti. In our times, foreigners sometimes wonder why Italians are so critical of Italy as a nation. On the night of 10 July 1992, a Friday, without advising Italian citizens in advance, the government deducted monies equal to 6/1000 lire of the total from every current (checking) account in the country, either private or commercial, in a so-called *prelievo forzoso,* "forced withdrawal." To avoid the possibility of account holders withdrawing their own money before the government's act of thievery, the law authorizing this maneuver was approved in secret and then retro-dated. (The author was in Italy when this occurred and saw the deduction from an account.) This tactic reappeared on 1 July 2020, when the government deducted 34.20 euros from every personal checking account in the country, and 100 euros from each commercial account; this is now deducted *every* year. The legal precedent for this was *decreto legge* number 201/2011 of 6 December 2011, the so-called *Salva Italia* ("Save Italy") bill, while the tax imposed in 2020 was technically an increase of the *imposta di bollo* ("stamp tax") on all bank accounts; see the *Gazzetta Ufficiale della Repubblica Italiana,* general series number 106, of 23 April 2020, pages 3-4, for the decree by the Ministry of Economy and Finance on 5 March 2020. Economists have characterized this kind of deduction as an insidious "wealth tax." Meanwhile, the general value-added (sales) tax on most retail products was 22 percent with an increase (to 25 or 26 percent) projected; in Britain and France it was 20 percent and 19 percent in Germany. Italians refer to the *stato ladro,* "the thieving state," when they are not employing even less flattering expressions (the translation of *un paese di merda* will be left to the reader).

38. Many feudal towns had to borrow money to pay the head tax, which was beyond the means of the ordinary subject. In Cammarata, in Sicily, this debt was not repaid until 1843. See De Gregorio, Domenico, *Cammarata: Notizie sul Territorio e la Sua Storia* (1986), pages 260-261.

39. While Louis XIV, whose precise motives are the subject of scholarly debate, has often been identified as the culprit in the events leading to this war, Europe's patchwork of states both large and small created myriad political complexities that could threaten the balance of power. Alliances changed frequently, and many nations besides France were greedy for territory. Louis probably feared his nation being geographically "encircled" by Hapsburg monarchies in the future. A fine overview is *The War of Succession in Spain, 1700-1715* (1969) by Henry Kamen. For details and background, a useful reference is *The Treaties of the War of the Spanish Succession: An Historical and Critical Dictionary* (1995) by Linda Frey. More generally, see *The Wars of Louis XIV 1667-1714* (1999) by John Lynn. The war had global consequences; its North American theatre was referred to by British colonists in the future United States as "Queen Anne's War."

40. For the reign of Vittorio Amedeo of Savoy in Sicily see Simone Candela's *I Piemontesi in Sicilia 1713-1718* (1996).

41. As regent for her young son, Frederick II, Queen Constance is believed to have renounced the apostolic legateship, the right to approve episcopal appointments in Sicily in return for the pope's protection of her only heir. In the event, Constance died in 1198 and no pontiff ever defended the boy's interests with much conviction. The next monarch to assert such rights, or at least the next one to do so openly and formally (as a legal declaration), was Ferdinand the Catholic late in the fifteenth century. King Philip II of Spain instituted the juridical office of *Judex Monarchiae Siciliae* in 1597. In 1715, Pope Clement XI revoked the privileges of the so-called *Monarchia Sicula,* but this did not end the academic (or juridical) debate. An early treatise is Nicola Maria Tedeschi's *Istoria della Pretesa Monarchia di Sicilia,* published in Rome in 1715, followed by Pietro Giuseppe Zappata's *Difesa Storica della Monarchia Siciliana,* published in Turin in 1716. For a more recent analysis see Salvatore Fodale's *Comes et Legatus Siciliae: Sul privilegio di Urbano II e la Pretesa Apostolica Legazia dei Normanni in Sicilia* (1970).

42. "King of Sardinia" thus became the principal title of the Savoy monarchs, who continued to rule Piedmont and Savoy (see note 40). The dynasty was often referred to as the "Royal House of Sardinia," which of course it was. At its foundation in 1297, the Kingdom of Sardinia and Corsica was ruled from Aragon.

43. The historian most often credited with formulating this paradigm is Pietro Giannone in his *Istoria Civile del Regno di Napoli* published during the reign of Charles VI of Austria in 1723, although others had postulated such ideas under different names, sometimes linking the origin of the concept to the reign of Frederick II. An early proponent was Giovanni Antonio Summonte in his *Dell'Historia della Città e Regno di Napoli,* published in 1601. This "Neapolitan Nation" should not be confused with the phrase as it was later used (or abused) by Benedetto Croce. See also Marino, John, *Becoming Neapolitan: Citizen Culture in Baroque Naples* (2011).

44. Many of Tanucci's letters survive, offering insight into his thinking and the function of the court under his influence. Time would reveal him to be biased and dogmatic, perhaps exercising excessive control over young Ferdinand I, but for now he was an efficient reformer. See *Lettere di Bernardo Tanucci a Carlo III di Borbone 1759-1776* (1969), edited by Rosa Mincuzzi.

45. The Holy Office was the successor to the Holy Inquisition, which had technically been abolished in 1542. However, an "inquisition" continued in the Spanish dominions. It was abolished in the Kingdom of Sicily in 1782 (see the next chapter). In this volume reference to "the Inquisition" in the Kingdom of Naples is made generically.

46. For the text of the *Codice Carolino* and the complex body of law that preceded it, see *Codice delle Leggi del Regno di Napoli* (1794), a multi-volume compilation by Alessio De Sariis. The uniform legal code of Charles III receives little attention, either here or by other historians, because it was supplanted by another following the unification of the kingdoms of Naples and Sicily under Ferdinand I (see note 11).

47. See Monziani, Limonta, Monti, Demai, Cantarelli, "Il Movimento dei Prezzi nel Regno di Napoli dal 1695 al 1755," *Giornale degli Economisti e Annali di Economia,* March-April 1966 (New Series, year 25, numbers 3-4), pages 354-375.

48. This is still in force, though it no longer entails excommunication. Subsequent reform proved difficult because it was not easy, either theologically or juridically, for a later pontiff to abrogate that which had been formalized by a recent predecessor. It will be seen that freemasonry played a part in the Italian unification movement.

49. The mere fact that the church never condemned the Palermitan movement implies that it was nothing more than a small, loosely-formed group, if indeed it ever actually existed under the name later ascribed to it. Its historicity is questionable. It was first described as the "Beati Paoli" in a story written by Luigi Natoli during the early years of the twentieth century. It is quite possible, however, that there existed small, informal groups of aristocrats who opposed the Inquisition and secretly shared forbidden books amongst themselves. This is suggested by the discovery of such books as the first (1763) edition of Voltaire's *Treatise on Tolerance* in the private library of a Sicilian nobleman, with contemporary, handwritten annotations in Italian. The myth that the novel referred to the Mafia was concocted when certain criminals in that organization began to identify with some of its characters long after its publication.

50. For some insights into the thinking of the king, see his letters to Spain, published as *Carlo di Borbone: Lettere ai Sovrani di Spagna* (2002), edited in 3 volumes by Imma Ascione. For some correspondence of young Ferdinand I to his father, see *Il Regno di Napoli dalla Tutela all'Emancipazione 1775-1789* in Sources.

51. One of the better histories of the Kingdom of Naples during the reign of Charles III is Michelangelo Schipa's *Il Regno di Napoli al Tempo di Carlo di Borbone* (1904). A fine timeline is offered in Luigi del Pozzo's *Cronaca Civile e Militare delle Due Sicilie sotto la Dinastia Borbonica dall'Anno 1734 in Po*i (1857), published by the Stamperia Reale of Naples as the "official" chronology of events in the twin kingdoms into 1857. Another reliable reference is Pietro Colletta's multivolume *Storia del Reame di Napoli dal 1734 sino al 1823* (1838).

52. Amongst the numerous works written about the French Revolution, fine recent introductions in English are *The French Revolution: From Enlightenment to Tyranny*, by Ian Davidson (2016); *Citizens: A Chronicle of the French Revolution*, by Simon Schama (1989); *The Oxford History of the French Revolution*, by William Doyle (second edition, 2003).

NOTES

53. The precise scope and impact of Maria Carolina's machinations are much debated. Though doubtless substantial, these seem to have been overstated by modern scholars seeking to demonstrate the influence of royal women. See, for example, Recca, Cinzia, *The Diary of Queen Maria Carolina of Naples 1781-1785: New Evidence of Queenship at Court* (2017).

54. For the rapport with the United States of America, see Howard Marraro's *Diplomatic Relations between the United States and the Kingdom of the Two Sicilies* (2 volumes, 1951-1952).

55. Events in the Kingdom of Naples were predicated on those across Europe and the Mediterranean. Specific foreign policy was conditioned by the actions of the great powers in a setting where smaller nations like the Italian states were little more than pawns. (In Naples, however, another factor was Queen Maria Carolina's contrarian influence on Ferdinand's actions; see note 53.) The successive unification movements in Italy and Germany were, in part, a response of smaller states to the hegemony of larger nations in conflicts like the Napoleonic Wars. For excellent overviews, see *Napoleon's Wars: An International History 1803-1815* (2009) by Charles Esdaile, and *The Napoleonic Wars: A Global History* (2020) by Alexander Mikaberidze.

56. For the Kingdom of Naples see Lanzellotti, Angelo, *Costituzione Politica del Regno di Napoli dell'Anno 1815 sotto Gioacchino Murat* (1820). For the Kingdom of Sicily see, amongst works by many other scholars, Grimaldi, Angelo, "La Costituzione Siciliana del 1812," *Revista de Derecho, Universidad del Norte,* number 48 (2017), pages 208-233. For statistics during Murat's reign, which was a reasonably prosperous period for the Neapolitans, see the works by Domenico De Marco and Stefania Martuschelli in Sources.

57. For a contemporary analysis see Saverio Cangiano's *Lezioni di Diritto Positivo* at note 11. A useful contemporary treatise on criminal law in the Two Sicilies will be found in Pietro Ulloa's *Amministrazione della Giustizia Penale nel Regno di Napoli* (1835), which compares the laws of this nation to those of others.

58. According to an enduring urban legend, *spaghetti alla carbonara* owes its name, though not the recipe itself, to the *Carbonari*.

59. The Rothschild Bank operated until, in view of the decline of the local economy with the annexation of the Two Sicilies to the Kingdom of Italy, it was forced to close in 1863.

60. This led to the leaders of the subsequent unification movement frequently being characterized by the papacy as freemasons, whether they were or not. Some, such as Giuseppe Garibaldi, were indeed freemasons, while others simply adopted quasi-masonic rituals. Even so, to describe the majority of them in this way would be overzealous and misleading. In this regard, it is worth noting that freemasonry itself took various forms based on its own "rites" and local practices. In its essence, freemasonry was not specifically monarchist or republican, nor was it intrinsically revolutionary.

61. See the collection *Delirious Naples: A Cultural History of the City of the Sun* (2018), edited by Pellegrino D'Acierno, and Jordan Lancaster's *In the Shadow of Vesuvius: A Cultural History of Naples* (2019).

62. The most recent legislation is based on the concordat signed 18 February 1984 between the Italian Republic and the Vatican, and ratified by Italy in March of the following year. This updated the Lateran Treaties of 1929. Among other effects, it established that Roman Catholicism is no longer the state religion of Italy and determined that a civil divorce was necessary before the church could annul a Catholic marriage. Article 1 reiterates the sovereignty not only of Vatican City but the church itself; article 5 governs the authority of law enforcement to enter churches or other property owned by the church. Italians' reverence for the church was one of the factors that effectively undermined the moral and social authority of the Italian crown, especially before the Lateran Treaties were signed in 1929. Until then, foreigners, such as Catholic clergy in Ireland, sometimes referred to the pope as being "a prisoner in the Vatican."

63. Much has been written about this in recent years. A typical, though by no means definitive, study with a focus on the years after 1860 is Sciarra, Federico, "Il Matrimonio nell'Ottocento Italiano fra Potere Civile e Potere Ecclesiastico," *Historia et Ius,* 9/2016 (2016), pages 1-14. Ecclesiastical weddings were not recognized from 1870 until 1929 because a state of war existed between the Kingdom of Italy and the Vatican (see the previous note).

64. See Alio, op.cit. in note 35. Also: Volpe, Enrico, *Piatti Tipici della Cucina*

NOTES

Napoletana e Lucana: Tradizioni, Storia, Descrizine, Usi e Costumi (1980); Lombardo, Francesca, *Sicilian Food and Wine: The Cognoscente's Guide* (2015); Spieler, Marlena, *A Taste of Naples: Neapolitan Culture, Cuisine and Cooking* (2018); Francesconi, Jeanne, *La Cucina Napoletana* (1974); Santasilia, Franco, *La Cucina Aristocratica Napoletana* (1987).

65. See, amongst numerous studies, Ventura, Piero, "La capitale e le élites urbane nel Regno di Napoli tra XVI e XVIII secolo," *Mélanges de l'Ecole Française de Rome*, 121/1 (2009), pages 261-296.

66. Goodwin, John, "Progress of the Two Sicilies Under the Spanish Bourbons from the Year 1734-35 to 1840," *Journal of the Statistical Society of London*, volume 5 (1842), page 73. Listing various agricultural statistics, Goodwin's reports are informative, though hardly surprising to those familiar with the kingdom's economic prosperity.

67. See De Crescenzo, Gennaro, "Le Scuole al Tempo dei Borboni," *Quaderni per la Verità Storica*, volume 2 (2018); Agresta, Salvatore, *L'Istruzione in Sicilia* 1815-1860 (1995); Sindoni, Caterina, *Scuole, Maestri e Metodi nella Sicilia Borbonica 1817-1860* (2012); Baldacci, Giuseppe, "L'istruzione nell'Italia pre e post unitaria, il caso Catania," *Archivio Storico per la Sicilia Orientale*, year 105, series 2 (2009), pages 290-316; Ricuperati, Giuseppe, "L'insegnamento della storia nella scuola italiana fra appartenenza e identità," *La Nazione tra i Banchi* (2012), pages 145-170; Scotto di Luzio, Adolfo, "Gli insegnanti degli italiani: Formazione e reclutamento dei docenti dagli Stati preunitari al Regno d'Italia," ibid, pages 93-108. See also Broccoli, Angelo, *Educazione e Politica nel Mezzogiorno d'Italia 1767-1860*, Fazio, Ida, "Istruzione ed Educazione delle Donne nella Sicilia Borbonica," Salvemini, Raffaella, "L'Istruzione del Povero," and the work of Alfio Crimi, in Sources.

68. As surely as the *fuitina* (elopement) described in the previous chapter has disappeared, the long shadows cast by many social practices of this era are still omnipresent throughout Italy, where the infamous *raccomandazione* (preferment), nepotism, clientelism (with its bribes and political favors) and sexism (sexual harassment and gender inequality) are a normal part of life, hence the Italian adage that *siamo ancora nel Medioevo*, "we're still in the Middle Ages." News of these phenomena sometimes makes its way into the international press. As regards nepotism, *The Economist* (in "Higher Education in Italy: A Case for Change," 15 November 2008, page 32) states that "this

week news emerged of a university rector who, the day before he retired on October 31st, signed a decree to make his son a lecturer," going on to explain that, "At Palermo University, as many as 230 teachers are reported to be related to other teachers." The Italian neologism for *nepotism* in one place on a grand scale is *parentopoli*. See also the article "The Ins and Outs: Italians are deeply anti-meritocratic" in the same publication, 9 June 2011, where the term *raccomandazione* (preferment) is explained. More recently: "Seven Professors Arrested in Florence University Nepotism Row" by Thomas Kington in *The Times* (London), 27 September 2017, reported from Rome; "Concorsi truccati all'università: indagati sette docenti siciliani," *Giornale di Sicilia* (Palermo), 25 September 2017. For a description of student life at Italy's public universities, see Pacitti, Domenico, "No Holiday in Rome" in *The Guardian* (London), 8 October 2002. For the high prevalence of plagiarism in Italy's universities, see Sutherland-Smith, Wendy, *Plagiarism, the Internet, and Student Learning: Improving Academic Integrity* (2008), pages 88-89. A perusal of Italian newspapers and websites will confirm that these problems infect Turin, Milan and Bologna as well as Naples, Palermo and Rome. It comes as no surprise that not a single Italian university is ranked in the world's top hundred according to recent annual reports published by the Times Higher Education Survey (timeshighereducation.com); see also "Young Italians abandon la dolce vita to move to Britain" by Nick Squires (in *The Telegraph,* 8 October 2014), which states that, "the registered population of Italians living in London is 220,000, but officials believe the true figure to be closer to half a million. Italians make up the fourth largest European community in the capital, after Poles, Irish and French." Recent analyses by Transparency International place Italy among the most corrupt nations of the European Union and western Europe. For reports and statistics on issues related to gender, see "Sicily's Women Today" in Jacqueline Alio's *Women of Sicily: Saints, Queens and Rebels* (pages 193-200). While one is reluctant to characterize twenty-first century Italy as a misogynistic gerontocracy little changed since the days of its monarchies, some statistics are startling; only around fifty percent of Italian women are employed in the workforce, with the figure hovering around thirty-five percent in Sicily. In 2015, the politically-appointed director of Palermo's chamber of commerce (a public agency that administers business licensing and other services) pleaded guilty to corruption; he had demanded a payoff of a hundred thousand euros to grant an exclusive concession to a pastry maker for vendor space at the Palermo airport, and was exposed when the victim wore a "wire" during their meeting while police were listening at the other end.

This case was not atypical. A wry but insightful glimpse of life in Italy is to be found in *The Italians* (2014) by John Hooper. A comedy, *Tuttoapposto*, released in 2019, accurately portrays the sexism, nepotism and corruption that characterizes Italy's universities; it is rather difficult to imagine a film depicting student life at Oxford or Harvard in the same way.

69. Born in 1777, Francis I was appointed to his father's council of state (cabinet) as a young man in 1795. He was well-educated. Interested in botany, about which he wrote concise treatises, he established a large nature reserve in Palermo whilst in the city during the French occupation of Naples. This Boccadifalco reserve, near Baida, later became the site of a military airport occupied by the Allies in 1943. Some historians believe that Francis was weak; it seems more likely that he was simply submissive to a domineering father.

70. This was enacted by decree number 131 on 4 January 1831, published on 24 January of that year. It may be consulted in *Collezione delle Leggi e de' Decreti Reali del Regno delle Due Sicilie, Anno 1831, Semestre I* (1831), pages 46-50. For a concise summary of a few similar laws of this era see Salvemini, Raffaella, "Tra Necessità e Quotidianità: La gestione della povertà a Napoli nell'Ottocento preunitario," *Proposte e Ricerche,* volume (year) 37, number 73 (2014), pages 153-166.

71. As stated in this book's Introduction, the unified Italy instituted nothing quite like this until 2019 (the *reddito di cittadinanza* initiated not by an established political party but by the recently-founded Five Star Movement), although there were already other programs in place, such as the *assegno di famiglia* to assist poor mothers with young children. Indeed, it is quite possible that the *reddito di cittadinanza* was inspired not only by similar programs in the United Kingdom and other European countries but by the statute of Ferdinand II.

72. In the Kingdom of the Two Sicilies, the ducat was a unit of currency but not a coin, q.v. Appendix 5. The schedule of monthly payments: 1 ducat for an individual living alone, 1.80 ducats for a family unit (household) of two persons, 2.50 ducats for a family consisting of three persons, 3 ducats for a family consisting of four persons, 4 ducats for a family of five persons or more.

73. Historians and observers criticize the inefficiency of the Kingdom of Italy and the republic that followed it (see note 68). It would appear, however, that the government and administration of the Kingdom of the Two Sicilies were efficient for their time if measured against those of other nations in western Europe. Compared to John Goodwin (see note 66), who was highly objective, many British commentators were extremely biased, often for political or economic reasons. See, for example, Elizabeth Dawbarn's *Naples and King Ferdinand: An Historical and Political Sketch of the Kingdom of the Two Sicilies* (1858). Much of the work published by Britons reflected a certain "selective morality" insofar as the authors discerned flaws in Neapolitan social policies that they failed to recognize in Britain's policies toward Ireland and India; of course, British commentators also criticized other nations.

74. Caricatures of this kind were a prominent feature in propaganda after 1860 as the new regime sought to denigrate the previous one. A leading scholar has keenly observed that in school history books Ferdinand II was "disparaged as the wicked 'King Bomba' for his bombardment of the civilian population of Messina in 1847, whereas the subsequent Piedmontese bombardment of Genoa, Ancona and Gaeta was either applauded or ignored." See Denis Mack Smith's "Documentary Falsification and Italian Biography," in *History and Biography: Essays in Honour of Derek Beales* (Cambridge 1996), page 181. While every blemish of the Two Sicilies was highlighted, Savoyard blights like the infamous "Piedmont Easter Massacre" of 1655 were conveniently expurgated from the Italian history imparted to school children. (See also Appendix 7.)

75. There is no doubt that the revolutions were, in the end, essentially political, but some scholars are inclined to point out that the root cause was simply economic even if, in certain cases, this was merely a pretext. The bad harvests, and the resulting food scarcity, combined with an industrial slump, were key factors across central and western Europe. See "Economic Crises and the European Revolutions of 1848," by Helge Berger and Mark Spoerer, in *Journal of Economic History*, volume 62, number 2 (2001).

76. The greatest beneficiaries of telegraphy in 1848 were those in central and western Europe; the impetus in Italy came with electric telegraph lines around Naples in 1852.

77. Even if the role of Sardinia-Piedmont were, *arguendo,* excluded, the international nature of things to come after 1859 was downplayed by Italianist historians writing between 1861 and 1946, who would have us believe that the unification movement and the ensuing war were exclusively domestic (Italian) efforts achieved without foreign diplomatic or military support. The "official" (government) views of two more recent events noted in this book's Introduction are equally incomplete, or "selective." The Americans and British are rarely mentioned in the Liberation Day (25 April) festivities marking the end of the Second World War in Italy in 1945, with some extremist politicians actually ascribing the victories in Turin and Milan almost exclusively to the Italian partisans rather than to the American Fifth Army. The roles of King Umberto II and the Allies who forced his hand are seldom mentioned in connection with Sicilian Autonomy Day (15 May), which commemorates Sicily's regional autonomy being granted in 1946 by the Kingdom of Italy and not, as many erroneously presume, by the Italian Republic, which did not yet exist. (These phenomena are a simple matter of observation for anybody who lives in Italy.)

78. Some historians place the beginning of the *Risorgimento* movement in the eighteenth century. The beginning of the political unification movement is often dated to the Congress of Vienna. In common parlance the proper nouns *Unificazione* and *Risorgimento* are often used interchangeably in Italy, where the more patriotic-sounding *Unità d'Italia* is also heard.

79. The achievement of Catholic "emancipation" in Britain in 1829 lent an air of legitimacy to British criticisms of the Two Sicilies, yet Britain still had an established church, while its Ireland policy left much to be desired, realities which made certain British criticisms of other states seem hypocritical. Although far fewer criticisms emanated from the United States, these might be seen to reflect still greater hypocrisy coming from a place where slavery still existed. Beyond moral equivalence arguments of this kind, it is true that most of the critics themselves were viewed as progressives in their own countries.

80. See Appendix 6.

81. While a discourse on the merits of his work lies beyond the scope of this history, it is worth considering Antonio Meucci (1808-1889) perfunctorily as an example of Italian nationalist propaganda and misinformation.

The telephone in use in Italy in 1930 when the Fascists took up the cause of Meucci was based on the patented design of Alexander Graham Bell (1847-1922), by then recognized as the inventor of the telephone, and this fact was conveniently ignored by overzealous Italian nationalists. For an essay regarding Meucci's work, see John Klooster's *Icons of Invention: The Makers of the Modern World from Gutenberg to Gates* (2009), volume 1, pages 207-208, 210-217. A treatise on the invention of the telephone would be a lengthy one; in passing, it should be noted that Johann Philipp Reis and Elisha Gray conceived what some have described as functional "telephone prototypes." The crux of the matter is that Meucci's *telettrofono* was never actually patented and no *prima facie* evidence survives to support the thesis that this device, of which only a few crude schematic diagrams exist, was even capable of achieving true voice transmission. (Scholarly debates on "priority" focus on the designs of Reis and Gray, with very little consideration of Meucci's work.) The telephone example is indicative of Italian historiography. In 2020, the online *Enciclopedia Treccani*, successor of the *Enciclopedia Italiana*, still identified Meucci as *inventore del telefono*, "inventor of the telephone." For an example of recent censorship see note 17.

82. The comparative wealth of the pre-unitary Italian states *circa* 1859 was calculated by Italian economists and bankers who were by no means advocates of regional autonomy. Based on deposits in millions of gold lire, indicative as a proportional measure even without converting its exchange value into today's currencies, this was: Two Sicilies (Naples and Sicily) 443.2, Papal State 90.6, Grand Duchy of Tuscany 84.2, Kingdom of Sardinia (including Liguria) 27.1, Venetia (under Austria) 12.8, Lombardy (under Austria) 8.1, Duchy of Parma 1.2, Duchy of Modena .4. Published in Francesco Saverio Nitti's *Scienze delle Finanze* in 1903, these statistics were subsequently confirmed by other economists following the fall of the Kingdom of Italy, for example by Anteo d'Angio in *La Situazione Finanziaria Italiana dal 1796 al 1870* in 1973 and by Nicola Zitara in *L'Unita d'Italia: Nascita di Una Colonia* in 1971. See also the monograph by Nicola Ostuni in Sources.

83. Italian unification was indeed important, but mostly to a population numbering just shy of twenty million in an area significantly smaller than California. The expanding United States already had a population of thirty million during the same period, while the population of the vast Russian Empire was around seventy million (more than Italy today). Italy's unifica-

tion is studied very little outside of Italy because, unlike the *Magna Carta,* the American constitution or even the works of Karl Marx, it reflected no novel political principles that ever had an impact outside one country. Giuseppe Mazzini, the lone exponent of the movement whose ideas ever gained (or merited) much currency outside Italy, was marginalized, appreciated by his own people more after his death than during his life.

84. See note 11 and "Women" in Chapter 4. The *Codice per lo Regno delle Due Sicilie* was published by Domenico Capasso of Naples in 1848.

85. Accompanied by several companions, Francesco Crispi, a native Sicilian fluent in the Sicilian language and the Albanian dialect spoken in Sicily, arrived *incognito* on the island before Garibaldi to drum up support among the population. It is thought that he bribed several Sicilian generals in western Sicily, something that would not seem out of character for a man inclined to opportunism and even duplicity. Naturally, documentary proof of bribery is elusive, but if actions speak louder than words several Sicilian generals' ready capitulation to inferior forces is, at the very least, deserving of suspicion. It is obvious enough that the new government would not conserve traces of activities such as bribery, but these early actions established the precedent of censored documents "disappearing," a phenomenon to which the erudite Denis Mack Smith sagely dedicates the greater part of his Introduction in *Italy and Its Monarchy* and an essay, "Documentary Falsification and Italian Biography," in *History and Biography: Essays in Honour of Derek Beales* (Cambridge 1996), pages 173-187. Foreign policy was equally deceptive. The practice of preventing access to important records was continued by the Italian Republic, especially with regard to war crimes (see notes 13 and 17). In the resounding words of the American statesman Daniel Patrick Moynihan: "Everyone is entitled to his own opinion, but not his own facts."

86. These citizens, perhaps expecting to be "liberated" from the Bourbons, made the mistake of seeking control of a town that belonged to an important British family whose assets, naturally, were to be protected by the invading forces supported by the British. This the rebels could not have known, but there is clear evidence of collusion, or at least cooperation, between the Piedmontese and the British. See Riall, Lucy, *Under the Volcano: Revolution in a Sicilian Town* (2013), and *Garibaldi: Invention of a Hero* (2008). One of the first works to openly challenge the Italians' hagiographies of

their unificationist heroes was Denis Mack Smith's *Cavour and Garibaldi 1860: A Study in Political Conflict* (1954, 1985); see also his *Mazzini* (1994). In the version of the invasion of 1860 taught to Italian children and still believed by many of the nation's adults, Garibaldi landed in Sicily with a thousand volunteers, the "patriotic" red-shirts, with no additional support whatsoever, conquered the island from the evil "Spanish Bourbons" to the acclaim of the grateful populace, then (still with only a thousand troops) did the same in Calabria and Campania *en route* to "liberate" Naples while Basilicata, Abruzzi and Puglia simply "surrendered." (If only the task of Patton and Montgomery some eight decades later could have been so easy.)

87. Acton, Harold, *The Last Bourbons of Naples* (1961), page 523. The passage quoted is Acton's translation.

88. Scholars debate whether this revolt was initially anti-Savoy or pro-Bourbon. It probably began as the former, quickly evolving into the latter, affecting Monreale and other towns as well as Palermo itself. Although it seems to have begun amongst the common folk, the early involvement of local aristocrats and bureaucrats strongly suggests a political scope. Other suppositions are based on a theory that it was simply an anti-government insurrection. Like most such riots, it found prisoners freed from the local Ucciardone prison. See Maggiorani, Vincenzo, *Il Sollevamento della Plebe di Palermo e del Circondario nel Settembre 1866* (1866) and, for a more objective analysis, Riall, Lucy, "Legge Marziale a Palermo: Protesta popolare e rivolta nel 1866," *Meridiana*, volume 24 (1995), pages 65-94. An interesting look at Sicily's social and legal situation just fifteen years after unification is Leopoldo Franchetti's *La Sicilia nel 1876: Le Condizioni Politiche e Amministrative* (1876). For insights into the status of the urban poor beginning around 1868, see "Assistenza e Beneficenza a Palermo dopo l'Unità ed il Progetto 'La Casa dei Poveri' di Giacomo Cusmano" by Maria Teresa Falzone, in *Archivio Storico Siciliano,* series 4, volume 10 (Palermo 1984), pages 154-177.

89. "Sulphur Mines in Sicily" a consular report of 1888, was published in *Scientific American Supplement* in 1891. Obviously, the Italian government could not censor what was published abroad. This is one of many examples of the censorship enforced in the Kingdom of Italy long before the advent of Fascism.

90. The most detailed biography of King Francis II is *L'Ultimo Re di Napoli* (1982) by Pier Giusto Jaeger. Arrigo Petacco's *La Regina del Sud* (1992) concentrates on Queen Maria Sophia; in English, a concise biography of the queen appears in Chapter 12 of Jacqueline Alio's *Women of Sicily* (2014). Another fine entry is John Van der Kiste's *The Heroine of Gaeta: Queen Maria Sophia of the Two Sicilies* (2019). Not to be overlooked is Tschudi, Clara, *Maria Sophia, Queen of Naples* (1905).

91. In the infamous Article 17 of the Treaty of Wichale negotiated with Ethiopia in 1889, the Italian translation disseminated by Italy stipulated that henceforth Ethiopia's foreign affairs were to be conducted exclusively by the Italian government while the Amharic text stated nothing of the kind. Based on this deception, Italy sought to claim Ethiopia as its protectorate, an assertion challenged by Russia and France (both nations contested Italy's intentions and the translation's veracity) as well as Ethiopia itself. For details see Chapter 6 in Marcus, Harold, *A History of Ethiopia* (1994).

92. This emphasis on the group over the individual may foster certain inclinations toward conformity that still persist in our century. For a recent study see Burton, Delvecchio, Germani, Mazzeschi, "Individualism/Collectivism and Personality in Italian and American Groups," *Current Psychology,* volume 38, issue 6 (18 December 2019).

93. According to the decree, Prince Gennaro (1857-1867) was to succeed to this income upon his thirty-second birthday. From Article 1 of decree number 3854 of 16 March 1857, witnessed by three high officials of the kingdom but nobody representing the order itself: "The annuity of 26,000 ducats of this income shall consist of 21,965 ducats drawn from the revenue of vacant commanderies of the Royal Constantinian Order placed at our disposal by the Ministry of the Presidency of the Council of Ministers." Whether the king's decision was appropriate based on the statutes of the order is moot as it was uncontested, though one could argue that it reflected his view of the institution as royal property. Nevertheless, the king did not plan to draw the greater part of the monies for his son's stipend from the general tax base of the state. It is worth noting that Prince Gennaro would receive the revenue generated by the agricultural estates, but not the estates themselves, which remained the property of the order and the crown. At all events, this was not the first instance of such an

arrangement, as the king undertook a similar use of revenue from vacant Constantinian commanderies for his son, Vincenzo, Count of Milazzo, six years earlier; see royal decree number 2445 of 4 August 1851. With decree 2444 under the same date, the assets and revenue of a specific Constantinian commandery, Monticchio ed Acquatetta, were established as a trust for Prince Giuseppe, Count of Lucera. (Young Vincenzo lived from 1851 to 1854, and Giuseppe from 1848 to 1851.)

94. This is merely a concise introduction. A fine overview and historiography is presented in Seward, Desmond, *Italy's Knights of Saint George: The Constantinian Order* (1986); see also the volume by Antonio Spada published in 2002 (in Sources). For a concise view of the orders and their work today see Mendola, Louis, *The Royal House of the Two Sicilies: An Introduction to the Orders of Chivalry* (2020). A great deal has been published in Italian. As regards Roman Catholic dynastic orders generally, including those of the House of the Two Sicilies, the most reliable reference in English remains Peter Bander van Duren's *Orders of Knighthood and of Merit: The Pontifical, Religious and Secularised Catholic-founded Orders and their Relationship to the Holy See* (1995).

95. Scipione Maffei questioned this kind of lax research methodology in his *De Fabula Equestris Ordinis Constantiniani,* published in 1712. The Holy See soon placed Maffei's work in its index of prohibited books.

96. This is the most important pontifical declaration regarding the Constantinian Order. In effect, it "reconstitutes" the order by establishing its form and function henceforth, as if the pope were approving a charter of foundation. It should be noted that pontiffs no longer involve themselves in dynastic orders in this way. The present policy of the Vatican regarding dynastic orders beyond the explicit purview of the Holy See is stated in its *Bollettino* of 16 October 2012 (B0585), "Precisazione della Segreteria di Stato in Merito agli Ordini Equestri."

97. King Charles transmitted the Constantinian Order to his son, Ferdinand, on 16 October 1759 with a decree that followed the Pragmatic because the Farnese inheritance was separate from the crowns of Naples and Sicily. This successively received pontifical confirmation. The fact was noted by one of the foremost experts on Catholic orders of chivalry, who wrote that, "Carlos III of Spain indeed handed the grand mastership over to his son Ferdinand, but that was at a later date and separately from his

renunciation of the throne of the Two Sicilies." See Cardinale, Hyginus, *Orders of Knighthood, Awards and the Holy See* (revised edition edited by Peter Bander van Duren 1985), page 146. As recently as 1796, Ferdinand explicitly referred to the Farnese inheritance being separate from the Neapolitan crown. See also the following note.

98. Ruo, Raffaele, *Saggio Storico degli Ordine Cavallereschi Antichi e Moderni, Estinti ed Esistenti, Istituiti nel Regno delle Due Sicilie sotto le Varie Dinastie* (Naples 1832), page 37 ("l'ordine restò costantemente attaccato alla corona di Napoli" and "l'ordine, oltre la dignità di gran maestro, ch'è sempre inerente alla corona"); *Rito e Forma da praticarsi nell'arme uno o più cavalieri del Real Ordine Costantiano di San Giorgio nella Capitale di Napoli, estratto dalle Costituzioni dell'Ordine, che ha comandato osservarsi la Maestà del Re Nostro Sovrano Francesco I, Gran Maestro del Real Ordine* (Stamperia Reale, Naples 1826). For a decree in 1822 referring to the "Royal" Constantinian Order, see *Collezione delle Leggi e dé Decreti Reali del Regno delle Due Sicilie* (Semestre I, Jan-Jun), Stamperia Reale, 1822, decree 241 (5 June 1822), page 314. More recently, the *Almanacco Reale* for 1857 (on page 408), states that "the grand master is always the king," *è sempre il re.*

99. The *Almanacco Reale del Regno delle Due Sicilie* (Stamperia Reale, Naples), for 1841, pages 100-101, under "Reali segreterie e ministeri di stato," describes the responsibilities of this *Secondo Ripartimento* (Second Division) as: Concessione de' diversi ordini cavallereschi. Collazione delle commende Costantiniane e de' benefici Antoniani. Spedizione de' reali diplomi e delle reali cedoli per tali collazioni. Corrispondenza colla real Deputazione Costantiniana per l'esame de' titoli che danno dritto al godimento delle commende familiari; per la formazione de' processi occorrenti per la fondazione delle nuove commende, e per le pruove di nobiltà degli aspiranti alla croce Costantiniana di giustizia. Corrispondenza cogli' Intendenti e cogli' Inquisitori Costantiniani nelle provincie del regno per tutto ciò che riguarda l'economica amministrazione del real Ordine Costantiniano. Affitti ed amministrazione delle commende vacanti dell'ordine medesimo. Concessione delle pensioni pel real Ordine di S. Giorgio della riunione. Permessione per domandare a far uso di decorazioni estere. Concessione delle Medaglie del Merito civile, in seguito de' rapporti de' rispettivi Ministri Segretarii di Stato. Redazione del protocollo delle conferenze com S.M. per gli affari di questo ripartimento. Spedizione de' reali rescritti alle diverse dipendenze. The *Almanacco Reale* for 1857 (page 89) contains virtually the same text.

100. The last major commandery of *giuspatronato* was granted to Nicola d'Elia of Seminara, in Calabria, in 1858, dedicated to his patron saint, Nicholas of Bari; this was confiscated with other properties of the Constantinian Order following the annexation of the Kingdom of the Two Sicilies to the Kingdom of Italy. Nevertheless, the titular right to it was inherited by the founder's heirs in the line of male primogeniture, who eventually emigrated. A page from the notification of the commandery's foundation is shown at the end of this appendix; interestingly, it was certified by Raffaele Ruo, still the order's notary, who wrote a book, *Saggio Storico* (see note 98) about the dynastic orders in 1832. (In the Two Sicilies, as in Italy today, a notary was a barrister, an attorney, holding a special qualification; Ruo was an expert jurist authorized to make important rulings within the Constantinian Order, where his position was similar to that of a chancellor. He was, in fact, the leading legal scholar specialized on the order toward the end of the life of the kingdom, when his book, complemented by a lengthy treatise written in 1841, was the standard reference on its orders of knighthood. No study of the status of the Constantinian Order during the reigns of Ferdinand II and Francis II is complete without an examination of Ruo's work.)

101. See Mendola, Louis, "English and Italian Legacy of the Norman Knight Figures of Monreale," *The Coat of Arms,* journal of The Heraldry Society, London, edited by John P. Brooke-Little, Norroy and Ulster King of Arms; NS volume X, number 166, summer 1994 (ISSN 0010-003X), pages 245-254. This is extracted in Chapter 18 of the author's *Sicilian Genealogy and Heraldry* (2013).

102. For a demonstrable indication of literacy levels, we look to *stato civile* (vital statistics) records of birth, marriage and death kept in the Two Sicilies, which required signatures or otherwise stated that the registrant could not read and write; those for acts of birth are especially useful. These were instituted in 1809 in the Kingdom of Naples and 1820 in Sicily. Having examined many thousands of such registrations, the author estimates general literacy at approximately 24 percent by 1860 in the Two Sicilies. To the very limited extent such records existed pre-1860 elsewhere in Italy, a more-or-less comparable estimate for other regions is valid. The problem is that most of the pre-unitary states that constituted the Kingdom of Italy (after 1860) lack sufficient records to consult. Speaking generally, very few documents of any kind issued before 1860 referring to specific persons required signatures

(which would prove literacy), and in most of Italy there were no vital statistics records in the decades immediately prior to 1860. Normally, something like a census form would not have to be signed by the person being interviewed, and no original records survive of the haphazard, incomplete census of 1861 (sometimes cited to "prove" that only 10 percent of southerners were literate), the accuracy of which cannot be confirmed and plainly conflicts with the author's findings. Nor are there original records of the census of 1871. The only civil record existing for *every* citizen, not merely soldiers or students, was a birth registration, but *only in the states that implemented these before 1860*. Acts of baptism were not usually signed by the parents or godparents. In the course of performing genealogical research over many years (the book *Sicilian Genealogy and Heraldry* considers research methodology), the author has also consulted many vital statistics records issued in the Kingdom of Italy beginning in 1866; not all of the birth registrations during this era required a parent's signature. It is interesting that in Sicily from 1860 until 1865 there were still civil birth registrations, a holdover from the Two Sicilies, even though they had yet to be implemented in northern Italy; these can readily be consulted in the Gancia division at the Palermo Archive of State. There were no universal "literacy tests" to ascertain reading ability in the general population. At the most, a school might have a list of students which could be compared to lists of local citizens to determine, in a general way, the percentage of local residents who attended schools. The number of schools in the Two Sicilies itself suggests a fairly high level of literacy (see note 67). Compulsory public instruction for children in primary grades was instituted in 1877 (mandatory education to the age of 14 years was made law in 1962), but rather few public (state) schools were built by the new government in southern Italy, and certainly not in Sicily, before 1880. The first state schools established by this law opened in Tuscany, Piedmont and other regions north of Rome. Certain proponents of the "illiteracy theory," such as Luigi Settembrini, being outspoken advocates of unification and detractors of the kings of the Two Sicilies, brought obvious "confirmation bias" to their pronouncements, and it should be remembered that, much like the original census data for 1861 and 1871, a great deal of documentation in the Kingdom of Italy, such as records regarding the occupation of Ethiopia, has been made to disappear; see Denis Mack Smith's "Documentary Falsification and Italian Biography" (cited elsewhere). In 1943, long after the unification, illiterate Italian soldiers held prisoner in camps in the United States of America were being taught to read and write the Italian language whilst in captivity; most of these men were born in the twentieth century, after Italy claimed to have conquered illiteracy and could no longer blame such problems on the pre-unitary states.

103. See Nickerson, Raymond, "Confirmation Bias: A Ubiquitous Phenomenon in Many Guises," *Review of General Psychology*, volume 2, number 2 (1998), pages 175-220.

104. Van Cleave, Rachel, "Rape and Querela Law in Italy: False Protection of Victim Agency," *Michigan Journal of Gender and Law*, volume 13, January 2007 (Ann Arbor 2007), pages 273-310. See also: Galli, Natalie, *The Girl Who Said No: A Search in Sicily* (2019); Bubola, Emma, "Locker-room talks: Italian politics and normalized sexism," *Al Jazeera* (11 March 2018); Donadio, Rachel, "The Missing Piece in Italian Politics: Women," *The Atlantic* (10 March 2018); Pianigiani, Gaia, "Women Could Decide Italy's Election, But They Feel Invisible," *The New York Times* (3 March 2018); Siri, Simona, "Having a misogynist leader has consequences. And no, I don't mean Trump," *The Washington Post* (14 December 2017); Soncini, Guia, "The Failure of Italian Feminism," *The New York Times* (26 October 2017); Giuffrida, Angela, "Italy's highest court accused of victim blaming over rape case," *The Guardian* (17 July 2018); Horowitz, Jason, "In Italy, #MeToo is More Like 'Meh'" in *The New York Times* (16 December 2017); Vigo, Julian, "Tight Jeans, Rape and Technology," *Forbes* (22 July 2018); Winfield, Nicole, "Italian Court Ruling That a Woman Was Too Ugly to Be Raped Sparks Outrage," *Time* (14 March 2019); Reynolds, James, "'I'm full of fear': Italian Woman's Story Exposes Rape Law," *BBC News* (12 April 2019). In 2018, the *Global Gender Gap Report* published by the World Economic Forum found Italy in 70th place compared to France in 12th, Britain in 15th and Spain in 29th. During the same year, Italy (with a population of some 58 million), had 142 femicides. ISTAT, the Italian national statistics agency, reports that 43.6 percent of Italian women (nearly 9 million) between the ages of 15 and 65 have been sexually harassed in the workplace, 15.4 percent in the three years immediately prior to the report; see *Statistiche Report: Le molestie e i ricatti sessuali sul lavoro 2015-2016* (13 February 2018), published in English in condensed form under the same date as *Sexual Harassment and Sexual Blackmail at Work*. See also Bastiani, Federica, et al., "Mental Distress and Sexual Harassment in Italian University Students," *Archives of Women's Mental Health*, volume 22, number 2 (April 2019), pages 229-236; Romito, Patrizia, et al., "Sexual Harassment and Menstrual Disorders Among Italian University Women: A Cross-sectional Observational Study,"

NOTES

Scandinavian Journal of Public Health, volume 45, number 5 (May 2017), pages 528-535; Marzano, Flavia, "Le Dinamiche di Reclutamento e di Carriera delle Donne nel Sistema Universitario Italiano," *Rassegna ASTRID,* number 77 (12 September 2008), year 4, number 15; Balloni, Bisi, Sette, *Gender-Based Violence, Stalking and Fear of Crime: EU Country Report for Italy* (University of Bologna 2012). An increasing number of cases have been reported in the press in the last few years, such as Campicelli, Lino, "'Vuoi laurearti? Resta nuda sotto la toga': nei guai un professore universitario," *Il Messagero* (9 May 2019); Foschini, Giuliano, "Bari: Docente universitario accusato di violenza resta in servizio," *La Repubblica* (25 May 2019); Vigne, Aurora, "Abusi sessuali su studentesse a La Sapienza: Indagato un professore," *Il Giornale* (29 May 2019). The Italian version of #MeToo is #QuellaVoltaChe.

105. Zamoyski, Adam, "The Hero of Italian Unification," *The Telegraph,* "Books" section, 31 May 2007, reviewing *Garibaldi: Invention of a Hero* by Lucy Riall. For commentary by Italian scholars on corrective revisionism in historiography by 1990, and certainly by 2011, see the papers by Maurizio Isabella, Antonino Recupero, Pasquale Villani and others in Sources.

106. Maria Carolina of the Two Sicilies (1856-1941), a granddaughter of King Francis I through his youngest son, Francesco, Count of Trapani (see Table 2), wed Count Andrzej Zamoyski.

107. See Wineburg, Sam, "Undue Certainty: Where Howard Zinn's *A People's History* Falls Short," *American Educator,* winter 2012-2013, pages 27-34.

DELL' HISTORIA
DELLA CITTÀ, E REGNO
DI NAPOLI,
DI GIO. ANTONIO SVMMONTE
NAPOLITANO.
TOMO SECONDO.
NEL QVALE SI DESCRIVENO I GESTI DI SVOI RE
Normandi, Tedeschi, Francesi, e Durazzeschi,
Dall'anno 1127. infino al 1442.

CON L'EFFIGIE DI ESSI RE, ALBERI DI DESCENDENTI,
& Epitaffij delle loro sepolture.

SI FA ANCO MENTIONE DI SVOI ARCIVESCOVI,
e Chiese, con altre cose degne.

SECONDA EDITIONE.

IN NAPOLI L'ANNO SANTO M. DC. LXXV.
A spese di ANTONIO BVLIFON Libraro all'insegna della Sirena
Con licenza de' Superiori, e Priuilegio.

Summonte's history of the Kingdom of Naples, 1675

Sources and Bibliography

This is a "select" bibliography insofar as its focus is the period after 1700, and because only the most immediately relevant works are included, though it constitutes a reasonably adequate "syllabus." Not every work cited in the endnotes is listed here; only a few sources appear which are directly pertinent to the Middle Ages, or to Italy after 1870. Nor are there many books listed that were written specifically about the *Risorgimento,* to which countless volumes, made from the timber of entire forests, have been dedicated.

As stated elsewhere, the major archives and libraries in Naples, Palermo, Bari, Messina, the Vatican, Parma, Barcelona, Madrid and Simancas were consulted over the last three decades. This includes the *Archivio Borbone,* acquired in 1951 from the royal family by the Naples Archive of State (which received it in 1953), and additional papers of King Francis II and his brother, Alfonso, now held in the archive of the royal family in Rome. Appendix 7, which deals with historiography, considers the conservation, consultation and interpretation of original sources.

Catalogues of many archival sources, though not usually the documents themselves, may be available online. To mention just a few in the Naples Archive of State: Ministero della Presidenza, Ministero dell'Interno, Ministero di Grazia e Giustizia, Ministero della Guerra, Casa Reale Amministrativa (indexed by the reigns of the sovereigns after Charles III), Catasti Onciari.

Apart from these, there are various collections of letters, such as those of Tanucci, and the almost-weekly letters from Charles III to Ferdinand I from 1775 to 1785, of which some duplicates are conserved in Spain. These reflect, amongst other phenomena, the subtle conflicts of interest between the kingdoms of Naples and Spain during that era. Very few of these original records have been translated into English.

A fair amount of academic scholarship has been published during the first two decades of our century about the Two Sicilies, and a number of those recent monographs and papers are listed here. By no means is this volume (or this bibliography) the "last word" on the topic. Rather, as the first major monograph about the kingdom (rather than the dynasty, the unification movement or some aspect of microhistory) to be published in English, it is intended as a foundation to "frame" this subject while attracting more attention to it.

The secondary literature includes edited collections as well as monographs and papers (articles or chapters). Both casual readers and scholars may find this "canon" useful for further reading; there are even a few guides to Neapolitan and Sicilian grammar. As one would suppose, most of the primary sources are in Italian, but an effort has been made to include a few secondary works that were published in English. The author consulted most of these works, and numerous others, directly, in their print format (yes, as actual paper books), some long before the internet simplified such research. Today, some of these works are available online from sites like Google Books, Archive.Org and Academia.Edu. The inclusion of a secondary work in this list does not necessarily imply agreement with everything presented in it.

Primary and Contemporary Sources

Almanacco Reale del Regno delle Due Sicilie. Court circular.

Annali Civili del Regno delle Due Sicilie. Ministry of the Interior.

Archivio Borbone. Collection of royal papers at Naples Archive of State.

Archivio Familiare. Papers retained by the royal family in Rome.

Bullettino delle Leggi del Regno di Napoli. Legislation during Murat's reign.

Carlo di Borbone: Lettere ai Sovrani di Spagna. Edited by Imma Ascione (2002).

Catasti onciari. Occasional tax census, peninsular regions, Naples Archive of State.

Codice Penale per gli Stati di Sua Maestà il Re di Sardegna (1859).

Codice delle Leggi del Regno di Napoli. Edited by Alessio De Sariis (1794).

Codice per lo Regno delle Due Sicilie (1819). Code of 1819.

Codice per lo Regno delle Due Sicilie (1848). Revised code, 1848.

Collezione delle Leggi e de'Decreti Reali del Regno delle Due Sicilie.

Constitutionum Regni Siciliarum (Naples 1773). Constitutions of Melfi.

SOURCES AND BIBLIOGRAPHY

Costituzione Politica del Regno delle Due Sicilie (1821).

Costituzione Politica del Regno delle Due Sicilie (1848).

Corriere della Sera, Milan, 14 August 2011, page 41.

Elenco Alfabetico delle Province, Distretti, Circondari, Comuni e Villaggi del Regno delle Due Sicilie. Compilation by Gabriello De Sanctis (1854).

The Ferraris Chronicle. Translation and notes by Jacqueline Alio (2017).

Gazzetta Ufficiale della Repubblica Italiana, general series number 106, of 23 April 2020, pages 3-4.

Giornale del Regno delle Due Sicilie. Newspaper of record, 1815-1860.

Lettere di Bernardo Tanucci a Carlo III di Borbone 1759-1776. Edited by Rosa Mincuzzi (1969).

Lezioni di Diritto Positivo secondo il Codice per lo Regno delle Due Sicilie. Compilation and notes by Saverio Cangiano (1841).

The Liber Augustalis or Constitutions of Melfi. Translation by James Powell (1971).

Nati Vivi: Nati dentro e fuori dal matrimonio (ISTAT 2018).

La Reggia in Trionfo per l'Acclamazione e Coronazione di Carlo, Infante di Spagna, Re di Sicilia, Napoli e Gerusalemme (1736). Compilation by Pietro La Placa.

Il Regno di Napoli dalla Tutela all'Emancipazione 1775-1789: Lettere di Ferdinando IV a Carlo III ed Altri Documenti Inediti. Edited by Carlo Knight (2015).

Riveli. Occasional wealth tax census, or *donativo,* Sicily, in *Tribunale del Real Patrimonio* and *Deputazione del Regno,* Palermo Archive of State, Catena division.

Roger II and the Creation of the Kingdom of Sicily. Translations of Assizes of Ariano and several chronicles, with notes, by Graham Loud (2012).

Scienza della Legislazione. Series by Gaetano Filangieri (1780).

Sicily's Rebellion against King Charles. Translation and notes by Louis Mendola (2015).

Stato Civile 1809-1860. Vital statistics records for peninsular regions. Provincial archives of state (Naples, Bari, Salerno, Potenza, Brindisi. etc.).

Stato Civile 1820-1865. Vital statistics records for Sicily, Palermo Archive of State, Gancia division.

Trattato di Accomodamento tra la Santa Sede e la Corte di Napoli Conchiuso in Roma tra i Plenopotenziari della Santità Papa Benedetto XIV e della Maestà di Carlo, Infante di Spagna, Re delle Due Sicilie. Edited by Francesco Ricciardo (1741).

"Tre Ordines per l'Incoronazione di un Re e di una Regina del Regno Normanno in Sicilia," *Atti del Congresso Internazionale di Studi sulla Sicilia Normanna* (Palermo 1974), pages 438-459. Notes by Reinhard Elze.

Verso la Riforma della Spagna: Il Carteggio tra Mara Amalia di Sassonia e Bernardo Tanucci 1759-1760. Edited by Pablo Vazquez Gestal (2016).

Secondary Literature

Acton, Harold. *The Bourbons of Naples* (1956).
Acton, Harold. *The Last Bourbons of Naples* (1961).
Adone, Pasquale. *Elementi della Storia del Regno delle Due Sicilie* (1853).
Agresta, Salvatore. *L'Istruzione in Sicilia 1815-1860* (1995).
Ajello, Raffaele. *Il Problema della Riforma Giudiziaria e Legislativa nel Regno di Napoli Durante la Prima Metà del Secolo XVIII* (1965).
Ajello, Raffaele. *La Vita Politica Napoletana sotto Carlo di Borbone: La fondazione ed il tempo eroico della dinastia* (1972).
Ajello, Raffaele, and D'Addio, Mario (editors). "Bernardo Tanucci: Statista, Letterato, Giurista," *Atti del Convegno Internazionale di Studi per il Secondo Centenario 1783-1983* (Naples 1988).
Alessi Palazzolo, Giorgia. *Giustizia e Polizia, Volume 1: Il Controllo di Una Capitale, Napoli 1779-1803* (1992).
Alio, Jacqueline. *Queens of Sicily 1061-1266* (2018).

Alio, Jacqueline. *Sicilian Queenship: Power and Identity in the Kingdom of Sicily 1061-1266* (2019).
Amabile, Luigi. *Il Santo Officio della Inquisizione in Napoli: Narrazione con Molti Documenti Inediti* (1892).
Andolfi, Colomba. *Facile, Facile: Impariamo la lingua napoletana* (2016).
D'Angio, Anteo. *La Situazione Finanziaria Italiana dal 1796 al 1870* (1973).
Antonelli, Attilio (editor). *Cerimoniale dei Borbone di Napoli 1734-1801* (2017).
Aprile, Pino. *Terroni: All that has been done to ensure that the Italians of the South became southerners* (2011).
Ascione, Gina Carla. *Vita di Corte al Tempo di Carlo di Borbone nel Palazzo Reale di Napoli* (2014).
Atkinson, Rick. *The Day of Battle: The War in Sicily and Italy, 1943-1944* (2007).
Baldacci, Giuseppe. "L'istruzione nell'Italia pre e post unitaria, il caso Catania," *Archivio Storico per la Sicilia Orientale,* year 105, series 2 (2009), pages 290-316.
Ballarati, Antonino. *La Storia Proibita dei Borbone* (2018).
Bander van Duren, Peter. *Orders of Knighthood and of Merit: The Pontifical, Religious and Secularised Catholic-founded Orders and their Relationship to the Holy See* (1995).
Barbagallo, Francesco. "Discussioni e Progetti sul Commercio tra Napoli e Costantinopoli nel '700," *Rivista Storica Italiana,* volume 83, number 2 (1971), pages 264-296.
Barra, Francesco. *Il Regno delle Due Sicilie: Studi e Ricerche* (2018).
Bascapè, Giacomo. *L'Ordine Costantiniano di San Giorgio e l'Ordine di San Gennaro della Casa di Borbone delle Due Sicilie* (1972).
Beccatini, Francesco. *Storia del Regno di Carlo III di Borbone* (1790).
Bedani, Gino (editor). *The Politics of Italian National Identity* (2000).
Belmonte, Guido. *Il Regno delle Due Sicilie: Liberali, ecclesiastici, fuorusciti, traditori* (2015).
Berger, Helge, and Spoerer, Mark. "Economic Crises and the European Revolutions of 1848," *Journal of Economic History,* Volume 62, Number 2 (2001).
Bianchini, Lodovico. *Della Storia delle Finanze del Regno di Napoli* (1839).
Bianchini, Lodovico. *Storia Economica-Civile di Sicilia* (1841).
Bonetta, Gaetano. *Istruzione e Società nella Sicilia dell'Ottocento* (1981).
Brevetti, Giulio. "Il Re Bomba e l'Eclissi della Natura: Una Lettura Iconografica della Raffigurazioni di Ferdinando II di Borbone," *Per la Conoscenza dei Beni Culturali,* volume 5 (2014), pages 185-204.

Briganti, Tommaso (editor). *Pratica Criminale delle Corti Regie e Baronali del Regno di Napoli* (1770).
Broccoli, Angelo. *Educazione e Politica nel Mezzogiorno d'Italia 1767-1860* (1968).
Buccaro, Alfredo (editor). *Storia e Immagini del Palazzo Reale di Napoli* (2001).
Buccaro, Alfredo. *Opere Pubbliche e Tipologie Urbane nel Mezzogiorno Preunitario* (1992).
Bucher, Michael. "Re-Discovering the Italian Kingdom of the Two Sicilies," *Time* ("Lightbox" section), 25 August 2016.
Bulgarelli Lukacs, Alessandra. *Alla Ricerca del Contribuente: Fisco, Catasto, Gruppi di Potere, Ceti Emergenti nel Regno di Napoli del XVIII Secolo* (2004).
Bulgarelli Lukacs, Alessandra. *L'Imposta Diretta nel Regno di Napoli in Età Moderna* (1993).
Buonanno, Michael. *Sicilian Epic and Marionette Theater* (2014).
Burton, Delvecchio, Germani, Mazzeschi, "Individualism/Collectivism and Personality in Italian and American Groups," *Current Psychology*, volume 38, issue 6 (18 December 2019).
Buttà, Giuseppe. *Un Viaggio da Boccadifalco a Gaeta: Memorie della Rivoluzione 1860-1861* (1875).
Calabrò, Vittoria. *Istituzioni Universitarie e Insegnamento del Diritto in Sicilia 1767-1885* (2002).
Calaresu, Melissa. "Making and Eating Ice Cream in Naples: Rethinking Consumption and Sociability in the Eighteenth Century," *Past and Present*, number 220 (August 2013), pages 35-78.
Campbell, Ian. *The Addis Ababa Massacre: Italy's National Shame* (2017).
Candela, Simone. *I Piemontesi in Sicilia 1713-1718* (1996).
Cangiano, Saverio. *Lezioni di Diritto Positivo secondo il Codice per lo Regno delle Due Sicilie* (1841).
Cannistraro, Philip. *Historical Dictionary of Fascist Italy* (1982).
Cantalupo, Benedetto. *I Principi e gli Effetti del Sistema Governativo delle Due Sicilie dal 1830 al 1848* (1850).
Cantone, Gaetana (editor). *Il Teatro del Re: Il San Carlo da Napoli all'Europa* (1987).
Capozzi, Eugenio. "Risorgimento e Identità Nazionale nel Cattolicesimo Politico Italiano," *La Nazione tra i Banchi* (2012), pages 77-90.
Cardinale, Hyginus. *Orders of Knighthood, Awards and the Holy See* (revised ed, 1985).
Caridi, Giuseppe. *Carlo III: Un Grande Re Riformatore a Napoli e in Spagna* (2014).

Carpanetto, Dino, and Ricuperati, Giuseppe. *L'Italia del Settecento: Crisi, Trasformazioni, Lumi* (1986).
Carreca, Salvatore. *Viaggio tra le Meraviglie della Due Sicilie 1735-1860* (2018).
Carroll, Philip. "Sulphur Mines in Sicily" *Scientific American Supplement* (1891).
Carta, Francesco. *Storia del Reame delle Due Sicilie dall'Epoca della Repubblica Romana fino ai Dì Nostri* (1848).
Caruso, Alfio. Garibaldi, Corruzione e Tradimento: Così crollò il Regno delle Due Sicilie (2020).
Cavallera, Hervé. "La rilevanza del tema educativo nella Napoli di Carlo Borbone," *Carlo di Borbone e la Stretta Via del Riformismo in Puglia* (Bari 2019), pages 175-196.
Chiosi, Elvira. *Lo Spirito del Secolo: Politica e Religione a Napoli nell'Età dell'Illuminismo* (1992).
Chiosso, Giorgio. *Alfabeti d'Italia: La lotta contro l'ignoranza nell'Italia Unita* (2011).
Ciano, Antonio. *One Nation Under Blood* (2018).
Cicciò, Sebastiano. *Gli Stati Uniti e il Regno delle Due Sicilie nell'Ottocento: Relazioni Commerciali, Culturali e Diplomatiche* (2020).
Ciconte, Enzo. *La Grande Mattanza: Storia della Guerra al Brigantaggio* (2018).
Cipolla, Gaetano. *Learning Sicilian* (2013).
Cirillo, Filippo. *Il Regno delle Due Sicilie Descritto ed Illustrato* (1853).
Cognasso, Francesco. *I Savoia* (1971).
Cognetti, Biagio. *Passato e Presente nel Reame delle Due Sicilie* (1862).
Colletta, Pietro. *Storia del Reame di Napoli dal 1734 sino al 1823* (1838).
Coniglio, Giuseppe. *I Borboni di Napoli* (1999).
Correnti, Santi. *Storia di Sicilia come Storia del Popolo Siciliano* (7th ed, Catania 1995).
Corsi, Carlo. *Difesa dei Soldati Napoletani* (1860).
Corsi, Pasquale (editor). *Carlo di Borbone e la Stretta Via del Riformismo in Puglia* (Bari 2019).
Cotugno, Raffaele. *Giovan Battista Vico e il Suo Secolo* (1890).Cotugno, Raffaele. *Massari del Risorgimento* (1921).
Crimi, Alfio. *Teoria Educativa e Scuola Popolare in Sicilia nel Tempo dei Borboni* (1978).
Crimi, Alfio. "L'Istruzione Femminile tra il Sette e l'Ottocento in Sicilia," Nuovi Quaderni del Meridione, volume 84 (1983), pages 465-471.
Croce, Benedetto. *Storia del Regno di Napoli* (1925).
D'Acierno, Pellegrino (editor). *Delirious Naples: A Cultural History of the City of the Sun* (2018).

Dalbono, Cesare. *Quadro Storico delle Due Sicilie* (1853, 1858).
D'Amora, Rosita. "The Diplomatic Relations Between Naples and the Ottoman Empire in the Mid-Eighteenth Century: Cultural Perceptions," *Oriente Moderno,* year 22, number 3 (2003), pages 715-727.
D'Amore, Manuela. *The Royal Society and the Discovery of the Two Sicilies: Southern Routes in the Grand Tour* (2017).
D'Angelo, Fabio. *Scienze e Viaggio: Ingegneri e Architetti del Regno delle Due Sicilie* (2014).
Davidson, Ian. *The French Revolution: From Enlightenment to Tyranny* (2016).
Davies, Norman. *Vanished Kingdoms* (2012).
Davis, John. *Conflict and Control: Law and Order in Nineteenth-Century Italy* (1988).
Davis, John. *Naples and Napoleon: Southern Italy and the European Revolutions 1780-1860* (2006).
Davis, John (editor). *Society and Politics in the Age of the Risorgimento* (1991).
De Cesare, Raffaele. *La Fine di un Regno* (2nd edition, 1900).
De Crescenzo, Gennaro. "L'Altro 1799: Massacri, Saccheggi e il Giudizio (negativo) di Mazzini sulla Repubblica Napoletana," Quaderni per la Verità Storica, volume 1 (2018), pages 1-8.
De Crescenzo, Gennaro. "Le Scuole al Tempo dei Borboni," *Quaderni per la Verità Storica,* volume 2 (2018), pages 1-13.
De Francesco, Antonino. "La Diversità Meridionale nell'Età del Liberalismo Postunitario," *La Nazione tra i Banchi* (2012), pages 47-60.
Del Boca, Lorenzo. *Italiani, Brava Gente?* (2014).
Del Boca, Lorenzo. *Savoia Boia! L'Italia unita come non ce l'hanno raccontata* (2018).
De Lorenzo, Renata. *Borbonia Felix: Il Regno delle Due Sicilia alla Vigilia del Crollo* (2013).
De Marco, Domenico. *La "Statistica" del Regno di Napoli nel 1811* (1988).
De Simone, Eugenio. *Atterrite Queste Popolazioni: La Repressione del Brigantaggio nel Carteggio Privato Sacchi-Milon 1868-1870* (2016).
De Sivo, Giacinto. *Storia delle Due Sicilie dal 1847 al 1861* (1868).
D'Este, Carlo. *Bitter Victory: The Battle for Sicily, 1943* (1988).
De Vincentiis, Emma. "La Caduta della Monarchia Borbonica in un'Opera Inedita di Ludovico Bianchini," *Archivio Storico Italiano,* series 7, volume 4, number 3 (1925), pages 77-84.
Di Biasio, Aldo. "Ingegneri e Territorio nel Regno di Napoli dal Decennio Francese all'Unità: L'attività del Corpo di Ponti e Strade," *Scienzati Artisti: Formazione e Ruolo degli Ingegneri nelle Fonti dell'Archivio di Stato e della Facoltà d'Ingegneria di Napoli* (2003), pages 91-106.

Di Blasi, Giovanni. *Storia del Regno di Sicilia* (1844).
Di Cesare, Raffaele. *La Fine di un Regno: Napoli e Sicilia* (1900).
Dickie, John. *Cosa Nostra: A History of the Sicilian Mafia* (2005).
Dickie, John. *Darkest Italy: The Nation and Stereotypes of the Mezzogiorno, 1860-1900* (1999).
Di Costanzo, Angelo. *Le Istorie del Regno di Napoli dal 1250 fino al 1498* (1572).
Di Fiore, Gigi. *1861, Pontelandolfo e Casalduni: Un Massacro Dimenticato* (1998).
Di Fiore, Gigi. *Controstoria dell'Unità d'Italia: Fatti e Misfatti del Risorgimento* (2010).
Di Giovine. *Pagine di Storia Militare del Regno delle Due Sicilie* (2018).
Di Lauro, Raffaelle. *L'Assedio e la Resa di Gaeta 1860-1861* (1928).
Di Rienzo, Eugenio. *Il Regno della Due Sicilie e le Potenze Europee 1830-1861* (2011).
Doyle, Wiliam. *The Oxford History of the French Revolution* (2nd ed, 2003).
Dunbabin, Jean. *Charles I of Anjou: Power, Kingship and State-Making in Thirteenth-Century Europe* (1998).
Durelli, Francesco. *Colpo d'Occhio su le Condizioni del Reame delle Due Sicilie nel Corso dell'Anno 1862* (1863).
Elliott, John. "A Europe of Composite Monarchies," *Past and Present*, volume 137, number 1 (November 1992), pages 48-71.
Erwin, Dale, and Maria Teresa Fedele. *241 Neapolitan Verbs* (2014)
Erwin, Dale, and Maria Teresa Fedele. *Modern Neapolitan Grammar* (2011)
Esdaile, Charles. *Napoleon's Wars: An International History 1803-1815* (2009).
Esposito, Gabriele. *Armies of the Italian Wars of Unification, Volume 1: Piedmont and the Two Sicilies* (2017).
Falzone, Maria Teresa. "Assistenza e Beneficenza a Palermo dopo l'Unità ed il Progetto 'La Casa dei Poveri' di Giacomo Cusmano," *Archivio Storico Siciliano,* series 4, volume 10 (Palermo 1984), pages 154-177.
Farinelli, Antonio. *Le Dogane di Confine tra Stato Pontificio e Regno delle Due Sicilie* (2020).
Fazello, Thomas. *De Rebus Siculis* (1558-1560).
Fazio, Ida, "Istruzione ed Educazione delle Donne nella Sicilia Borbonica," *Contributi per un Bilancio del Regno Borbonico* (1990), pages 116-135.
Felice, Costantino. *Mezzogiorno tra Identità e Storia: Catastrofi, Retoriche, Luoghi Comuni* (2017).
Fernandez Diaz, Roberto. *Carlos III: Un Monarca Reformista* (2016).
Ferrara, Francesco. *Storia Generale della Sicilia* (1831).
Ferrari, Alessandro. *Ristretto della Storia di Napoli e Sicilia* (1857).

Ferraro, Giuseppe. *Il Prefetto e i Briganti: La Calabria e l'Unificazione Italiana 1861-1865* (2016).
Fierro, Aurelio. *Grammatica della Lingua Napoletana* (1989).
Finocchiaro, Vincenzo. *La Rivoluzione Siciliana del 1848-1849 e la Spedizione del Generale Filangieri* (1906).
Fiore, Antonio. *Camorra e Polizia nella Napoli Borbonica 1840-1860* (2019).
Fiorelli, Vittoria (editor). *La Nazione tra i Banchi: Il Contributo della Scuola alla Formazione degli Italiani tra Otto e Novecento* (2012).
Focardi, Filippo. *Il Cattivo Tedesco e il Bravo Italiano: La rimozione delle colpe della seconda guerra mondiale* (2016).
Fodale, Salvatore. *Comes et Legatus Siciliae: Sul privilegio di Urbano II e la Pretesa Apostolica Legazia dei Normanni in Sicilia* (1970).
Fortunato, Giustino. *Il Mezzogiorno e lo Stato Italiano: Discorsi Politici 1880-1910* (1911).
Fortunato, Giustino. *Ricordi di Napoli* (1874).
Fragnito, Gigliola (editor). *Elisabetta Farnese, Principessa di Parma e Regina di Spagna* (2009).
Francesconi, Jeanne. *La Cucina Napoletana* (1974).
Franchetti, Leopoldo. *La Sicilia nel 1876: Le Condizioni Politiche e Amministrative* (1876).
Fraschetti, Mario. *Pontelandolfo e Casalduni Bruciano Ancora* (2018).
Frey, Linda. *The Treaties of the War of the Spanish Succession: An Historical and Critical Dictionary* (1995).
Galasso, Giuseppe. "Appartenenze e identità dagli Stati preunitari alla nuova Italia," *La Nazione tra i Banchi* (2012), pages 24-36.
Galasso, Giuseppe. *Napoli Capitale: Identità politica e identità cittadina. Studi e ricerche 1266-1860* (1998).
Galasso, Giuseppe. "Il Regno della Due Sicilie tra Mito e Realtà," *Mezzogiorno, Risorgimento e Unità d'Italia: Atti del Convegno, Roma, 18, 19 e 20 Maggio 2011* (2014), pages 17-23.
Galasso, Giuseppe. *Storia del Regno di Napoli: Il Mezzogiorno Borbonico e Napoleonico 1734-1815* (2007).
Galli, Natalie. *The Girl Who Said No: A Search in Sicily* (2019).
Garnier, Charles. *Journal du Siége de Gaëte* (1861).
Garnier, Charles. *Le Royaume des Deux-Siciles: Mémoire par Charles Garnier* (1866).
Gatti, Stanislao. *Della Filosofia in Italia* (1846).
Giammattei, Emma. "Letteratura e Risorgimento Meridionale," *Mezzogiorno, Risorgimento e Unità d'Italia: Atti del Convegno, Roma, 18, 19 e 20 Maggio 2011* (2014), pages 291-310.

Giannone, Pietro. *Istoria Civile del Regno di Napoli* (1723).
Giannone, Pietro, and Pecchia, Carlo. *Storia Civile e Politica del Regno di Napoli* (1796).
Gilmour, David. *The Pursuit of Italy: A History of a Land, Its Regions, and Their Peoples* (2011).
Giustiniani, Bernardo. *Historie Cronologiche dell'Origine degl'Ordini Militari e di Tutte le Religioni Cavalleresche* (1692).
Goodwin, John. "Progress of the Two Sicilies Under the Spanish Bourbons from the Year 1734-35 to 1840," *Journal of the Statistical Society of London*, volume 5 (1842).
Gregorio, Domenico. *Cammarata: Notizie sul Territorio e la Sua Storia* (1986).
Grimaldi, Angelo. "La Costituzione Siciliana del 1812," *Revista de Derecho, Universidad del Norte,* number 48 (2017), pages 208-233.
Guarino, Gabriel. "Public Rituals and Festivals in Naples 1503-1799," *A Companion to Early Modern Naples* (2013), pages 257-279.
Guasti, Niccolò. *Lotta Politica e Riforme all'Inizio del Regno di Carlo III: Campomanes e l'espulsione dei gesuiti dalla monarchia spagnola 1759-1768* (2006).
Guerri, Giordano Bruno. *Il Sangue del Sud: Antistoria del Risorgimento e del Brigantaggio* (2010).
Hooper, John. *The Italians* (2014).
Houben, Hubert. *Roger II von Sizilien* (1997).
Iachello, Enrico (editor). *I Borboni in Sicilia 1734-1860* (1998).
Imbruglia, Girolamo (editor). *Naples in the Eighteenth Century: The Birth and Death of a Nation State* (2000).
Isabella, Maurizio. "Rethinking Italy's Nation-Building 150 Years Afterwards: The New Risorgimento Historiography" *Past and Present*, volume 217, number 1 (2012), pages 247-268.
Jaeger, Pier Giusto. *L'Ultimo Re di Napoli* (1982).
Joranson, Einar. "The Inception of the Career of the Normans in Italy: Legend and History," *Speculum,* volume 23, number 3 (July 1948), pages 353-396.
Kamen. Henry. *Philip V of Spain: The King Who Reigned Twice* (2001).
Kamen, Henry. *The War of Succession in Spain, 1700-1715* (1969).
Katz, Robert. *The Fall of the House of Savoy* (1972).
Koenigsberger, Helmut. *The Government of Sicily under Philip II of Spain: A Study in the Practice of Empire* (1951).
La Cecilia, Giovanni. *Giustificazioni: Ferdinando II, il Migliore dei Rei* (1851).
Lancaster, Jordan. *In the Shadow of Vesuvius: A Cultural History of Naples* (2019).

Lang, Francesco. *Compendio Elementare della Storia delle Due Sicilie: Ad uso delle scuole* (1858).
Lanzellotti, Angelo. *Costituzione Politica del Regno di Napoli dell'Anno 1815 sotto Gioacchino Murat* (1820).
Lavalle Cobo, Teresa. *Isabel de Farnesio: La Reina Coleccionista* (2002).
Ligresti, Domenico. *Dinamiche Demografiche nella Sicilia Moderna 1505-1806* (2002).
Lima, Bruno. *Due Sicilie 1860: L'Invasione* (2008).
Li Vecchi, Alfredo. *La Finanza Locale in Sicilia nel '600 e '700* (1994).
Lombardo, Francesca, and Alio, Jacqueline. *Sicilian Food and Wine: The Cognoscente's Guide* (2015).
Lombardo, Maria. *Sotto il Segno dei Borbone* (2016).
Lupo, Maurizio. *Tra le Provvide Cure di Sua Maestà: Stato e Scuola nel Mezzogiorno tra Settecento ed Ottocento* (2005).
Lupo, Salvatore. *L'Unificazione Italiana: Mezzogiorno, Rivoluzione, Guerra Civile* (2011).
Lynn, John. *The Wars of Louis XIV 1667-1714* (1999).
Mack Smith, Denis. *Cavour and Garibaldi 1860: A Study in Political Conflict* (1954, 1985).
Mack Smith, Denis. *Italy and Its Monarchy* (1989).
Mack Smith, Denis. "Documentary Falsification and Italian Biography," *History and Biography: Essays in Honour of Derek Beales* (Cambridge 1996), pages 173-187.
Mack Smith, Denis. *The Making of Italy 1796-1866* (2nd edition, 1988).
Macry, Paolo. "Immagini Riflessi: Il Regno delle Due Sicilie negli Occhi dell'Europa Ottocentesca," *Mezzogiorno, Risorgimento e Unità d'Italia: Atti del Convegno, Roma, 18, 19 e 20 Maggio 2011* (2014), pages 147-156.
Macry, Paolo. *Ottocento: Famiglia, Elites e Patrimoni a Napoli* (1988).
Maestro, Marcello. *Gaetano Filangieri and His Science of Legislation* (1976).
Mafrici, Mirella (editor). *All'Ombra della Corte: Donne e Potere nella Napoli Borbonica 1734-1860* (2010).
Maggiorani, Vincenzo. *Il Sollevamento della Plebe di Palermo e del Circondario nel Settembre 1866* (1866).
Makdisi, John. "The Islamic Origins of the Common Law," *North Carolina Law Review* (June 1999).
Mallett, Robert. *Mussolini in Ethiopia 1919-1935: The Origins of Fascist Italy's African War* (2015).
Mangone, Angelo. *L'Armata Napoletana dal Volturno a Gaeta 1860-1861* (1972).

Marcus, Harold. *A History of Ethiopia* (1994).
Marino, John. *Becoming Neapolitan: Citizen Culture in Baroque Naples* (2011).
Marino, John. *Pastoral Economics in the Kingdom of Naples* (1988).
Marraro, Howard. *Diplomatic Relations between the United States and the Kingdom of the Two Sicilies* (2 vol, 1951-1952).
Martuschelli, Stefania. *La Popolazione del Mezzogiorno nella Statistica di Re Murat* (1979).
Matthew, Donald. *The Norman Kingdom of Sicily* (1992).
Maucieri, Danilo. *Leggi e Decreti Monetari del Regno delle Due Sicilie* (2007).
Mayer, Carl August. *Neapel un die Neapolitaner oder Briefe aus Neapel in die Heimat* (1840).
Mazzarese Fardella, Enrico. "La Condizione Giuridica della Donna nel Liber Augustalis," *Archivio Storico Siciliano,* series 4, volume 21-22 (Palermo 1997), pages 31-44.
Mellone, Viviana. "La Rivoluzione Napoletana del 1848: Fonti e metodi per lo studio della partecipazione politica," *Meridiana,* volume 78 (2013), pages 31-52.
Mendola, Louis. *The Kingdom of Sicily 1130-1860* (2015).
Mendola, Louis. *Sicilian Genealogy and Heraldry* (2014).
Meriggi, Marco. *Gli Stati Italiani Prima dell'Unita: Una Storia Istituzionale* (2002).
Merrill, Charles. *Colom of Catalonia: Origins of Christopher Columbus Revealed* (2008).
Mikaberidze, Alexander. *The Napoleonic Wars: A Global History* (2020).
Mitcham, Samuel, and von Stauffenberg, Freidrich. *The Battle of Sicily: How the Allies Lost Their Chance for Total Victory* (2007).
Moe, Nelson. *The View from Vesuvius: Italian Culture and the Southern Question* (2002).
Montessori, Maria. *La Scoperta del Bambino* (1950).
Monziani, Limonta, Monti, Demai, Cantarelli. "Il Movimento dei Prezzi nel Regno di Napoli dal 1695 al 1755," *Giornale degli Economisti e Annali di Economia,* March-April 1966 (New Series, year 25, numbers 3-4), pages 354-375.
Musella, Luigi. "Tra Analfabetismo e Politica: Scuola e Democrazia tra Otto e Novecento," *La Nazione tra i Banchi* (2012), pages 209-220.
Musto, Ronald. *Baroque Naples: A Documentary History 1600-1800* (2000).
Nicoletta, Antonio. *La Scuola e l'Ordinamento Scolastico nel Regno delle Due Sicilie* (eleaml.org/sud/borbone/nicoletta09.html). Retrieved October 2019.
Nicosia, Filippo. *Il Podere Fruttifero e Dilettevole* (1735).

Nisticò, Ulderico. *Epitome di Storia Politica del Regno delle Due Sicilie dall'8 Dicembre 1816 al 13 Febbraio 1861, e Ancora* (2017).
Nitti, Francesco Saverio. *Scienze delle Finanze* (1903).
Nuzzo, Enrico. "Caratteri delle Nazioni e Identità Patrie nella Cultura Filosofica Meridionale," *Mezzogiorno, Risorgimento e Unità d'Italia: Atti del Convegno, Roma, 18, 19 e 20 Maggio 2011* (2014), pages 311-326.
Oliva, Gianni. *L'Alibi della Resistenza* (2003).
Oliva, Gianni. *Un Regno Che è Stato Grande: La Storia Negata dei Borboni di Napoli e Sicilia* (2011).
Onnis, Pia. *L'Abolizione della Compagnia di Gesù nel Regno di Napoli* (1928).
Orlandi, Andrea (editor). *Memorie del Sud* (1999).
Ostuni, Nicola. *Finanza ed Economia nel Regno delle Due Sicilie* (1992).
Pace, Antonio. *Benjamin Franklin and Italy* (1958).
Pagano, Giovanni. *Storia di Ferdinando II dal 1830 al 1850* (1853).
Palmieri, Giuseppe. *Cenno Storico-Militare dal 1859 al 1861* (1861).
Palmieri, Niccolò. *Storia della Rivoluzione di Sicilia nel 1820* (1848).
Palmieri, Pasquale. *I Taumaturghi della Società: Santi e Potere Politico nel Secolo dei Lumi* (2010).
Panico, Guido. *La Storia e il Suo Racconto* (2017).
Patriarca, Silvana. "Italian neopatriotism: debating national identity in the 1990s," *Modern Italy*, volume 6, number 1 (2001), pages 21-34.
Patriarca, Silvana. *Italian Vices: Nation and Character from the Risorgimento to the Republic* (2010).
Patriarca, Silvana, and Riall, Lucy (editors). *The Risorgimento Revisited: Nationalism and Culture in Nineteenth-Century Italy* (2012).
Payne, Stanley. *A History of Fascism 1914-1945* (1995).
Pecora, Gaetano. *Il Pensiero Politico di Gaetano Filangieri: Una Analisi Critica* (2007).
Pedio, Tommaso. *Reazione alla Politica Piemontese ed Origine del Brigantaggio in Basilicata 1860-1861* (1961).
Pedrini, William. *L'Eccidio di Decima, 5 Aprile 1920: Niuna esitanza, niuna debolezza* (2017)
Pellegrino, Bruno. *Leali o Ribelli: La Chiesa del Sud e l'Unità d'Italia* (2012).
Pellicanò, Stefano. *Genocidio: La Conquista del Regno delle Due Sicilie* (2012).
Pellicciari, Angela. *I Panni Sporchi dei Mille* (2011).
Pellicciari, Angela. *Risorgimento da Riscrivere* (2007).
Peluso, Pasquale. "The Roots of the Organized Criminal Underworld in Campania," *Sociology and Anthropology*, volume 1, number 2 (2013), pages 118-134.

Pennington, Kenneth. "The Birth of the Ius Commune: King Roger II's Legislation," *Rivista Internazionale del Diritto Comune,* Number 17 (2006).
Pescosolido, Guido. "Una Società Immobile? Sviluppo pre-unitario e questione meridionale," *Mezzogiorno, Risorgimento e Unità d'Italia: Atti del Convegno, Roma, 18, 19 e 20 Maggio 2011* (2014), pages 73-82.
Petacco, Arrigo. *La Regina del Sud* (1992).
Pilliteri, Francesco (editor). *Contributi per un Bilancio del Regno Borbonico* (1990).
Pinto, Carmine. *La Guerra per il Mezzogiorno: Italiani, Borbonici e Briganti 1860-1870* (2019).
Pinto, Carmine. "La Guerra entre Nápoles y Turín: Nacionalismos, Revolución, Legitimismo," *La Historia: Lost in translation?* (Cuenca 2017).
Pinto, Carmine. "La Rivoluzione Disciplinata del 1860: Cambio di regime ed élite politiche nel Mazzogiorno italiano," *Contemporanea,* volume 1 (Jan-Mar 2013), pages 39-68.
Pinto, Carmine. "Sovranità, Guerre e Nazioni: La crisi del mondo borbonico e la formazione degli Stati moderni 1806-1920," *Meridiana,* volume 81 (2014), pages 9-25.
Pinto, Carmine. "Tempo di Guerra: Conflitto, Patriottismi e Comunità Politiche Opposte nel Mezzorgiorno d'Italia 1859-1866," *Meridiana,* volume 76 (2013), pages 57-84.
del Pozzo, Luigi. *Cronaca Civile e Militare delle Due Sicilie sotto la Dinastia Borbonica dall'Anno 1734 in Poi* (1857).
Porzio, Annalisa. *Il Palazzo Reale di Napoli* (2014).
Putnam, Robert. *Making Democracy Work: Civic Traditions in Modern Italy* (1993).
Quandel, Pietro. *Giornale della Difesa di Gaeta da novembre 1860 a febbraio 1861* (1863).
Racioppi, Giacomo. *Moti di Basilicata* (1867).
Raffaele, Giovanni. "Istruzione ed Educazione nell'Ultimo Cinquantennio Borbonico," *Contributi per un Bilancio del Regno Borbonico* (1990), pages 137-180.
Raffaele, Silvana. *La Bottega dei Saperi: Politica Scolastica, Percorsi Formativi, Dinamiche Sociali nel Meridione Borbonico* (2005).
Raffaele, Silvana. "La Politica Assistenziale nella Sicilia Borbonica," *Contributi per un Bilancio del Regno Borbonico* (1990), pages 181-198.
Recca, Cinzia. *The Diary of Queen Maria Carolina of Naples 1781-1785: New Evidence of Queenship at Court* (2017).
Recupero, Antonino. "La Monarchia Amministrativa dei Borboni in Sicilia: Verso una Revisione del Giudizio Storico," *Contributi per un Bilancio del Regno Borbonico* (1990), pages 283-294.

Renda, Francesco. *L'Espulsione dei Gesuiti dalle Due Sicilie* (1993).
Riall, Lucy. *Garibaldi: Invention of a Hero* (2007).
Riall, Lucy. "Legge Marziale a Palermo: Protesta popolare e rivolta nel 1866," *Meridiana,* volume 24 (1995), pages 65-94.
Riall, Lucy. *Sicily and the Unification of Italy: Liberal Policy and Local Power 1859-1866* (1998).
Riall, Lucy. *Under the Volcano: Revolution in a Sicilian Town* (2013).
Ricca, Erasmo. *La Nobiltà del Regno delle Due Sicilie* (1859-1865).
Ricuperati, Giuseppe. "L'insegnamento della storia nella scuola italiana fra appartenenza e identità," *La Nazione tra i Banchi* (2012), pages 145-170.
Rinaldi, Gustavo. *Per Non Dimenticare: La spietata repressione militare piemontese e italiana dal 1860 al 1870 nei territori conquistati del Regno delle Due Sicilie* (2018).
Rinaldi, Gustavo. *Il Regno delle Due Sicilie: Tutta la Verità* (2001).
Roselli, John. *The Life of Bellini* (1996).
Runciman, Steven. *Sicilian Vespers: A History of the Mediterranean World in the Later Thirteenth Century* (1958).
Ruo, Raffaele. *Saggio Storico degli Ordine Cavallereschi Antichi e Moderni, Estinti ed Esistenti, Istituiti nel Regno delle Due Sicilie sotto le Varie Dinastie* (Naples 1832).
Russi, Luciano. *Studi su Carlo Pisacane: Realtà e Utopia di un Rivoluzionario* (2012).
Russo, Giuseppe. *La Scuola d'Ingegneria in Napoli 1811-1967* (1967).
Russo, Rocco. *La Magione di Palermo negli Otto Secoli della Sua Storia* (1975).
Salerno, Eric. *Genocidio in Libia* (2005).
Salvemini, Gaetano. *Cronologia dei Primi Scritti Mazziniani 1831-1834* (2006).
Salvemini, Raffaella. "L'Istruzione del Povero: il Capitale Umano nella Napoli del 700," *Scuola e Società: Le istituzioni scolastiche in Italia dall'età moderna al futuro* (2002), pages 95-120.
Salvemini, Raffaella. "Tra Necessità e Quotidianità: La gestione della povertà a Napoli nell'Ottocento preunitario," *Proposte e Ricerche,* volume (year) 37, number 73 (2014), pages 153-166.
Santasilia, Franco. *La Cucina Aristocratica Napoletana* (1987).
Sarcone, Michele. *Istoria Ragionata de' Mali Osservati in Napoli nell'Intero Corso dell'Anno 1764* (1765).
Schipa, Michelangelo. *Il Regno di Napoli al Tempo di Carlo di Borbone* (1904).
Sciarra, Federico. "Il Matrimonio nell'Ottocento Italiano fra Potere Civile e Potere Ecclesiastico," *Historia et Ius,* 9/2016 (2016), pages 1-14.

Scotto di Luzio, Adolfo. "Gli insegnanti degli italiani: Formazione e reclutamento dei docenti dagli Stati preunitari al Regno d'Italia," *La Nazione tra i Banchi* (2012), pages 93-108.
Scotto di Luzio, Adolfo. "Scuola, Istruzione, Libri e Giornali," *Mezzogiorno, Risorgimento e Unità d'Italia: Atti del Convegno, Roma, 18, 19 e 20 Maggio 2011* (2014), pages 335-342.
Scotti, Giacomo. *I Massacri di Luglio: La storia censurata dei crimini fascisti in Jugoslavia* (2017).
Seldes, George. *Sawdust Caesar: The Untold History of Mussolini and Fascism* (1935).
Seward, Desmond. *Italy's Knights of Saint George: The Constantinian Order* (1986).
Seward, Desmond. *The Monks of War: The Military Religious Orders* (1995).
Simonsohn, Shlomo. *Between Scylla and Charybdis: The Jews in Sicily* (2011).
Sindoni, Caterina. *Scuole, Maestri e Metodi nella Sicilia Borbonica 1817-1860* (2012).
Sodano, Giulio (editor). *Io, la Regina: Maria Carolina d'Asburgo-Lorena fra Politica, Fede, Arte e Cultura* (2016).
Soresina, Marco. *Italy Before Italy: Institutions, Conflicts and Political Hopes in the Italian States 1815-1860* (2020).
Spada, Antonio. *Ordini Cavallereschi della Real Casa di Borbone delle Due Sicilie* (2002).
Spagnoletti, Angelantonio. *Storia del Regno delle Due Sicilie* (1997).
Spieler, Marlena. *A Taste of Naples: Neapolitan Culture, Cuisine and Cooking* (2018).
Spinosa, Nicola (editor). *I Borboni di Napoli* (2009).
Spurio, Lorenzo. "La Protesta del Popolo delle Due Sicilie di Luigi Settembrini," *Lumie di Sicilia,* number 138 (May 2020), pages9-10.
Sterling, Claire. *Octopus: The Long Reach of the International Sicilian Mafia* (1990).
Stone, Harold. *Vico's Cultural History: The Production and Transmission of Ideas in Naples 1685-1750* (1997).
Summonte, Giovanni Antonio. *Dell'Historia della Città e Regno di Napoli* (1601).
Takayama, Hiroshi. *Sicily and the Mediterranean in the Middle Ages* (2019).
Tedeschi, Nicola Maria. *Istoria della Pretesa Monarchia di Sicilia* (Rome 1715).
Tedesco, Antonio. *Quella Voce Fucilata nella Piazza: L'Eccidio di San Giovanni Rotondo del 14 Ottobre 1920* (2012).
Topa, Michele. *I Briganti di Sua Maestà* (1993).
Traniello, Francesco. "Chiesa, Mezzogiorno e Risorgimento," *Mezzogiorno, Risorgimento e Unità d'Italia: Atti del Convegno, Roma, 18, 19 e 20 Maggio 2011* (2014), pages 83-94.

Tschudi, Clara (trans Ethel Hearn). *Maria Sophia, Queen of Naples* (1905).
Tufano, Roberto. "Il 'Popolo' nel Governo di Bernardo Tanucci: L'emergenza della questione sociale nel Regno di Napoli 1734-1774," *Un'Isola nel Contesto Mediterraneo* (2018), pages 103-147.
Ulloa, Pietro Calà. *Amministrazione della Giustizia Penale nel Regno di Napoli* (1835).
Vacca, Giuseppe. *La Situazione delle Provincie Napoletane e il Riordinamento del Governo Locale* (1861).
Valenti, Calogero. "Due Episodi di Peste in Sicilia, 1526 e 1624," *Archivio Storico Siciliano*, series 4, volume 10 (Palermo 1984), pages 5-88.
Valletta, Nicola. *Delle Leggi del Regno Napoletano* (1786).
Valsecchi, Franco. *Il Riformismo Borbonico in Italia* (1990).
Van Cleave, Rachel. "Rape and Querela Law in Italy: False Protection of Victim Agency," *Michigan Journal of Gender and Law*, volume 13, January 2007 (Ann Arbor 2007), pages 273-310.
Varvaro, Alberto. *Vocabolario Storico-Etimologico del Siciliano* (2014).
Ventura, Piero, "La capitale e le élites urbane nel Regno di Napoli tra XVI e XVIII secolo," *Mélanges de l'Ecole Française de Rome*, 121/1 (2009), pages 261-296.
Venuti, Antonino. *De Agricultura Opusculum* (1516).
Vick, Brian. *The Congress of Vienna: Power and Politics after Napoleon* (2014).
Vico, Giambattista. *Principi di Una Scienza Nuova* (1858 edition compiled by Giuseppe De Cesare).
Viglione, Massimo. *1861, Le Due Italie: Identità nazionale, unificazione, guerra civile* (2011).
Villani, Pasquale. *Mezzogiorno tra Riforme e Rivoluzione* (1973).
Villani, Pasquale. "Tentativo di un Bilancio Storiografico sul Regno delle Due Sicilie," *Contributi per un Bilancio del Regno Borbonico* (1990), pages 295-310.
Viterbo, Michele. *Gente del Sud: Il Sud e l'Unità* (2012).
Vitignano, Cornelio. *Cronica del Regno di Napoli* (1595).
Vocino, Michele. *Primati del Regno di Napoli* (1960).
Volker, Sellin. "Il Mezzogiorno nella Diplomazia Europea 1806-1848," *Mezzogiorno, Risorgimento e Unità d'Italia: Atti del Convegno, Roma, 18, 19 e 20 Maggio 2011* (2014), pages 165-174.
Volpe, Enrico. *Piatti Tipici della Cucina Napoletana e Lucana: Tradizioni, Storia, Descrizione, Usi e Costumi* (1980).
Zappata, Pietro Giuseppe. *Difesa Storica della Monarchia Siciliana* (Turin 1716).
Zazo, Alfredo. *L'Istruzione Pubblica e Privata nel Napoletano 1767-1860* (1927).
Zazo, Alfredo. *La Politica Estera del Regno delle Due Sicilie nel 1859-1860* (1940).

Zeldes, Nadia. *The Former Jews of this Kingdom: Sicilian Converts After the Expulsion 1492-1516* (2003).
Ziblatt, Daniel. *Structuring the State: The Formation of Italy and Germany and the Puzzle of Federalism* (2006)
Zilli, Ilaria. *Carlo di Borbone e la Rinascita del Regno di Napoli: Le Finanze Pubbliche 1734-1742* (1990).
Zitara, Nicola. *L'Unita d'Italia: Nascita di Una Colonia* (1971).

Websites

These websites are indicated for information and convenience only. Neither the author or publisher assumes responsibility for their content. Website addresses change from time to time. Those marked by an asterisk (*) have an English text.

archiviodistatonapoli.it - Naples Archive of State.

reggiadicaserta.beniculturali.it - Royal palace at Caserta.

teatrosancarlo.it - San Carlo opera house, Naples.

realcasadiborbone.it - Bourbon descendants of Ferdinand II.

cademiasiciliana.org - Study of the Sicilian language.*

neoborbonici.it - Two Sicilies history and culture.

eleaml.org - Two Sicilies history and culture.

argenionapoli.it - Fashion items bearing Two Sicilies coat of arms.

italianpower.com - Two Sicilies apparel and memorabilia.*

italianamericanpodcast.com - Italian diasporic culture.*

ilregno2s.blogspot.com - Two Sicilies history, faith, culture.*

bandiere.it - Maker of flags of the Kingdom of the Two Sicilies.

bottega2sicilie.net - Flags and other Two Sicilies items.

N. 49.

Avviso:

Le associazioni si ricevono nella Pietà de' Turchini, n. 17. Né lettere né danaro saranno ricevuti se non sono francati.

GIORNALE
DEL REGNO DELLE DUE SICILIE.

Mercordì, 27 febbraio 1822.

Prezzo di associazione.

Per un mese . . due. 1. 10.
Per tre mesi . . . . . 3. 80.
Per sei mesi . . . . . 4. 80.
Per un anno . . . . . 8. 70.

Gli atti del Governo inseriti nel Giornale del Regno delle Due Sicilie sono officiali.

NOTIZIE ESTERE.
RUSSIA.

Pietroburgo, 7 gennaio.

L'ukase indiritto da S. M. l'imperatore al generale d'infanteria Signor Jermoloff in data degli 8 ottobre (1) contiene quanto segue:

Ogni negoziante russo e straniero, il quale nello spazio di diesi anni, principiando dal 1822, aprirà una casa di commercio in quelle contrade, sarà registrato nella prima classe (*gild*) degli abitanti : durante quel tempo essi saranno esenti dalle capitazioni, dagli alloggi militari, e godranno il privilegio nell' acquisto delle terre franche d' ogni imposta, messe in vendita dal governo. I porti della Mingrelia avranno le stesse regole sanitarie de' porti del Mar Nero ec.

— Leggesi nel nostro *Osservatore Imparziale* il seguente articolo: » L'anno 1821 è terminato: secondo di casi come i precedenti, la storia ha sovra esso, con quelli incontestabile signoria. Dall' un canto vediamo troni commossi, e ben tosto assodati, altri dalle rivoluzionarie procelle tuttora scossi, epidemie, dottrine antisociali, l' anarchia mascherata sotto i nomi di riforma e di costituzioni, intenta con lena affannata a distruggere l' opera dei secoli, ed a sciogliere i vincoli di civiltà; e finalmente un tal genio di vertigine, e di cecità generale, frutto del *sovvertimento delle moderne idee*, padroneggiare le deboli, ed inesperte menti dei due emisferi: dall' altro verso, possenti monarchi dalle stesse massime, e dalle stesse intenzioni condotti, conservare la maggior fermezza fra le politiche tempeste, e far uso della loro preponderanza per tener i popoli nei limiti dei loro doveri, ed i re nel possesso dei legittimi loro diritti. Sotto questi aspetti l' anno teste finito si affacciò allo sguardo dell' Osservatore ».

(*G. di Pietr.*)

SPAGNA.

Madrid, 22 gennaio.

Sta per essere sottoposta al congresso una quistione importante nelle attuali circostanze: « Allorquando i deputati delle Corti delle province di America giunsero a Madrid recarono seco 40,000 *duros*, ossia 200,000 franchi, per supplire agli emolumenti che la costituzione concede loro durante la legislatura. Questa somma venne deposta nel tesoro delle Corti, ed i deputati percepirono si dovuti tempi il loro avere fino al mese di ottobre; ma d'allora in poi, i fondi sono esausti, e molti di essi chiesero al governo, se non la totalità dei loro onorari, almeno *acconti*, che li mettano in istato di provvedere ai propri bisogni, sopra tutto essendo cessata ogni comunicazione con una parte delle provincie di America, e richiedendosi lungo tempo onde ricevere sussidi di colà.

Il tesoro generale rifiutò finora tutte le loro domande, quindi molti deputati dovettero privarsi dei loro effetti per sovvenire ai primi bisogni della vita. Questi deputati si sono riuniti poc' anzi, ed hanno diretto alle Corti una rappresentanza, nella quale domandano una risposta categorica, per prendere poi quelle risoluzioni ch' esige la loro situazione, e lo stato attuale delle cose fra le Americhe spagnuole e la penisola. Ciascheduno vede che questo passo è in parte mossa dal desiderio dei deputati americani di separarsi dalle Corti, e di uniformarsi al nuovo ordine di cose stabilito nelle colonie.

(*Jour. de Paris.*)

(1) Vedi il nostro Giornale num. 46.

VARIETA'
Politico-Letterarie.

Gl' incontri

Non dell' incontro d' Ulisse coll' amata Penelope, nè di quello di Edipo coll' infelice Laio, nè di quello di Mario col figliuolo sulle calde arene della spenta Cartagine; ma degl' incontri a favellare imprendo in cui s' imbattono e quelli che le arti belle coltivano, e quelli ancora che alle scienze ed alla letteratura son dediti. Spesso nelle opere di costoro rinvengonsi ancor diverse, nel rappresentare un Giove che scuota l' olimpo con un sol cenno suo, gli diano, la stessa figura, la stessa mossa, la stessa espressione? O che un cantore nelle montagne di Calidonia ti faccia sentire lo scroscio del fulmine nei suoi versi, colla stessa forza del primo pittore delle antiche memorie, senza averlo mai conosciuto? O che un filarmonico colle stesse note inventi una cantilena, la qual coincida con altra inventata da un secondo, con cui non ci fa uh ci può essere nessuna corrispondenza? Per negar questo bisognerebbe dire che gli stessi fenomeni della natura, messe certe circostanze, siano incapaci d...

ACKNOWLEDGMENTS

Any historian worth his salt is but a link in a chain, part of a community of scholars. This book has been long in the making and some who contributed to it are no longer among us. Herewith are brief epitaphs for a few of them.

Douglas Fairbanks was a thespian, a confidant of kings who played his greatest role in military intelligence; he trained a specialized unit that saw action in Operation Husky, the Allied invasion of Sicily. Achille di Lorenzo was an anti-Fascist close to the surviving Bourbons of Naples; he was part of the rescue mission to save Umberto Nobile's last, ill-fated Arctic expedition. Cardinal Jacques Martin was Prefect of the Pontifical Household and assisted Pope John Paul II in exorcisms; he facilitated my unrestricted access to the Vatican library and archive. James Charles Risk was an American naval officer present at the invasion of Sicily in 1943, serving in the Allied Military Government, and later a numismatist and sometime diplomat; he knew Queen Elizabeth II and the last King of Italy. Cyril Toumanoff was a native of Saint Petersburg, where he witnessed the Russian Revolution; he was a longtime history professor at Georgetown University, where one of his students was a young Bill Clinton, and in retirement High Historical Consultant of the Sovereign Military Order of Malta. Sir Steven Runciman wrote defining works on the Crusades, the Byzantine Empire and the Sicilian Vespers, unbiased histories presented from two or three perspectives rather than just one as was customary since Gibbon's time; he was a gentleman scholar in the best Oxbridge tradition.

Invaluable context for certain details was provided over the years by Urraca de Bourbon of the Two Sicilies and her cousin, Giovanni de Bourbon of the Two Sicilies.

Among military personnel consulted were two American veterans who stood out for their keen knowledge of Sicilian society just before the fall of the Kingdom of Italy. Richard Tambe was a soldier present in Sicily during Operation Husky. Anthony Di Carlo, a multilingual army officer who worked in American military intelligence in France and Germany, had spent a few years in Italian schools during the Fascist era. Both men were highly conversant with the history of Sicily from the Vespers to the Second World War.

Nuggets of information sometimes emanated from less exalted quarters. Published histories mention the fact of medical supplies, including the antimalarial chloroquine, being introduced in Italy by the Americans, but it was interesting to hear the account of an old man in Sicily of how people died in the malarial marshes until the Americans arrived.

Equally interesting was the commentary of Eleonora Sara, who worked in the censorship division of the Palermo post office in the years immediately before 1940. Stefania Mantegna, the author's cousin, who was also in Palermo during the Second World War, offered informative comments from an aristocratic point of view.

Among the living, Baron Robert La Rocca and Archbishop Lorenzo Casati offered useful suggestions. Jacqueline Alio edited the manuscript. Special thanks to John Viola, Patrick O'Boyle and Karen La Rosa.

Thanks are due the staffs at archives and libraries in Italy, particularly the state archives of Palermo, Naples and Rome, and the Vatican Secret Archive. Thanks also to Carlo de Bourbon, Duke of Castro, for permitting consultation of some records of the royal family. Sincere gratitude is conveyed to the two colleagues who found time to make suggestions based on a thorough peer review of the manuscript just a few weeks before this book went to print.

Special thanks to the Metropolitan Museum of Art, New York, and the Royal Collection Trust, London, for permission to publish (respectively) the photographs of the pendant of Queen Margaret kept in The Cloisters in Manhattan and the gold coronation spoon of England's Norman kings retained in the Crown Jewels collection displayed in the Tower of London. Thanks are due the Bibliothèque Nationale of Paris for the photograph taken by Gustave Le Gray in 1860.

Any shortcomings which might present themselves in the preceding pages are, of course, solely my responsibility as *auctor et scriptor* of this work.

King Roger II shown holding his sword, Mikalis, in an engraving in the 1675 edition of Summonte's history of the Kingdom of Naples.

INDEX

abortion, 140
Abruzzi (Abruzzo), 20, 32, 33, 88, 131, 181, 300n86
Acton, Harold, xvi, xviii, xx, 24, 300n87
Acton, John, 111, 134
Adams, John, 126
Adelaide del Vasto, Great Countess of Sicily, 30, 45, 62
adoption, 94, 141
Adrianople (Edirne), battle of, 40
adultery, 140
Adwa, 13
Africa. *See* Egypt, Libya, Tunisia, *etc*
Agatha, Saint, 18, 137
Aghlabids, 8, 11, 42, 186
agriculture. *See* farming, latifondi, olives, wheat, *etc*
Agrigento, 32, 34, 38, 131
Akragas. *See* Agrigento
Alaric, 41
Alban Hills, 88
Albania, Albanians, 6, 55, 85, 136, 226, 280n14
Alcamo, 179

Alcamo, Cielo of, 285n31
Alfonse the Magnanimous, 54-55
Alfonso, Count of Caserta, 31, 181, 189, 230
aldermen. *See* jurats
algebra, 47
almonds, 53, 96
Alto Adige. *See* Tyrol
American Civil War, 190
American Revolutionary War, 111
Amiens, Peace of (1802), 117
anarchists, 106
Ancona, 296n74
Angevins, 10, 30, 51-54, 266
Anglo-Spanish War (1727), 77
Anglo-Spanish War (1779), 111
Anjou dynasty. *See* Charles I, Louis IX, *et al*
anticlericalism, vi, 166, 168
anusim. *See* Jews
apostolic legateship, 45, 47, 74-75, 77, 91, 288n41
Apulia. *See* Puglia
aqueducts, 84. *See also* kanats
Arabic language, 45, 46, 50, 53, 62, 283n23

Arabic numerals. *See* Hindu-Arabic numerals
Arabs. *See* Aghlabids, Fatimids, Kalbids
Aragon, x, 6, 30, 46, 52, 54-55, 126, 213
arancina (rice ball), 8, 138
architecture, 7, 24, 25, 38, 40, 53, 60, 61, 66-70, 84, 106-107, 113, 145, 152, 186, 237
Ardinghelli, Maria Angela, 92
Ariano, Assizes of, ix, 48, 58, 127, 239, 284n27
aristocracy. *See* nobility
armies, 13, 16, 17, 18, 40, 76, 79, 80, 88, 111, 116, 118, 170, 179, 180, 190, 195. *See also* carabinieri
aspirin, 146
astronomy, 84, 92, 117
atrocities, 13, 17, 58, 189, 270, 278n12
Augustus III of Poland, 81
Austerlitz, Battle of, 118
Austria, 72-73, 75-80 passim, 93, 110, 116, 125, 133, 140, 150, 162, 165-166, 198
Avellino, 203
Aversa, 147
Balbo, Italo, 271
Bal'harm. *See* Palermo
Ballarò market (Palermo), 8
Balsamo, Giuseppe, 99
Balsamo, Paolo, 113
banditry, vi, 90
banks, 18, 117, 133, 166, 173, 181, 190, 259, 287n37, 298n82
Barbapicciola, Giuseppa, 92
Barbary pirates, 91, 109
Barcelona, 54, 213
Bari, 18, 42, 44, 49, 53, 54-55, 78, 131, 144
baron (title), 92, 240, 244-245
baronage. *See* nobility
Baroque architecture, xii, 7, 24, 25, 60, 83-84, 106, 145
Basilicata (Lucania), 26, 32-33, 42, 43, 55, 95, 99, 131, 190
Bava-Beccaris Massacre, 23, 195
Bavaria, 72, 198
Beati Paoli, 59, 90, 290n49
Becket, Thomas, 46, 65
Bell, Alexander Graham, 23, 297n81
Bellini, Vincenzo, 144
Belloc, Hilaire, 198
Benedict XIII, Pope, 77
Benedict XIV, Pope, 85, 108
Benevento, Battle of, 51-52, 266
Bentinck, William, 119-120
Berbers, 43
betrothals. *See* marriage practices
birth records. *See* vital statistics
births outside marriage 8, 94, 172, 277n7. *See also* foundlings, orphanages
Bixio, Nino (Gerolamo), 180, 189
Black Death. *See* bubonic plague
blazon, 252, 254

boar, 54, 93, 122
Boccaccio, Giovanni, 266
Boccadifalco, 295n69
Bonaparte, Caroline, 119
Bonaparte, Joseph, 119
Bonaparte, Napoleon, 115-120 passim, 140
Borboni *name,* 212
Borsellino, Paolo, 273
botany, 113, 115, 295n69
Bourbon dynasty. *See* Charles III, Ferdinand I, Louis XIV, *et al*
Bourbon, Urraca, xvii, 201
Bresci, Gaetano, 196
Brindisi, 32-33, 78, 144
Britain. *See* United Kingdom
Bronte, 180, 189
bubonic plague, 53-54, 57, 60, 87, 287n36
buffalo, 54
Byzantine Greeks. *See* Byzantines.
Byzantines, ix-x, 11, 25, 41-47 passim, 49, 85, 136, 248
Byzantium. *See* Constantinople
Cagliostro. *See* Balsamo, Giuseppe
Cairo, 44
Calabria, x, 11, 32-33, 39, 42, 43, 45, 49, 55, 76, 84, 95, 100, 126, 131, 135, 139, 146, 159, 181
Calatafimi, 34, 179
Caltabellotta, Peace of, 52-53
Caltanissetta, 131
Cammarata, 288n38

Camorra, 90-91, 100-101, 197-198
Campania, 100, 130-131, 277n7. *See also* Naples, Salerno
Canada, 4, 18
canals. *See* kanats
canna, 192
Cannizzaro, Stanislao, 144-145
cannolo, 53
cantaro, 192
Canterbury, viii
Capitanata, 131
Capodimonte, 83, 84
Capuan Castle (Naples), 52
Capuchins, 56
carabinieri, 198
Caracciolo, Domenico, 113, 114, 134
carbonara recipe, 291n58
Carbonari, 132-133
Carditello, 93
Carlo III, King. *See* Charles III
Carlo Alberto Savoy, King, 156, 163, 165, 193
Carlo Felice Savoy, King, 118-119, 133
carozzo, 192
Carroll, Philip, 194
Carthaginians, 38, 88
Casalduni, 189, 278n12
Caserta, 25, 83-84, 93, 106, 113
Castel dell'Ovo (Naples), 48, 55, 69
Castellamare di Stabia, 85, 263
Castel Nuovo (Naples), 52, 70

castles, 44, 48, 52, 55, 61, 66, 69, 70, 186, 193
Catalogus Baronum, 239-240, 250
Catalan language, 53, 267
Catalans, 52, 54, 56, 73, 213, 267
Catalonian. *See* Catalan
Catania, 18, 32, 34, 52, 54, 58, 73, 76, 78, 131, 137, 144, 157-158
catasti onciari, 89, 243. *See also* riveli
Catholic church. *See* Jesuits, papacy, *etc*
cattle theft, 100
cavallo (monetary unit), 60
Cavour, Camillo Benso di, 164-169 passim, 175, 178
censorship, vi, 12, 16, 19, 59, 74, 86, 112, 123, 168, 191, 266-268
census, 305. *See also* catasto, riveli
ceramic art. *See* majolica
Ceres (planet), 117
challenges. *See* disabilities
Charlemagne, 22, 42
Charles I of Anjou, King of Sicily, x, 6-7, 27, 30, 51-52
Charles II of Anjou, King of Naples, 30, 52, 70
Charles III de Bourbon, King (VII of Naples, V of Sicily, III of Spain), xi, xvii, 31, 71-109 passim, 110, 210-220
Charles V, Holy Roman Emperor, 56, 57
Charles VI of Austria, 72-77 passim, 87
cheeses, 137
chemistry, 92
Chiara, Santa (Naples), 201
children's rights, 47, 94, 110, 128, 141-142, 194. *See also* schools, *etc*
China, 42, 47, 53, 86
Chinese Villa, 118
chivalry, orders of. *See* knighthood
chocolate, 8, 56, 196
cholera, 157
Churchill, Winston, 182
Cilento, 150, 164
cinema, Italian, xvi, 19, 295n68
cirneco, 54
citizenship, 4, 78, 130
city-states. *See* communes
Civitella del Tronto, 181
Clement XI, Pope, 227, 288n41
climate, 54, 111, 138
coats of arms. *See* heraldry
Codice Carolino (1739), 89
codici. *See* legal codes
coffee, 137
coinage, xv, 48, 192, 259-262
collecta. *See* donativo
Collodi (Lorenzini), Carlo, 142
Columbus, Christopher, 56

INDEX

commerce, 48, 53, 58, 79, 82, 87, 113, 128, 145-146, 153, 157, 159-160, 173
commodities exchange, 112, 172
communes, 9, 51, 78, 241
composers, musical, 60, 144
Confederate States of America, 190
confirmation bias, 270, 305, 306n103
Congress of Vienna, 125-126, 156, 162
Conrad I, King of Sicily, 50
Conrad II (Conradin), 50, 51
Constance of Aragon, Queen of Sicily, 46, 64
Constance Hohenstaufen, Queen of Sicily, 52, 54
Constance Hauteville, Queen of Sicily, 49-52, 288n41
Constantine the Great, 40, 225
Constantinian Order of St George, 211, 225-229, 236-238
Constantinople, 40, 41, 43-44, 52, 55, 225
constitution: of 1820, 130-131; of 1848, 163; of 1860, 180; American, xxii, 112, 127; Bolognese, 123; British, 123; Italian, 17; Sardinian (Piedmontese), 25, 163, 193; Sicilian, 120-123, 126; Spanish, 130
Conversos (Anusim). *See* Jews
copper coinage, 256, 259-262

Corleone, 118
coronations, 46, 63-65, 104, 119
Correnti, Santi, 26
Cosenza, 32, 33, 131, 147, 159
cotton, 118, 171
Cottone, Gaetano, 117
Cotugno, Domenico, 98
count (title), 244
Counter Reformation, 56, 101, 226
crimes against humanity. *See* war crimes
Crispi, Francesco, 180, 195
crocchè, 138
Croce, Benedetto, 13, 26, 272, 289n43
crowns, 46, 63, 64, 200
crusade: First, 45; Second, 49; Sixth, 50
cuccagna, 138-139
cuccìa, 137
cuisine, 24, 53, 136-138, 196
cultural appropriation, xiv, 272
Cumae, Battle of, 38
Curzio, Carlo, 88
Dante Alighieri, x, 266
Daunia, 131
deaf, school for, 204
death penalty. *See* executions
deconstructionism, 25, 272
Denmark, 162
dentistry, 146
deer, 54, 93, 122
De Felice, Renzo, 268

De Gregorio, Leopoldo, 82
deforestation. *See* forests
De Martino, Pietro, 84
denialism, historical. *See* historiography
De Roberto, Federico, xvi, 195
dialects. *See* Neapolitan, Sicilian
disabilities, mental and physical, 147, 154, 212
Diaspora. *See* Jews
diasporic Italians, 4, 5, 196
Di Blasi, Francesco, 114
Diodorus Siculus, 275
divario, 19, 163
diversity, social. *See* homosexual rights, immigrants, multiculturalism, women's rights
Divine Comedy. *See* Dante
divorce, 13, 24, 58, 129-130, 140, 278n11
diwan, 44
DNA. *See* genetics
dog breeds, national, 54
Dominicans, 102, 142, 193
donativo (tax), 59, 74, 89-90, 119, 120. *See also* riveli
droughts, 159-160
ducat, xv, 48, 192, 259-260, 262, 295n72
duke (noble title), 243
dynasty *defined,* 212-213
earthquakes, 113, 197, 205, 207, 209
Easter Massacre (1655), 193

Eastern Roman Empire. *See* Byzantines, Constantinople
economy, 48, 53, 58, 79, 82, 87, 98, 113, 128, 145-146, 153, 157, 159-160, 166, 173, 190, 194
Edrisi. *See* Idrisi
education, 2-3, 22, 23, 45, 50, 59, 81, 86, 91, 92, 102, 113, 130, 142-144 passim, 147, 192-193. *See also* literacy, schools, universities
Egypt, 15, 55, 115
elections. *See* referendum
electoral fraud: in 1860, 188, 271; in 1946, xvii, 277n8
Elena, Queen of Italy, 197
elopements. *See* fuitina
Elvira of Castile, Queen of Sicily, 47
emigration (from Italy), 12, 18-19, 168-169, 194, 196, 268
Enciclopedia Italiana, 269
engineering, 84, 92, 146, 158, 171
England pre-1707, viii, 44-46 passim, 48, 65
England post-1707. *See* United Kingdom
Enlightenment, xxii, 59, 87, 91, 112, 113, 116, 196
epidemics, 21, 57, 84, 87, 98, 157. *See also* bubonic plague, cholera, typhus

INDEX

epistemology, historical. *See* historiography

Escorial, Treaty of the, 80

Ethiopia, 14, 195

ethnic groups, ix-x, 5, 6, 51, 55. *See also* multiculturalism

ethnie *defined,* 3-4

Etna, Mount, 137

Etruscans, 38

executions, 114, 159, 202, 270, 278n12

excise taxes, 74

expression, freedom of, 59, 120, 123, 267

extortion. *See* Camorra, Mafia, Ndrangheta

family: importance of, 8, 58, 77, 123, 212; size of, 140

famines, 95, 98, 113, 131, 159, 195

farming, 37, 89, 96, 100, 113, 143, 137, 192, 195, 197. *See also* latifondi, olives, rice, wheat, *etc*

Farnese, Antonio, 80, 227

Farnese, Elisabeth (Isabella), 73, 79-80, 227

Farnese Palace (Rome), 189

Fasci Siciliani, 195, 198

Fascism, 19, 23, 267-269 passim

Fascist Legacy (film), 281n17

Fatimids, 42-44 passim, 47, 51, 68

Fazello, Thomas, 275n1

feasts and festivals, religious. *See* Saint Januarius, Saint Rosalie, *et al*

federalism, 22, 156, 166-167

feminism. *See* women's rights

Fenestrelle (prison), 190

Ferdinand I, King, xi, 31, 96-97, 109-134 passim, 138, 142, 149

Ferdinand II, King, 31, 153-173 passim, 175, 176

Ferdinand the Catholic, 288n41

Ferdinandea (Graham Island), 155-156

Ferdinando I (steamship), 132

Fermi, Enrico, 271

Ferraris Chronicle, xv

feudalism. *See* manorialism

Ficuzza, 118

Filadelfi movement, 150, 158

Filangieri, Carlo, 180

Filangieri, Gaetano, xxii, 112, 116

films. *See* cinema

First Family Pact, 80

First World War, 198

fishing, 138

Florio, Vincenzo, 145

follaris (coin), 256, 262

food. *See* cuisine, farming

foundlings, 94

forests (and deforestation), 54, 59, 87, 95, 124

Francavilla, Battle of, 76-77

France, 35, 54, 71, 72, 73, 75, 76, 80, 97, 101, 114, 115, 125, 143, 150, 159

Francis I, King, 31, 119-120 passim, 130, 149-152
Francis II, King, 31, 175-183 passim, 195
Franciscans, 53
Franklin, Benjamin, xxii, 112
Frederick II, King of Sicily, Holy Roman Emperor, x, 24, 49-51, 59, 92
freemasonry, 90, 91, 132, 166, 180, 290n48
French Revolution, 114-116 passim, 120
Frentania, 131
Friars Minor, Order of. *See* Franciscans
Friulian, 7, 267
fuitina, 139-140
gabellotti, 99-100, 124
Gaeta, 32, 33, 79, 181, 189
Gagliano River, 42, 146
Gancia monastery, 180
Garibaldi, Giuseppe, 17, 168, 178-181 passim, 190
Garnier, Charles, 266
gattò, 138
Gattopardo, Il (novel). *See* Leopard, The
gay rights, 278n11
gelato. *See* ice cream
gender equality. *See* homosexual rights, women's rights
genealogy, xv, 5, 305
genetics (DNA), 43

Gennaro, Saint. *See* Januarius
Genoa, 98, 144, 151, 168
genocide, 3, 19, 281n17
Genovesi, Antonio, 91-92
George III of the United Kingdom, 114
Germans and Germany, 49, 56, 72, 73, 93, 133, 279n13, 291n55. *See also* Bavaria, Holy Roman Empire, Prussia, Swabia, *etc*
Ghibellines, 51, 266, 258
Gibraltar, 77
Giglio delle Onde (steamship), 264
Giornale del Regno delle Due Sicilie, 26, 328
Giovane Italia (Young Italy), 151, 165-166
Girgenti, province of, 131. *For the city see* Agrigento
Giura, Luigi, 146
giurati. *See* jurats
Giustiniani, Bernardo, 226
Gladstone, William, 163
globalization, xii, 23
glove-making, 171-172
Goethe, Johann W, 93, 99
goiter, 194
gold, xii, 46, 65, 74, 101, 170, 190, 259-262
Golden Militia, 226
Gothic architecture, 53
Goths, 40-42

Gozo. *See* Malta
Graham Island (Ferdinandea), 155-156
grain. *See* rice, wheat
grana (monetary unit), 260
Grand Alliance, 71-73 passim
grand tour, 93
grapes. *See* viticulture
Great Britain. *See* United Kingdom
Great Schism (1054), 44
Greeks, ancient, 37-40, 61
Greeks, Byzantine. *See* Byzantines
Greek language, 39, 40, 45, 46, 53, 62
Greek Orthodoxy. *See* Orthodox Church
Gregory XVI, Pope, 156
Guelphs, 258, 266
guilds (maestranze), 90, 141
Guiscard. *See* Robert Hauteville
gunpowder, 110
Guzzoni, Alfredo, 17, 279n13
habeas corpus, 121
Hague, Treaty of (1720), 77
Hales, Stephen, 92
haplogroups, 43
Hapsburg dynasty. *See* Charles V, *et al*
harems, 51
Hastings, Battle of, 44
Hauteville dynasty. *See* Roger II, William I, Constance, Tancred, *et al*

head tax, 59
healthcare. *See* medicine
Henry II of England, 47-48, 65
Henry VI, Holy Roman Emperor, 30, 49, 252
Henry of Guise, 57
heraldry, 251-258
Herculaneum, 86
Hindu-Arabic numerals, 47
historiography, xvi, 19, 23, 191, 265-271
Hohenstaufen dynasty. *See* Henry VI, Frederick II, *et al*
Holy Alliance, 133
Holy Land. *See* Palestine
Holy Office. *See* Inquisition
Holy Roman Empire, x, 22, 35, 49, 56, 118
Holy Trinity basilica. *See* Magione
homosexual rights, 278n11
honor killings, 140
Hospitallers. *See* Malta, Knights of
hospitals, 56, 57, 84, 147. *See also* medicine
hound, Sicilian, 54
Humbert I. *See* Umberto I
Huns, 40
Husky, Operation, 329
Ibadi sect, 43
Ice Age, Little, 54
ice cream, 137, 196
Idrisi (Edrisi), Muhammed, 53

illegitimacy. *See* births outside marriage
illiteracy. *See* literacy
immigrants (in Italy), 8
India, 42, 47
Industrial Revolution, 99, 111, 140, 145
industry, 132, 146, 149, 150, 158, 171-172
Inferno. *See* Dante
Ingham, Benjamin, 111, 137
Ingrassia, Giovanni, 57
Inquisition (Spanish) and Holy Office, 55-58 passim, 77, 88, 112, 113
internet, 23
Ireland, 79, 159
Irpino, 131
irrigation. *See* aqueducts, kanats
Islam. *See* Muslims
Istanbul. *See* Constantinople
Istria, 198, 280n13
Italia, onomatology of, 39
Italiani brava gente, 16
Italianità *defined,* 20
Italian Republic, 17, 22, 129, 189
Italian States, League of, 156
Italian unification. *See* unification movement
itria, 24
Jacobites, 76
Januarius (Gennaro), Saint, 58, 83, 224
Jay's Treaty (1795), 114
Jefferson, Thomas, 111, 115, 126
Jesuits, 56, 91, 101-102, 118, 126
Jesus Christ, 39
Jesus, Society of. *See* Jesuits
Jews, 15, 43-49, passim, 55-56, 85, 102, 117, 135, 269
Jiménez dynasty. *See* Elvira, Margaret
Joanna I, Queen of Naples, 54
Joanna II, Queen of Naples, 54
Joanna of England, Queen of Sicily, 46, 65
John of Procida, 6
Joseph, Saint, 137
bin Jubayr, 49
Judaism. *See* Jews
Judeo Arabic, 46
July Revolution (1830), 150
jurats (giurati), 141, 241, 247
Justinian, Code of, 48, 127
Kalbid dynasty, 42
kanats, 53
Kasteel, Karel, 202
Kastriot. *See* Scanderbeg
knighthood, 221-238
Lampedusa, 109
land reform, 197
Lanza, Ferdinando, 180
lasagna, 10, 137
Lateran treaties, 292n62
latifondi (estates), 124, 197
law. *See* legal code
Lazarus, Saint, 222

INDEX

Lazio. *See* Rome; Velletri

legal code: of 1739 (Carolino), 89; of 1819, 127-130; of 1848, 24, 172-173; of Ariano (1140), 48; of Melfi (1231), 72; Italian, 13, 129; Maliki, 48; Sardinian (Piedmontese), 129, 278n11

legislation. *See* constitution, legal code, voting

Leopard, The (novel), xvi

Leopold II of Tuscany, 156

libel law, 123

Libya, 16, 49, 198

Lion of the Desert, The (film), 280n17

Lipari Case (1711), 74-75

literacy, xv, 11, 47, 60, 188, 192, 268, 304n102

literature, xvi, 6-7, 142, 285n31, 290n49

Lombards (medieval civilization), 11, 22, 41-44, 239, 240

Lombardy, 95, 162, 195

London, Treaty of (1718), 76

Longobards. *See* Lombards

Longo, Maria, 56

lottery, 88

Louis IX of France (saint), 51

Louis XIV of France, 31, 71, 75

Louis XVI of France, 114

Louis the Grand Dauphin, 31, 72

Lucania. *See* Basilicata

Lucanians, ancient, 37

Lucera, 32, 33, 51, 266

Lucy, Saint, 137

macaroni. *See* maccheroni

maccheroni, 53

macinato (tax), 59

Mack Smith, Denis, xx, 24, 268

Madrid, xi, 57, 75, 78, 95

maestranze. *See* guilds

Maffei, Scipione, 302n95

Mafia, xviii, 90-91, 100-101, 197-198

magic. *See* witchcraft

Magione (Holy Trinity) basilica, 201, 227, 237

Magna Carta, 127

Magna Graecia, ix, 38-40, 275n1

majolica (ceramic), 7

malaria, 330

Maliki Law, 48

Malta, 56, 91, 115

Malta, Knights of, 56, 115, 221, 223

Manfred Hohenstaufen, King of Sicily, 30, 50-52

Maniakes, George, 43

manorialism (feudalism), 44, 89, 123-124, 239, 240, 245. *See also* latifondi

manslaughter, 74, 140

Mantegna, Stefania, 330

manufacturing, 84, 171-172

Marches region, 32, 33, 244

Marconi, Guglielmo, 271

Marco Polo, 24, 53

Margaret of Navarre, Queen of

Sicily, viii, 46, 49, 87, 240
Maria Amalia, Queen of Naples and Sicily, 81, 85, 93
Maria Carolina, Queen of Naples and Sicily, 110, 114, 118-120 passim, 125, 138
Maria Cristina Bourbon, Queen of Sardinia, 118
Maria Cristina Savoy, Queen of the Two Sicilies, 156-157, 175, 200
Maria Luisa Savoy, Queen of Spain, 75
Maria Sophia, Queen of the Two Sicilies, 181, 184, 189, 191, 198, 201
Maria Teresa, Queen of the Two Sicilies, 180
marionettes, 144
marquess (title), 244
marriage practices, 8, 94, 136, 139. *See also* divorce, fuitina, women's rights
marriage records. *See* vital statistics
Marsala, 34, 179
Marsala wine, 111, 137
Marsia, 130-131
Martin, Saint, 137
Martorana church, 46, 48, 63
Marvuglia, Giuseppe Venanzio, 118
Marx, Karl, 169
Mary (Mother of God), 40
Maschio Angioino, 52, 70
masons. *See* freemasonry
mastiff, Neapolitan, 54
mattanza *defined,* 138
Mazzini, Giuseppe, 151, 159, 165, 166
measurements. *See* weights and measures
Medici, Gian Gastone, 81
medicine, 45, 50, 53, 56, 57, 84, 87, 88, 97-98, 147, 157. *See also* epidemics, obstetrics, *etc*
Meehan, Brenda, xvii
Megara Hellas. *See* Magna Graecia
Melfi, Constitutions of, 50, 58, 127, 240
mental health treatment. *See* disabilities, psychiatry
mercantile exchange, 112, 172
Messina (city), 7, 34, 43, 53, 87, 113, 119, 160, 181, 197
Messina, Strait of, 16, 73, 76
Metastasio, Pietro, 83
Metternich, Klemens, 125, 140
Meucci, Antonio, 23, 169, 270
Mezzogiorno *defined,* 194
midwifery, 146
migration. *See* emigration
Mikalis (sword), 46, 332
mikvehs, 7
Milan, Edict of, 40
Milan Massacre. *See* Bava-Beccaris Massacre

INDEX

Milazzo, 76
Mileto, 43-44
military. *See* armies, navies
mining, 84, 111, 124. *See also* sulfur
Miraglia, Biagio, 147
misinformation. *See* historiography, propaganda
Modena, 36, 169, 178
Modica, 8
Molise, 32, 33, 131
Monarchia Sicula. *See* Apostolic Legateship
Mongiana, 84, 146
monoculture, 51
Monreale Abbey, 25, 68, 256
monsù *defined,* 138
Montesquieu, Charles-Louis, 112
Montessori, Maria, 171, 196-197
mosaics, 25, 46-48 passim, 63, 67
movies. *See* cinema
multiculturalism, ix, 47, 51, 266
muqarnas, 47
Murat, Joachim, 119, 123, 126, 130
murder, 74, 144
music, 60, 83, 139, 144, 145, 251. *See also* composers, opera
Muslims (and Islam), ix, 42-51 passim, 56, 266
Mussolini, Benito, 15
Mycenaeans, 37

Naples (city), x, xi, xiii, 8, 18, 24, 45, 51, 52, 58, 60, 78, 79, 81, 82, 87, 93, 97, 112, 116, 118, 126, 132, 146, 154, 172
Naples, Kingdom of, *defined,* x, xi, xiii, 51-52, 54
Naples, University of, 50, 57, 59, 84, 86, 91-92, 139, 171
Napoleonic Wars, 115-120 passim, 125
Navarre, 6, 46, 213
navies, 15, 38, 59, 75, 79, 109-110, 117, 118, 119, 179, 180, 181
Naxos (in Sicily), 37
Nazione Napoletana, xiii, 78-79, 83, 289n43
Ndrangheta ('ndrangheta), 100
Neapolitan language, x, 5, 7, 10, 53, 85, 145
Neapolitan Nation. *See* Nazione Napoletana
Neapolitan School (of opera), 60
Neapolitan War, 126
Neo-Bourbon movements, 22-23
nepotism, 82, 268
newspapers, 26, 328
New York, viii, xi, 97, 107, 196
Nicholas, Saint, 18
Nicholas I, Tsar of Russia, 159
Nilos Doxopatrios, 48
Nine Years' War, 71

nobile (title), 245-246
Nobile, Umberto, 171
nobility (aristocracy), 48, 71, 77, 89, 117, 124, 143-144, 156, 197, 221, 239-250
Nola, 203
Norman Palace (Palermo), 47, 66, 67
Norsemen (Vikings), 43, 240
Norwich (Cooper), John Julius, 24, 271
Noto, 34, 131
nutrition, 113, 194. *See also* cuisine, famines, farming
obstretics, 146
Odoacer, 41
oleoculture. *See* olives
olives, 37, 96, 137, 192
oncia (onza), 89, 192, 260
opera, 60, 83, 88, 144, 145
orders of knighthood. *See* knighthood
orders, religious. *See* religious orders
organized crime. *See* Camorra, Mafia, Ndrangheta
orphanages, 141-142
Orthodox Church, 46, 48, 63, 135, 136, 283n24
Oscan language, 39
Ostrogoths. *See* Goths
Ottoman Empire, 56, 87, 91, 99, 109, 136, 198
ovine livestock, 138

Pacte de Famille, 80
Padania, 22
Paestum, 38, 93
palaces, royal, 7, 47, 66, 67, 83, 93, 106, 118. *See also* castles
Palatine Chapel. *See* Norman Palace
Palermo, ix, x, xi, 7, 8, 18, 42, 45, 46, 47, 51, 60, 80, 83, 86, 87, 88, 90, 102, 111, 113, 114, 116, 126, 144, 160, 179-180, 191
Palestine (Holy Land), 45, 49, 50, 211, 225, 253
Palmieri, Luigi, 171
Palma, 203
palmo, 192
Pantelleria, 155
papacy, x, 40, 50, 74, 85, 92, 156, 163, 175. *See also* Papal State, Pius IX, *etc*
papal legateship. *See* apostolic legateship
Papal State(s), 41, 55, 129, 156-156, 167, 199, 260. *See also* Rome
paper making, 24, 42, 45, 62
Paris, Congress of (1856), 164
parliaments, 60, 83, 86, 119, 120-130 passim, 132-133, 196
Parsifal, 144
Parthenopaean Republic, 116
Partinico, 179
Passito, 137
pasta. *See* lasagna, maccheroni,

INDEX

spaghetti
pastries. *See* cannolo, cuccìa, sfincia, zeppola
patrizio (title), 245
Paul of Tarsus, 131
Pax Romana, 39
peerage, Sicilian, 121, 242
pellagra, 194
penal codes. *See* legal code
Peter I, Tsar of Russia, 103
Peter III of Aragon (Peter I of Sicily), 6-7, 52, 54
Peucezia, 131
pharmacies, 84
Philip V of Spain, 10, 31, 71-73, 80, 227
Phoenicians, 37, 38
phylloxera blight, 194
physics, 92
piastra (coin), 192, 259-261
Piazzi, Giuseppe, 117, 124, 144
Piedmont, 8, 10, 24, 73, 75, 80, 133, 156, 162-170 passim, 177-181 passim, 188, 189, 191. *See also* Sardinia, Kingdom of
Piedmont Easter Massacre, 23, 193
Pietrarsa, 158, 159, 171
pigs, 138
Pinocchio, 142
Pinto de Fonseca, Manuel, 91
Pio, Luigi, 112
piracy, 91, 109
Pirandello, Luigi, 271

Piria, Raffaele, 146
Pisacane, Carlo, 164
Pius VII, Pope, 133
Pius IX, Pope, 163, 167, 175
pizza, 8, 137
plague. *See* bubonic plague
plebiscites. *See* referendum
Plombières Agreement (1858), 177
poetry, x, 50, 272
police, 79, 100, 129, 173. *See also* carabinieri
Polish Succession, War of (1733), 80
polyculturalism. *See* multiculturalism
Pontelandolfo, 14, 189, 270
Poor Clares, 56
popes. *See* papacy, Pius IX, *et al*
population, 79, 89, 188, 263
porcelain, 84, 171
Portici, 83, 146
Portugal, 101
postal service, 147
potato blight, 159
del Pozzo, Luigi, 26, 211, 290n51
Pragmatic of 1759, 96, 211-220
Preachers, Order of. *See* Dominicans
press freedom. *See* expression, freedom of
Pretuziana, 131
Primate of Sicily, 47-48
prince (noble title), 243

Principato, 131
Principi di Una Scienza Nuova, 87
Pringle, John, 98
propaganda, political, 12, 13, 190, 191, 267, 272. *See also* historiography
Protestants, 57, 135, 199. *See also* Reformation, Waldensians
provinces identified, 130-131
Prussia, 86, 133
psychiatry, 147
Puglia (Apulia), 11, 26, 32, 33, 39, 42, 55, 95, 98, 100, 131, 277n7. *See also* Bari, Taranto, *etc*
Punics. *See* Carthaginians, Phoenicians
Punic Wars, 38
Quadruple Alliance, War of, 76
Quandel, Pietro, 266
Queen Anne's War, 288n39
ragù, 138
railroads (railways), 146, 161
rape, 13, 58-59, 140-141, 189, 269, 270, 278n11, 284n27
Ravenna, 41
Rebellamentu di Sichilia, 6-7, 27
reddito di cittadinanza, 23, 148 154-155
referendum: of 1860, 11, 187-189; of 1946, 8, 277n8
Reformation, Protestant, 56. *See also* Protestants, Waldensians
regalia, 46, 63-65, 200

Reggio Calabria, 32, 33, 131, 160
Regno *defined*, 93
religious orders: 130, 192; Dominicans, 102, 142, 193; Franciscans, 53; Jesuits, 56, 91, 101-102, 118, 126; Poor Clares, 56
Renaissance, 55, 266
reparations, 280n14
republics, 17, 22, 114, 116
revisionism, historical. *See* historiography
revolt: of 1795, 114; of 1799, 116, of 1820, 132; of 1848, 160-161; of 1866, 191
rice, 8, 19, 53, 95
Ripa, Matteo, 86
Risk, James, xvii
Risorgimento. *See* unification movement
riveli, 5, 168, 243, 274, 287n37. *See also* donativo
Robert (Guiscard) Hauteville, Duke of Apulia, 43-45
Roger I, Great Count of Sicily, 44-45, 256
Roger II, King of Sicily, ix, xv, 45-51 passim, 53, 63, 137, 239, 262, 332
Roman Empire. *See* Romans
Romanesque Gothic, 53
Romans, 4, 11, 38-42
Rome, 12, 22, 39, 40, 41, 79, 88, 116, 163, 167, 189

Rosalie, Saint, 18, 58, 137, 168
Rothschild Bank (Naples), 133, 190
rotolo, 192
Ruffo, Fabrizio, 116
Ruffo, Paolo, 178
Runciman, Steven, 24
Ruo, Raffaele, 228, 235, 238, 303n98, 304n100
Russia, 99, 103, 117, 118, 133, 135, 143, 156, 159
Ryswick, Treaty/Peace of, 71, 72
sagre (culinary and harvest festivals), 137
Salemi, 137, 179
Salento, 131
Salerno, 42, 44, 45, 48, 51, 54, 246
salicylic acid, 146
salma, 192
Samnites, 38
San Carlo opera house, 83
Sanità district (Naples), 172
San Leucio, 84, 113
Sannio, 131
Santiago, Order of, 222
Sapri, 164
Sara, Eleonora, 330
Saragossa. *See* Zaragoza
Sarcone (Piacenza), Michele, 98
Sardinia (region), 17
Sardinia, Kingdom of, 24, 73, 76, 119, 129, 156, 163, 168. *See also* Piedmont
sardines, 94
Sarno, 203
sartù, 138
Scanderbeg, George Kastriot, 226
Scarlatti, Alessandro, 60
Schism (1054). *See* Great Schism
schools, public: 130, 142, 147; for deaf, 204. *See also* Dominican order, education, literacy, Montessori, universities
Sciacca, 94, 155
scleroderma, 88
Scotland, 76, 172
seafood, 138
secession movements, xix, 16, 22, 190, 269
Second World War, 13, 17, 18, 28
Segesta (Egesta), 38, 61
Segré, Emilio, 271
seismometer (and seismograph), 171
separation, marital. *See* divorce
separatism. *See* secession
Serao, Francesco, 98
Settembrini, Luigi, 160, 305n102
Seven Years' War, 96, 97
Seville, Treaty of, 77
sfincia, 53, 137
sfincione, 137
Shakespeare, William, 57
sheep, 54, 138
shipping, commercial, 99, 132,

145, 158
Sicanians, 37
Siceliots. *See* Greeks
Sichelgaita of Salerno, 44-45
Sicilianità *defined,* xiii
Sicilian language, x, 6-7, 11-12, 27, 53, 85, 274
Sicilian School (of poetry), x, 50, 285-286n31
Sicilian Succession, 92
Sicilian Vespers War, x, 6, 52, 54
silk making, 42, 113
silver, 48, 259-262
Siracusa (Syracuse), 34, 38, 40, 131, 137, 157
slavery, 39, 54, 85, 102, 117, 194
Slovenian, 6
social programs, 109-110, 148, 154-155
Society of Jesus. *See* Jesuits
souks (suks), 8
spaghetti, 8, 24, 53, 291n58
Spain, 55-59 passim, 71-73, 79-83 passim, 95, 96, 97, 101, 110, 133, 211. *See also* Aragon, Barcelona, Catalonia, Madrid, Navarre
Spanish Succession, War of, 72-73
Spinelli, Giuseppe, 88-89
spumoni, 196
steamships, 132, 145, 264
stock exchange, 112
Stupor Mundi *defined,* 50

Swabians, 52
suffrage, women's, 13, 141, 280n15
sugar cane, 53, 56, 94
sugo (sauce or gravy). *See* ragù
sulfur, 110-111, 158, 163, 176, 181, 194
sulphur. *See* sulfur
Summonte, Giovanni, 289n43, 308, 332
supplì, 138
sword, royal, 46, 332
synagogues, 117
Syracuse. *See* Siracusa
Tagliacozzo, Battle of, 51, 266
Tancred Hauteville, King of Sicily, 30, 49, 227
Tanucci, Bernardo, 82, 97, 109, 110
Taparelli d'Azeglio, Massimo, 12, 188-189
Taranto, 15, 32, 33, 53, 78
tarì (coin), 260, 262
Tasca, Giuseppe, 201
taxes. *See* catasti onciari, donativo, excise taxes, head tax, macinato, riveli
Teano, 181
Teatro San Carlo. *See* San Carlo opera house
telegraph, 146, 161
telephone, 12, 23, 169
Templars (knights), 222, 258
temples, ancient, 38, 61, 93

Terra di Bari, 131. *See also* Puglia
Terra di Lavoro, 130, 131
Terra d'Otranto, 131. *See also* Puglia
Teutonic Knights, 201, 222, 227, 237, 258
Theotokos, 40
Third Coalition, 118
Thirty Years' War, 59
Thomas Becket, 46, 65
Thousand Cities, 93, 145
timballo, 138
tobacco, 56, 74
de Tocqueville, Alexis, 162
Togliatti, Palmiro, 277n8
Tomasi di Lampedusa, Giuseppe, xvi
tomolo, 192
Torino. *See* Turin
tornese (coin), 192, 260-261
torture, 57, 120, 278n12
Toscanini, Arturo, 171
Toumanoff, Cyril, xvii
transportation. *See* railroads, shipping
Trastámara dynasty, 55
Treaty of Paris (1763), 97
Troia, Michele, 98
tumolo, 192
tuna, 138, 145
Tunisia, 11, 42, 49, 56
Turin, 20, 73, 76, 133, 156, 163, 182
Turkey, 40. *See also* Byzantines, Ottoman Empire
Tuscan language, x, 11, 53, 266, 274
Tuscany, 81, 97, 156, 167, 169, 178
TuttoAPPosto (film), 295n68
Two Sicilies: defined, ix-x; use of name pre-1816, 58, 108, 211, 215, 220
typhus, 97
Tyrol, South (Alto Adige), 6, 17, 198
Umberto I of Italy, 195-196
Umberto II of Italy, 269, 297n77
unification movement, 16-17, 165-171 passim, 266
United Kingdom, xi, 73, 75, 76, 97, 110-111, 114-120 passim, 145, 156, 158-167 passim, 176, 177, 179. *See also* England pre-1707, Scotland
United States of America, xi, xxii, 97, 111, 112, 114-115, 159
universities: 263; Catania, 73; Genoa, 144; Naples, 50, 57, 59, 84, 86, 91-92, 139, 171; Palermo, 19, 113, 115, 204; Turin, 269
unwed births. *See* births outside marriage
Urban II, Pope, 45
Ustica, 109
Utrecht, Treaty of (1713), 73

Valletta, 116
Vandals, 41, 42
Vanvitelli, Luigi, 84
Vatican. *See* papacy, Papal State(s)
Velletri, Battle of, 88
Veneto. *See* Venice
Venice, 22, 41, 54, 87, 226
Vespers War. *See* Sicilian Vespers
Verdi, Giuseppe, 88, 144
Vesalius, Andreas, 57
Vesuvius, Mount, 84, 171
viceroys, 57, 60, 74, 75, 77, 81, 111, 113
Viceroys, The (novel), xvi
Vico, Giambattista, 87, 92
Victor Emmanuel I of Sardinia, 113, 156
Victor Emmanuel II of Italy, 166, 181
Victor Emmanuel III of Italy, 197
Vienna, Congress of. *See* Congress of Vienna
Vienna, Peace of (1738), 80-81
Vienna, Treaty of (1731), 80
Vietri, 7
Vikings. *See* Norsemen
viscount (title), 244
Visigoths. *See* Goths
vital statistics records (birth, marriage, death), 94, 119, 136, 139, 174, 304n102
viticulture, 111, 137, 194

Vittorio Amedeo II, 72-75 passim
volcanic eruptions, 84, 132, 203, 205
Voltaire (François Arouet), 82, 290n49
Volturno River, Battle of, 181
voting, 8, 11, 12, 13, 121, 122, 141, 187-189, 242, 271, 277n8. *See also* referendum, suffrage, etc
Wagner, Richard, 144
Waldensians, 193
war crimes (and crimes against humanity), 2-3, 13-14, 17, 19, 189, 198, 278n12, 279n13
Washington, Booker T, 197
Washington, George, xi, 105, 114
water management, 53, 84, 100
weights and measures, 192. *See also* coinage
wheat, 95, 98, 99, 137, 159. *See also* farming, latifondi
wheat berry pudding, 137
Whitaker, Joseph, 111, 137
William I, King of Sicily, 46, 49
William II, King of Sicily, 46, 49
wines, 111, 137. *See also* viticulture
Winter's Tale, The (play), 57
witchcraft (magic), 136
women's rights: abortion laws, 140; betrothals, 140; divorce,

13, 19, 24, 58, 129-130, 284n27; elopements, 139; higher education, 92; honor killings, 140; literacy, 47, 142; midwifery, 146; property inheritance, 92, 240; rape laws, 13, 58, 278n11, 284n27, 306n104; spousal violence, 48, 140; suffrage (voting), 13, 141, 280n15; surnames, 94

Woodhouse, John, 111

World War I. *See* First World War

World War II. *See* Second World War

Young Italy. *See* Giovane Italia

Zamoyski family, 271, 307n106

Zaragoza, 54

zeppola, 53, 137

This book was first printed simultaneously in Italy and in the United States of America in September 2020, set in Garamond, a typeface developed in Paris by the engraver Claude Garamont during the sixteenth century.

Conradin Hohenstaufen arrives for the Battle of Tagliacozzo of 1268 in this engraving from Summonte's history of the Kingdom of Naples